The World
of Benjamin of Tudela

The World
of Benjamin of Tudela

A Medieval Mediterranean Travelogue

Sandra Benjamin

Madison • Teaneck
Fairleigh Dickinson University Press
London: Associated University Presses

Associated University Presses
440 Forsgate Drive
Cranbury, NJ 08512

Associated University Presses
25 Sicilian Avenue
London WC1A 2QH, England

Associated University Presses
P.O. Box 338, Port Credit
Mississauga, Ontario
Canada L5G 4L8

The paper used in this publication meets the requirements
of the American National Standard for Permanence of Paper
for Printed Library Materials Z39.48-1984.

Library of Congress Cataloging-in-Publication Data

Benjamin, of Tudela, 12th cent.
    [Masa' ot shel Rabi Binyamin. English]
    The world of Benjamin of Tudela : a medieval Mediterranean
travelogue / [edited by] Sandra Benjamin.
        p.   cm.
    Includes bibliographical references and index.
    ISBN 0-8386-3506-7 (alk. paper)
    1. Benjamin, of Tudela, 12th cent.   2. Voyages and travels.
3. Jews—Social life and customs—Early works to 1800.
I. Benjamin, Sandra.   II. Title.
G370.B5B4613   1995
910.4'1'09021—dc20   92-54882
                                                              CIP

PRINTED IN THE UNITED STATES OF AMERICA

Contents

Acknowledgments

Historical research, writing, and preparing a manuscript for publication are occupations at which one works essentially alone. Nonetheless I could not have completed this book without the help and support of several people to whom I'm deeply indebted.

In London, where I developed the idea for the book and began work on it: To Sandra Blackman, to Rabbi Michael Rosen of Yakar, and to librarian Ezra Kahn at Jews College.

In Tudela, to archivist Julio Segura.

In Israel, to Moshe Shavit, for preparing more than forty maps, for help in transliterating from Hebrew, and for enthusiastic researching of the medieval Middle East.

In Italy, to Professor Cesare Colafemmina at the University of Bari, historian of medieval Jewish life in southern Italy.

In Washington, to Doris Ross for the generous use of her apartment and writing facilities; to Ori Soltes at B'nai B'rith, for the use of the library and for his insights into medieval Judaica; and to Bosco Nedelcovic, for twenty years of practice in writing letters about socioeconomic matters.

In New York, to Professor Robert Heilbroner for my early interest in economic history, and now for his franc/frank/Frank comments, and for reviving my flagging spirits; to Mrs. Yael Penkower and the staff of the library at the Jewish Theological Seminary; and to librarian Henry Reznick at Hebrew Union College, upon whom I descended bleary-eyed for the uncreative task of citation checking, to find a wise and willing collaborator in the research; to Miles and Barbara Cohen, rabbi and psychologist, book people, intelligently sympathetic to my writer's needs and uncommonly generous, who provided solutions to problems of Hebrew terminology, storing cartons of papers, and word processor perversity.

And to my *extra-terrestre* traveling-companion JBAS, who showed his love, while I worked on the book, by providing me with Belgian chocolates and photocopies beyond counting.

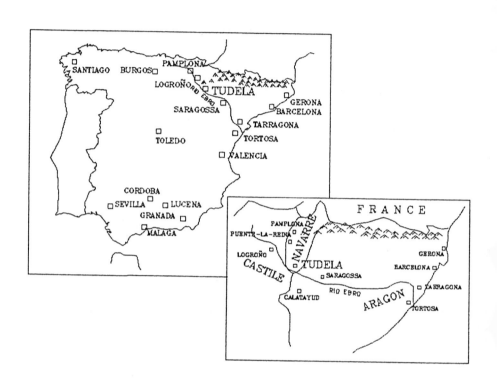

Introduction

Although nowadays few Jews live in Spain, during the Middle Ages more Jews lived on the Iberian peninsula than in any other European land. They generally lived well there, prosperous and secure, or at least more so than in the Christian kingdoms to the north. From the eighth century, when Mohammedans had imposed their sovereignty over the peninsula, communities of Moslems, Christians and Jews associated with each other in a spirit of mutual toleration and often cooperatively and amicably. At the end of the period that European history labels the Dark Ages, Spain's Jews were experiencing a Golden Age.

Jews lived all around the sparsely inhabited peninsula, though mostly in its eastern half. Each Jewish community was small—only a very few cities (Toledo, Valencia, Cordoba) had more than a hundred Jewish families—yet even in small communities Jewish life and culture flourished.

The era's most renowned figures, including Ibn Gabirol, the poet, and Maimonides, the physician-philosopher, came from the Andalucian communities of the south. But the northeast of the peninsula held many Jewish communities as well. Compared with the southerners who lived in arid country, the people of the northeast tended to be of a more practical turn of mind, because the well-watered valleys below the Pyrenees encouraged agriculture and consequently trade—so it's not surprising if the most famous Jewish figure from Spain's northeast, whose story has come to us across eight centuries, was a merchant.

His contemporaries knew him as Benjamin ben Jonah. Historians know him as Benjamin of Tudela, and they know him because, for several years ending in 1173 or thereabouts, he traveled around the Mediterranean littoral taking notes on the places and people. His chronicle reads rather like a Mediterranean Jewish Year Book, for he reported on sights of Jewish interest and he named the leaders of each community and their occupations, as well as tantalizing us with touristic comments on wonders we shall never see. Benjamin was by no means the first person to travel extensively in this region, nor even the first to write about it, but he was the first (whose journal has survived) who wrote in a straightforward manner, more fact than fable. For this reason, his chronicle is a valued source of information about Mediterranean lands in the Middle Ages.

9

Who was this chronicler who journeyed through half the known world? Benjamin didn't tell us he was a merchant (that's a scholars' deduction); indeed, he wrote nothing at all about himself. From the fact that he traveled and from his commentary we know him to have combined an adventurous spirit with a methodical mind. But about his appearance, his family, his financial position, his age when he traveled, he gave not the slightest hint.

A few commentators on his chronicle have called him "rabbi," but medieval Jews used "rabbi" as a title of respect for any man with some knowledge of the Law; Benjamin certainly wasn't a rabbi in our sense of the word. There's nothing in his chronicle to suggest particular learning or piety. He mentioned prayer services seldom and briefly, just noting practices that a visitor would find "different," and he made no mention of law or philosophy.

He wrote in a Hebrew that is inelegant, simple, as a merchant would write. For while nothing is known of Benjamin as an individual, quite a lot is known about traders and merchants at the end of the Jewish Golden Age.

Merchants and traders furnished the leaven in medieval economic life. Transporting the goods and knowledge of the East to Europe and to Iberia, they brought fresh air into societies stale with Christian scholastics and Mohammedan sybarites. Jews had predominated among the carriers for at least three hundred years prior to Benjamin's time.

During these centuries feudalism came to dominate the European social order, especially in France: the highly structured feudalism that occupies so much space in our medieval history textbooks. Jews had no place in feudalism, and only tangentially did it affect Jewish life. While Christians were perforce absorbed in monastery or manor, a large number of Jews were self-employed in crafts or commerce.

Our capitalistic system had its beginnings in crafts and commerce, but mundane matters rarely receive attention from serious scholars of Judaica. For the non-expert, "Jewish studies" tend to center on Bible and Talmud, the Holocaust and Israel, the holidays and cooking—a substantial menu, but one that omits the common activities of ordinary Jews in ten centuries prior to the modern period. During this "age of faith," writers Jewish and non-Jewish limited themselves largely to formulations about the sacred; anyhow, Jews have always been "the people of the Book." From a vast literature, outstanding essays and poems of tenth to twelfth century Jews are now easily found, often duly anthologized—and too often dully, for many of them were finely crafted masterworks, yet they are presented one after another, without any explanation of the contemporary conditions to which each writer was reacting. These writers weren't incorporeal. The Talmudists, a thousand years earlier, composed the life pleasing to God with notes on everyday business.

Even where it goes beyond religious practice to social life, "Jewish history" skips so quickly from Herod to Herzl that many students are left with mistaken ideas, for example, that all medieval Jews were confined to ghettos and moneylending.

Benjamin tells us of a great variety of ways in which Jews earned their living and of the prosperity they enjoyed. He recorded, for many towns, whether Jews were living in their own quarter or throughout the area. In writing about such secular concerns, Benjamin was unusual for his era, perhaps unique. In any case, he was there, and the breadth of his observations makes him a natural as guide.

The life of Benjamin and his merchant contemporaries centered in the Jewish community yet extended beyond it. Benjamin describes the officials governing world Jewry from Baghdad; he likewise talks briskly about Christmas celebration in Constantinople and flood measurement in Cairo. Sometimes he gives non-Jewish phenomena a peculiar Jewish interpretation.

He combined an interest in foreigners' practices with the credulity of his era. Among his factual items on politics and geography he interspersed hearsay accounts of the fabulous. Such stories, albeit not our "truth," illustrate his perception of the world.

Benjamin knew about war and about Jewish sufferings in war. He traveled through the Balkans and the Middle East some two generations after the Crusaders overran Palestine, the same duration as that separating us from the Nazis. In Palestine he reported time after time on the towns emptied of Jewish residents, and he described incidents in the Crusaders' conquest and aspects of their government, all with his usual calm, here a strange calm. Today's few remaining Holocaust survivors, and their children, plead that we not forget the slaughters of that decade of darkness; surely Benjamin heard from the victims of the Crusaders' brutalities.

I'm finishing the preparation of this book in a room where the television is turned on low, anxious for the latest developments in another Middle East conflict. Now, they keep saying, it's a war of technology. To the armed participants in that long-ago fighting over the Holy Land, the modern war matériel would be incomprehensible. Yet I doubt there has been much change in the experience of hearing your defenses crash or of seeing a village annihilated or of being burned alive.

Benjamin and I shared, along with many of our people, a particular concern for the Jews of Eretz Yisrael not waging a war but suffering nonetheless at its center.

In a fundamentally Christian society it's natural enough, in narrating a history of the Middle Ages, to accentuate feudalism and the Crusades, but Jews had another viewpoint. Following Benjamin around provides some impressions of twelfth-century life in Mediterranean lands as lived and seen by Jews, in a world remarkable for its activity and diversity.

Benjamin affirmed his membership in the Jewish community; he was probably less conscious of belonging to a community of writers. Texts of other travelers collaborate portions of what Benjamin wrote; furthermore, they give additional information about a particular place at his time.

Details come from three more kinds of contemporary material. The first is legal in nature, royal decrees and Jewish case law. The second is Hebrew poetry, especially the secular poems. The third is correspondence, on varied but mainly commercial topics.

We don't know of any letters that Benjamin wrote back to Tudela, though he may well have written some. Scholars have guessed that the chronicle as we have it consists of just extracts from his travel notes. Part 2 of this book, "Benjamin's Travels," incorporates virtually all the notes in Benjamin's chronicle and expands on them. I have written part 2 in the form of letters home, letters describing things that Benjamin probably saw and heard.

But before the letters, part 1, "Benjamin's Tudela," gives glimpses into the world from which Benjamin came. To appreciate any traveler's reactions, one must know about the life he left behind. Even more so, as far as Benjamin goes, for his origin in the milieu of Tudela surely influenced his project of going so far.

The World
of Benjamin of Tudela

Part One
Benjamin's Tudela

1

Tudela's Marketplace

Although medieval Tudela numbered only several thousand inhabitants—a small place in comparison with renowned cities like Barcelona and Toledo—Tudela had some importance as a market town. For in Benjamin's time even a skilled rider leaving Tudela on a fast horse would need to ride two full days before reaching another town as large.

And not many people had horses. Most people walked or rode donkeys. Small traders carried their burdens on their backs, or loaded them onto their animals, or packed them into carts to be drawn by their animals or by themselves. A merchant would employ numerous pack animals to move his stock of goods over land; his transportation differed from that of the beggar in amount but not in speed. However, money could purchase water transport, and where waterways existed, it was generally safer and more comfortable to use them than the roads—so much so that access to navigable waters usually determined the size of population centers.

Tudela was a major crossing point on the Rio Ebro, which from the northern mountains flows southeast through Logroño and Tudela and Saragossa and finally empties into the Mediterranean at Tortosa. From Tudela to Tortosa is about three hundred kilometers, for Benjamin a boat trip of at least four days . . . downriver.

Merchants from Tudela commonly sailed down the Ebro to the coast and then traveled northward to the quays of Barcelona, abundantly stocked with imported items—salt and soap, tin and timber, needles and nutmeats—to return home weeks later with an assortment of wares to sell in the local market and with tidbits of information about the world beyond the Great Sea.

Tudela's marketplace, like that of most towns, occupied the big square beside the central church, this location having been chosen in ancient times to encourage the peace of God and continued although now most of the traders were Moslems and Jews. Streets of stone buildings bordered the market square, among them inns catering especially to foreign traders. (Jewish traders could usually find a bed in a Jewish home, so seldom patronized these inns.)

Traders always entered the town in groups, the men and their mules laden with bags and bales, accompanied by bowmen. Despite the risks, costs, and discomforts of travel, many traders found it worth their while to go to distant markets to display their wares, especially when they had something new to offer.

The likelihood of something new to see, to acquire, to learn—that is what made the market the highlight of town life. Held one or two days a week, markets attracted people from a wide area. On market days, peasants in their drab workshifts, sacks slung over their shoulders, began arriving at dawn; some of them had walked though the night in hopes of selling their produce. Others with bulkier loads came pushing a two-wheeled cart or pulling an open-sided four-wheeled chariot which could carry triple the weight. The vendors arranged themselves with their poultry or pastry or fabricated products around the marketplace, where they were joined an hour or two later by more men and women who arrived on the barge, with more sacks and casks and animals. The local townspeople offered their crafts and services. Markets meant a mingling of buyers and beggars, seekers and sellers, countrymen and officials and scholars, Christians and Moslems and Jews.

The marketgoers knew how to rank people socially by the differences in dress: the rough rule was that the greater the number of items of apparel worn, the higher the status of the wearer. The poorest might have only a flimsy tunic to cover his body, and go barefoot and bareheaded; townspeople of the trader- and artisan-class always covered themselves completely, including hair and feet.

The townspeople among whom Benjamin lived could afford dress reflecting personal taste. The more traditional among them donned a few robes, one over the other, robes essentially the same for men and women, the outer robe probably of silk and cut especially loose of body to hide the body-outline. The sleeve was also cut wide, to accommodate the sleeve-kerchief, which might hold purse, prayerbook, or playing cards. People concerned themselves especially about their garments' quality and hue. Gentlemen preferring a modern style wore doublet and hose: with each piece a different bright color, the wearer exhibited his ability to purchase expensively dyed garments. A gentleman, Jew or non-Jew, generally carried a sword. At least to the casual observer, no particular way of dress distinguished Jews from other townspeople.[1]

Jews participated along with others in the market activities. They laughed at the antics of the trained animals and they gambled. They nibbled those sweetmeats which kashrut permitted. As vendors, they shouted their prices to the crowd and they bargained with their customers. As shoppers, they sniffed the spices, fingered the brocades, skimmed the books, and checked lengths of cloth against the market's official cubit measure. They queried the vendors about where the articles had come from and commented on how they were made. Ladies, pinching fruit at one stall, comparing pink and red silk scarves at another, stroking a wooden spindle to test its smoothness or grimacing into a silver-backed mirror; gentlemen, haggling over the value of a saddle or kibitzing at a game of chess—unless you heard chatter in Hebrew, you wouldn't know who was Jewish.

Yet if you were looking to meet with some Jews in Tudela's market, you'd find them easily enough. The local silversmiths and goldsmiths, mostly Jews, leased space in the *alcaiceria*, the fortified bazaar adjoining the commercial center. This gave them the security they needed while they carefully weighed their customers' coins and examined them for fineness of detail and state of preservation. From the booths there came the incessant tinkle of coins that characterized the marketplace.

In this spot you'd also hear talk of Jewish matters, of which Jews in casual conversation were bound to talk, like the singing voice of the new cantor or the legal impediment to a desired marriage or the treatment of Jews in a distant land. You'd hear comments on some novelty in the market. And you'd certainly hear laments and complaints, for while Tudela's Jews could count Moslems and Christians among their friends, one expects a more sympathetic understanding from friends in one's own community. How often Tudela's Jews must have quoted to each other from the delightful grumble of their own scholar-poet Abraham ibn Ezra:

> The planets and spheres in their stations
> Changed their order when I first drew breath.
> If I were to be a seller of lamps,
> The sun would not set till after my death!
> The stars in my heaven have ruined my life.
> I cannot succeed however I strive.
> If I were to be a seller of shrouds,
> No one would die while I was alive![2]

2

Tudela's Jews under Moslem Rule

The Tudela markets where Benjamin did his business were much the same as markets that had taken place around the Mediterranean for a thousand years. Yet by listening to talk on a Tudela market day one could have located it in time, as the traders exchanged reports of sieges and battles and new rulers. Brief allusions sufficed to communicate important news, for the context was familiar; it was a war-weary world.

Tudela itself had passed from Moslem to Christian rule some decades previously, but farther south the Christian armies were still beating back the Moors.* Many of the Christian soldiers, coming from France, passed by Tudela en route to these battlefields. Other soldiers went eastward from France, to the Holy Land, where in their grandfathers' time an army of Franks had captured the Moslem-ruled Jerusalem and massacred its Moslem and Jewish inhabitants; and the French Christians were still making war in the East. Even though the Jews in Tudela were living well enough under Christian rule, their sympathies lay with the Moslems—because most of the world's Jews, it seemed, were living in peace within Moslem kingdoms, and because, in the East just as in Spain, it was the violent Christians who had invaded lands that for centuries had been part of the Moslem empire.

For the three centuries when the Rio Ebro marked the boundary of Moorish Spain, Tudela lay at the Moslem empire's northern edge. Christians ruled the mountainous area north of Tudela and the strip of land extending eastward to Barcelona and the Mediterranean. Tudela, a cross point between the two kingdoms, served them both as a commercial center.

Thus, quite cosmopolitan for its size, Tudela under the Moors could support a great number of craftsmen. Jewish craftsmen abounded, in part because Moslems avoided manual labor. In contrast, Jews considered handicrafts not only licit but admirable: "Artisans maintain the fabric of the world, and in the handwork of their craft is their prayer."[1] Given the prohibition

---

*"Moslem" and "Mohammedan" are used interchangeably. "Moor" refers specifically to those Moslems who had settled in Spain and constituted the ruling class.

against earning money from Torah,[2] many Jewish scholars earned their living from crafts. They could specialize as they wished, since Tudela provided enough custom, for example, for several smiths, from jewelers to horseshoers, and for several workers in leather, from tanners to saddlers and bookbinders.

Although Jews in Moorish Spain were as free as anyone else to enter any line of work, among the crafts they had their specialties. Tudela's Jews worked as tanners and cobblers, and as gold- and silversmiths. Above all they worked in textiles: as silk weavers and embroiderers, as spinners, dyers, tailors, and furriers. They traded in wool. Despite the disrepute attached to the weaving trade, a few Jews wove the wool of the good Pyrenees sheep.

The Jewish community encouraged its men not only toward learning a trade but also strongly toward self-employment.[3] In reality some men would have to spend their lives as scribes or clerks in the service of communal enterprises or larger merchants; nonetheless, to be employed by another was considered unsatisfactory, fictionalized as "temporary," or denigrated by calling a man so employed (whatever his age) a "boy."[4]

Not all Tudela's Jews worked at urban occupations. Farming too had traditionally been held in high esteem in the Jewish world.[5] Tudela and the surrounding Ebro Valley prospered through agriculture, and no local laws or customs excluded Jews from working the land or owning it. The poor fund of the Jewish community owned land and gardens.[6] Individual Jews owned a large number of estates, gardens, and vineyards, especially outside the town in the district of Mosquera. Most of these landowners cultivated their own fields. At the least, they supervised the production of cheese and wine to assure that their products satisfied the laws of kashrut. Actually the line between town and country was blurred. Men made wine at the vineyard, and expensive candles and honey near the beehive. Women turned milk into cheese near where the sheep grazed. The townspeople were never very far from nature, and a Tudela farmer could live within a Sabbath's walk of a synagogue, send his children to a teacher, and seek treatment of a physician.

Within the town most craftsmen worked from their own houses, their workshops on the ground floor and their living quarters upstairs. Producers of similar goods would live adjacent to each other, the potters in one lane, the glaziers in the next, the carpenters in another. By and large Jews worked in the same locations and at the same occupations as non-Jews (the exceptions being for religious reasons, e.g., Jews did not raise pigs). Sometimes a Jew and a Moslem would choose to work together as partners, for the Jew the advantage being that someone could always be there to tend the shop or milk the animals, even on Saturdays and the days of Jewish festivals.

Such propinquity did not extend to housing. Jews, especially Jewish women, tried to avoid sharing a house with Moslems, for then they too would be constrained by purdah. Eventually the Jewish authorities forbade

Jews to sell or rent any part of their house to Mohammedans. This limited the market and raised the price of houses owned by Jews. Similarly, all-Jewish apartment houses were expensive, but Jews liked to live in them. In this sense, at least, the Jews had a conservative, close-knit community.

For the most part, Jews lived in neighborhoods predominantly though not entirely Jewish. Cities throughout the Moslem world were composed of "quarters," each of which housed a particular religious or ethnic group— Jewish, Christian, Arab tribe, and so forth. The empire-building Moslems of the eighth century, consolidating their rule over peoples of several religions and languages, organized their new cities into ethnic quarters for ease of administration; it was not their intention either to humiliate or to exclude. The Moors, at least, did not oblige any individual to dwell in the quarters assigned to his people. Jews in any case had always tended to live close to their synagogue and, consequently, to one another.[7]

Doubtless some Jews were more observant than others, but the community did not divide into separate synagogues on that basis. In cities with many Jews, rather, synagogues might be organized according to the homeland of the worshipers, for traditions differed from place to place.

Everywhere the Jew, shortly after dawn, would walk to the synagogue's morning service. In Moorish Spain he carried along his breakfast, which, after the prayers, he would eat with the other men in the synagogue courtyard. Most likely he entered the synagogue through a courtyard around which stood several buildings housing Jewish-community services. The synagogue itself generally had a simple exterior rather like a small mosque. Mosques, however, provide no interior seating, whereas Jewish prayer services, being comparatively long, alternate seated with standing worship. Rugs and mats covered the synagogue floor, and congregants wishing additional comfort supplied their own cushions on which to sit or recline.

Members of the congregation also provided their own prayerbooks. As codexes of the entire Bible were bulky to carry and awkward to read from, the Torah reading for the week would be copied in its own small booklet, of which many worshipers possessed a copy. Most books for prayer were decorated, for it was considered a mitzvah to beautify them, and wealthier congregants tried to surpass each other in the luxury of the decoration.

The weekly portion of the Bible, the *geonim* had decreed, should be read only on Shabbat and not on weekdays, although a brief initial section of it might be read at the Monday and Thursday morning service. In order to hear these short readings from the Torah, a greater number of men would attend the morning service on Mondays and Thursdays than on other weekdays. Thus Monday and Thursday became the days for dealing with community affairs, the prayer service being followed by the reading of any new government proclamation and by announcements of taxes, of articles lost or found, of property sales, of charitable activities, and so forth.

An infrequent yet major issue of community business was the election of its spiritual and moral leader, for although any congregant might lead the morning, noon, and dusk services on workdays, by Benjamin's time even a small community wanted an expert to lead prayers on the Sabbath and on festivals. One could no longer even hope for a prayer leader with *semikha* (ordination), as in the good old days; the title had simply lapsed. The prayers might be led by a permanent or a visiting scholar from one of the academies, certified as *haver*. Most likely the prayer leader would be a cantor, one of an occupation that had developed to cope with the poems being added to the services and with the changing melodies. Cantors were a peripatetic lot, many of them rivaling traders in their international connections.

When a community engaged a cantor, or appointed a high official such as a *rosh yeshiva* or a judge, it submitted his name for approval to Baghdad. This practice went back to the time of the geonim, when Spanish Jews looked to Babylon for decisions based on *halakha*. (This practice was not peculiar to the Jewish communities, for in major administrative matters the Moslems too consulted Baghdad, and the Christians, Rome.) Baghdad still sent out scholar-messengers with *responsa*, or to teach or preach, or to establish courts; and to solicit funds to continue their essential Jewish work. Spanish Jews all knew about Baghdad. Men also came from academies in Spain and elsewhere, disseminating new Jewish law or literature and requesting contributions. Some visiting scholars were just roaming from place to place in search of a post, carrying little besides news.

Every Jewish community supported a number of scholars, including some from abroad. Doing so was a sacred obligation, as was the education of one's own children. Religion and learning being interdependent, study was not only a way to obtain knowledge but was also an act of worship.

Study was considered a right and an obligation of all children—or at least of boys—not excepting orphans and the sons of poor families. Among some other peoples, boys might have to be denied schooling so that they could earn a living, but among Jews this was discouraged and rare: knowledge of the Law was incumbent upon all Jewish men. As befitted the honor of studying Torah, each pupil had to come to school well dressed—if necessary, at community expense. Their classes might be held in the synagogue, or the teacher might hold them in his own house or in a house he had rented for the purpose; wherever "school" was, the pupils were known as "synagogue boys," and correspondingly they learned young that school was a serious matter. The schools granted no vacations, apart from Jewish holidays, although the boys could take time off to travel with their parents, as on family visits.

First the boys had to learn to read. Early on, some attempt had been made to teach Hebrew by identifying complete words and phrases, that is, without reference to the sounds of individual letters; but by 1100 the scholars had given up that system as being ineffective. The pupils learned their letters and words from books, although the expense of books precluded the possession of a book by each boy; usually several pupils shared a text. Men teaching privately would lend books to their pupils. Whatever was required, all Jewish boys learned to read.

Education meant preparation to participate in the synagogue service. Boys learned Pentateuch, Prophets, and Psalms. From the age of five, they studied Torah; at ten, they began Mishnah; at fifteen, Talmud. The schools did not teach prayers, for the boys attended synagogue regularly and would hear them repeated often there.

Even in school, the boys learned by repetition and memorizing. In ancient times, before a system had been developed to indicate pronunciation and cantillation, one had to know the Bible more or less by heart in order to read it. By Benjamin's time, the accuracy of Bible reading had long since been assured by markings; but still the boys had to memorize. And they memorized without hearing any explanation of the significance of what they were memorizing, for teachers believed that knowing a text by heart must precede the understanding of it.

Efforts were made to influence the boys' spirit by teaching them poetry. Through choral recitation of biblical poetry, the more recent sacred poetry, and the occasional somber secular poem, pupils (it was hoped) would develop appreciation of wisdom and of the need to follow the *mitzvot*.

The children's fathers, however—not the schools—bore the responsibility for their religious and moral education. The Jewish community also insisted that fathers prepare their sons to earn a living. This was true of non-Jews too, but Jews like to have a Jewish reason for doing things, and the Talmud says: "He who does not teach his son a trade is as guilty as though he teaches him to steal."[8] A father generally prepared his sons to follow his own occupation, but Jewish tradition made him responsible only to teach his sons "a clean and easy trade."[9] For sons who learned quickly, or for boys who were to follow an occupation different from the father's, there were renowned craftsmen who understood the training of boys and were paid to undertake it.

For boys of the age preparing to earn a living, the schools did complement the religious studies with some basic vocational training. No arithmetic had been taught at the elementary stage, but schoolboys of bar mitzvah age studied arithmetic so that they might prepare complicated accounts with the aid of an abacus. Boys aspiring to be international traders were sent to work as employees in the larger trading firms. Although boys learned to read when very young, only at this rather advanced stage did they learn to write. Writing was taught to the level where a boy could take down dictation without mistakes in spelling. More advanced calligraphy—in Hebrew and in Arabic—was taught only to those preparing to be merchants or government officials, physicians or religious scholars. Many Hispano-Jewish merchants could speak Arabic well, but not write it. Doubtless many Jewish merchants wrote even their Hebrew hesitantly.

For employed men, the synagogue service on weekdays (especially Mondays and Thursdays) was often proceeded or followed by a short course of study. Now adult, the student could be initiated into the mysteries of logic or the philosophies of religion. He would hear formal lectures by scholars, and he would with other worshipers read texts connected with the daily service and discuss them. A man had to be considered learned by his fellows before they would name him to any position of community responsibility.

All Jewish men were expected to study for at least a short period every day. A traveler could freely participate in the studying of the community where he found himself. Religious scholars and men working at worldly vocations might study together. A scholarly man might be an artisan, although learning was mostly the domain of the mercantile middle class. But to anyone who could profit from it, learning was available. And learning rewarded a man with higher status in his community.

Jews were bound into the Jewish community not only by inclination but, under Moslem rule, by Islamic law. Islam, holding that all non-Moslems are inferior beings, imposes laws on all infidels to remind them of their inferiority. The code expressly labels Jews and Christians less inferior than other non-Moslems, however, treating them within a special category of *dhimmis,* or protected peoples. Like all non-Moslems, dhimmis were forbidden to speak disrespectfully of Mohammed or his religion; nor could they prevent one of their number from joining Islam. Dhimmis were permitted their own forms of worship in their own religious buildings, although no synagogue or church could stand higher than a neighboring mosque. Neither could they construct new houses of worship, nor even repair their existing ones. Nor could they proselytize. Dhimmis had to pay a head tax in return for their protection and for their exemption from military service. They were required to wear distinctive clothing and they were forbidden to hold public office. That was Islamic law. But the Moors never applied the laws against dhimmis very harshly, and generally they didn't enforce them at all.

On the other hand, the Islamic code explicitly authorized a dhimmi-people to administer its own religious community, called *aljama.* Each aljama held a man to certain duties and responsibilities, it gave him certain benefits, and it imposed on him a certain pattern of life. To be sure, everywhere in Europe and the Mediterranean lands during this period, every individual belonged to a religious community and could hardly have survived outside one. Since it was as a member of his religious community that each individual was taxed and judged, the lines between the religious communities were sharply drawn. This seemed only natural at a time when religion was the framework of life, when the fundamental issues with which a man concerned himself related to the nature of God and of good and evil.

Within the Moslem empire, the aljama (Jewish or Christian) denoted a kind of substate, a "state" based on religious affiliation rather than on territory. Whatever the residence of the Jew, in any part of town or even outside the walls, he was part of the Jewish aljama. In each city or town the Jewish aljama ran its own houses of worship, schools, charitable organizations, and judicial system, based on its own laws and traditions.[10] No such services existed outside one or another aljama.

While the Jewish and Christian communities were entirely responsible for providing services for themselves, they had also to provide virtually all the funds for the Moorish government. The rulers allowed the Spanish peoples to work at whatever they found most profitable, the better to tax them. Because the Moors occupied the positions as officials and soldiers, the Christian and Jewish Spaniards employed themselves in agriculture, handicrafts, and commerce; and the Moors taxed farming, land ownership, and the trades. They also imposed a head tax, the *jizya*, on their subject peoples, that is, on Christians and Jews as such. This was a heavy burden on all the dhimmis, even though the Moorish officials taxed progressively: that is, they specified the jizya of a certain amount for persons of ordinary income, then required payment of twice that amount from wealthy individuals and of half the amount from poor persons. As for those Jewish individuals too poor to pay, gradually men from a few wealthy families took over the tax burdens of the poor as a sacred duty.[11] Thereby the benevolent rich gained status in the community on a par with the earlier aristocrats, namely the scholars.

Some aspects of taxation on Jews peculiarly reflected their relations with the Moorish sovereigns. For one thing, representatives of the Jewish aljama to the court commonly received, among their emoluments, a percentage of the profits of the kosher butcher or a regular supply of fresh meat. The head taxes they had to pay as dhimmis naturally rankled, but even more the Jews resented a common system of collecting taxes. Certain Christian and Jewish traders became "tax-farmers," paying the government for the right to collect the tax from a particular customs house or from a group of artisans, for example. The tax-farmers paid a sum less than they could obtain as tax payments, and they kept the difference. The system easily lent itself to corruption.

Although they suffered as a minority people, the Jews prospered under Moorish rule. The aljama system endorsed Jews' determination to live in accordance with their own laws and customs, to maintain a Jewish way of life. As dhimmis they paid high taxes, but they were free to work, to worship, and to organize their community as they wished, and to meet with their coreligionists from other lands; and they were free in their everyday lives to deal with Moslem individuals on a basis of virtual equality.

To the degree that the Moors behaved with moderation, the Jews found them congenial. Like Jews, the Moslems exalted scholarship. They devoted Sunday and Wednesday evenings to study outside the mosque, and Jews left their synagogue libraries to join Moors and Christians in the main square, where learned men of the town, such as physicians and judges, lectured on music, astronomy, mechanics, natural sciences, and metaphysics ("the first among sciences"). Sometimes visiting scholars held disputations, where speakers for each religion argued its superiority over the other two.

Even earlier, as conquerors of Spain, the Moslems had been tolerant, insofar as they had made no attempt to force their religion or their language on their new subjects, Christians and Jews. But Moslem hegemony occasioned the peninsula-wide circulation of books and ideas in Arabic, so Jews learned Arabic. They never stopped using Hebrew for worship or for speaking among themselves, yet long before Benjamin's time the Spanish Jews had adopted Arabic as their principal language. They spoke Arabic in their dealings around the vast Moslem empire, and they used it to study the Greek-Arab sciences of astronomy, mathematics, geography, and medicine. Jews likewise worked together with Moslems in artistic and literary endeavors, developing a great culture during Moorish Spain's many generations of peace. Jews as much as Moslems contributed to the intellectual ferment and benefited from it. Much more than any other people of the West, Spanish Jews had access to knowledge in many fields, in depth.

The Jewish aljama maintained an active cultural life of its own. As the Arabic poetry that filled the air expressed the soul of the Moslem upper classes, Jews fervently wrote and recited poetry in Hebrew as an assertion of pride in their own glorious people. Just in the generation or two prior to Benjamin's, Tudela had nurtured the master poets Judah Halevi and Abraham ibn Ezra, and in the preceding century the neighboring town of Saragossa had fostered Solomon ibn Gabirol. It was ibn Gabirol who in these lines caught the quality of Jewish oppression:

> Six years were decreed for a slave to wait
> When his freedom he sought at his master's hand;
> But the years of my bondage lack term or date—
> It is hard, O Master, to understand.[12]

Not that Tudela's Jews were familiar only with the work of local poets. From school and synagogue they knew the sacred poetry written in the East in biblical times, and they had also heard sacred and secular poems of the Jewish Andalucians, such as this by Moses ibn Ezra:

> Let man remember all the days of his life
> He moves at the grave's request.
> He goes a little journey every day
> And thinks he is at rest;
> Like someone lying on board a ship
> Which flies at the wind's behest.[13]

Poets often philosophically passed their lives seeking patrons. They dedicated their lines to Moorish kings and lords and to Jewish princely merchants, in hopes of a gift or a paying position. They even dedicated poems to each other, and sent their poems back and forth to each other, for criticism and for pleasure certainly, but also with the idea that doing so might lead to some financial reward. Or they wrote on commission—in the Jewish community, wealthy families traditionally commemorated events like a birth, a wedding, or a death by having a poem written about it.[14] Abraham ibn Ezra earned some of his modest living by humorously marking events of importance to his patrons and pupils. He could not always have found it amusing, however, when his trip to collect his fee proved in vain:

> I come in the morn
> To the house of the nobly born;
> They say he rode away.
> I come again at the end of the day,
> But he is not at his best,
> And needs a rest.
> He is either sleeping or riding afar.
> Woe to the man who is born without a star![15]

Audiences seeking the romantic, the historic, the philosophic, and the comic—each could find poems to its taste. Yet a large share of the poetry written in this Golden Age, as in ancient times, dealt with sacred matters, for one stream of Jewish thought discouraged secular writings. That emphasis on religious poetry, plus the desire of Moslems to keep the use of the Arabic alphabet for themselves, resulted in Jews writing almost all their poetry in Hebrew.

About the content of poems, too, the well-traveled Abraham ibn Ezra had something to say:

> Arabs like singing of love and desires,
> Christians of battlefields and vengeful fires,
> Greeks of wisdom's fruits and speculation,
> Hindus of proverbs and divination,
> But Israel chants to the Lord of Hosts.[16]

Like the Moors around them, the Jews preserved their important poems in writing. All Jewish families, even the poor, had a few books.[17] Books were possessed proudly, like jewelry bought and valued as investment. At the same time, since most books concerned religion, books assumed the status of ceremonial objects and were beautified as such. Their covers were leather-bound and gilt-lettered.[18] Their pages were elaborately patterned and bordered. Decorated pages without lettering were sometimes inserted at the front or back of a book just to glorify the book, or to glorify God, by their art. Calligraphy was stylized and intricate, as though the Hebrew letters were woven into exquisite designs that happened to be words. The Jewish interest in fine arts being restricted by the biblical commandment against graven images, and the surrounding culture's Moslems likewise frowning upon representational art, Jews developed an artistic appreciation of *words*.

As Jews liked Hebrew poems, so they liked Jewish stories. Evenings and Shabbat the whole community would assemble to hear recitals about biblical times, little caring whether the stories were true or legend. They would listen to accounts of ancient personalities and demand to know exactly where they had dwelt, who were the enemies in the long-ago battles. The story-tellers answered, for they dared not admit ignorance, and who could check the validity of what they said?

The tales told by Christians and Moslems often glorified warriors and kings. The Jews, lacking recent warriors and kings of their own, had to dramatize their own heroes: R. Sheshet who was blind and frail and yet founded an academy; R. Hisda, born poor but become so rich as a brewer that he paid for the entire rebuilding of the Sura academy; R. Judah ben Ezekiel, who studied with so much concentration that he sometimes forgot to pray, yet who through prayer and the doffing of a shoe could make it rain. The Jews of Spain made national heroes of Talmudic scholars who had lived in the distant East a thousand years before, celebrating them for exploits of scholarship and piety.

In Benjamin's Tudela as elsewhere and always, the synagogue served not only as house of worship and house of study but also as a house where Jews could meet other Jews. The whole community would gather there on the arrival of a merchant or scholar from afar, to hear discourse on his homeland and the news from communities en route. The strong Jewish interest in distant places reflected, doubtless, a minority people's instinctive fear of being forced to emigrate as well as the Jews' traditional commercial occupations.

One of their heroes was Samuel ben Joseph ha-Levi ibn Nagrela, a businessman in international trade in the first years of the eleventh century.

Hostilities among Moslems had driven him from his native Cordoba; he went to Malaga, then was summoned by the king to Granada. Under those circumstances he overcame the Jewish aversion to working in the service of others to accept work as a translator, calligrapher, and scribe. Whereas most Jewish merchants wrote their Arabic in Hebrew characters, Samuel could write with Arabic letters and did so in a fine hand, excelling in a skill and art highly regarded among the Moslems. Employed by the vizier, Samuel became his private secretary and eventually he himself served as vizier of Granada. During decades of continuing civil commotion and military aggression, he served the king as diplomat and general.[19] As a pastime he wrote poems on many themes, from religious faith to market scenes, and, unusually for a Jew since ancient times, on war:

> In their land wicked men stoned with the rocks
> Of their tongues the children of the living God.
> They conspired against them and took weapons
> And purchased shackles for their feet
> In order to destroy the Jewish community
> And lay waste both high and low, the suckling infant and he that is weaned!
> And when the king grew arrogant and spoke
> With a disdainful mouth, we looked upon him with derision
> And crossed over to his land with a mighty force
> To take revenge for the leaders that were ravaged.
> With us were men like young lions
> And a host as numerous as a swarm of locusts.
> They were not heavy with excess flesh
> Nor with fat upon their flanks,
> Each was dressed for war on that day of wrath.
> And each removed his cloak for the battle.
> Each one hastened to his sword and ran to his death
> With a willing heart and joyfully
> In coats of armor that gleamed like the waves,
> And shields crimson like dyed parchment
> With rounded helmets and brow-plates
> Upon horses like fleet and darting clouds.
>
> . . . .
> We returned after the carnage and the burning
> And our hands were filled with spoils.
>
> . . . .
> Mine is the Lord that said: "Trust me
> And I will make your steps to fall in pleasant places
> For you I will break the teeth of the young lions
> And cause the giants to fall before you."[20]

Another, pithier:

> War at first is like a young girl
> With whom every man desires to flirt.
> And at the last it is an old woman,
> All who meet her feel grieved and hurt.[21]

And from his experience at court came this extraordinary simile:

> A royal favorite
> Is like a lion rider:
> Feared by all who see him,
> He trembles at his bearer.[22]

In a life busy with diplomacy and poesy, Samuel ibn Nagrela also became expert in Jewish law, and, in recognition thereof, the first Spaniard to be honored with the title Nagid (prince). Samuel was even admired widely beyond the Jewish community, as illustrated in this outrageous flattery written to him by a Moorish contemporary:

> If man could tell the true and false
> And could the difference understand,
> Instead of kissing Mecca's stone
> He would, O Samuel, kiss thy hand.[23]

His brilliance and his generosity notwithstanding, Samuel ha-Nagid failed in one way common to successful men: he raised his son and heir Joseph as a prince, and once Joseph assumed the positions of vizier of Granada and head of the Jewish community, he proved himself greedy and arrogant. He lived in a marble palace, dressed ostentatiously, filled high offices with his relatives and Jewish friends, and appeared to dominate the king. Thereby he awakened general resentment and he earned the especial enmity of high-placed Moslems, who eventually (on the last Shabbat of the year 1066) attacked his palace, killed him, and strung up his body on a cross. This sparked Christian mobs to riot against Jews, looting and killing. Fortunately the rioting was contained within Granada, but Granada's Jewish survivors all had to leave the city. Jewish deaths numbered in the thousands.[24]

Jews in communities caught up between warring Moslems and Christians, as in northeast Spain, particularly enjoyed stories about Jews living as autonomous people, like the early Bible stories. If in addition such a story had a hero in some way connected with Tudela or its region, the Jews of Benjamin's Tudela would naturally, enchantedly, tell and tell again that story . . . as they did the life of Hasdai ibn Shaprut.

The earliest of Spain's Jewish secular heroes, Hasdai was born about 915 in Andalucia. He worked as physician and medical translator (Greek into Arabic), and when he became known he was asked to join the court of the khalif 'Abd al-Rahman III at Cordoba. Despite Hasdai's success in the broader world, despite his winning the great respect of Jews as well as Moslems, the Jewish community never named him to any official position.

He contributed in other ways. As a wealthy member of the Jewish aljama he sought out Hebrew books to buy in other lands, he wrote to Jewish communities abroad, and he encouraged Jewish scholars from other countries to come to Spain. He was proud of Andalucia's supremacy in contemporary Jewish culture, and dreamed of establishing there some kind of Jewish independence.

The Moorish administration posted him to Navarre, to the very district of Tudela. About that time he heard from some traders returned from the East of a Jewish tribe living far to the east, even to the east or the north of Baghdad. Hasdai sent off a letter to the king of this allegedly independent tribe called Khazars, first introducing himself and his country:

> The name of the country in which we live is, in Hebrew, Sefarael; and in the language of the native Ismaelites, 'al-Andalus'[Andalucia]. . . . Our land is fertile, and abounds in springs and reservoirs—a land of grain, wine and oil. It is rich in fruit and sweetness . . . it has orchards and gardens, trees of all sorts—fruit-bearing and silk-bearing. . . . Merchants and traders gather here from all the countries. . . .
>
> We, the remnant of Israel in the Diaspora, lived peacefully here at first; but when we sinned against God, He induced the rulers to appoint tax collectors over us; and they burdened us with tributes, they oppressed and humiliated us.

And then Hasdai stated his purpose:

> I am anxious to learn the truth whether there really exists a place in the world where the dispersed Israel has its own government, which is subservient to no one. And if I knew that this were true, I would renounce all my honors, would abandon my high post, would leave my family, and would make my way over mountains and valleys, over land and sea, until I would get to that locality where my master, the Jewish king, lives.[25]

Hearing of some struggle in that part of the world between Byzantines and Mohammedans, and knowing that elsewhere such as Italy Byzantines were persecuting Jews, Hasdai appealed on the Khazars' behalf to the Byzantine rulers.

In due course Hasdai got a letter from Joseph, king of the Khazars. King Joseph was most cordial, inviting Hasdai to come east and serve him as minister. But Hasdai's earlier enthusiasm may have cooled, or Eastern politics may have intervened; in any case, Hasdai never saw the Khazars' Jewish kingdom.

Curious as Jews were about faraway peoples, not all of them relished the thought of traveling, or once embarked, wanted to continue. A visiting scholar, queried for the hundredth time about his travels, could well have responded in the words of the poet Moses ibn Ezra who, from around 1100, had wandered for many years through northern Spain:

> I am tired of roaming about the world,
>   surveying its breadth; and I am not
>   yet through; . . . .
> Journey follows journey, but I find no
>   resting-place, no calm repose.[26]

3

Santiago, Reconquista, and Crusades

Benjamin's Tudela—he knew it as "Tuteila"—was the major town in the southern part of the small Christian kingdom of Navarre. Since before the Romans Tuteila or Tullonium had graced the south bank of the Rio Ebro as a village, but Navarre didn't exist at all until the eighth century, when the Moslems invaded Iberia from the south, establishing their sovereignty over a submissive populace as they swept northward to the Ebro Valley and seized it. About the year 800 these conquerors fortified Tudela to control passage across the river.[1] Then they pushed farther northward, but the northern mountain people would not be subdued; instead these developed the concept and institutions of "Navarre" as a defense against the invaders and succeeded in driving them back. The Ebro Valley remained the northern limit of the Moslem empire for three hundred years, and Tudela a Moorish frontier town.

The Jews were content under Moslem rule: they could live comfortably and practice their religion undisturbed. They would be under the rule of non-Jews in any case, and it seemed that Moslem was more tolerant than Christian. For Spain's Christians, however, it was *their* land that the foreigners had overrun. The victors had allowed them their religious autonomy, but the Spanish Christians were a vanquished people. Stronger Christians would fight to throw off the Moslem yoke. By Benjamin's time they had half-thrown it off.

The move to recover Spain from the Moors started in France. Not long after the peninsula fell to the Moslems, Charlemagne sent soldiers over the Pyrenees but they were routed at Saragossa.

Then, early in the ninth century—as Christians tell the story—a tomb was discovered a few hours' ride inland from Spain's northwest coast. It held the remains of the apostle Saint James (in Spanish, Santiago), which had floated from Jaffa in Palestine. Christians, desperately desiring a leader, rallied around Santiago. Pilgrims from France trekked across the Pyrenees and traversed northern Spain to visit the shrine at Santiago. Tudela, lying just south of the main pilgrim route, watched the pilgrims and traded with them as Santiago formed a link between northern Spain and the rest of Christendom, and as the idea of Santiago intensified the Christian urge for reconquest. Within a century, a wide strip of northernmost Spain, from Barcelona to the Atlantic, was again Christian.

Saint James had ousted the Moslems from his shrine and from the whole pilgrim route—how glorious it was to follow that route in Christian rejoicing, to visit that shrine! To encourage the pilgrims, Christian religious orders built new roads across northern Spain and put up hundreds of bridges and hostels. In droves the pilgrims crossed farmlands that had heretofore been tranquil, and whose farmers included Jews. Now the whole region was invaded by peasants and knights freed from their feudal constraints yet wishing to establish a feudal pattern of land ownership. The Jews moved into the towns.

From all parts of France and beyond, men and women, many tens of thousands of them every year, journeyed to pray at the shrine of Santiago. In winter a trickle, in summer a wide river, Christians from all nations streamed across northern Spain to attain Santiago. Their various routes from France joined at Puente la Reina, just southwest of Pamplona and a two-day ride north of Tudela. Around Puente la Reina, as far as the eye could see, camped small and large groups of pilgrims, each person in his group with a scallop on his cap and with walking stick and beggar's cup for support. Each individual would purchase little; still, the vast numbers of them assured a continual market for vendors of candles, sweetmeats, and footwear. Commercial motives, mostly, impelled Tudelan merchants to Pamplona, to Puente la Reina, and to Logroño (the Ebro port farther west on the pilgrim route). The miracle of Saint James sustained pilgrims in the millions; thousands like the Tudela merchants went to see *them* as a marvel of Christian religiosity.

Not that Tudelans had to leave home to see pilgrims. During two centuries all of northern Spain swarmed with pilgrims, and through Benjamin's time Tudelan merchants traded with them.

The pilgrims from France duly returned home with news about the land south of the Pyrenees. French Christians resented the Moslems' continued occupation of three-fourths of the peninsula, and certain monks fed the dreams of reconquest. In Provence, experience led the Christians to detest Moslems: Mohammedan pirates were continually raiding Christian ports from Barcelona to southern Italy. This piracy gave the popes another reason to approve a Christian fight for Moslem lands.

The feudal system in France had no vent for the energies of its younger sons and adventurers. If these men were to recapture Spain, they would gain both material and spiritual benefits. The popes stressed religious solidarity: the carrying the cross to Spain, *la croisade*, the Crusade, would be for the defense and liberation of fellow Christians. Among the cross carriers were some who thought the recapture of Spain from Moslems a good excuse to attack Jews, with excesses of violence so great that in 1066 Pope Alexander admonished the Franks to leave the Jews alone.[2]

Although the *re-conquistadores* nevermore indulged themselves in gross abuse of Jews, some Christian soldiers still molested Jews on the grounds that Jews had traditionally cooperated with the Moors. Reacting to the Christian invasions, the Moslems persecuted first their Christians, then all their dhimmis, Jews too. During the long years of Christian-Moslem warfare, the Jews huddled in the middle, fearful of both camps.

In many towns of Christian-ruled northern Spain, the Christians encouraged the Jews to live in the citadel or fortified areas for their protection as merchants and as Jews, allowing them complete autonomy within their fortified quarters. This had the consequence that whenever Jews fought to defend their own homes from invaders, they were willy-nilly fighting on behalf of the ruling power.

In the very center of the Iberian peninsula lies Toledo, the capital of Spain since its rule by the Visigoths centuries before. The Jews of Tudela knew Toledo as the peninsula's oldest Jewish community, settled by exiles of the tribes of Judah and Benjamin. The city's very name came from the Hebrew "Toledot" (generations); thus, "city of the (many) generations." Beloved by its Jewish residents, who included some very wealthy merchants, Toledo under the Moors was large and dynamic, cosmopolitan, the cultural center of Christian Spaniards, Mohammedans, and Jews. In 1085, the extensive Moorish kingdom of Toledo fell to the Christians.

After this conquest, the Franks concentrated their fighting in the Pyrenees-Ebro region. They sang, among their marching songs, the "Chanson de Roland," glorifying the incursions of Charlemagne across the Pyrenees three hundred years before. By attributing Charlemagne's invasions to advice from Santiago, the song strengthened the link between the soldiers and the pilgrims, giving hatred of the Moslems a religious justification.[3]

Not only the Christians threatened Moorish Spain. The country suffered continual warfare among Moslems. Around 1090, armies of puritanical and fanatical Moroccan warriors called Almoravids, fearful of Christian invasion and zealous against the laxity of the Moors, made incursions all along the Mediterranean coast. Regarding the Jews, the Almoravids claimed that Mohammed had given them five hundred years to await the Messiah, after which they could wait no longer, if their Messiah had not come they would have to embrace Islam. Anticipating by a few years the end of this period, the Almoravids demanded immediate conversion, but then they withdrew their ultimatum in response to money payments by Jews and a plea for tolerance on their behalf by a Moslem *qadhi* (judge).[4] In the Almoravids' devastation of Andalucia, they destroyed Granada, a city with many Jews.

Moses ibn Ezra, born in Granada in 1055, knew firsthand of the Almoravid warfare and its consequences, of the cruelties committed so that castles and kingdoms might change hands. Considering the wreckage, he wrote:

> Before me, entombed from ancient days,
> Lie people asleep forever.
> Here they know neither scorn nor praise,
> Their neighbor they neither love nor hate,
> They envy not another's endeavor.
> I cannot detect, regarding a grave,
> If it contains a master or a slave.[5]

The Almoravids attacked around the Spanish Mediterranean as far north as Valencia. To Valencia's defense came riding out from Burgos, west of Tudela, a Christian adventurer called El Cid, who took up arms for Saragossa's Moorish rulers. At that time Valencia had a Jewish community of some 160 families—traders, merchants, and craftsmen, not scholars. El Cid won the city in 1094. His treaty included stipulations for minority peoples, which, vis-à-vis the Jews, superseded those of Charlemagne. Besides forbidding Jews to insult or proselytize Moslems, it held that henceforth Jews could not purchase Moslem prisoners of war or use Moslems as slaves. It held that no Jew could be placed in a position of authority over Moslems or their property. It made no declaration about Jews' employment or landholding. It's hard to say whether El Cid in Valencia was good for the Jews or bad for the Jews.

Soon after El Cid took Valencia, while the Christians were fighting for and winning the area around the Ebro, while they were assuring the Jews that they might live securely again in a Christian region, Jews in Spain heard reports about armies of Franks departing for Palestine. Now, French Christians wanted to do more than recover Spain from the Moslems; they had determined also to recover the Moslem-held Jerusalem. And the Franks, after massacring whole communities of Jews en route, did seize Jerusalem in 1099—upon which, they burned most of the Jews alive and expelled the survivors.

The Jews of Andalucia felt deeply ravaged. Their Spanish home invaded, their spiritual home incinerated. Andalucia prided itself on having the world's finest *yeshivot*; but in the overwhelming horror their rabbis sat intransigent, believing all to be God-determined. Some Jews despaired of them, and instead consulted astrologers and diviners. They implored God to send the Messiah. The Jews of Cordoba impatiently picked one of their own pious men, Ibn Aryeh, to fill that role, to whom they rendered corresponding homage until the leading scholars could tolerate it no more.[6]

Tudela fell to the Christians in 1115. Perhaps it was about then that Benjamin was born; more likely, he was born in a Tudela already Christian for a few years. Either way, in his youth, he heard endless stories about the battle-old Jews recounting how they had nearly died of starvation during the siege; about swordfights on the ramparts; about how physicians (Moslems, Jews, and Christians) had risked their lives to help the wounded; about certain Moslems and Jews fleeing Tudela at the time of its capitulation.

But once the Christians had won Tudela and incorporated it into Navarre, their leaders allowed the Jews to return home. (In contrast, although they permitted the Moslems to remain in the area, they obliged them to give up their homes and mosques inside the town walls.) The change of sovereignty from Moslem to Christian hardly disturbed the Jews' position. Christian theology from the time of Charlemagne had held Jews to be a people apart, a community related to the sovereign in a special way. The Moslems had segregated the Jews as dhimmis; the Christians segregated the Jews by making them wards of the king. From the Jews' point of view this had at least one advantage. Should war come again, Jews taken captive would not be sold into slavery like other captives. As the property of the king, Jews would be ransomed . . . with Jewish money, of course.

Following the lines of the treaty laid down twenty years before by El Cid at Valencia, the new Christian rulers guaranteed the Jews possession of their houses and other property. They left the Jews free to worship as they wished and to run their own community affairs. The Mohammedans, those who remained, could hardly be counted on to serve the new order, but the Christians hoped for Jewish loyalty.

The new rulers had economic reasons too for wanting the Jews to stay. After the long period of warfare, the re-establishment of agriculture and commerce would require skills and dedication. Of the main products grown around Tudela, cereals could be made to grow again in a year or two, but olives and grapes would need more time. To be sure, Christians were coming to populate the newly conquered towns, erstwhile pilgrims and soldiers, but a Frank here was likely to be an adventurer who might shift his allegiance to another of the petty lords, and with it his residence. And for the most part, these Franks lacked experience in farming and trading. Of the Moors who were staying, many had been scholars and administrators; as a people they shied away from farming and handicrafts. The Jews, in contrast, were successful at farming and crafts, and renowned for their commercial activities.

In the northeast of the peninsula the pattern developed that when the Christians won a town they would encourage Jews to come and settle there, often by granting them lands that under the Moors had lain neglected or that in the wars had been devastated. Jews did come, particularly from the south. Northern Spain was falling to the Christians because the Moors, with centuries of rule, had become physically and morally weak. The same weaknesses were rife among the overlords in the south, perhaps even more so in the hot climate. The Christians had not invaded southern Spain; still, Andalucia had for decades been suffering intra-Moslem warfare.

Around 1145, a group of Moslem-Berber fundamentalists in North Africa, the Almohads, decided that the Moors of Andalucia should be brought back to the pure Islamic faith. Almohad doctrine related only to Moslems. But once the Almohads had conquered Andalucia, arrogant in victory and zealous in setting up new offices, they began inquisitions that led them to persecute Moslems and non-Moslems. They closed synagogues and churches, forcing Christians and Jews to choose between conversion, exile, and death. Unable to worship freely, unable to educate their children in their faith, many Jews converted or went underground. Many other Jews fled. They fled to the Christian lands, which suddenly (or so it seemed) offered more security than the Moslem.

If this grievous persecution had to come, its timing was fortunate. By now the Christian rulers around Tudela had seen for themselves the loyalty, stability, and industry of the Jews, native and refugee. Those given farmland had not much gone into the production of grain or wool; instead they established vineyards and dairy farms, which required more capital and less land to produce a livelihood. These would also require more time before the investment would pay off—evidence that the Jewish farmers planned to stay. Monasteries, themselves known for developing wine and cheese by improvements generation after generation, sometimes worked together with the Jews here in exploiting the land.

Then too, the Jews, being essentially a city people, stimulated trade; their commerce, like their estates, had soon become a good source of taxes and loans for the crown. The Christian rulers had also come to appreciate their Jews' experience with Moors. The new officials had necessarily to deal with and encourage those Moslems who remained, and because Jews in the former administration had worked with Moslems in high and low capacities, the Christian rulers used the Jews as advisers and go-betweens. Similarly, those Christians who appreciated the scholarly and civilized ways of Mohammedans and wished to emulate them found they could learn these ways from the Jews.

So Christian rulers welcomed the many Jewish refugees from Almohad persecution. Jews fled Andalucia in such great numbers that after 1148 Jewish life on the peninsula was concentrated in the Christian part. By the reign of Sancho VI ("the Wise"), whose rule of Navarre, starting in 1150, spanned the period of Benjamin's adulthood, Jews were being appointed to high positions at court.

Decades and decades of war around the peninsula had wearied all of Spain's peoples. Even the Christian victors in the north were tired of war, tired of waving the banner of Santiago over infidel heads more sagacious than their own. Neither the Franks nor the Spanish Christians had much interest in matters intellectual; now, anyway, they were devoting their resources to physical construction and political integration. For men seeking greater excitement, war was still raging in the south. The Moors, being booted out of their glorious governorships, had lost the optimism, energy, and funds necessary for scholarship. Where recently ten astronomers or theologians had worked, now just one or two remained. The bright lights of Moorish culture had dimmed.

So for various reasons Spanish Jewry was separating from the Moslem east and becoming closer to the Christian north. Tudela's Jews lived under generally favorable conditions. Still, there were portents, dribbling down from across the Pyrenees—portents indicating a new sort of Christian consciousness.

1. In France, Christian craftsmen were organizing into groups to talk shop, to drink together, to assure mutual help for legal cases and burials . . . and to pray together. In this they sought the sanction of the Church and required oaths that served to exclude Jews. If, as a consequence of these unions, Jews were to be restricted in handicrafts as well as in land-ownership, no wonder more and more Jews in France were entering the insecure trade of moneylending. French ideas were taking root in Christian Spain; would Tudela's textile and silver trades be closed to Jews?

2. El Cid—the adventurer who had conquered Valencia—stories were now circulating about him and his valor, and about how he had financed his expedition with a loan from two shrewd Jewish moneylenders in the citadel at Burgos . . . though old-timers who knew Burgos swore that Jews first went to that citadel only some years after El Cid's death. Had El Cid patronized Jews, they would more likely have been court Jews. The concept of crafty Jewish moneylenders was French.

3. The Franks were warring against the Moslems in Palestine. The Moslems had won back some of the land fallen to the Christians forty years earlier, including, in 1144, Edessa, an ancient Christian religious center. So the Franks had again gone to war in the Holy Land, molesting Jews on the way. Reports of this reached Tudela, though old folks said that the violence seemed not so bad as that on the Franks' earlier march to Jerusalem. On the other hand, a preposterous story was circulating among the French Christians to the effect that Jews used Christian children's blood in Passover ceremonies. . . .

Tudela's Jews were suffering economic as well as religious consequences of the French-Christian wars in the Holy Land. In the economic impetus to the wars, Jews themselves, namely Jewish traders, had played no small role. Over many generations Jews had dominated the trading chain for goods produced in the East and imported throughout Christian lands. These goods stimulated desire for more goods and for knowledge about the distant lands from which they came. If feudal rigidity "pushed" the Christian adventurers eastward to Jerusalem, it was eastern riches that "pulled" them.

The Franks returned from the East with rare goods as booty, and a wish for more, and the money with which to buy. Their crusades had established routes to the East, over which Christian traders now dared to venture. The French Christians in their fighting had developed a Christian chauvinism that encouraged them to buy from Christians. As *Spain* became increasingly Christian, and as *trade* became increasingly Christian, commerce between lands north and south of the Pyrenees no longer depended on Jews. And just at the time when the East was becoming more commercially interesting and accessible, Jews were being excluded from that trade too. With Christian expansion, the crusaders, after so horribly murdering the innocuous Jews of Jerusalem, were adding insult to infamy by extinguishing Jewish trade. Would there be no place at all for Jews in the Christian Holy Land?

The Christian Holy Land?—that's the *Jewish homeland.* Jerusalem was a city of Jewish pilgrimage eons before any Christians existed. But, Benjamin might well have reflected, now there are so few Jews in the world, and these live so far from Jerusalem. Now there are so many Christians in the world that they can send a thousand times more pilgrims than can the Jews to the holy Jewish city. A Jewish pilgrimage can have but one possible destination: Jerusalem. Whereas the Christians have other places to go: Rome, Santiago. . . .

Santiago and its pilgrims! To Tudela come just a few pilgrims to sleep, eat, and visit, but enough of them so that Tudelans all see what it means to be a pilgrim: the devotion that causes a man to trek week after week, even month after month, over potholed and often dangerous roads, feet weary and bleeding, stomach complaining of strange food, yet with spirit joyous in adventure. Humble men and rich men alike, loquaciously missing the comforts they left behind while exulting in their strengthened religious faith.

Was it like this in ancient times when Jews in Eretz Yisrael went up to Jerusalem?

The Jews from Andalucia, of a more spiritual and cultural bent than the Jews of Navarre, who are now in Tudela—these refugees are always referring to Jerusalem, speaking passionately of it as the Jews' spiritual home. They particularly delight in the poems of Judah Halevi, who in his youth moved south to Andalucia, where his writings brought him fame early in the century. How vividly he expressed his longing for Jerusalem:

> Beautiful height! O joy! The whole world's gladness!
>   O great king's city, mountain blest!
> My soul is yearning unto thee—is yearning
>   From limits of the West.
>   .   .   .   .

And who shall grant me, on the wings of eagles,
    To rise and seek thee through the years,
Until I mingle with thy dust belovèd
    The water of my tears?

I seek thee, though thy King be no more in thee,
    Though where the balm hath been of old—
Thy Gilead's balm—be poisonous adders lurking,
    Winged scorpions manifold.

Shall I not to thy very stones be tender?
    Shall I not kiss them verily?
Shall not thine earth upon my lips taste sweeter
    Than honey unto me?[7]

Halevi was still a boy when the Christians conquered Toledo, in his early thirties when they killed his benefactor there, about forty when they besieged Tudela. All the years of his life, that never-ending war. Toledo. Granada. Almoravids. Almohad ruffians despoiling the sere countryside. Swordplay. Riots. Plunder. Murder. Streams of refugees. Great military victories or small squabbles among soldiers, they somehow always led to violence against Jews. He saw it in the Christian north, cursed it with his comrades in Moslem Seville and Granada. Halevi was disillusioned with life, yet anxious in the growing awareness that his own life would not last forever.

Are you still, at fifty, pursuing your youth
Though your days are flying to their end?
Will you flee from serving God
And strive to be serving men?
. . . .
Make yourself acceptable to your Creator
For the rest of your days which rush by.
Seek not with a double heart for His favor
And go not to meet enchantments,
But to do His will be strong as a leopard,
Swift as a roe, and mighty as a lion.[8]
. . . .

Could he please God, and enjoy himself at the same time, by traveling again?

My heart is in the East, though I'm deep in the West.
How can I savor food, partake of it with zest?
How can I fulfil those bitter oaths I vowed,
With Zion crushed by Edom, while I'm to Arabs bowed?

It would not be hard to leave the good things of Spain,
Knowing that I might the Temple site attain.[9]

Halevi's phrases were genius. His thoughts were those of many a middle-
aged man moldering away in Tudela.

4

Leaving Tudela

A trip to Jerusalem? to the "home" of his people? Such a long trip? Maybe even to Baghdad, long since the center of the Jewish world? Dare he embark on a journey like that?

We shall never know what impelled Benjamin eastward, nor the doubts that beset him. Was his main motive pilgrimage? or commerce? or adventure? or even escape from family responsibilities? We just don't know. We can, however, be fairly certain that he didn't make his decision overnight. First as dream, then as plan: most likely he shared his idea, sought counsel of the rabbis and advice of the merchants of Tudela, then of all those scholars and foreigners he could buttonhole in nearby Pamplona and Saragossa and in the coastal towns.

Jewish refugees from Andalucia reminded him of Jews' many ties to the East, to the Bible lands, and of the glory of being a Jew there. Old Moors babbled Moslem tales, evidently learned fifty or more years ago from parents or grandparents come here during the era of Moorish rule: amazing stories of Cairo and Baghdad "in the East." The Franks who had settled in Tudela and the French-Christian pilgrims ever trudging along the roads to Santiago, they repeated what they had heard about the Kingdom of Jerusalem and about pilgrims to the Holy Land.

Clopping along on his donkey, gliding along on a river-boat, Benjamin would reflect on the Hebrew poems of longing for Jerusalem. Could he himself go there? Even Judah Halevi, so desirous of seeing Jerusalem, so eager for new adventure, had hesitated before leaving on the long trip:

> Can bodies of clay be prison-houses
> For hearts bound fast to eagles' wings—
> For a man life-weary whose whole desire
> Is to lay his face in the chosen dust?
> Yet he fears and trembles with falling tears
> To cast Spain from him and seek shores beyond;
> To ride upon ships, to tread through wastes,
> Dens of lions, mountains of leopards—
> But he rebukes his dear ones and chooses exile,
> Forsakes shelter and inhabits deserts. . . .[1]

Nor could Benjamin find much reassurance in the Talmud: "Travel is hard on clothes, person, and purse";[2] "Three things sap one's strength—worry, sin, and travel."[3] He would return from the East an old man . . . if he were lucky enough to return at all. To be sure, others had done it, and how they loved to talk about it. Stories enough for ten lifetimes. They would tell their tales whether or not one wanted to listen, for the pleasure of re-living a bit of the adventure.

However experienced the travelers, however much they enjoyed new places, merchants and pilgrims alike spoke of their loneliness en route and their concern about people at home, and stressed the importance of finding a good traveling companion. Of course, if only for safety's sake, he wouldn't travel alone. For each segment of his journey he would necessarily join a caravan of merchants and other travelers, with its contingent of armed men; although in a party the men would sleep and eat together and not seek out persons who lived locally. In any case he would meet men in the caravans and on board ship, but of these men he had better be suspicious and, at most, he would have their company for only a few months. He should indeed travel with a friend, for the whole trip. The Arabs have a saying: "The companion is more important than the route taken."[4] Rabbi Meir made another point: that "travelers should go in threes, for a single traveler is likely to be murdered, two are likely to quarrel, but three will always make their way in peace."[5]

Apart from murder, which would vitiate all his planning, Benjamin had to consider other hazards. War burst out intermittently along the Spanish coasts; although international trade continued despite it, no wise trader who had an alternative sailed from a Spanish port now. If one did set sail safely, then there were sure to be storms at sea—agonies of thrashing and keeling and vomiting, as the survivors described them. His baggage might have to be jettisoned. And sea monsters! . . . not that anyone had ever returned to tell of having been eaten by a sea monster . . . excepting Jonah. One might even come through the voyage unharmed and then meet disaster, as some people say happened to Judah Halevi himself: that when he arrived at the very gates of Jerusalem he was met by a Moslem horseman and slain.[6]

Then there were the normal risks of living, like theft and illness, that one might meet at home too but which seemed worse when one was abroad. At least being Jewish would mitigate such hardships. Jewish traders over the centuries had developed an effective network of mutual aid, so that by Benjamin's time, in commercial centers everywhere—indeed wherever a Jewish community existed—any Jew found "family." This proved largely true despite the Talmudic warning: "Business does not make brothers."

Notwithstanding the diversity of their origins, Jewish traders shared, along with their religion, their membership in a particular and minority group. Camaraderie grew, moreover, because of their common experience of long months and years away from their homes. Since they often acted as agents for one another, they were constrained to conduct their business so as to merit the mutual trust.[7] Their "shop talk" included reports of pirates at sea and highwaymen by land: disasters risked by each of them. The moral obligation developed that, if harm should come to a trader or to his merchandise, businessmen from the nearest Jewish community had to aid him in any way possible.[8]

Even on reaching a destination safely, the Jewish traveler would go first to a synagogue. Arrival in town would be a relief after the preceding nights spent on board ship or, en route between towns, in uncomfortable inns. At synagogue he would be received warmly. Some local man—often the cantor—would invite him home, offer him bed and meals for the duration of his sojourn, and, as he prepared to move on, furnish him with victuals, an animal, and detailed directions for reaching the next town. Should the sojourner need them, his host (or the host community) would provide him with clothes or medical care. For the traveler inclined to sponge, his expenses while abroad could be less than those at home.

Not that all Jewish travelers imposed on the local communities. Those whose sojourns lasted more than a week or so, and who could afford it, would take their own rooms or apartments and then accept the invitations of local people for Shabbat and feast or fast-days. The regular system of hospitality, however, did enable poorer men to travel—for example, men without work in their own regions, who hoped to find greater opportunity in a foreign land. They'd say that "the change of one's domicile brings good luck."

The traveler might be a scholar or a cantor seeking a new post or on his way to take up a new post. Or a courier with an important query for a rabbi in a larger center, or a response or a notification from Jerusalem or Baghdad for distant communities: like merchants, judges corresponded frequently. The traveler might be a lady, accompanied just by her servants, going to visit her distant family: it was not unusual for a trader, sometimes for business reasons, to take a wife from a merchant family across the sea. For all such travelers the synagogue arranged sleeping places and Shabbat hospitality. The variety of visitors obliged the community to heed the maxim "Treat him like a rabbi, watch him like a thief."

In the synagogue of any sizable Jewish community, a traveler from abroad would likely find other sojourners from his own country, or at least news of some landsman who had recently passed through. Besides keeping him informed about the commercial world and the Jewish world, this reminded him of his own part in them. If he were, for instance, a fugitive husband, chances are that he would be found out, since an abandoned wife would give power of attorney to men traveling to countries where her roaming husband might be, and, wherever located, the erring husband could be brought to the Jewish court.[9]

These travelers journeyed through vast lands served by roads and sea routes of varying advisability. Before setting out from Tudela, Benjamin would have considered three general itineraries:

1. If he were to embark on a sea voyage from Tortosa, he could sail to Genoa or Venice and thence to the Holy Land. This was the usual route of pilgrims from northeast Spain. Intermittent battles regardless, sea travel was safer than land travel. But that itinerary would mean long months at sea and little chance to visit the communities of different regions.

2. If he were first to go south, he would follow the old Roman road (although it was in bad condition, and impassable after a rain). It led from Saragossa via Toledo to Cordoba. From Andalucian ports, large ships sailed regularly across the Great Sea to Egypt, not far from Jerusalem. By going south, he would avoid lengthy travels through Christian lands north of the Pyrenees and eastward; and, everything considered, a Jew would still be better off in Moslem territory than in Christian. In the south of Spain he would visit the culturally rich and Jewishly significant Andalucia, with its fabled cities of Granada and Cordoba, the Jewish town of Lucena,[10] renowned for its scholars, and the port of Malaga, from which ibn Gabirol had come. But now, sadly, Andalucia's Jewish communities were fast disintegrating, and if caught in a war down there, he would risk his whole trip.

3. If he were to travel north, through the Christian lands, he would see the world of Jews who had never known Moslem rule, Jews of a different nature and strange customs. He would reach Genoa or Venice by traveling overland and continue overland to Rome, the destination of many Christian pilgrims. Rome had a large old Jewish community, doubtless with men who could tell him how best to proceed to Jerusalem.

Would that last itinerary be best? Indeed, should he make the trip at all? In matters of such great moment, people commonly sought an answer of God, and a Jew would do so in a Jewish manner. He might open a Torah scroll at random and divine God's will from the columns and verses that appeared . . . though the rabbis inveighed against so doing. He would call upon his mother or some other older woman to intercede with God for him and would solicit her prayers for his journey.

He would need to apply to the synagogue congregation for permission to leave, a permission virtually always granted on condition that the voyager arrange for his taxes to be paid to the community during his absence. Announcement at the synagogue of his impending departure would put any creditors on notice to present their claims. If no objections were sustained, he would receive the community's laissez-passer, without which he'd risk being turned away by the Jews in the next town.[11]

From local scholars and merchants known abroad, he would request letters of introduction, for these attestations of his worthiness would ease his way in foreign Jewish communities, especially where he was not sojourning on commercial business. These letters were the only documents he'd need from Tudela for travel. On crossing into Moslem territory, he would be required to pay a dhimmi-protection tax, imposed in lieu of the annual head tax paid by dhimmis resident in Moslem lands. He'd get a receipt, which he would have to carry on his person; if he couldn't show it on demand, he would have to pay again. Jewish and Christian travelers reported that this purchased "protection" was indeed effective . . . provided the traveler had friends in local high places.

Travelers carrying merchandise met customs barriers, and laws of Moslem lands required non-Moslem traders to pay duties at a double rate. Generally, however, Moslem customs men considered this unfair and seldom demanded the double duty. Some traders nevertheless took it into their own hands to evade the discriminatory tax: for example, a non-Moslem coming from abroad might present himself as an agent delivering goods to a local Moslem, a friendly ad hoc accomplice.

But there was no escaping the road tolls. Traders never ceased griping about the road tolls exacted at the entrance to every principality and every town. The more cynical traders insisted that lords and princelings constructed new roads and arranged detours on old roads just to be able to collect another toll. Surely a man from Tudela would find the tolls in foreign lands no worse than those he had to pay in his home region. In northern Spain and southern France—that is, on routes to Santiago—a vast number of pilgrims required shelter and food; bishops and abbots, to finance these "free" services, imposed road tolls ubiquitously. Whenever traders could, wherever the volume of traffic warranted it, they would tread a new path; but before long some bishop found a way to put up a gate there too and demand his toll. Mohammedan lands probably knew similar skirmishes.

Whenever a traveler crossed into a new territory, officials would subject him to all sorts of questions (and in Moslem lands ask to see his tax-receipt). Arriving by sea, a traveler at his home port would probably be passed through quickly, whereas a foreign traveler might have to wait on board a day or more before he could disembark. The ruler didn't seem to care where the traveler came from or where he was going, provided he paid the tolls.

Boundaries defined lands over which sovereigns fought; they did not impede peaceable travel or trade. Money crossed borders easily, coins from one territory being taken at face value in exchange for coins from another territory, so long as the money-changer recognized them. In effect, some coins served as international currency, while others were spendable only near the territory in which they had been minted. Travelers paid their tolls and such small expenses with gold and silver coins, while traders paid larger commercial bills with negotiable paper.

Benjamin composed a detailed picture of what he might find on the different routes, based on travelers' morsels of remembrance and advice. He himself would doubtless even visit towns that no one had mentioned. Although previously he had written only business letters and kept simple accounts, he would, he decided, keep a diary of all the places he saw and the people he met.

What should he take along to write on—parchment or paper? Parchment was certainly more durable—that's why it was always used for Torah scrolls, contracts, and the like—and as he would be traveling for years through wind and rain, durability was important. On the other hand parchment, being made of animal skins, was expensive, and he would need many sheets of it. The new paper from Valencia now, made of linen and hemp rags by the Jativa Jews[12] that paper was cheaper than parchment and lighter to carry because it was thinner—indeed he might be judged penurious for using it — although the letters coming into Tudela from the East, even from prosperous merchants, were written on paper. It was said that the prelates in Rome disliked paper because it was so much used by Moslems and Jews.[13]

He would carry paper.[14] And a writing case, as a scribe carries it, hanging from his belt, with his quill pens, and ink-sticks, and a small, strong sack of sawdust for drying his freshly written phrases.

Just thinking about what he would write, he felt exhilarated. He'd be a writer, a chronicler, a historian, a scholar. . . . He built fantasies on the verse of Samuel ha-Nagid:

> A man's wisdom is in his writing,
> Through his pen his ideas take wing;
> By his pen he may ascend to the rank
> That the scepter attests for a king.[15]

It remained only to choose a day for departure. People thought Tuesday a lucky day to start trips, Wednesday unlucky. Jewish travelers on longer trips generally preferred to spend Shabbat at home and then leave on Sunday. A convoy of Jews would likely schedule its departure for just after Shabbat or for just after a fast day or festival.

Chances are that some of his friends and colleagues arranged to accompany Benjamin on the first segment of his trip, down the Ebro at least to Saragossa.

The moment came. He went to the synagogue for morning prayer, breakfasted copiously, inspected his pack on the mule that would carry it to the landing, and gazed blinkingly at his house. Would he ever see it again? Soberly he murmured:

    May it be Thy will, O Lord my God,
to lead me forth in peace, and direct my
steps in peace, and uphold me in peace,
and deliver me from the hand of every
enemy and ambush by the way, and send a
blessing on the works of my hands, and
cause me to find grace, kindness,
and mercy in Thy eyes and in the eyes of all
who see me. Blessed art Thou, O Lord,
who harkenest unto prayer.[16]

Part Two
Benjamin's Travels

N.B. The text in boldface type comes from Benjamin's chronicle (primarily from the translation of A. Asher, *The Travels of Benjamin of Tudela*).

Letter from Barcelona

I first set out from the city of SARAGOSSA, its Jewish quarter in the south-eastern part of the city inside the old Roman walls. Jews have been active here for hundreds of years.

Solomon ben Judah ibn Gabirol called Saragossa a "second Gomorrah." Of course he had his particular reasons for considering it so—do you know his story? Born in Malaga, always sickly, Solomon lost his parents early and had to earn his living, so that he was very lucky to be blessed with a genius at writing. And he knew it, that is, he knew about the genius:

> I am the master, and song is a slave to me.
> The harp of all poets and minstrels am I.
> My song is a crown to all kings of the earth,
> And a miter on the heads of the noble and high.
> Though my body treads on the earth here below,
> My spirit soars to the clouds in the sky.
> Sixteen though I am, yet my wisdom excels
> The wisdom of one who is eighty well-nigh.[1]

Somehow the poor but talented young poet came north, and Saragossa's learned Yekutiel ben Isaac ibn Hassan took him under his wing. In this way, during his impressionable youth, Solomon sojourned in the upper-class world of courtiers and poets. There he knew the anxieties of boy-becoming-man, and he wrote poetry as youngsters do, though to be sure more profound than most, as when in homage to his patron's father he brought allusions to his own life into his lines about an apple:

> My lord, take this delicacy in your hand.
> Perceive its scent. Forget your longing.
> On both sides it blushes, like a young girl
> At the first touch of my hand on her breast.
> An orphan it is without father or sister,
> And far away from its leafy home.
> When it was plucked, its companions were jealous,
> Envied its journey, and cried aloud:
> "Bear greetings to your master, Isaac,
> How lucky you are to be kissed by his lips!"[2]

But soon Solomon suffered further bereavement: in 1039, his beloved patron Yekutiel was killed in some horrid civic business. Aged eighteen, the grieving Solomon wrote:

53

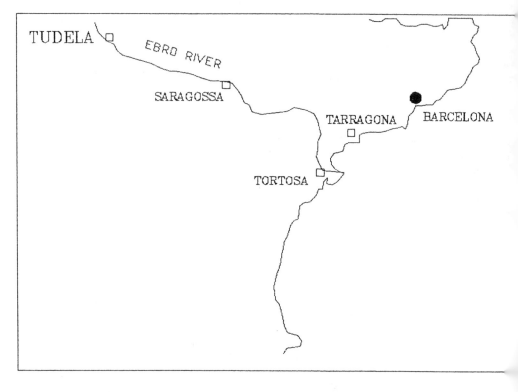

And now the sun, in scarlet decked,
Descends for evening. Behind her
She trails the colors from north and south,
Arraying the west in deep purple.
The earth she denudes of color,
Leaving it faint in the shadow of night.
With her departure the skies are black
As though in mourning for Yekutiel.[3]

Despondently, he reached out for the world with his pen. Always interested in language and especially the Hebrew language, during the next year
or so he wrote four hundred stanzas elucidating Hebrew grammar[4] . . . and
doubtless other poems as well. But the self-important young poet and the
Jewish community of Saragossa didn't get on well together, and with the
death of Yekutiel, he had lost his patron, so that finally in 1045 Solomon
was forced to leave the city. Alone, sensitive, morose, bitter, he despaired
of where he was, and (like many young Jews in Moorish Spain at the time)
he decided to go to Palestine. In any case, he couldn't wait to leave Spain:

Woe to thee, land of my foes,
In thee I have no portion,
Whether joy or sorrow be thy lot. . . .[5]

Meanwhile, he kept on writing melancholy poetry in Hebrew, filled with the awe of God.

> When all within is dark
>   And former friends misprize,
> From them I turn to Thee
> And find love in Thine eyes.[6]

So concerned was he about God and man that to develop his own ideas he studied Aristotle, upon whose works he then wrote commentaries. He wrote a book too, in Arabic, called *The Well of Life*, on man's relationship to God and man's purpose in life.

In the same strain, the poetry flowed, nay, gushed.

> My thoughts astounded asked me why
> Towards the whirling wheels on high
> In ecstasy I rush and fly.
>
> The living God is my desire,
> It carries me on wings of fire,
> Body and soul to Him aspire.
>
> God is at once my joy and fate,
> This yearning me He did create,
> At thought of him I palpitate.
>
> Shall song with all its loveliness
> Submerge my soul with happiness
> Before the God of Gods it bless?[7]

And he did virtually all this in *rhyme* . . . and you certainly realize how much harder it is to rhyme Hebrew than Arabic. Before Solomon, really, no one had much success in doing it.[8]

His great talent and the depth of his thinking made other scholars jealous of him, and they harassed him. His reaction was to write more poems, poems about his rivals, contemptuous lines like these:

> . . . fools parading as wise men . . .
> They deem their song superior to mine
>   whereas they do not even understand it . . .
> Tiny little ants that they are, they
>   venture to compare themselves with me.[9]

> . . . sceptics . . . weaklings . . . prisoners of the senses.
> And every fool and every spendthrift
> Thinks himself as great a master as Aristotle.
>   You think that they have written poems?
> You call that a Song?
> To me it seems the cackling of ravens.[10]

They say it was one of his rivals who murdered him, age 37,[11] near Valencia. Perhaps he was on his way "home" to Malaga or Saragossa . . . or Palestine?

From Saragossa **I proceeded down the river Ebro to TORTOSA.** The Jewish community of Tortosa is very old; they say that Jews were already in Tortosa when the ancient Romans arrived. A tombstone here has lettering in Latin, Greek, and Hebrew.

You probably know that a Jewish community of scholars flourished here in the days of Moslem rule, but that many of the Jews fled (as did the Moslems) while the Christians were gaining control of the city, and that by the time Count Ramon captured Tortosa in 1148, few Jews remained.

As it happened, Count Ramon (Ramon Berenguer the fourth, who died a few years ago) turned out to be a good man, who made efforts to restore the Jewish community. He gave the Jews orchards for grapes and figs and olives, orchards which Moslems had held, to encourage the Jews to remain there. Jews did not have to pay any taxes at all during the first four years of Don Ramon's rule, and even after that their tax burden was mild. He decreed that Jews could not take Moslems as slaves or insult them; but also that Jews were never to be under the authority of a Moslem. He appointed Jewish officials to his court.

He set aside a fortified area, between the river and the seacoast—this must have been a thriving neighborhood, under the Moslems—where he decreed that Jews might build sixty houses; and besides, he promised more land for houses for any Jews who might return to Tortosa or come to settle here. But sixty houses proved ample for the Jewish population.

The count also set aside a part of the port area for the houses of the Genoese, who had come from Italy to fight with him. Don Ramon wanted to make Tortosa into a big commercial seaport. Although he ruled for fourteen years, his hopes for Tortosa never blossomed into reality. Even today, Tortosa is just a mediocre seaport. And the Jews did not fare so well either, for Don Ramon was obliged to share his power with other nobles who had fought with him against the Moslems, and these other nobles lacked interest in enlarging Tortosa's seaport or in working with the Jews toward the development of the city; these other nobles wanted only to amass a fortune, quickly.

Two days journey brought me to the ancient coastal city of TARRAGONA, with its ruins of many Greek and Roman buildings constructed with huge, irregular stones; buildings like these are to be found nowhere else in the whole

Kingdom of Spain. The massive walls here are also magnificent. It is a very old city, built by the Phoenicians.

I am told by Jews here—and I have read in the writings of Edrisi and other Arab geographers—that Tarragona was a Jewish city when the Moslems came here. There are many Jews throughout this region, working mostly as traders and farmers. In the city itself, Jewish merchants live in different parts of the fortified areas. With Tarragona now under Christian rule, the Jews still live well here and some Jews have become officials in the city administration.

Tarragona has been governed by the family Burdet for forty years. The Robert Burdet who took part in the capture of Tudela and then became castellan of the Christian Tudela: they say his forefathers in Normandy were just petty nobles. Yet by winning the battle for Tudela he founded a whole dynasty of governors of Tarragona. How a single wartime adventure can change the world for a man and his heirs!

Two days hence lies BARCELONA. The city though small is handsome and is situated on the seashore. Merchants resort hither for goods from all parts of the world: from Greece, from Pisa, Genoa and Sicily, from Alexandria in Egypt, from Palestine and the adjacent countries. Every day ships arrive with silks and spices, glassware and jewels. All the merchants praise Barcelona for its beautiful scenery, just as Jewish travelers and poets sing the city's praises.

Once upon a time, Jewish merchants did most of the trading out of Barcelona, between the Christian and the Moslem ports. But no longer, for now trade with the East is conducted by Christians. Goods from Damascus are carried to the ports of Syria and Palestine, whence Italian-Christian merchants ship them to Venice and Genoa and then on to the ports of Provence and that of Barcelona.

The main area of Jewish residence is close to the harbor, in the *callis iudaicus* in the center of the old city, thus also near the cathedral, the count's castle, and the main gate. **There is a congregation of wise, learned and princely men. Among them are R. Shesheth**, and **R. Shealthiel** who is descended from R. Judah ben Barzilai al-Barceloni. R. Judah ben Barzilai wrote the *Sefer ha-Shetarot* about fifty years ago, and these days it is known to all scholars. He based it on existing *shetarot* (legal instruments) which Jews use in dealings among themselves. In cases of a legal matter between a Jew and a Christian for decision in a Spanish court, naturally the legal document is written in Latin; but often a *shetar* in Hebrew is appended. Barcelona is the head city of all the Jewish communities in Catalonia and Aragon.

R. Shesheth ben Isaac ben Joseph Benveniste is one of the family of

Benveniste long important in Barcelona and Narbonne. They were the first of the local nasi'im, and served the counts as advisers, negotiators, and money lenders. Young R. Shesheth, born in Narbonne, is just thirty years old, yet already he is one of the outstanding physicians of Barcelona. As he reads widely, he is familiar not only with the medical literature but also with Moslem scholarship generally, and with history, and with Hebrew poetry. He himself has written some poems of merit.

There is also Abraham Alchakim, who was physician to the count. He started his royal service as physician to King Alfonso (the first of that name), king of Aragon and our Navarre. When King Alfonso died in '34, he was succeeded by his brother Ramiro (the second), whose daughter and heiress (named Petronilla) Don Ramon married in '37, thereby uniting Aragon to Catalonia under his rule, and R. Abraham became physician at the court of Don Ramon. (Another Jew who had served King Alfonso before serving with Don Ramon was Eleazar of Saragossa, who joined the count's household as steward.)

For R. Abraham, one reward from Don Ramon was a large garden, where R. Abraham was to construct a public bath. The count and the physician shared the cost of furnishing the bathhouse, the count paying two-thirds and the physician one-third. The bathhouse was run under the sole control of R. Abraham the physician, who received one-third of its income, in perpetuity, for himself and his heirs. Don Ramon decreed that no other public bath might be established in Barcelona. On which account, the elderly R. Abraham is very rich.

Don Ramon died in '62; now it's the fifth Ramon Berenguer who is count and sovereign of Barcelona and who rules as King of Aragon under the name of Alfonso (the second).

Another Barcelona physician, an intelligent young man named Joseph ibn Zabara, entertains us with his wit. He says things like: "Do not swallow poison because you know an antidote." To a wealthy man who disparaged his undistinguished ancestry, R. Joseph retorted: "Your noble line ends with you, mine begins with me." One of his patients received a visit from a bore, who asked him, "What's ailing you?" to which the sick man replied: "Your presence."[12]

In ancient times, this city was founded by men from Carthage. Later on, during many generations, the Visigoths—Christians—ruled Barcelona, and they persecuted Jews. The Jews rejoiced when the Mohammedans came and conquered the city. But soon afterward they lost it again, to the Christian emperor Charlemagne.

Charlemagne was happy to have the Jews in his domain because of their skills in trading, thus he placed no limits on their business dealings. He himself is said to have frequented Jewish merchants, especially a jeweler, and to have placed Jews in high positions at his court. One of these officials, a certain Isaac, went as interpreter with a delegation of Charlemagne's to Harun al-Rashid, khalif in Baghdad. Isaac was the only one to return from the mission, and across the Great Sea and over the Alps he led Harun al-Rashid's gift: an elephant.[13]

But Charlemagne dared not be too lenient with his Jews. In court, when a Jew brought a charge against a Christian, the Jew was required to have more witnesses than a Christian. The emperor forbid the sale of any Church property to a Jew. If a Jew took in pledge any property belonging to the Church, he risked the loss of his own property—and of his right hand. There were other such decrees. Charlemagne was trying to appease both Jews and Christians—the eternal ploy of the political man.

Charlemagne made Barcelona part of his Spanish March, his Spanish border-country stretching along the whole southern border of France, at the Pyrenees. Barcelona stood at the southern edge of the March, which became closely linked with the lands of the counts of Provence, the sea coast province in the southeast corner of the empire of the Franks. There was much maritime commerce between Barcelona and Marseille.

And there was much fighting around Barcelona between Christians and Moslems. The Mohammedans won Barcelona back from the Christian counts, with the help of Jews, not only from this city but from the whole seacoast region (and with the help especially of the Jews from Tarragona; they told me so in Tarragona). But the Christians, under the first Ramon Berenguer, won it back again. That's why Barcelona is much less Moorish in its culture than is Tudela—it was ruled by the Moslems for such a short time.

During the generations when Tudela was the northernmost town of the Moors, Barcelona was usually at the southern edge of the Christian empire, and a war zone. Lasting peace returned to this city only in our own century.

The local Jewish community has naturally shared the ups and downs of Barcelona's history. There have been some very prominent Jews in the city, and the Jewish community is prominent in the region. Some Jews own land outside the city walls and are good farmers; they say that Jews own one of every three or four estates in and around Barcelona. And yet the position of Jews is not like that of other men: although Jews here might own any land they wish, the count virtually owns the Jews. They are little more than his vassals, not quite free men. But then (it seems to me) lords always calculate taxes, fines, and indemnities differently for Jews than for others. Because the county of Barcelona was part of Charlemagne's Spanish March and is linked with the counts' fiefs in Provence, this corner of Spain holds to policies of land-ownership like those of the lands across the Pyrenees, a system requiring loyalty and oaths to one's lord. And in this Jews have no part.

The local Jews engage in many crafts, making cloth and clothing and shoes and jewelry. Most of their shops and stalls stand outside the city walls in the marketplace near the old fort. Wealthier Jews earn a good living by lending money to the nobles. Money changers serving the merchants and travelers, who must always keep a supply of coin on hand, have traditionally accepted the money of others for safekeeping and for lending.[14]

But now, so they tell me, much to the north of the Pyrenees, beyond Provence, a great number of Jews work primarily as moneylenders because they are obliged to do so, being prohibited other employments. There, they say, even some poor Jews join with others so that together they can lend money to rich lords. Up in France few Jews are smiths. Here in Barcelona, as in other cities south of the Pyrenees, Jews prefer to work fashioning gold and silver into vessels and ornaments because merchants would rather sell these than sell the base metal.

The Bible tells us that even in antiquity Jews worked with gold and silver. They refined these metals and cast and beat and filigreed them to make articles for use in synagogue rituals and in home ceremonies. And of these metals they also made vessels for the house and ornaments for the person, for which they had no problem finding buyers. And then, much more recently, Jews perfected their great skills while living under Moslem rule, since Moslems disdain artistry and left it mostly to Jews. One consequence is that now in Barcelona (as generally in northern Spain where Christians rule), many of the goldsmiths who work for noble households are Jews. Of course most men in this craft, Jews and non-Jews, work both gold and silver, just as is customary in Moslem lands. You probably know that the Arabic word sā'igh refers to gold- and silver-smiths together and means simply "one who fashions."

Such an intricate craft, this working in gold and silver. Much more complicated than making that copper cooking–ware, for instance. The Jewish silversmiths make all sorts of things, from the tiny bells for hanging around donkeys' necks that you always hear jangling in the streets to big magnificent candlesticks and decorations for the Torah scrolls. But perhaps the silver items made here are not so fine as those which come from the lands of Byzantium, usually small delicate pieces inlaid with colored stones or decorated with enamel.

Some Jews have been employed in the Barcelona mint. It makes my heart jump and my greed rise to see how many coins are made in a single day. It is not very skilled work, making coins. Besides the metals, the coin maker just needs a small furnace, an anvil, and basic tools like a die and a punch, that is, the metal plates with the design cut into them. And of course he needs a fine balance, for he must weigh the metal very very carefully before melting it and forming it while still hot into small balls. He places the die on the anvil and a small ball of metal on the die. Then he lays the punch on the metal ball and hits it sharply once or twice with a hammer, thereby flattening the metal ball into a flat round shape and simultaneously cutting the design from the die and punch into the two faces of the round flat metal, producing the coin. On the other hand, the cutting of the designs into the thick metal plates requires some skill. Some of the gold coins here are named after the men, Jews, who cut them.[15]

Many Barcelona Jews fear that they may be forced to leave their skilled work. From time to time over the last fifty years Franks have passed through Barcelona on their way to Palestine, To'im,[16] misguided wanderers, and these Franks believe that only Christians have a right to live and work, and they are very aggressive toward the Jews. They scream that Jews should not be allowed to live and work like men because the Jews killed Christ, but more likely these Franks are envious of the skills and the wealth in the Jewish community.

Letter from Narbonne

From Barcelona, **a journey of a day and a half brings you to GERONA, which city contains a small Jewish congregation**, with its cemetery and its ritual bath. Those Jews who own land in Gerona and outside its walls have to pay a tithe to the Church. Only a few years ago did the Jews receive permission to rent shops beyond the walls.

< <   < <   > >   > >

Three days further lies NARBONNE, a city of Jewish importance since around 800, when King Charlemagne drove out the Mohammedans. Local Jews now vaunt the fact that their forefathers supported the Holy Roman Emperor. They like to talk about how King Charlemagne rewarded Narbonne's Jews for supporting him, by giving them special rights and even naming a "Jewish king" here—perhaps what we call a *nasi,* or prince.[1]

In Narbonne today **the number of Jews amounts to about three hundred.*** Most of their dwellings are in and around the Villa Judaica, but the Jews rent properties scattered over a wide area in the northern part of the city; while in the Villa Judaica reside many Gentiles who replaced former Jewish inhabitants. In the last twenty years, because of fighting between Narbonne and Toulouse, many Jews have left Narbonne.[2]

Narbonne remains **a place of eminence in consequence of the studies carried on**. Scholars from Moslem Iberia and Christian France and Italy meet here, and the city is an intellectual center for Jews, with fine Jewish schools, among the best in the world for the sciences and medicine,[3] and **from here the study of the Law spreads over all countries.**

This city contains many very wise and noble men, principally R. Calonymus, son of the great and noble R. Theodoros, o.b.m., a descendant of the House of David, as proved by his pedigree. Some scholars, to be sure, express skepticism about such pedigrees. They say that any records of David and his descendants must have been lost even in ancient times, owing to all the

---

*We cannot assume the accuracy of Benjamin's population figures. Medieval writers used numbers for effect, and Benjamin's figures sometimes seem inconsistent. Furthermore, the numbers he gives for "Jews" or "Jewish inhabitants" probably refer only to men or to heads of households. (Extant writings from the twelfth-century Mediterranean lands make only bare allusions to women.)

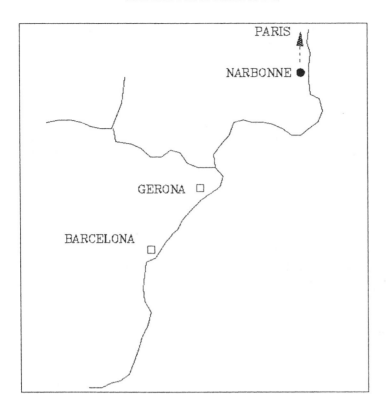

wars and dispersions. Doubtless some men in all times have claimed relationship to ancient nobility and expressed pride therein even if it wasn't
true. Such men use the false connection to help them associate with men of
greater wealth and renown. This dishonest practice often continues through
several generations of a family, so that those who today boast of noble
ancestors may not even know if the vaunted relationships were true ones.
The Christians have been teaching for a thousand years that Mary came
from the line of David. And from King David the Karaites also claim a
descent which is in fact uncertain.

Be that as it may, the eminent R. Calonymus **holds landed property from
the sovereign of the country, of which nobody can deprive him by force.** The
lords here do act as protectors of the Jews. When a few years ago some
To'im sailing from Provence to the Holy Land attacked Jews, the viscount
and the archbishop sent the Frank attackers away, the Jews fortunately
escaping without harm.[4]

Another prominent Narbonnais is **R. Abraham** ben Isaac, **the President of
the Academy,** that yeshiva which attracts so many scholars to Narbonne. As
R. Abraham is *rosh yeshiva*, they generally call him Ab-beth-din (president
of the Court of Law) or its acronym, Abad. In his fifties now, he first came to

the attention of the older men of Languedoc and Provence by his Talmudic commentaries and by his responsa. Now he is a leading figure in Jewish Provence among the partisans of law and customs from Spain.

The book that made him famous is his Eshkol, a compendium of Jewish law based on the Babylonian Talmud. They say that although Rabi Abad isn't very original, he puts forth other scholars' ideas in a clear fashion and with great wisdom. He broke new ground in his Eshkol by organizing all the Talmudic laws and regulations according to topic. Now students and the younger judges can find the rulings they seek much more easily than they could in the older books. Scholars greatly admire Rabi Abad as the first Jew between the Pyrenees and Paris to write a major book of Jewish law.[5]

Paris, far north of here in **the Kingdom of France (called by the Jews Tsarphat)**, is **the metropolis of it and has six days in extent. This city, situated on the River Seine, belongs to King Louis** (the seventh of that name) **and contains many learned men** among its numerous Jews, **the equal of which are to be met with at present nowhere upon earth; they employ all their time in the study of the Law, are hospitable to all travelers and on friendly terms with all their Jewish brethren.**

Paris and the north of France and the Norman country to the west of Paris are the regions from which have come the greatest number of pilgrim-warriors to the Holy Land, especially in the years just before 1100 and again just before 1150. The first waves of Franks, and their confrères from the Rhineland, decimated the Jewish communities along their routes, on the grounds that if they were to tramp for months to put down the infidels of the Holy Land they should equally put down the infidels closer at hand. Seventy years it is now since the Jews suffered a horror greater than any they had ever known, or at least not since the times of the Romans. These massacres were the extreme outcome of the long Christian tradition of abusing Jews for their refusal to accept Jesus as God.

Twenty years ago, to encourage Franks on a second big Eastern adventure, Pope Eugenius (the third of that name) proclaimed that any man taking up the cross for the Holy Land need not pay interest on debts to Jews. This time the Christian leaders of France—namely, Abbot Bernard of Clairvaux (the main preacher of this second invasion) and the then-young King Louis and his minister, the abbot Suger—rejected the idea of violence against Jews and preached and decreed against it, so that there were no massacres of Jews like fifty years earlier and the Franks contented themselves with plunder of Jewish property. Through such plunder, in addition to the official confiscations and special taxes, the Christians took the wealth of the Jews to outfit themselves for their invasions of the Holy Land.[6]

Furthermore, since the Franks' first invasions, the ports of the Great Sea from Italy to the Holy Land have favored Christian over Jewish travelers, so that fewer Jews can live from trading in goods. At the same time, the Church has proclaimed increasingly against Christians lending money for interest. As a result, north of here now, moneylending is being carried on by a great number of Jews.[7]

These changes in Jewish fortunes are considered to be so serious that, for the first time since the days of the Talmud, a synod has been called to discuss the problems. The assemblies, attended by hundreds of rabbis and scholars from France and from Germany, meet in cities east of Paris, namely in Rheims and in Troyes, at times to coincide with the fairs,[8] under the direction of Jacob ben Meir Tam (a grandson of Rashi). The synod has forbidden all Jewish traders to purchase or to take as security for a loan, or to obtain in any way whatsoever, any ornament of Christian significance (such as a crucifix) or any article belonging to a church, for if such an item is seen in Jewish hands, the Christians may punish the whole Jewish community.[9]

Letter from Lunel

Four parasangs* from Narbonne **lies the city of BEZIERS, containing a congregation of learned men,** some of whom live in the part of town belonging to the bishop and others in the part belonging to the count, for thus is the city divided in two. Both the bishop and the count have appointed Jews to administer their businesses and their taxes, and both the bishop and the count impose their taxes on the Jews.

According to an old tradition here, the Christians used to go out every year on the Sunday before Easter to stone the Jews and their houses; but, blessed be the Name of God, the bishop stopped that annual violence a few years ago.[1] He demanded in return that the Jews pay him another tax each year. Among the taxes that the Jews have to pay the count is a spice tax, specifically on honey, pepper, and cinnamon.

Beziers has a new synagogue, with beautiful inscriptions in Hebrew and with pavements of mosaic.

MONTPELLIER, called by the Jews Har Ga'ash, is conveniently situated for the purposes of trade, being within two parasangs of the coast. You meet here with Christian and Mohammedan merchants from all parts: from Algarve, Lombardy, the Roman Empire, from Egypt, Palestine, Greece, France, Spain and England. People of all tongues come here principally in consequence of the traffic of the Genoese and of the Pisans. In the time of our grandfathers, until Franks settled in the Holy Land, the principal importers here of goods from the East were Jews; but now there are many Christian traders and fewer Jewish merchants.[2]

The Jews of this city belong to the wisest and most esteemed of the present generation. Among them are many learned men, for the city contains several *yeshivot.*

---

*Benjamin generally gives distances in "parasangs," one parasang being equal to about three-and-a-half English miles. Sometimes he uses other measures, many different systems being current.

Travelers would consider five parasangs a common day's journey.

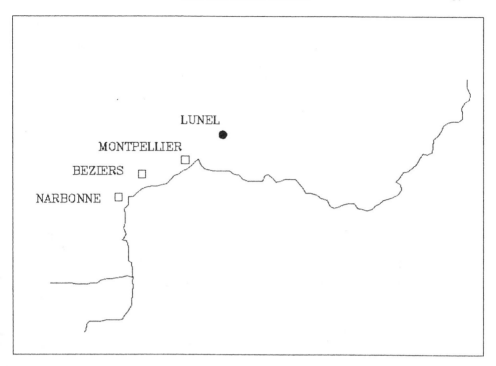

LUNEL

MONTPELLIER

BEZIERS

NARBONNE

Here medicine is also taught, to Jews and Gentiles alike, in earlier times in Hebrew and in Arabic, nowadays in Latin.[3] From the old Jewish idea of the *Bet heqdesh la 'aniyim* (house consecrated to the needy),[4] the Christians of Montpellier have dedicated a building entirely to the cure of disease; they named it after the Holy Ghost, and use it especially for the Franks returning from their wars in the East. That is, the good and benevolent local Christians have adapted an old Jewish activity of mercy for the benefit of violent Christians who massacre Jews!

If it is true that more of the Jews than of other peoples study medicine, then it is not only because of their greater interest in healing the sick. It is also because Jewish physicians can rise to positions of influence with non-Jewish rulers. And because—should that influence prove ineffective—physicians can readily employ their skills in other countries.[5]

Many different rulers control the cities on this coast eastward from Barcelona: the French king, the German emperor, the count of Provence (who is the king of Aragon), and the count of Toulouse and Saint Gilles. The coastal people, that is, the Christians, are of an openness of spirit and a high cultural level; they are liberal in their views, being critical of the opulence of their Church and treating the Jews well.[6]

The Jews of this region are great scholars, writers, and philosophers.[7] **They are also very rich and benevolent toward all those who apply for assist-**

ance. Their bête noire is the pirate. Pirates delight in capturing Jews, for they know a Jew will always be ransomed.[8] It becomes very expensive for the rescuers here, as for any Jewish community on the seacoast. The ransom money is only the beginning. The pirates will have taken the victim's garments, so the local Jews must re-clothe him. They have to pay for his lodging and food not only while he remains with them, but in one way or another also during his journey home. Plus the fares.

< <   < <   > >   > >

From Montpellier **four parasangs to LUNEL, which stands within two parasangs of the coast, a city also containing a holy congregation of Jews who employ all their time in the study of the Law.**

This town is the place of residence of celebrated rabbis, among them **R. Asher, an ascetic, who does not attend to any worldly business but studies day and night, keeps fasts, and never eats meat. He possesses an extraordinary degree of knowledge of everything relating to Talmudic learning.** He surprises me, for I was under the impression that it is contrary to Jewish law to refrain from the good and permitted things in life.[9] Judah ha-Levi wrote that it is proper for a man to delight in living, for living in this world gives him the chance to merit the world to come.[10] Asceticism is more a practice of Christians, who look down on us Jews for not castigating our sinful selves through pain and deprivation.

The local Jews are in constant connection with Palestine and the East for their religious studies. The first Jews here came from Jericho, in ancient times after Jericho was conquered by the Canaanites. Many of the current Jewish inhabitants of the towns in the valley of the Rhone are descended from refugees who left Spain in the time of the Visigoths. Then there are those who themselves migrated: since the time of our grandfathers Jews have lived more securely in this region, Provence, than north of here in the lands of the Franks or south of here in lands torn by battles between Christians and Moslems. As with geography, so with scholarship: the towns of Provence are intermediate between the Moslem and Christian cultures, and often it is Jews who form the bridge between the two. Provence has many men learned in Torah and in Arabic.

Among the new **inhabitants of Lunel** is **the physician Judah ben Saul ibn Tibbon of Spanish origin,** who left Granada (his birthplace) because of religious strife there and settled here several years ago. Now in his midforties, R. Judah works as physician and also as translator, and it is due to his literary work that he is well known among the Provençal scholars. Translators abound in Provence, because it is here that the Greek sciences of the Mohammedans are translated for dissemination in Europe, to aid Christians in discovering and understanding the thoughts of the ancients. Here Jews do the translating, then it's left to the Christian scholars to compile, summarize, and write commentaries on these works. Meanwhile, more often than not, it's Jewish traders who carry Arab ideas and techniques to the north, along with Eastern incense and rich vestments for the Church.

Apparently scholars fluent both in Arabic and in Latin (or in one of the vernaculars of the Christians) are to be found almost only among the Jews, who translate either directly from Arabic into Latin or else in two stages from Arabic into Hebrew and then from Hebrew into Latin or a vernacular. Generally Jews don't *speak* Latin, as it's the language of the Roman destroyers of the Temple and of the modern Christian church, but some Jews here and in Spain have learned it for correspondence and diplomacy.[11]

R. Judah is one of the many Jewish physician-translators who transmit the great medical works of the Greeks. However he does not confine himself to medicine; he has translated other works from Arabic into Hebrew. He says that most Jews of Christian lands are fluent only in Hebrew, for the languages of their sovereigns are not strong in works of scholarship or science as Arabic is; whereas the Jews of the Moslem lands have made the Arabic language their own so as to study great works of science and philosophy in Arabic books, sometimes books by Jews; and he says that the Arabic language is richer and clearer than the languages spoken in Christian Europe.[12] On the other hand, he tells me, some men argue that the Jews of northern Europe, whose only or principal language is Hebrew, speak better Hebrew than we Arabic-speakers for whom Hebrew is a second language.[13]

R. Judah translates poetry between the two languages, and has done a few of the expressive Hebrew poems by Solomon ibn Gabirol. He translates philosophy, from Arabic into Hebrew, notably Bahya ben Joseph ibn Paquda's wonderful book on ethics, *Hovot ha-Levavot* (Duties of the heart), where R. Bahya expounds on ten spiritual commandments as being pivotal to Jewish life; and he is just finishing the translation of Judah ha-Levi's *Kuzari*.[14] R. Judah ben Saul says that in order to translate such works honestly, one must understand the subject well in addition to having a scholarly knowledge of the two languages;[15] and that (even when going directly from the original into the Christian language) the qualified translator will proceed in two stages, first making a literal translation into the new language, then rewriting the literal translation for clarity and beauty, as though it were an original production of his own.[16]

R. Judah has had opportunity to compare bad translations with good ones—and so has made himself into a good and respected translator—because he reads voraciously. He has a large collection of books, with two or three copies of some titles, and of this library he is very proud.[17] He appreciates that his collection of books incorporates the labor not only of their authors and perhaps translators but also thousands of hours of work of numerous copyists; and that books contain the knowledge and wisdom of

the ancients for generations yet unborn. R. Judah speaks with disdain about
men who collect books despite indifference to the ideas contained in them,
a disdain shared with (and perhaps inherited from) an earlier native son of
Granada, the vizier-statesman Samuel ha-Nagid. Samuel ha-Nagid is
R. Judah's hero.[18] R. Judah must have delighted in translating R. Samuel's
verse:

> A man who spends money to buy himself books
> Not for their contents, just for their looks,
> Is like a cripple who on wall or in sand
> Sketches legs and feet but cannot stand.[19]

Samuel ha-Nagid became legendary for encouraging people to read by
giving books away to impecunious scholars and even sending books as donations to poor Jewish communities abroad;[20] of course he was wealthy enough
to do so. R. Judah may love reading, and love his books, and want to
encourage scholars just as much, but he is not quite in Samuel ha-Nagid's
financial position; still, he lends his books willingly to the scholars and
others here. (He makes certain to get them back!)[21]

R. Judah is not unusual among Lunel's Jews in supporting scholarship.
**All foreign students who resort hither with the intention of studying the law
are supplied with food and raiment at the public expense during the whole
time of their stay in the academy.**
Many students come hither from the north, from the valley of the Rhine,
a great region of Jewish scholarship. One legal scholar who came here from
the Rhineland was Rabbenu Gershom, among whose decrees were that a
woman could not be divorced without her consent; that an apostate son
who died should be mourned as any other child; that a traveler carrying
another's letter may not read it; and—an idea reiterated by R. Judah—that
a scribe copying a document or book must copy it exactly as it was written,
and not make any change however he might wish to correct or improve it.
Rabbenu Gershom had many pupils who spread his words, among whom
the famous Rashi. Rashi too came from the north, where many Jews earned
their living in agriculture and where one hundred years ago Rashi was a
vintner and trader. But when Frank warriors passed down the valley of the
Rhine massacring Jewish communities, the elderly Rashi left his vineyards
and his home. Many other Jews along the Rhine were likewise forced from
their lands, and now their heirs are trying to survive as moneylenders.
Montpellier and Lunel having many physicians and scholars, a few men
have reminded me of Rashi's censure of physicians: he blamed them for
over-confidence in their craft, which results in their trusting in it instead of
in God; and he blamed them for commercializing their profession to the

extent that they sometimes fail to attend the poor.[22] In the north, that is, in France, few Jews are physicians.[23]

Here in Provence the Jews speak highly of medicine from the East and of luxury goods from the East; on the other hand they disparage the Jewish philosophy of the East as being too "spiritual." **The Jews of this city, amounting to about three hundred, are wise, holy, and benevolent men, who support their poor brethren near and far.**

Letter from Marseille

From Lunel to **POSQUIÈRES**[1] **two parasangs. This is a large community, containing about four hundred Jews and a fine academy under the presidency of the renowned rabbi, R. Abraham ben David,** called Rabad. Son-in-law of the renowned Rabi Abad (R. Abraham ben Isaac in Narbonne, from whom I brought greetings), Rabad is **a scholar of the very greatest eminence and skill, both in the Scriptural and the Talmudic branches of learning. He attracts students from distant countries whom he teaches and whom he lodges in his own house.** To be sure, every community feels a sacred obligation to support scholars, being that study is an act of worship, and many pious Jews foster young scholars from abroad. Still, the students hold R. Abraham ben David in the highest esteem because **he provides them with all necessities of life from his own means and private property, which is very considerable.**

< < < < > > > >

From Posquières **to NOGRES or Bourg de St. Gilles, three parasangs.** The town has **about one hundred Jewish inhabitants.**

It is the place of residence of R. Abba Mari, son of R. Isaac o.b.m. who holds the office of steward to Count Raymond.

This town, a place of Christian **pilgrimage visited even by the inhabitants of distant countries and islands, is situated within three parasangs of the sea on the very banks of the large river Rhone which flows through all Provence.**

< < < < > > > >

To ARLES, three parasangs, with two hundred Israelites.

< < < < > > > >

From Arles, **three days to MARSEILLE, a city containing many eminent and wise men. The three hundred Jews form two congregations, one of which resides in the lower town on the coast of the Mediterranean** (the bishop's land) **and the other in the upper part near the fortress** (the viscount's land). **Both** communities are under the bishop's authority. The community in the upper part **supports a great academy and boasts of many learned scholars.**

As in any congregation, the scholars and the others argue about the proper

72

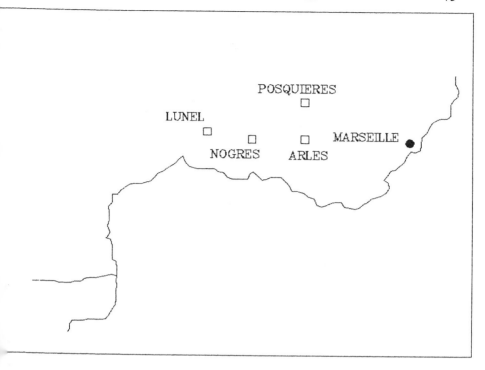

way to conduct the service. The Amidah is to be prayed silently, while standing up; the Sh'ma is to be recited very loudly, for the Talmud says so, but during the quintessential Sh'ma should the worshipers stand as for the Amidah or should they sit as Saadia Gaon decreed? Should a psalm be recited as part of the closing prayers, or is that a sectarian practice not to be emulated? The psalms and poems which lift so many hearts in private prayer—men able to spend more hours in public worship would like to add some of them to the synagogue service, and everyone agrees that they are beautiful and worthy to praise the Lord—but what about working men who cannot spare the additional time for a longer service?[2] Congregants want familiar prayers and a familiar order of prayers, these making it easier to follow the service; but the sages declared that praying should not be a fixed task,[3] that each worshiper should add something new to his prayers every day. The tenth-century poet Joseph ibn Abitur (native of Spain, migrant to Palestine) put this idea into a song, which perhaps you know:

> Each day I compose a new blessing
> On God's works and feats,
> He who renews Creation daily
> With his mighty deeds.[4]

An extensive trade is carried on in this city, which stands on the very coast. They tell me that in the trade which has flourished here since the time of

Charlemagne, Jews have always been active. Once the Mohammedans had conquered the lands from Babylonia in the east to beyond Santiago, that is, to the edge of the earth in the west, they had to devote their energies to controlling and administering their immense empire, and at that time, the commerce between the parts of the empire and beyond its borders became the work of Jews.

Although their pirates kept busy, honest Mohammedans eschewed the trade over the Great Sea. When they traveled abroad to trade, as to govern and to study, they did so within their own vast Arabic-speaking empire. They also preferred land travel to sea travel. Other than their invasions into Spain, they never crossed the Great Sea, thus never became familiar with the kingdoms north of it. They couldn't speak the Europeans' Latin anyway, just as the Europeans were ignorant of Arabic—whereas Jews everywhere could communicate with one another in Hebrew. Consequently Jews, although they carried on most of their trade within the Moslem empire, forged the thin trading links that did exist between Moslem and Christian worlds.[5]

Brocades, furs, slaves, and pharmaceuticals made up most of the cargo in the boats sailing frequently between Marseille and Barcelona at this corner of the Great Sea and Constantinople and Alexandria on the eastern shores; the dealers in these items were predominantly Jews. North of the Pyrenees, up in central France, the Jewish traders held such a monopoly of international commerce that the words *Judaeus* and *mercator* were used as synonyms. Not that all traders around the Great Sea were Jewish. The Christian Greeks and Italians, skilled sailors, traded too. When in 1081 Venice—a city unfriendly to Jews—took over the trade between Constantinople and the East, the Jews lost their near-monopoly of international commerce.

If they were to continue to profit, Jews would have to do better than others.

By the time Venice grew into a strong commercial nation, Jews were trading in virtually everything that can be traded and they had a regular network of contacts with traders in all goods throughout most of the world. Back and forth they sent detailed records of their goods and their transactions. Their business letters were carried by traders and other travelers, even between very distant countries. They would entrust a letter to a traveler going part of the distance, then that traveler would turn the letter over to another. Even though it takes a year or so for a letter between (for instance) Marseille and Baghdad,[6] and it may have been entrusted to several travelers before reaching the addressee, the letters usually arrived. Merchants wanting greater assurance that their message would reach its destination soon learned to dispatch two copies by different couriers.[7]

In a letter, a trader might inform a distant colleague of the imminent arrival of a shipment of goods, and ask him to pay for it on his behalf. From this sort of communication merchants developed a way of paying for goods at a distance, namely with letters of credit or bills of exchange. Using one of these, a trader could transport large sums of money without having to carry coin.[8]

Small Jewish merchants would ask others, traveling abroad, to sell and to buy for them in foreign lands.[9] It also became common for Jews to pool their resources, into partnerships. Talmudic dicta against being employed by another encouraged Jews to develop partnerships, often with one partner investing the capital and another traveling on the road. Partnership arrangements had the further advantage of dividing among two or more men the losses that inevitably occur in the long-distance transport of luxury goods.

In most towns, one of the leading Jewish businessmen would receive the letters sent to a foreign merchant and hold them for his arrival. The same businessman would accept money from a foreign merchant to pay out later for the merchant's purchases. Acting as representative of the merchants, he would also deal with the rulers in case of a merchant's difficulty or death. (Otherwise, when a merchant died, the ruler would confiscate his goods.) This consular role seems to have originated with Italians in the eastern part of the Great Sea rather than with Jews. Now it is common among both Jews and Italians.[10]

Not only Jews collectively, but often an individual trader dealt in a vast variety of goods—for example, perfume, pitch, pearls, peppers. Since every item (and each item in its several qualities) has to be priced separately, traders began to call upon a specialist to set the prices for the goods to be sold—another stimulus for businessmen to work together.[11]

All this sharing of information and activities among Jews has created a pool of knowledge particular to Jews, which Gentiles believe is a Jewish ethnic aptitude for business. Unconcerned about the origins of the acumen, sovereigns seek to profit from it. Just as, in the good old days, the Moorish rulers of Andalucia and Tarragona employed Jewish merchants in their courts, along this coast the Christian princes depend on Jews for imported wares and for coin, the rulers and the Jews serving each other's interests.

In Marseille Jews own some of the merchant ships, by themselves or in partnership with Christians. Most of the vessels though are Italian. They are of both types, the rounded navis with sails and the thin galley with oars.[12] Ships go from here to every port in the Great Sea, carrying every sort of merchandise from spices to slaves. Arabs seldom run the ships, even though most laden ships arrive from the East, with goods especially for traders to carry north to Frankish knights who sojourned in Palestine, and for their ladies: luxury articles for body care and adornment, like perfumes, and herbal lotions and unguents and ointments, and dyes for the hair. For each man who travels with the merchandise, there are many who never leave the port cities but work with the traders, such as merchants, brokers, inspectors, translators, insurers, and packagers. Many of these are Jews, as is common in the ports of Provence.

The city is abustle not only with traders, but also with pilgrims evident by the red cross sewn on their outer garment, and especially with the Frankish warriors who are the most conspicuous. A knight walks tall, the center of his entourage of squires and grooms. In the scabbard on his left side he carries his famous heavy double-edged sword, which is his weapon for hand-to-hand combat. (In the East the knights also fight with battle lances, in length twice the height of a man, but one hardly sees these weapons except when the armies are boarding ship.)[13] Most Franks are beardless when they leave their homeland, but as they move east they begin to grow beards in accordance with local custom.[14]

We're all aware that ever since the time of Charlemagne the Franks have sent their soldiers climbing over the Pyrenees to oust the Mohammedans from Spain; and now for more than sixty years the Franks have been sending their soldiers over the Great Sea to oust the Moslems from Palestine, many of which soldiers board ship or end their sea voyage at Marseille. On their outward voyage the Franks are aggressive and empty-handed; on their homeward voyage they seem chastened and carry rich booty. All of the returnees, in their different ways, express amazement at the vast amounts of coin and culture they found in the East; even among the ones eager to get home, some are going to feel disappointed in their old routinized rural lives. After observing any Frank here for just a few minutes, you know from his manner of speech and his demeanor where his hometown is, whether he has yet been to Palestine, and if so, about how long he stayed there.

From all that I have heard, I think I shall like the Kingdom of Jerusalem, except for its people.

Letter from Pisa

From Marseille, people take ship for GENOA, which also stands on the coast and is reached in about four days. The city is surrounded by a wall. No king governs over it, but senators chosen by the citizens from among themselves. Every house is provided with a tower and in times of civil commotion war is carried on from the tops of these towers.

Two Jews, from Ceuta on the North African coast, **reside here.** They are said to be refugees from Almohad persecutions. There is no real Jewish community here. According to Genoese law, the visit of a Jew or a Moslem is limited to just three days.[1] Another law subjects any Jew sojourning here to a tax of three *solidi* annually to pay for the lighting of some church.[2] In fact, a few Jewish traders do drift in and out of the city without much hindrance. They cannot take up official residence, yet the people of Genoa treat them well enough so that they continue their precarious sojourns, the attraction being the great amount of trade along this coast.

The Genoese are masters of the sea and build vessels called galleys by means of which they carry on war in many places, against Christian and Moslem alike, and bring home a great deal of plunder and booty, to Genoa. They are at war with the Pisans. They use their galleys as trading ships too, mostly for short distances, as for bringing textiles here from Marseille. But they have also built some galleys for longer distances, such as for sending goods to Sicily or to Barcelona. These oar-propelled ships, the largest, they build with two floors or decks, on which merchants sailing with their merchandise can rent space to build themselves rooms. Such wealthy merchants often stipulate that animals and pilgrims be forbidden or restricted on the deck. But traveling this way is unusual, for most merchandise is carried by sailing ships.[3]

Many of the pilgrims to Palestine, mostly Christians and especially Franks, arriving in the north of Italy, cross overland to Venice, whence they sail eastward. Venice is said to be a city that grows no grains or fruits at all, but depends entirely upon commerce. Apparently Jews are even less welcome in Venice than in Genoa, although until modern times Venice tolerated Jews who traded with the East. Now Franks go to the East in far greater numbers than Jewish traders ever did, so the Venetians support the Franks, supplying them with food and arms, money, even warships. Venice is the richest port in the world, its merchants the masters of commerce with the East. Some Jews do participate in that magnificent mart, but they have to

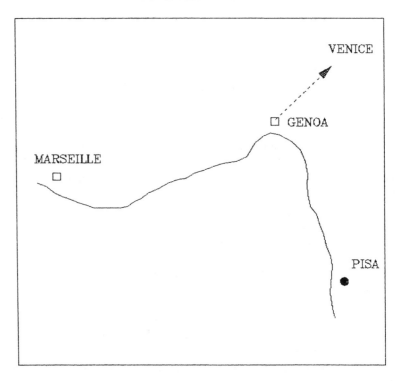

deal shiftily, never announcing to the world at large that they are Jews, because Jews cannot trade as citizens of Venice and they cannot trade legitimately as foreign merchants, for they don't come from another trading nation.

And yet, even in Venice and Genoa, where Jews must use subterfuge to trade, it is trade which provides the Jewish communities of northern Italy with the major part of their livelihood. And brings substantial customs duties into the cities' coffers.

From Genoa **to PISA is a distance of two days' journey. The latter city is of very great extent, containing about ten thousand fortified houses, from which war is carried on in times of civil commotion.** Success in its wars against the Moslems has furthered Pisa's prosperity, making it into the leading town of central Italy and enabling it to begin new and beautiful buildings such as the cathedral which they say will be the largest in central Italy and will have ornate interior decoration and a freestanding tower.[4]

The city has no walls. It stands about four miles from the sea, yet its harbor is the best (almost the only) harbor on this coast of central Italy, making Pisa a major trading port. **The navigation is carried on by means of vessels**

which ply upon the Arno, a river which runs through the very city. Pisa trades in its own vessels, it carries hither great quantities of dyestuffs from the East and sells them in the renowned textile cities of Lucca and Florence. Rivaled as a merchant port by Genoa and Venice, Pisa controls markets throughout the lands bordering the Great Sea,[5] it boasts of having three times as many agents in Constantinople as does Genoa,[6] and it has colonies in Egypt and Syria.[7]

In contrast to Genoa and Venice, Pisa welcomes people from different lands. French and German merchants come here from the north, and Turks and Persians from the east. These Eastern peoples are Moslems, about whom the Church often complains, calling them heathens.[8] But the people of Pisa pay the Church no mind in this regard; **all Pisans are brave,** and tolerant and confident. **No king or prince governs over them, the supreme authority being vested in senators chosen by the people.** Their legislation treats Jews kindly, and as a result there is a Jewish community, whose members take part with impunity in the Eastern trade.[9] Now there are **twenty Jews resident at Pisa.**

I'll cut this letter short, because I've just heard that berthed in the harbor there's a ship bound for Barcelona, so I'll go out now and deliver this at the quay.

Letter from Lucca

From Pisa **four parasangs to LUCCA, a large city** and an independent republic. It's a major way station on the *via regia*, which road runs between
France and the south of the Italian peninsula. Controlling this road, Lucca
tries to keep the Pisans from using it,[1] for the two cities are traditional
rivals. When not engaged in armed conflict against each other, the cities
maintain commercial warfare, so that the prosperity of each depends on
good merchants. Of course such rivalry is advantageous for Jews. The city
contains about forty Jews, which makes Lucca's the biggest Jewish community in Italy north of Rome.

Several generations ago, Lucca's flourishing commerce attracted some
Jewish silk-weavers from the south of Italy.[2] They and their descendants
continued to work at silk-crafts, and now Lucca is the center of Italy's
silk industry.[3]

The silk industry depends not only on its skilled craftsmen but also on
its merchants. The merchants in fact come first, because the region around
Lucca produces no raw silk for its craftsmen to weave. Some of their raw
silk comes from the south, from Calabria and Sicily; but most of it comes
from the East. Whenever a cargo ship from the East docks at Genoa, several
of Lucca's merchants travel there to buy. Some buy only for the manufacture
which they themselves control; while bigger Luccan merchants may buy
large quantities of raw silk in Genoa, for resale to silk manufacturers in
Lucca. Some big Luccan merchants keep a permanent agent in Genoa. From
time to time a merchant from Genoa comes to Lucca with raw silk to sell.
Always Genoa—Lucca doesn't obtain raw silk from Pisa or from Venice.[4]

Some of Lucca's merchants go abroad themselves, to Constantinople or
other eastern ports of the Great Sea. In addition to raw silk, they buy silver
and gold for use as thread, and dyestuffs.[5] All these are very expensive, and
the merchants must have the money to pay for them, even if they need not
always pay in coin.[6] In whatever way they purchase the raw silk, they will
transport it to Lucca via the Genoa road, in long narrow bales which the
pack animal bears on either flank.[7]

For the most part, Luccan merchants who bring in the raw silk do not
sell it to the craftsmen but themselves maintain ownership of it and merely
distribute it, first to throwsters and then to dyers and weavers.[8] (Patterned
silk is woven of threads already dyed different colors; while a monocolored
cloth can be dyed after it is woven.) The craftsmen work in their own homes

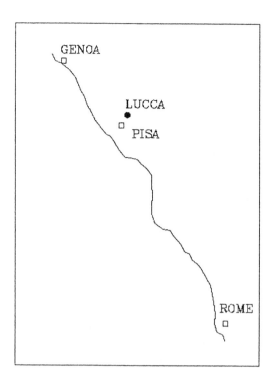

or workshops, with their own tools; the merchants pay them by the piece, then take the finished cloths to sell them.[9]

Silk cloth being produced from expensive materials brought from afar, it must be sold at a high price. Traditionally only very wealthy people could afford to buy it, and no single locality housed enough wealthy people to support a silk industry. Lucca had the advantage of location on the route between Rome and the northern countries—Christian pilgrims and prelates on their journey homeward from Rome passed through Lucca and bought its good-quality silk, thereby stimulating the manufacture of it. As Luccan weavers produced more silk, Luccan merchants sought customers for it from a wide area.[10]

The Christian conquest of Jerusalem, and the consequent journeying of great numbers of northern Europeans to the lands of the East, gave impetus to Lucca's silk industry. Many of the Franks saw how colorful the Eastern silks were and how many of the Eastern people wore them; they were eager to purchase silk for their own use at home, even if they could afford only a small piece of it. Some knights and officials returning home from the Holy Land passed through Lucca. To meet the Franks' tastes, Lucca's craftsmen produced silks with new Oriental patterns (for example, with hawks and falcons),[11] and Lucca's merchants sallied northward to sell the silks on the Franks' home grounds, especially at the great fairs of Champagne.[12] They also sell great quantities of silk to churches: it is said that Lucchese silk is used for vestments and church decorations in all the lands of Europe.[13] Now Lucca's silk is so well-known that merchants come here from France and Germany to buy it.[14]

Despite the high price there is no lack of buyers for good silks. People buy them for their beauty, of course, but also for their durability—they know that in case of need they can sell them for coin. Traders in luxury textiles will buy silks and resell them at a higher price. Such merchants, already knowledgeable about textiles, gained skill in the money arrangements, keeping the textiles in their possession until the seller could buy them back or until a propitious moment to offer them on the market. From these financial dealings with textiles grew the skills in pawnbroking and moneylending which have sometimes enraged the Christian debtors. Now Jews in the communities of France and Germany are forced into financial trading in order to survive.[15]

The Jews of Lucca have long had particular ties with the Jews of the Rhineland. Two hundred years ago, when Lucca was a center of Jewish scholarship, its most prominent family was Calonymus; it was one of the rabbis Calonymus who established the Talmudic academy here. Around the year 1000 of the common era some members of that family and of that academy migrated to the Rhineland and established an academy there too, in the city of Mainz. The Luccan community has kept in touch with the Talmudic scholars up there, and in Lucca one hears a lot about Germany.

The Jewish congregations of Germany live along the banks of the great river Rhine, from Cologne where the empire commences unto Regensburg at **the** other **frontier of Germany which is fifteen days' journey** distant. **Germany is called Ashkenas by the Jews and is a country full of hills and mountains.**

These are the cities of Germany which contain congregations of Israelites: Metz and Treves situated on the River Moselle: Coblenz, Andernach, Kaub, Kartania, Bingen, Worms and Mistran. On the river Rhine are the cities Mainz, Strassburg, and Speyer. It was along these two rivers that the Jewish communities suffered the worst of the atrocities of Franks departing for the Holy Land, just before 1100 and again in 1145–47.

The second time, the archbishops of Cologne and Mainz spoke out against the violence and provided refuge for some Jews. Meanwhile, the murderous Christian fanatics were egged on by a Cistercian monk named Rudolf. One of the leaders of the Cistercian order, Bernard of Clairvaux from Burgundy, learned of the massacres while he was in Flanders preaching for men to do their Christian duty in the Holy Land; he hurried to Germany to calm the rioters, to order Rudolf back to his monastery, and to condemn anti-Jewish persecutions.[16] But not before hundreds of defenseless Jews had been slaughtered, which we shall bemoan for the rest of our days.

These cities of Germany **contain many eminent scholars. The congregations are on the best terms with one another and are friendly towards the far and near; whenever a traveler visits them they are rejoiced thereat and hospitably receive him. They send letters to one another by which they exhort themselves to hold firm in the Mosaic law. Those that spend their time as mourners of the downfall of Zion and the destruction of Jerusalem are always dressed in black clothes and pray for mercy before the Lord, for the sake of their brethren.**

Besides the cities which we have already mentioned as being in Germany, there are Aschaffenburg, Würzburg, Xanten, Freising, Bamberg, Tsor, and Regensburg on the confines of the empire. All these cities contain many rich and learned men.

In the last century while the German Jews grew in learning and in wealth, Lucca declined as a center of Jewish scholarship. But it recently regained some of its eminence due to the sojourn here of a certain sage, another son of Tudela. It refreshes me to know that R. Abraham ibn Ezra lived in this city and liked it.

R. Abraham's life has been so fruitful. He was physician and astronomer, philosopher and grammarian. He wrote poems, religious and secular, even as a youth, some excellent poems; and growing older and wiser he wrote commentaries on the Bible. What genius! And what wit! They say he was always too busy to make much money or even to think about money; wherever he went he chose to be with scholars. From his boyhood he was quite friendly with Judah ha-Levi, o.b.m., though R. Judah was somewhat older than R. Abraham. The two traveled together to Andalucia and as far as North Africa. What a joy it would have been to travel in their company!

Until he was around fifty, R. Abraham was at home in Spain. Then, R. Judah having just gone off to Palestine and Isaac (R. Abraham's only surviving son) living as a Moslem in Baghdad, the lonely R. Abraham sought solace in traveling . . . and presumably in his writing, for he wrote a great deal during his sojourns, at least in Italy.

He went first to Rome, where he wrote a brief work on the prophets Daniel and Job, and a book on the structure of the Hebrew language. But Rome's Jewish scholars deprecated R. Abraham's ideas. Angry and sad, he left and wandered northward, arriving in Lucca in 1145. Here, evidently, the Jewish community and its scholars dealt better with him. He stayed a couple of years, during which he supported himself by teaching Bible and Hebrew grammar to synagogue boys. The rest of his hours he spent writing a commentary on the Pentateuch and an unusual work on the authorship of the Book of Isaiah, and works on grammar. I think it was here that he composed his *Yesod Mora* (Foundations of the fear of God), drawing from his Bible commentaries and newly classifying the mitzvot, and like R. Bahya delving into ethics.[17] In addition he wrote eight short works on astrology, which many people have told me they read with great interest.

Around 1150—several local men recall him clearly—R. Abraham moved on to Mantua and Verona (to the north in Italy), and after that he went to Beziers and Narbonne (in Provence). He journeyed to Baghdad, to be with his dying son . . . from which bereavement came this poem:

> Father of the child, draw near to mourn,
> For God has taken away from you
> Your son, your only son,
> The son whom you love, Isaac.
>
> I am the man who has seen
> Destruction, whose joy has fled.
> Alas, I have lost the fruit of my loins,
> And it never came into my mind;
> For I thought that in my old age
> He would be well and strong.
> But I have labored in vain,
> I have begotten a son, to dismay me.
> For how can my heart be glad
> At the death and departure of Isaac?
>
> .   .   .   .
>
> I shall lament and weep each minute,
> And raise a plaintive cry,
> When I remember how three years ago
> He died in a foreign land;
> How he journeyed from place to place,
> My soul yearning after him,
> While I wept night and day.
>
> How many sorrows befell me!
> These are the generations of Isaac![18]

And yet, glorying in life as he generally did, R. Abraham returned from the East with fascinating stories and practical ideas. He showed the merchants of our community a way of writing numbers—each numeral through ten being represented by a single letter of the Hebrew alphabet—which is simpler to use than the multiple-letter Roman numerals.[19]

By now R. Abraham is well in his seventies. When the Luccans last heard of him he was in northern France. They have not forgotten him, nor will he be forgotten: future generations are bound to study his commentaries on the Bible, and perhaps to delight as we do in his poems. For the years that remain to him, may he be blessed with a comfortable life!

Letter from Rome

ROME, the metropolis of all Christendom. The two hundred Jews who live here are very much respected. Some of them are officers in the service of Pope Alexander, who is the principal ecclesiastic and head of the Christian Church.

The princes of the Church, called cardinals, come from all over the world to elect the pope; they elected Alexander in 1159. But some of the cardinals frowned upon Alexander as pope and after his election they opposed him by naming their own pope called Victor. Frederick Barbarossa, king of Germany and called Holy Roman Emperor, headed the forces of Victor and his cardinals. The Pisans, along with the kings of Sicily, France, England, and Spain, and others, entered this religious war on the side of Pope Alexander.[1] The party of Victor seeming to be victorious, in '61 Pope Alexander fled to France. The churchly nobles make war just as do worldly nobles. Pope Alexander's side won after all, and Rome has just celebrated his triumphal entry into the city.[2]

Rome's Jewish community is pleased by the success and return of Pope Alexander, for he is a man learned in law, and fair, and they say he should prove a good leader if he ever has the chance to rule his Church during peacetime. In Rome it is a Jewish specialty to make cloth ornaments and banners, especially embroidered ones, and like all local craftsmen the Jewish banner makers worked hard for weeks preparing for Pope Alexander's official reentry. It was a great day when a large contingent of Jews, their rabbis at its head, went to greet him.

This was not the first time that cardinals split into factions and elected two men to be pope, who then fought to hold the office. It happened thirty-five years ago too, when the head of the Christian church in Rome was the Jewish pope. At least that was the sobriquet given to Pope Anacletus (the second of that name), who at birth had been Pietro Pierleoni, scion of the prominent Roman family Pierleoni, which had converted from Judaism several decades previously. I believe it was Pietro Pierleoni's great-grandfather, Baruch Benedict, who converted.[3]

Anacletus, in his pre-papal name of Cardinal Petrus Leonis, had served the Church admirably as papal legate in France.[4] Although the people of Rome defended Anacletus as the properly elected pope, a group of cardinals decried his Jewish ancestry and chose another cardinal as pope. This one, who took the name Innocent, received the support of two important Church councils, along with that of most of the bishops and most of Europe's kings

85

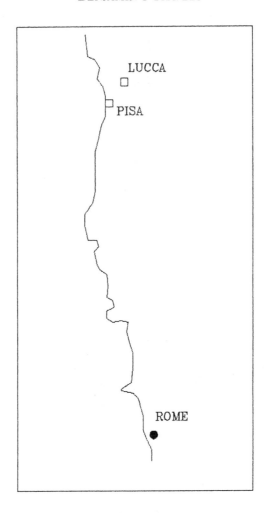

and princes. Innocent represented the reform wing, Anacletus the traditional wing, which drew its support from the common people.[5]

The Church and lay princes broadcast their objection to Anacletus's "Jewish blood," and they accused him of all sorts of corruption on behalf of
"his" Jewish community. The leader of the faction supporting Innocent was
a monk, Bernard of Clairvaux, who argued against having a pope of recent
Jewish family yet insisted that the Jews be left in peace; one hears rumors
that the Church is adding Bernard to its list of saints. The opponents of
Anacletus continued their invective and calumny throughout his eight years
as pope, though he managed to remain in the office until his death. His main
(almost his only) monarchical support came from Roger of Sicily, renowned
for his liberality. Anacletus's principal supporters were the brave people of
Rome. During these years of Church conflict about the pope's Jewish ances-

try, Rome's Jewish community suffered neither official persecution nor local animosity.[6]

The Jews generally live well here, in a sunny world unclouded by anti-
Jewish violence or even the fear of it. They have heard of the Franks' massacres of Jews to the north; but that was long ago and far away, and in a sense
the atrocities against Jews in the Rhineland redounded to the benefit of the
Jews in Rome, because consequently the popes assumed toward the Jews a
protective role. The pope issued a proclamation against the killing of Jews,
against using force to convert them, and against disturbing them or their
synagogues or their gravesites. He issued it twenty years after the massacres, to be sure; we thank God that subsequent popes have honored it.[7]

Unmolested in their Jewish community, the Jews worship in elegant synagogues and maintain important schools,[8] in the Jewish quarter on both banks
of the Tiber. Many prosperous families own a house in the countryside in
addition to a well-furnished home here; and some families have not only
servants but also slaves. (Jews are not forbidden to hold Christian slaves.)

Jews can enter freely into any employment (perhaps even the Church!),
but most Jews work in silk or other textiles, as manufacturers or traders.
The specialties here are cloths of high quality and carpets. Jews also trade
in pearls and gems, in perfumes and incense. And they trade in money
(buying and selling coins of various countries) and they make loans. In
Rome Jews are virtually the only traders in textiles; and unlike others, when
Jews sell an expensive item they may require only a part of the price in
immediate payment, arranging to receive the rest of the price in weekly
sums.[9]

Unlike Jews elsewhere, the Jews of Rome **pay tribute to no one**, that is,
they pay no special taxes as Jews.[10] That seems only fair, since Jews were
living in Rome long before Christians.

It was the Rome of eleven hundred years ago, in the very first years of
Christians, Rome as capital of a huge empire, whose soldiers invaded the
capital of the small Jewish kingdom and destroyed the Holy Temple. **In the
outskirts of Rome is the palace of Titus who was rejected by three hundred
senators in consequence of having wasted three years in the conquest of Jerusalem, which task, according to their will, he ought to have accomplished in
two years.**

**The city of Rome is divided into two parts by means of the river Tiber
which runs through it. In the first of these divisions you see the large place of
worship called St. Peter of Rome. There was the large palace of Julius Caesar.
The city contains numerous buildings and structures entirely different from
all other buildings upon the face of the earth.**

**The extent of ground covered by ruined and inhabited parts of Rome
amounts to four and twenty miles. You find there eighty halls of the eighty**

eminent kings who are all called Imperator, from King Tarquin to King Pepin the father of Charles who first conquered Spain and wrested it from the Mohammedans.

There is further the hall of the palace of King Vespasian, a very large and strong building; also the hall of King Galba, containing three hundred sixty windows, equal in number to the days of the year. The circumference of the palace is nearly three miles. A battle was fought here in times of yore and in the palace fell more than a hundred thousand slain, whose bones are hung up there even to the present day. The king caused a representation of the battle to be drawn, army against army, the men, the horses, and all their accoutrements were sculptured in marble, in order to preserve a memorial of the wars of antiquity. You find here also a cave under ground containing the king and queen upon their thrones, surrounded by about one hundred nobles of their court, all embalmed by physicians and in good preservation to this day.

Also St. Giovanni in Porta Latina in which place of worship there are two copper pillars constructed by King Solomon o.b.m. whose name "Sh'lomo ben David" is engraved upon each. The Jews of Rome say that every year, about the time of the Ninth of Ab, these pillars sweat so much that the water runs down from them.

You see there also the cave in which Titus the son of Vespasian hid the vessels of the Temple, which he brought from Jerusalem.

Opposite St. Giovanni di Laterano stands a statue of Samson with a lance of stone in his hand, also that of Absalom the son of David, and of King Constantine who built Constantinople, which city is called after his name. His statue is cast in copper; man and horse are gilt. Rome contains many other remarkable buildings and works, the whole of which nobody can enumerate.

In a cave on the banks of the Tiber you find the sepulcher of those holy men o.b.m., the ten martyrs of the kingdom. These sages lived in the century after the destruction of the Temple, a time of great persecution of Jews in the vast Roman Empire. The Roman Emperor decided to kill ten of the important Jewish scholars—ten in number, to correspond with the ten brothers of Joseph who had sold him into slavery—and the emperor's men picked ten teachers of Mishnah. The first one's turn came; he rose to Heaven, where he learned that the fate of the ten had been sealed. So informed, the other nine, violently tortured, went to their deaths with equanimity. They were all buried in the same tomb.

The scene brings to my mind some lines of a poem by Moses ben Jacob ibn Ezra:

> Where are the graves of all those who have died
> Since the very beginning of time?.   .   .   .   .
> Their bodies lain atop one another, Become ashes or dust,
> Mixed, together, in their sleep forever.[11]

Ever since the days of the Roman empire, the Jews of Rome have kept in very close contact with the scholars of Jerusalem. When the men here study Talmud, it's the Palestinian Talmud.[12] They follow traditions which developed in Palestine. While we in Spain read through the Pentateuch each year, the Romans take three years. And whereas we celebrate Rosh ha-Shanah for two days and we hold two Seders for Passover, the Romans celebrate each holiday only one day.

The exact rites used in the Italian synagogue were recently written into a book by the learned Roman R. Menahem ben Solomon. He also wrote a commentary on the Book of Psalms, titled *Midrash Sekhel Tob* (Midrash of good discernment), which has become very popular despite its preachy tone.[13]

The principal of the many eminent Jews resident here are R. Daniel and R. Jechiel. The latter is one of the Pope's officers, a handsome, prudent and wise man, who frequents the Pope's palace, being the steward of his household and minister of his private property. R. Jechiel is a descendant, a grandson, **of R. Nathan** bar Jechiel, **the author of the book Aruch and its comments.** The Aruch defines every word used in the Talmud, describes the customs mentioned therein, indeed explains the significance of every Talmudic subject. R. Nathan compiled his work from the writings of the geonim of Babylonia, although he himself was always resident in Rome,[14] Rome which follows the traditions of Palestine.

The Italian Jews are reputed to enjoy studying commentaries on the Bible, and arguments about the meanings of those commentaries, and the relevance of those commentaries for the observance of the Law, while lacking knowledge of the Bible itself.[15] R. Abraham ibn Ezra is said to have sneered at Rome's Jews for this, even going so far as to write disdainful verse about the leader of the congregation, R. Isaac ben Malkhi Tsedek:

> To his ignorant flock he exclaims,
> "Full well am I versed in Talmudic lore";
> He lifts up his voice, to reach the clouds,
> Yet in the easiest chapters he signally fails.
> Even the rank beginner can discover his errors.
> He reads in Taharoth, and knows not his Bible;
> Its very beginning, familiar to all, even to a child,
> Is to him a hard task.[16]

R. Abraham came here in 1140 and lived in poverty, teaching Bible and Hebrew. But he was never content here. He craved conversation about the astrology of the ancient Hebrews and the calculations of modern Spanish astronomers, while Rome's Jewish scholars would talk of nothing other than Torah and Jewish law.[17] The local Jews gave him no encouragement at all for his writing. In fact the scholars attacked R. Abraham for his interest in science, and as a result of the fracas R. Abraham's students left him.[18] He quit Rome disappointed and bitter, complaining (as ever, in verse) that no one appreciated him:

> I've returned to wandering in grief . . .
>   And my own thought frightens me;
> I feel my mouth and tongue chained in fetters.
>
>   In my earlier sojourns I could write poems;
> . . . .
> In every place I lived, I composed books,
> And (like a mirror) I made clear what was unperceived.
> And now I have fallen, In the dust I have grovelled.
>   Here, I dare not open my mouth.
> My spring of knowledge is sealed.[19]

Letter from Salerno

CAPUA is four days from Rome. The town is elegant and prosperous[1] **but the water is bad and the country unhealthy. Among the three hundred Jews who reside at Capua are many very wise men of universal fame,** among whom a few are employed by the town as financial advisers.[2]

< <   < <   > >   > >

From thence to Puzzuolo or SORRENTO, a large city built by Zur, son of Hadadezer, **who fled in fear of King David, o.b.m. The city has been inundated in two spots by the sea. Even to this day you can see the streets and towers of the submerged city. A hot spring, which issues forth from under ground, produces the oil called petroleum, which is collected upon the surface of the water and used in medicine,** as liniment and laxative, as well as in fumigation.[3]

There are also the hot baths, provided from hot subterranean springs, which here issue from under ground. Two of these baths are situated on the seashore and whoever is afflicted with any disease generally experiences great relief if not certain cure from the use of these waters. During the summer season all persons afflicted with complaints flock thither from the whole of Lombardy.

From this place a man may travel fifteen miles by a causeway under the mountains. This way was constructed by King Romulus, the founder of Rome, who feared David, King of Israel, and Joab, his general, and constructed buildings both upon and under the mountains.

< <   < <   > >   > >

The city of NAPLES is beautiful, populous, and thriving.[4] **It is very strongly fortified, situated on the coast, and originally built by the Greeks** at the site of a town called Cuma. They called their newer quarters Neapolis (new town) and then the whole city became known by that name.[5] Naples owes its prosperity to linen and linen cloth;[6] it is a mercantile center with many markets, famed for the variety of goods from all parts.[7]

The five hundred Jews who live in the city can own land and property and sell it or leave it to their heirs if they wish.[8] About ten years ago the Jewish community inaugurated a new synagogue and school, financed largely with the help of a certain Ahisamekh.[9]

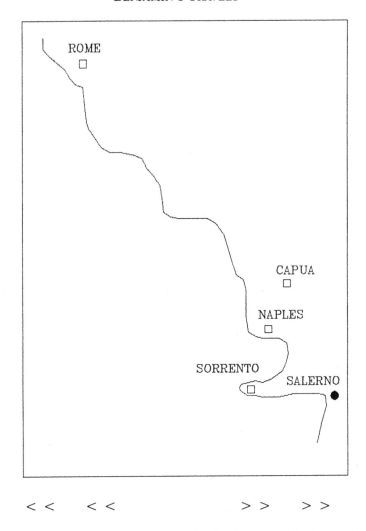

< <   < <   > >   > >

One day from Naples lies SALERNO. The city is surrounded by a wall from the landside, one part of it however stands on the shore of the sea. The fortress on the top of the hill is very strong. The land around Salerno is very fertile, and the city flourishes with the commerce in produce and fruit. They say, though, that Salerno used to be even more prosperous, until King Roger made it part of his kingdom of Sicily forty years ago.

The Jews live mostly in wooden houses in a section of the city reserved for Jews and called the Judaica, although a few Jews live elsewhere, in the town and on the farmland just outside the walls. Several Jews have left the land in recent years, but some still own vineyards and olive orchards and hire Christians to help in the work.

The number of Jews amounts to about six hundred, among which R. Malkhi

Tsedek, the grand rabbi, originally from Siponte, and **R. Elijah ha-Jevani** (the Greek), a physician, **deserve particular notice, being wise and learned men.** Jews here can choose their work freely. Some of them engage in money and finance, many work at producing pottery and bottles, but the greatest number are employed in dyeing and weaving.

One of the scholars here now was a student of R.Abraham ibn Ezra. His name is Solomon Parhon, and he comes from Calatayud in Aragon. A few years ago he completed a lexicon of the Bible, in Hebrew, titled *Mahberet ha-Aruch*. When he came to Italy he found even the scholars unaware of the modern Hebrew language as developed by Jews in Moslem countries, so he wrote this book with the aim of bringing Jews in Christian countries up to date.[10] He writes a very clear and truly beautiful Hebrew; his style would make R. Abraham proud of him.

Scholars in every field come here, and the city surges with the discussions of men of Roman, Italian, Byzantine, Moslem, and Jewish education. There is here an exchange of ideas greater even than in Spain, men who can discuss the thinking and the events of ancient times and relate them to the development and accomplishments of the Christian and Mohammedan peoples. The character of Salerno is very different from that of Rome. Jews in Rome seemed but few in a Christian sea; here Jews are one community among several, they are more friendly to strangers and more open to ideas.

The pride of Salerno is its medical academy, called the Civitas Hippocratica after the Greek physician of ancient times. It teaches all the medicine of the Greek and Roman schools. They say that this academy was founded, in the days before the Normans, by a Greek, a Roman, a Moslem, and a Jew.[11] In its early days many of the teachers were Jews from Arabia. The students heard lectures in Arabic, Hebrew, Greek, and Latin. When the Normans came, about a hundred years ago, among them were many noblemen who loved learning, who developed the academy. The Norman King Roger of Sicily was a grand patron of the academy. (However his son, King William of Sicily, who just died, took less interest in it.)

It's **the principal medical academy of Christendom,** but the Church does not control it; rather its benefactors are scholars and lay people. Persons of any faith, any man or woman who is at least twenty-one years old and has studied logic, may enroll at this cosmopolitan school. The professors include many monks, among them several from the monastery at Monte Cassino, where the medical manuscripts are copied. The monks at Monte Cassino have friendly relations with the physicians at Salerno, even though the most orthodox churchmen oppose the academy.

Physicians here attach great importance to proper diet, for one thing, for they (like the Talmudists) believe that a man's way of living can influence his health, and that illness is a consequence of natural causes. This conflicts with the Christian belief that disease is a punishment from God for some sin. These traditional Christians think that suffering should be endured until death provides the relief of a blissful afterlife. Abbot Bernard of Clairvaux— dead now over ten years but still much spoken of—declared any monk who consulted a physician or took medicine to be infirm in his faith.[12]

Here as in Navarre, the traditional monks urge the ill to fast, pray, repent, and prepare to die. These monks commonly advise petitioners to relieve their suffering by calling on the saints, a certain saint for each part of the body, for example, Saint Lucia for the eyes, Saint Apollonia for the teeth, Saint Blaise for the throat, Saint Bernadine for the lungs, and Saint Erasmus for the abdomen. But gradually Christian prelates are coming to tolerate the idea of modern medicine, and to recognize this academy which offers the Christian world the medical knowledge heretofore confined to Moslems and Jews.[13]

Since long before Christianity, Jews have taught that healing comes from God. One illustration is this prayer which Talmudic scholars recommended for a person about to undergo an operation or bloodletting:

> May it be Thy will, O Lord my God, that this operation may be a cure for me, and mayest Thou heal me, for Thou art a faithful healing God and Thy healing is sure, since men have no power to heal. . . . [14]

Physicians act as God's instruments, in Jewish belief; thus while recognizing that God ultimately determines whether a man shall be healed, Jews have always had the greatest respect for physicians and their skills. Yeshivot have always taught rudiments of medicine as part of the dicta for healthy living. Jewish scholars have studied and practiced medicine as a spiritual vocation,[15] for the Talmud says that the science of medicine is authorized by God Himself.[16] Jewish medical practitioners often link their observations, theories, and prescriptions with a verse from the Bible or halakha or a moral dictum of the rabbis, such as Ben Sira's "God created medicines out of the earth, therefore no discerning man should reject them."[17]

Many eminent physicians have also been great scholars of the Law[18]— just to remind you of a few important ones from the Spanish peninsula: Hasdai ibn Shaprut, Jonah ibn Biklarish, Judah ha-Levi, Abraham ibn Ezra, and perhaps among the next will be young Benveniste of Barcelona.

Even outside the Jewish community it is conceded that Jews make excellent physicians. Our religion compels a regard for human life that encourages them to make the most of their medical studies. The belief of Jewish doctors that life is significant and should be maintained as an end in itself doubtless explains why all peoples hold Jewish physicians in particular esteem, and why so many rulers call Jewish physicians to court.

Indeed, most Jews well known outside the Jewish community have been physicians; and it also seems that most of the prominent Jewish physicians have been called to treat a general or a governor, or even appointed to serve a vizier or khalif. Rulers are generally strong men, not sickly, so why do kings and khalifs surround themselves with physicians? It may have little to do with the royal bodies, more to do with what is in the physicians' heads, for most physicians' knowledge is very wide and deep. Rulers must know or at least sense that their power depends on knowledge, that knowledge is in books, and that it is the physicians who know the books.

At least one prince of royal blood came here from a great distance for medical treatment. Robert, duke of Normandy (a younger son of the King William who conquered England) led a group of Franks in the first of their invasions of the Holy Land, and there he took an arrow in his arm. He neglected the wound, which festered. So Duke Robert, accompanied by his wife, Sybilla, came to Salerno, where the physicians told him that the wound would not heal because of the poison in it, that the poison could be removed only by suction, and that the person performing the suction would be risking his own life. Duke Robert refused any treatment that might harm another person. But when the Duchess Sybilla learned of the situation, she had her husband drugged with opium and she herself lowered her mouth to his arm and sucked out the poison, curing Duke Robert at the cost of her own life.

About the treatment of particular maladies neither the Bible nor the Talmud says much, but they do say quite a bit about the prevention of disease for the individual and community. This ancient Jewish predilection is incorporated in the book written by Salerno's physicians for Duke Robert, called the *Regimen sanitatis*:

> Use three physicians still; first Doctor Quiet,
> Next Doctor Merryman, and Doctor Diet.
>
> Rise early in the morn, and straight remember
> With water cold to wash your hands and eyes,
> In gentle fashion stretching every member,
> And to refresh your brain when as you rise,
> In heat, in cold, in July and December,
> Both comb your head and rub your teeth likewise.
> If bled you have, keep cool; if bathed, keep warm;
> If dined, to stand or walk will do no harm.[19]

It was Greeks who created the art of medicine as we know it today: especially Hippocrates, and Galen who was born a Greek and studied in Greece before going as physician to the court of Marcus Aurelius in Rome. Their books form the basis of all medical study, at Salerno and elsewhere: Hippocrates for general medicine and Galen especially for anatomy. In the lifetimes of these Greeks and ever since, what they wrote has been studied by Jews; and Jews have transported the Greeks' remedies back and forth across the Great Sea and beyond.

Jews have traded in lapis lazuli stones and Palestinian ox tongues; cubeb from Yemen, scammony from Syria, and opium from the East; senna, from Mecca, used as a purgative, and myrobalan (Indian gooseberries) used for other intestinal troubles; and innumerable other drugs. One of the main herbs traded, epi-thymon (dodder of thyme), was a very important plant in the Greek pharmacology. The best quality of this plant came from the Byzantine island of Crete, and it was so well known that many people believed that the medical arts themselves developed on Crete. Not so, but it's because the Greeks developed the science of pharmacology by using local plants that all our pharmaceuticals have Greek names.

The trade in pharmaceuticals was active and rewarding—not just in money—because many Jews through trading learned about pharmacology, which led to many Jewish merchants becoming pharmacists. Jews enjoy the occupation of pharmacy because it combines international trade with the study of books. Pharmacists (Jews and non-Jews) being often consulted for medical treatment, in time some also qualified as physicians and practiced the two professions together. This dual employment seems to have increased in recent years.

When the Moslems came to rule the lands around the Great Sea, they added their knowledge of medicine from the East to that of the Greeks; they used the Greek pharmaceuticals and they translated the Greek writers into Arabic. Thereby they opened another employment for Jews: from their tradition of trade and their international contacts, Jews were the only people able to translate from Arabic into Latin and northern European languages. So it came about that for the Christians, the Jews held the key to modern medicine.

Like the Ab-beth-din of Narbonne, who recently compiled the *Eshkol* to classify all the decisions in the Talmud by topic, about 120 years ago the Persian physician Avicenna wrote his *Canons of Medicine*, which includes a classification of all scientific knowledge into disciplines and is said to be the most important medical work to be translated out of Arabic. It greatly facilitated studies at Salerno and other schools.

Jews learned medicine from scholars like these and became medical scholars themselves. One such, even prior to Avicenna, was Shabbetai Donnolo, who lived and wrote in the tenth century in the town of Oria on a small peninsula near Brindisi, which was then in the empire of the Greek church. Shabbetai was very learned, and spoke Greek and Latin as well as Hebrew and his native Italian tongue; and Arabic too, some say. A physician and pharmacist, he wrote *Sefer ha-Yakar* (The precious book) *of Drugs, Liquids, Powders, Emulsions and Ointments, for the instruction of Jewish physicians in preparing drugs in accord with the science of Israel and Greece.* . . . He wrote it *in Hebrew,* and listed over a hundred "simples"—single herbs, fruits, leaves, and roots—and explained how to compound them. He sought to tell physicians and pharmacists exactly what their drugs were and how to use them for curing various diseases, because the drug-merchants often recommended drugs that could be dangerous.[20] *Sefer ha-Yakar* is used here at Salerno. Just think: Hippocrates, Galen, Avicenna, and Shabbetai ben Abraham Donnolo!

On hearing that I am a Jew from northeast Spain, physicians here mention the more recent compilation by Jonah ibn Biklarish, physician to the sultan of Saragossa: a huge book of charts of remedies, with their names and uses and possible substitutes, in Spanish, Latin, Greek, Syriac, and Persian. What a polyglot! But then, in Lunel I learned that Jews were responsible for the greatest part of works translated into western languages not just from Arabic but also from Syriac, Egyptian, and ancient Greek.

Medicine is a cosmopolitan art, as it should be, given that illness afflicts all peoples. Don't let me exaggerate the Jewish role as physicians and pharmacists, for—as they keep reminding me here—medicine is more a creature of Greeks and Mohammedans, and modern physicians in Christian lands would be far less effective were it not for the good monks in their monasteries who maintain the herb gardens and compound the specifics and dispense these to myriad sufferers.

Salerno's physicians dream of a time when practitioners of all kinds of medicine, from all peoples, might work together toward some way of mitigating leprosy, which afflicts so many more people now than even sixty years ago—a wretched remembrance of some Franks' sojourns in the hot East. But then, so many more people are traveling long distances than ever used to.

The learning of Salerno goes all over the world, to anyone who wants to make use of it. Physicians, being scholars, are bound to stay in big cities, where they content themselves with looking at the patient and his various excreta, inquiring about symptoms, and prescribing treatment. Admittedly, most physicians (however proud-spirited) do at least work closely with surgeons and women-doctors and (some of them) with monks who live in the small towns and villages.

Jewish physicians seldom work as surgeons. They employ themselves in general medicine; or they especially treat victims of poison or sufferers from diseases of the eyes. Some Jewish oculists are women. Any Jew who is sick and indigent is entitled to free consultation with a Jewish physician—the sick person need only reach the physician! (In the Talmud physicians are reminded of their responsibility to treat the illnesses even of persons unable to pay their fees, and Rashi judged that "the death of the neglected poor is tantamount to homicide committed by the physician."[21] Sadly, there are still a few Jewish physicians who provide their services only in accord with the Talmudic dictum "A physician who takes no fee is worth no fee.")[22]

Although the physicians in these parts vaunt the magnificent scholarship at Salerno, I'm not sure that the ordinary sufferer is better off. Sometimes the remedies prolong life or alleviate pain, sometimes they don't, just as in Talmudic times. The surgeons keep busy treating wounds and setting fractures, cutting out stones and amputating limbs. The practitioners, apparently wherever they are, prescribe the familiar drugs—compounds of all kinds of vegetable matter—which enter the body as tablets, beverages, gargles, eye- ear- or nose-drops, or suppositories; or prescribe the external use of ointments or unguents. They might recommend a specialist for you to be cupped or have leeches applied: blood-letting is among their favorite treatments here too, as is purgation.[23] Or they might prescribe hot or cold baths, or bed rest or exercise, or taking more or less fresh air and sunshine, or performing more or less sexual intercourse.

Almost always they want to regulate your diet, according to your body humors: children should be denied fruit, elderly people should eat hot foods, and persons of choleric temperament should eat cold foods and abjure the hot ones. Only, the scholarly physicians can never agree on which are the "hot" foods and which the "cold." The one dietary matter on which all of them seem to concur is that their patients should eat less. As it says in the *Regimen sanitatis*:

> All pears and apples, peaches, milk and cheese,
> Salt meat, red deer, hare, beef, and goat: all these
> Are meats that breed ill blood and melancholy.
> If sick you be, to feed on them were folly.[24]

If the patient does refrain from eating all these foods, he will eat virtually nothing, reduce his expenses for nourishment, have more money to pay the physician, get weaker, make more calls on the physician . . .

Letter from Taranto

Half a day to the west of Salerno, on the coast, lies **AMALFI. The Christian population of this country,** a republic, **is mostly addicted to trade. They do not till the ground, but buy every thing for money, because they reside on high mountains and rocky hills. Fruit abounds, however, the land being well-supplied with vineyards, olive groves, gardens and orchards.**

Nobody dares wage war with them, for a city so situated is difficult to attack: its inhabitants can easily retreat into the mountains, as they did in 1135, when threatened by the forces of the Pisans. But the Amalfans having left their city unoccupied, the Pisans invaded Amalfi and pillaged it, in '35 and again in '37, causing great damage.

It used to be a splendid city, they tell me. Its trade with Constantinople was immense, and the merchants of Amalfi had their own quarter in that city. A legacy of this, still to be seen, is Amalfi's cathedral door, of silver-inlaid bronze, magnificently cast in Constantinople about a hundred years ago.

There used to be many Jews here, when Amalfi was richer and stronger. Then Amalfi rivaled Venice as one of the great ports of Italy, but now Venice dominates all the trade with the East. Amalfi likewise rivaled Venice in the beauty of its cloths. Jews have woven Amalfi's silk and woolen brocades for the last two hundred years; they specialize in dyeing cloths of as fine a quality as the best ones of Venice. The Christian rulers here, first Roman then Eastern church, encouraged Jewish manufacturers and traders, who could live here more securely than in the warring republics farther north on the Italian peninsula.

Now **Amalfi** is a subdued **city among the inhabitants of which you find twenty Jews.** Numerous Jews have departed, along with the city's great industry.

< <   < <   > >   > >

From Amalfi, northward **one day to BAVENTO** (Benevento), **a large city situated between the coast and a high mountain. The congregation of Jews numbers about two hundred.** They live from weaving and dyeing and reside in an ample Jewish quarter. The **principals** of the community include a **Rabbi Calonymus.**

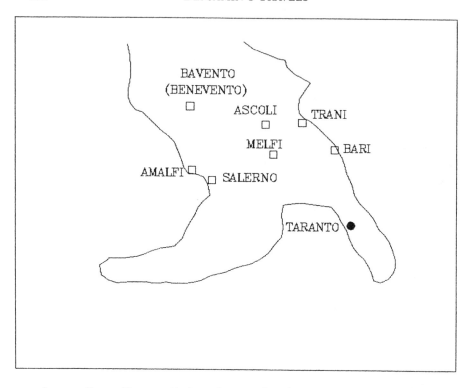

Among Jews, Bavento is best known for the sojourn here of Aaron ben Samuel ha-Nasi of Baghdad, some three hundred years ago. At that time the academies of Babylonia were still thriving and Baghdad was the center of Kabbalism. Aaron went from town to town in the south of Italy, performing miracles everywhere he went by making incantations with the Tetragrammaton (the four consonants in the unutterable name of God). In Gaeta, a village northwest of here, he came across a donkey which had once been a boy; Aaron reversed the witchcraft and returned the boy to his father.

Bavento's Jewish community was delighted to have this erudite miracle-worker among them. But then, at the local synagogue, Aaron noted that the cantor had omitted God's name when reciting the Blessings. It occurred to Aaron that if the cantor could not say God's name then he might be a resurrected corpse, for, as it is written, "the dead cannot praise God."[1] He talked to the cantor and made him confess. The cantor explained that as a boy he had been sickly and his father took him on pilgrimage to Jerusalem, where they consulted a holy man. This holy man informed the father that the son's life would be short. The father pleaded with the holy man for a way to save his son's life. The holy man agreed to save the boy, and to that end inserted under the skin of the boy's arm an amulet with the Tetragrammaton. The boy grew healthier, developed into a studious youth, and in due course became the cantor of Bavento. He feared ever to talk of his experience or to remove the name-of-God which kept him alive. But under Aaron's prodding he told all. Aaron removed the amulet from the cantor's arm, and immediately the cantor dropped dead.[2]

Wonder-workers like Aaron thrive in the south of Italy—apparently in greater numbers than in Spain, and of all religions.

From Bavento **two days to MELFI in Apulia, the Pul of Scripture, with about two hundred Jews.** The capital of the province of Apulia, it is a trading center.

< <   < <   > >   > >

Northward **one day's journey to ASCOLI. Forty Jews live there,** of importance in the town's commerce.

< <   < <   > >   > >

From Ascoli two days to **TRANI on the coast, a large and elegant town. All the pilgrims who travel to Jerusalem assemble here in consequence of the convenience of its port,** likewise many of the Frankish warriors and administrators of the Kingdom of Jerusalem.

As an important commercial center, rich from its trade with the East, Trani has a large and industrious Jewish community. Its common languages are Hebrew, Latin, Greek, and Arabic. **The city contains a congregation of about two hundred Israelites,** many of them come in the last twenty years from Andalucia, refugees from the Almohads.

Among the principal Jews of Trani is **R. Nathan the Darshan** (lecturer), so titled because he is capable of expounding Holy Scriptures in the ancient manner and is familiar with the Haggada. Just as we Jews in Spain looked in olden days to Babylonia in matters of scholarship and observance, the Jews of southern Italy have always looked to Palestine. The rites and order of service followed here in Trani, they tell me, are much the same as those followed in Jerusalem at the time of the Second Temple. However, although the community contains many pious men, on the whole the local Jews are less than observant, the men being lax in their study and the women (so I'm told) lax in their use of the ritual bath.

The very position on this coast which facilitates receipt of learning direct from the Holy Land probably also accounts for the laxity in religious practice. Many different peoples came here with new ideas. The region has been incorporated into a succession of empires, each with its own religion— Moslem, Byzantine, Norman. The Jewish community specifically has been influenced not only by its recent immigrants from Moorish Spain but in earlier times by immigrants of the Karaite persuasion.

Then too, in such great ports the men are diverted from religious duties by the urgencies of their business. Jews work in every branch of shipping, all along the coast, and Jews carry the imported wares from the ports to the interior. Besides shipping and trade, the local Jews work principally at the manufacture of glass and textiles.

This is a center for the weaving and dyeing of silk. Working with silk is laborious and requires great skills, of which Jews are masters. The Jews have always exported their silks through agents in the Jewish communities of Cyprus, Constantinople, and Syria, although recently they have had to deal with attempts to exclude them in those places. Here the Jews' dominance of the silk market was recognized by the king, who gave the Jewish community a monopoly of raw silk in Apulia and Calabria, so that in these two provinces of southernmost Italy, Jews control the distribution and the weaving of it. Of course this was not sovereign largesse. The production and export of silk being extremely lucrative, the king wants to keep tabs on the revenue, the better to tax it.

The Normans who rule southern Italy say that the Jews and their property are by rights the property of the Church, in other words, that Jews can live and work here only on sufferance of the Church so the Church has rights in Jewish income. In some communities if a Jew dies without leaving a will, the Church may claim his property. This idea of the rights of the Church in Jewish revenue has taken hold gradually throughout this land. In Salerno already before 1100 Duke Roger transferred his revenues from Jewish income to the archbishop, making this gift "for the salvation of his mother's soul." The Jews of Trani were spared such ignominy until about a dozen years ago, but now they too live under the authority of the Church, which exploits them for profit.

         < <   < <   > >   > >

From Trani, one day's journey to St. Nicholas di BARI, the large city which was destroyed by King William of Sicily and his Greek allies in 1156. **The place still lies in ruins and contains neither Jewish nor Christian inhabitants.** Almost the only buildings of importance that remain are the famous priory and church, the latter containing magnificent tombs. The church is called Saint Nicholas, for Christians consider Saint Nicholas the patron saint of sailors. Saint Nicholas di Bari has an excellent harbor.

Whatever the influence of the long-deceased Nicholas, the sailors of this region never lack for work, several generations of them having been employed in the warfare between Arabs, Byzantines, and Normans.

In one of the revolts around the middle of the last century, in an effort to please certain local Christians, some good citizens of Bari burned down the

Jewish quarter. Until then, this city housed a famous yeshiva, with eminent scholars; but the fire destroyed the yeshiva and all its sacred books.

The Jewish community of Bari was very old, for Jewish settlement along this coast goes back at least to the time of the Romans. During a thousand years Bari's Jews held many important posts in city and provincial administration, though at times Jews who were offered such posts declined them for fear of acting immorally or for fear of desecrating the Sabbath. In Bari and its province of Apulia the Jewish cultural tradition has been very strong.

In fact, an event of utmost importance for the Jewish world occurred right here just short of two hundred years ago, in 972. Four Talmudic scholars from the Babylonian academy at Sura were sailing to Andalucia when they were captured off the coast of Bari by Moslem pirates. Sold into slavery in different cities of Spain and North Africa, the rabbis were ransomed by the local Jewish communities. Each went on to establish a yeshiva in his new city, concurrently disseminating in the West their superlative knowledge of Talmud.[3] One of the four rabbis was Moses ben Enoch, who, in the Cordoba of Hasdai ibn Shaprut, founded the famous yeshiva (the one razed twenty years ago by the Almohads), in which yeshiva had studied great Talmudists like Joseph ibn Migash and great poets like Samuel ha-Nagid and Joseph ben Jacob ibn Sahl.

Getting back to Bari and the destruction of its Jewish quarter a hundred years ago . . . afterward the Jews had to pay heavy taxes. Sometimes it was the king who imposed the taxes, sometimes the archbishop. Jewish revenues were seen as "belonging" to the Church, as in Trani. Bari imposed this condition upon its Jews even earlier. A hundred years ago, the Norman prince-adventurer Robert Guiscard captured Bari from the Greeks and soon thereafter he transferred all the rights from Jewish income to his wife, Sichelgaita. That income, to be of such interest to the sovereign, must have been a substantial sum, reflecting a large and prosperous Jewish community. When Robert Guiscard died, his wife, Sichelgaita, and their son, Roger, transferred these rights to Jewish income to the archbishop, making the Jews in effect vassals of the Church.[4]

But the monetary affairs of Bari's Jews are now moot. Since King William the Bad and his devastation, no Jews remain in Bari. Nor for that matter, apart from the Saint Nicholas edifice, any church. There's an old saying that "from Bari shall go forth the Torah."[5] and so it always did, until recently . . .

From Bari, one day's journey and a half directly south across a small peninsula **to TARANTO. The city is large** and very old. **This is the frontier town of Calabria, the inhabitants are Greeks,** and the Jews speak the Greek language in addition to Hebrew. In this large center of Jewish learning live many eminent scholars. Jews have lived here since Roman times, when the

Emperor Titus ruled Palestine and settled Jewish prisoners here. **The three hundred Jews who live here** now are their descendants.

Still the Jews of Taranto are not citizens of Taranto. They are *affidati*, specially-protected non-citizens, living as tolerated aliens. Thus are Jews generally compelled to live, in Christian as in Moslem lands.

Yet it seems to me that Christians have less regard than do Moslems for people not of their own faith. The Christian disparages not only the Jew but the Moslem as well.[6] The Moslem empire in the East is a source of wondrous knowledge and a cornucopia of treasures. The practical paper for writing, the most beautiful silks and brocades, the most magnificent of animals the horse, the herbal medicines and drugs which cure man's body and comfort his soul—all these come from the Moslem East, which the Christian Franks seek to destroy.

Letter from Oria

From Taranto eastward across the small peninsula toward Brindisi, but just south of that road, shortly before reaching Brindisi, lies a city, ORIA, with an important Jewish community and tradition.

Oria's "son" who achieved the widest fame, well beyond Jewish circles, is a man of whom I first heard in Salerno (and about whom I believe I wrote you), the physician Shabbetai Donnolo. As it happens, Abraham ibn Ezra has published some of Donnolo's commentaries.[1] At Salerno's medical school Donnolo is renowned as the author of their pharmacology text; here they tell me that Donnolo also taught there. And they tell me stories of his unusual youth . . .

Shabbetai was bar mitzvah age when, in 925, Arabs attacked and conquered Oria and took many captives, among them Shabbetai and his parents. The parents were taken to Palermo and then to North Africa. Young Shabbetai remained captive only as far as Otranto, a Roman-ruled port-city two or three days journey from Oria. Otranto's Jews felt religiously bound to pay ransom for Jewish captives, and Shabbetai was among those freed.[2]

Very bright and of scholarly curiosity, Shabbetai in due course determined to acquire knowledge of the physical world, and he set about doing so despite many obstacles. Years later he would write of his youthful ambitions and his efforts:

> Eager to learn medicine and astronomy, I studied and copied many old Hebrew manuscripts. Then I sought Jewish scholars to elucidate them for me, but in this whole land I found no one who could explain properly; they told me that astronomy is the realm of Gentiles, that the Gentiles' treatises on astronomy are quite different from those of the Jews, and that the Jewish writings in this field are of little value.
>
> So I began to study the books of the Greek and Arab sciences, even writings from Babylonia and India. I paid a Babylonian scholar a considerable sum of money to instruct me about mathematics and the heavens. After much reading, discussion and reflection, I realized that the Jews' ideas on astronomy accord very closely with those of the Gentiles. All that which I learned, I began to compile in a book called Hakemoni.[3]

Hakemoni, in fact, deals mainly with religion and philosophy, but Donnolo did write of astronomy and astrology in another book (his commentary on the *Sefer Yezirah*).

On second thought, in Donnolo's mind evidently all those classifications of knowledge were intertwined. In *Hakemoni* he wrote of God's glory and the various ways in which it manifests itself. Then he developed the old idea that man is similar to the world, in that man's head is like the heavens, man's eyes like the sun and the moon, and so forth. This leads him to say that "whoever kills a man, it is as if he destroyed a whole world."[4]

All this work was a side line, for Donnolo earned his living through his practice of medicine and pharmacy, in which fields he gained such a reputation that he was appointed house physician to the viceroy of the emperor.

But, as is often said, no man is a prophet in his own land. One of Shabbetai's scholarly friends in Calabria was the monk and abbot Nilus of Rossano. One day Dr. Shabbetai heard that Abbot Nilus of Rossano was very ill. He went to the abbey, talked to Nilus, and knew from his medical studies that Nilus' sickness was caused by the fasting and other rigors of his ascetic monastic life. Shabbetai advised treatment, but Nilus refused, on the grounds that if he were cured by a Jew and it became known, pious Christians might hold it against him.[5]

Such prejudice is common among Christians,[6] most of whom (the monks excepted) live at a lower cultural level than the Jews in their midst. The Christians seem less willing to accept or just to explore new ideas than we are or than, in Spain, the Mohammedans are. And yet all the local people seem eager enough to learn from the Franks who pass continually through the nearby seaports.

The good monks, like our Jewish scribes and many of our scholars, spend their days copying books. Sometimes the scribes copy a book but neglect to append the name of its author—perhaps as a result of eyestrain. (Well, it's probably eyestrain that accounts for Jews especially suffering from eye diseases.) Should it happen, for whatever reason, that the copyist doesn't name the author, once the book has been delivered to its purchaser, there's nothing the author can do about it. Shabbetai Donnolo, very concerned about this, began one of his books with a long poem starting:

> May God reward him who copies this in Shabbetai's name
> And from my handiwork expunges not my fame. . . .
> Let him purge his heart of envy, lest he requite good with shame.[7]

He petitioned every scribe who would copy his book to be sure to copy the introductory poem as a plea to succeeding copyists to inscribe his authorship; and he went beyond begging honesty of his copyists, by writing this poetical preface in an acrostic using the letters of his name to introduce successive lines[8] . . . doing as much as one writer can to ensure he receives the credit for his work.

Oria's Jewish community had a second physician-astrologer of repute, a younger contemporary of Shabbetai's, named Paltiel. In the year 960 or thereabout, an imam called Al-Moizz came from Africa to southern Italy on military campaign, met Paltiel, and asked for an astrological consultation. Paltiel observed the heavens and prophesied that Al-Moizz would conquer Bari, Taranto, and Otranto, and later become king of Sicily. The concern of Al-Moizz centered on Egypt, but he appreciated the political support implicit in Paltiel's prediction and hired him as adviser, taking him to his home near Kairouan, on the North African coast. When in 969 Al-Moizz became khalif of Egypt, Paltiel went with him to the palace in Cairo as court astrologer.

We know so much about Paltiel the astrologer because a descendant of his wrote down all the details in his *Megillat Yuhasin* (Scroll of genealogy). The book makes difficult reading, for its Hebrew is awkward. (It illustrates the contention of R. Abraham ibn Ezra that Italian Jews don't write nearly as good Hebrew as Spanish Jews.)[9] Nevertheless the author, Ahimaaz ben Paltiel, provided us with a great deal of information about his ancestors and the times in which they lived. Some of the information is written in poetical form, such as an elegy to Animaaz's ancestor, the astrologer Paltiel.

Ahimaaz died over a hundred years ago, in 1060. His chronicle tells us about the two centuries prior to that, about his ancestors, and about events they considered important, such as the wars between Byzantines and Arabs and such as the miracles of Aaron of Baghdad in Bavento. The above-mentioned account of the astrologer Paltiel lies in the middle of the chronicle.

The chronicle starts with a description of the founder of the family dynasty, Amittai, who lived in the middle of the ninth century, wrote hymns, and studied not only orthodox doctrines but also mystical ones.

R. Amittai, the founder, had a son, R. Shefatia, whom Oria's Jewish community considers its savior. In the year 870 King Basil, then emperor in Constantinople, tried to force the Jews to convert to Christianity. When even his promises of riches didn't persuade the Jews to change their faith, he banned the practice of Judaism throughout his empire. R. Shefatia ben Amittai journeyed to Constantinople to urge or bribe the emperor into changing his mind. Some say that while he was there R. Shefatia cured the illness of one of the noble young ladies.[10] Whether or not that occurred, King Basil did moderate his edict, exempting from it those Jews who lived in Oria and in five nearby villages. Rejoicing, R. Shefatia wrote:

> Israel is saved forever by the Lord,
> Yea, saved this day,
> O Highest, by Thy word.
> Great to forgive,
> Lord of compassion, Thou.[11]

Because in all the Byzantine empire, only around Oria could Jews be Jews with impunity, Jews flocked there to settle. Oria grew into a fine Jewish city, a seat of Jewish scholarship with a long-established yeshiva.

Now that this region is ruled by Normans and no one cares any longer about the Byzantines, Jewish scholars argue that, despite his attempts to convert the Jews, Basil wasn't the worst of emperors, as Byzantine emperors go. Yet it was with reason that R. Shefatia reviled him, as in this story:

These events took place on Rosh ha-Shanah, when R. Shefatia was ill. As an eminent rabbi, he was to have the honor of blowing the shofar, but he felt too weak even to go to the synagogue. His congregation sent representatives to his house to urge him to go to the service, so eventually he pulled himself up from bed and went to the synagogue and, at the ordained time, started to blow the shofar, but he was too fatigued and the notes sounded weak. He went back home, accompanied by members of his congregation, and he returned to his bed.

After he had rested a few minutes, he spoke to them, saying: "My time has come. I'm going to my eternal rest . . . You don't know, as I do, that our oppressor Basil is already dead. He has just passed on, bound in burning chains, to be delivered to Gehenna. God is calling me now so that I can be a judge of Basil for all the crimes he has committed against our people." So R. Shefatia died.

The congregation noted the day and hour of his death. Some weeks afterward a proclamation arrived from Constantinople, as one always arrived to mark major events. The document announced the death of the emperor Basil and the time at which he had died, and the congregation saw that it was just prior to the hour of their rabbi's death.[12]

R. Shefatia's son Amittai (named after his grandfather) now headed Oria's Jewish community. Apparently he was less beloved than his father had been. In any case, it was R. Amittai's responsibility, as the leader of the community, to provide the poems and hymns for community celebrations, and he himself wrote many songs of praise and lament. Some men are blessed with the ability to improvise poetry!

One day, at the funeral of a Jewish traveler who had died in Oria, R. Amittai was chanting a dirge about the short duration of our residence in our home on earth. It began

> Woe to thee, lodging! Woe to thee, O Exile!
> Who doth not rebel nor against thee revile

He was about to continue

> Nor knowing thee, lamenteth all the while!

when one of the mourners chimed

Who knoweth thee? They who suffer from thy bile![13]

R. Amittai identified the offender as the schoolteacher Moses and threw him out of Oria.

Letter from Otranto

BRINDISI on the seacoast. A territory of the Byzantines (that is, of the Eastern Christians), Brindisi fell to the Normans in 1071. In the next generation the Normans' countrymen, the Franks, began their military invasions and then their soberer travels to the Holy Land; many of them passed through Brindisi, making it the prosperous town it is today.

Brindisi has about ten Jews, who are dyers. In the Italian peninsula south of Rome virtually all the dyers and weavers are Jews.[1] This city is a center of the dyeing craft.

The Franks who travel through the Greek empire and sojourn in the Holy Land return with a passion for silks and for bright colors, and with the coin to buy them. It seems that in the Christian lands of the north, until quite recently, most people didn't wear bright colors although the lords and their ladies wore them and the Church used them for its ornate decorations. Only the Church and the nobles could afford them, good dyed cloths being expensive as they are. Now purchasers clamor for all the cloths that the weavers and dyers can produce, and these are always very busy making colorful cloths not only for garments but also for curtains, rugs, carpets, and tablecloths.

Dyeing employs a great number of people, so that Jews rich and poor occupy themselves in it.[2] Merchants obtain the dyestuffs from lands near and far and distribute them to the people who actually do the dyeing. These have a horrid job: their hands reek from the dyestuffs and pucker from continual immersion in liquid, their eyes sting from the acids and puff in weariness from matching colors. These men and women are poorly paid, and yet they must know all about the dyestuffs and be skilled in applying them, for a dyer's bad judgment can ruin an expensive woven cloth.

Of course dyers work not only with cloth; they also work in the manufacture of glass, leather, and cosmetics. The dyers must know all about the substances they are dyeing, for the same dye will produce different results on different materials, even different color on different cloths.

The cloth-dyer must consider the material—unspun fiber, thread (or yarn), or fabric—which is to be dyed. Wool is generally dyed raw before it is spun, linen is generally dyed as spun thread before being woven, silk can be dyed before or after being woven into cloth. He must know if the color is to remain permanently in the cloth. Some purchasers, especially among Mohammedans, want a color that washes out after a few months; then they can

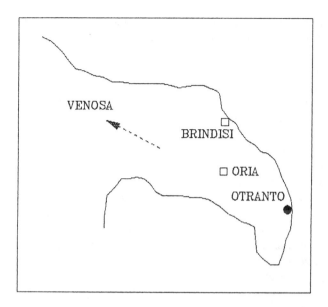

re-dye their turbans, for instance, in accord with the season. But in most cases a cloth is more precious if its color remains without fading, and indeed the highest prices are paid for the strongest, brightest colors. For these the dyer often uses mordants, certain salts which bite into cloth so that it holds color better. The dyer must know which salts to use with which cloth.

The white mordant salts called alum come here from Constantinople and smaller ports of that region, as do the dyestuffs indigo and brazilwood. Saffron and weld come from North Africa. Woad and madder grow in this region here, and seem to be the most common dyestuffs. Dyestuffs are numerous; wherever there are several dyers, each of them will produce only one color.

Red colors are usually created with madder. The madder plant must stay in the soil for a year or two because young roots yield only a weak color, so the dyers use older roots. Another red dye is crimson from the insect kermes, which must be collected at a certain time of year and its body then dried—this is the dyestuff which smells so bad. With either madder or crimson, a skilled dyer can produce several shades of red.

Blue colors are produced from the leaves of the woad plant; or from the flowers of indigo, a dye which turns cloth yellow in the vat, but the yellow changes to green, then blue, when the cloth is removed from the vat and left in the air. Woad produces the more lasting color; indigo produces the more brilliant blue, almost a purple.

Yellow comes from saffron or weld. The saffron dyestuff is made from the blossoms of the crocus, it is the dye *karkom* of the Song of Songs;[3]

people greatly admire this color, however it doesn't last long. Weld produces a more permanent color, a lemon-like yellow.

Brown develops best from the brazilwood dye, which is among the more expensive dyes and can produce shades from red to purple. Dyers often produce brown by first mixing a little brazilwood into a yellow and then mixing this shaded yellow together with the red of madder.

Green is the color most difficult for the dyers, which is surprising since nature is full of green plants. There are several dyestuffs which produce green, but applied to cloth, their color doesn't endure. Often dyers produce a green cloth by dyeing it first yellow with weld, then dyeing it a second time in a weak bath of woad or indigo.

Woad is used very commonly, for dyers can obtain a great range of colors from it depending on the quality and the amount used, and on how long the cloth remains in the dye bath. Cloth immersed in fresh woad will turn black; in a weaker woad, blue; and in the weakest woad, green. Dyers can even produce a purple by adding madder to the woad bath. Indigo too can produce shades from green to a blue-black.

The actual dyeing is rapid and easy after the preparation of the dyes. Indigo flowers must be left a long time to ferment; madder roots must be washed, dried, and ground up. Dyes come from different parts of plants: roots, leaves, flowers, or fruits. There is a purple dye which comes from insects, but it is extremely expensive. For a cloth or a garment of whatever color, the dyeing accounts for a large part of the price. The dyestuffs themselves are expensive, and many of them must be carried great distances.

The results of the dyeing process depend not only on the dye which is used and how it is prepared, but also on the dilution of the dye in the vat and the heat of the dye bath. The heat comes from a fire underneath the vat, which remains uncovered. Dyers place the material to be dyed in the vat and stir it around with their hands; or they hang the yarn or cloth around a pole and move the pole about in the vat. Dyers can also produce different shades by varying the time that a cloth remains in the dye bath. Dyers are very secretive about their dyeing processes and about how they produce their dyes.

The dyeing trade uses ingredients of small size and great value, it buys its materials abroad, and it has many trade secrets; consequently, tax collectors take a particular interest in it. The Jews' dye tax is a good source of income for many lords and bishops in the south of Italy.

< <   < <   > >   > >

From Brindisi, **two days to OTRANTO on the coast of the Grecian Sea.** This is the easternmost city on the Italian peninsula, a port flourishing from the trade with the East and especially with Palestine.

From Palestine the first Jews were brought to Otranto long ago, as prisoners of the Roman emperor Titus. In more recent times, this coastal region suffered greatly in constant warfare between Greeks and Arabs, that is, between Eastern Christians and Moslems. Starting before the time that the Arabs attacked this coast and captured Donnolo and continuing long afterward, each generation of men hereabouts was subjugated by a different conquering people. But since the Norman conquest of the south of Italy a hundred years ago, the diverse peoples of this region have known peace.

Except for the invasions of Franks in passage to the Holy Land! In contrast to the earlier invaders, however, the Franks have stimulated commerce and enriched the port cities. So as to share in the prosperity, some Jews have come here to trade or to work in textiles, especially Jews from Moslem lands. Far more Jews live in the south of the Italian peninsula than in the north. Jews here know all about the horrors perpetrated in the Rhineland by Franks en route to the Holy Land, but are sure that nothing like that could happen here. And in fact the Franks, through their travel and trade, have benefited Otranto and **its five hundred Jewish inhabitants** and the entire province of Apulia. The Jewish communities in this coastal region are many, large, and prosperous.

Otranto is an entrepôt not only for merchandise but also for Jewish learning. From Rome and from Spain, from Baghdad and from Palestine, Jewish ideas come to Apulia's port cities, where other Jewish travelers imbibe them and carry them thither to the four corners of the earth. Thus the saying of the rabbis of our fathers' generation: "Scholarship comes from Bari and the word of the Lord from Otranto."[4] Now of course, sadly, that's only half true: since 1156, when Bari lost its rabbis, Otranto remains as the sole major rabbinical center in southern Italy. (Some men of Otranto also perished in King William's raids.)

Despite its importance, Otranto—like all Jewish communities of Italy—looks to Rome, Rome's Jewish community being the biggest and best-organized of the whole peninsula. Although Apulia's Jews are familiar with the scholarship of Babylonia,[5] Otranto follows the directives from Rome about keeping the Palestinian ritual. Often the tidings about that ritual pass through Otranto on their way to Rome.

You know our *piyyutim*, those rhyming prayers of psalms and Bible verses. Well, here especially the men delight in chanting them during worship, and recount with strong regional pride how the piyyutim developed. They tell me that the very first rhyming prayers came from Palestine, but that it was poets in this corner of Italy who added greatly to their number and charm—long before the Jews of Rome incorporated piyyutim into their worship, to say nothing of composing any of their own. Indeed the very word piyyut comes from the Greeks.

They told me about one important writer of piyyutim, a certain Silano who was born some three hundred years ago in Venosa (northwest of here, up near Melfi), and studied with a *paytan* who came from Palestine. Here is a poem in which Silano beseeches God:

> The cry of those who praise Thee
> To Thy throne shall rise.
> Fulfil their wants who call Thee One, Thou,
> Hearing all that come before Thee now.[6]

If a man lived three hundred years ago and all we know about him is that he wrote religious poetry, we may think him to have been a sober individual. But apparently Silano was somewhat of a prankster; in any case, he became a legendary figure along this coast. Ahimaaz ben Paltiel, in his chronicle, tells this story about one of his ancestors and Silano:

Silano the paytan, having studied with a Palestinian, was familiar with the Hebrew Aramaic dialect, though most of the men of Venosa were not. One day there came to Venosa a great Palestinian scholar who spoke only this dialect; whenever he preached, Silano translated for him. The Jews of Venosa liked what the Palestinian had to say. So the Palestinian extended his sojourn there, preaching regularly in his Hebrew Aramaic, with Silano at his side repeating the words in Italianate Hebrew. Every Shabbat the Palestinian read from the Midrash, then delivered a sermon based on the Midrash text. Every Shabbat Silano stood by, interpreting each word of the Palestinian's phrases and allusions in order to make them intelligible to the local people.

One market day in Venosa, many villagers being in town, some commercial dispute between townsman and villager erupted into a fight and subsequently into a brawl. The men punched each other, the women attacked recklessly with their brooms and any other weapons they could reach. In due course peace returned; but naturally for several days the battle endured as Venosa's main topic of conversation.

Silano decided to add to the fun. On Friday he secretly removed the Palestinian's parchment Midrash. From the text which would be read the following day, he erased several lines, and in their place inserted a poem he had just composed about the marketplace fight—who had insulted whom, who had shouted what, who had hit whom and with what. Then he returned the altered parchment to its place. On Shabbat the great preacher, ignorant of the substitution, began to read. He quickly realized that this was like no Midrash he had ever read before. Nonetheless, it was the Midrash and he was obliged to read the Midrash, so continue reading it he did. All the while, sentence by sentence, Silano translated, with his usual calm and serious mien. As the Palestinian read and Silano translated the substitute version, the passivity of the worshipers turned to attention and then awe. God had proclaimed in the Midrash exactly what would occur in Venosa! What a blessing to be present at this revelation!

His congregation abuzz in wonder, the Palestinian yielded to his doubts and knew that a prank had been played on him, surely by Silano. Preacher and worshipers, incensed that Silano would joke with a sacred text, forced him out of town. He was destined to wander.

But a certain Ahimaaz, a pious Palestinian traveling in Italy, happened to meet Silano, heard his story, and took pity on him. Ahimaaz journeyed onward, but arranged to be in Venosa for Rosh ha-Shanah and Yom Kippur. He foresaw correctly that, as an eminent guest, he would be invited to lead a service. Back in those days, synagogue services followed no prescription of particular prayers or order of prayer; these were determined by custom or by the preference of the prayer leader. The prayer leader being a cantor or scholar, if he had composed a prayer or song of his own, in the way of cantors and scholars he would incorporate it into the service. When his time came to conduct the service, Ahimaaz led some familiar prayers, then chanted a piyyut unfamiliar to Venosa's worshipers. They found it exceptionally beautiful, and asked Ahimaaz whence it came. "Indeed it is beautiful," he agreed. "It is a composition of a poet bred in Venosa, the paytan Silano." The community grieved at having sent its talented son into exile, and invited him to return.[7]

That's a pleasant story, although a bit simplistic; perhaps it's for women. Local men, in another version, say that Ahimaaz, originally from this part of Italy but living in Palestine, was traveling in Italy to collect donations for the Palestine Academy. Now the good folk of Venosa had demanded Silano's excommunication, and it was the Palestine Academy which had, ultimately, issued the excommunication order. When Ahimaaz returned to Palestine, he had with him a piyyut written by Silano, one which criticized the Karaites and applauded the Rabbanites. It was this piyyut which Ahimaaz chanted when asked to lead a service in a Jerusalem synagogue. When the rabbis there heard about Silano and his exile, they lifted the ban from him.[8]

There are many piyyutim that denounce Karaites, but it is not only these piyyutim which anger the Karaites, it is piyyutim generally. Karaites become virulent about piyyutim for Yom Kippur and the lesser fast days, contending that there's no place for these songs in this worship, which should consist entirely of prayers and Bible passages.[9] In the good old days, they maintain, the worshipers could recite all the services easily, but now they feel it necessary to employ a cantor to lead the intricate chants;[10] and sometimes the cantor sings by himself; and, worse, they choose a cantor for his singing voice rather than for his scholarship. Despite the Karaite-Rabbanite animosity—and it must be admitted that some of the Rabbanites' piyyutim are very abusive of Karaites[11]—the worshipers here take great joy in the Apulian piyyutim.

Notwithstanding the vagaries of Apulian fortune, the frequent invasions and changes of rulers and rebuildings of towns here, local Jews constantly had Jerusalem in their thoughts. R. Amittai ben Shefatia, a contemporary of Silano's, wrote several expressive poems about Jerusalem, among which:

> Why do all my neighbors tend
> To rise from their afflictions
> Whereas I, for years on end,
> Bewail the two destructions?[12]

Many piyyutim had come from the pens of Silano and their followers and had been sent abroad before R. Solomon ben Judah ha-Bavli (the Babylonian) of Rome and certain rabbis of the Calonymus family up north wrote their liturgical poems.[13] Or so they tell me here. In any case, it does seem that beautiful piyyutim were being written in Italy before Solomon ibn Gabirol and Isaac ibn Ghayyat wrote in this vein in Andalucia, starting the long line of Spanish paytanim like Moses ibn Ezra and Judah ha-Levi even to our own Abraham ibn Ezra. . . .

This gets us a long way from Otranto, but here in Otranto discussions do range far and wide. As some of the local rabbis admit, Otranto is famous not for the originality of its work but for its role as mediator and expeditor.[14] They say (frequently) that "the Law has gone forth from Otranto,"[15] "from Otranto and Bari to Rome and then Lucca,"[16] and they tease me for going contrary to the Law.

Letter from Thebes

From Otranto you cross over in two days to the island of CORFU, which is the limit of the Kingdom of Sicily. Corfu contains but one Jew, a dyer.

King Roger ruled over this island, reinforcing its garrisons against the Franks. He was succeeded by his son, King William, but in 1149 the island was conquered by Manuel, emperor of Greece. The Greek empire, also called Byzantine, is said to be the greatest of the world's civilizations.

The Byzantine Christians (also called Eastern Christians or Christians of Constantinople) are a different sect of Christians from those of Spain, Provence, and Rome. Long ago, from the time of the Emperor Constantine, Constantinople was the capital of the Roman Empire, but over the centuries the eastern empire and the western empire drew apart. In the middle of the last century, these Eastern Christians broke away from the authority of the bishop of Rome. The Greeks venerate icons, and they celebrate Easter on a different day than the Romans, and they allow their priests to marry. When, at the end of the last century, the first armies of Franks passed through the Greek lands on their way to the Holy Land, the Eastern Christians did not join them to fight for Jerusalem. This angered the Franks, who ravaged parts of the Greek lands, and so the two Christian groups separated still further from each other. The Greeks fear that the land-hungry Franks will endeavor to rule the Eastern Christian empire too.

Their fears could well be justified. The Franks care only that their own pilgrims are free to visit the city where their man-god died and their religion began. Certainly they know little and care less about the history and hopes of Jews.

The Greeks are a more religious people than the Franks, and the bishops here have more to say about the governance of this empire than the bishops do in Christian Spain.

Unlike the bishops of Spain or France, those of the Eastern Church do not cavil about the lending of money at interest. In these lands dependent on trade, even the churchmen appreciate that placing money at risk in commerce must be encouraged by interest, indeed the church itself commonly lends money. Loans which bear interest can be advanced by members of any community.[1]

< <   < <   > >   > >

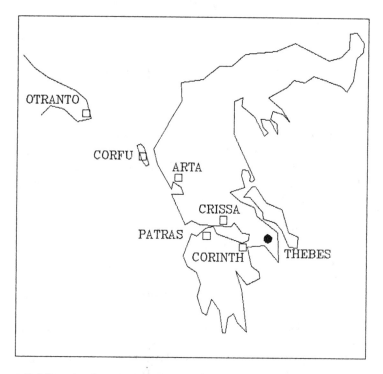

From Corfu, **two days journey by sea brings you to the coast of ARTA, the confines of the empire of Manuel King of Greece. On this coast lies a village with about one hundred Jewish inhabitants, the principal of them are R.Sh'lachiah and R. Hercules.**

< <   < <   > >   > >

Two days to ACHELOUS, with ten Jews, principal: R. Shabbetai.

< <   < <   > >   > >

Half a day in a northwesterly direction **to ANATOLICA on the gulf.**

< <   < <   > >   > >

One day's journey by sea to PATRAS. This is the city of Antipatros King of Greece, one of the four kings who rose after King Alexander. The city contains large and ancient buildings and about fifty Jews reside there.

< <   < <   > >   > >

Half a day by sea to LEPANTO on the coast. A hundred Jews reside there.

< <   < <   > >   > >

From Lepanto **one day's journey and a half to** the inland city of **CRISSA**, at the southern foot of Parnassus, on the gulf. **Two hundred Jews live there by themselves on Mount Parnassus and carry on agriculture upon their own land and property.** Jews are among the merchants who ship grains and other foods to Constantinople.

Jews have lived in the Greek lands since ancient times. In the last century many Jews came to these lands from Moslem countries, hoping to find better conditions. Greek Jews can move freely within the Eastern empire and even beyond, like all Greek citizens. The Eastern Christians make no separate legal community for Jews, in the sense that in Christian Spain and in parts of Italy the Jews are wards of the king, and in Moslem lands, dhimmis. The Greek lands include many peoples, of whom the Jews are one.

< <   < <   > >   > >

From Crissa, **three days to the city of CORINTH which contains about three hundred Jews,** silk weavers. When the Normans invaded this coast in 1147, they took skilled silk workers back to Sicily; these silk workers were Jews.

< <   < <   > >   > >

North of Corinth, SOUTHERN THESSALY is a fertile plain with many springs of water; indeed the plain is so wet that it is full of flies and mosquitos. They say it is unhealthy, but mostly I find it annoying and I rue the many occasions when I had reason to recall this verse:

> To whom shall I cry in my anguish?
>   And where shall I flee from the fleas?
> No breathing-space do they allow me;
>   They treat me as would enemies.
> They buzz in my ears all their love-songs,
>   And creep on my brow and my eyes.
> I try to partake of my breakfast—
>   They swarm on the coveted prize.
> They drink of my wine from the goblets,
>   Considering me in no wise.[2]

< <   < <   > >   > >

From Corinth, **three days to the** inland **city of THEBES.** Thebes is the third city of the Grecian empire, Constantinople being the first and Salunki the second.

The largest Jewish community in the Greek lands, **Thebes has about two thousand Jewish inhabitants. Among them are many eminent Talmudic scholars and men as famous as any of the present generation.** Rabbanites and Karaites, usually antipathetic, here join in scholarly disputations. **No scholars like them are to be met with in the whole Grecian Empire except at Constantinople.**

Thebes is the center of the Greeks' silk industry, and the **Jews here are the most eminent manufacturers of silk and purple cloth in all Greece.** The Byzantines foster the production of silk as a cultural art,[3] and silk is a traditional industry of Jews. We know that even in ancient Palestine Jews produced silk, for the Prophet Ezekiel mentions the silk garments of an Israelite woman.

They've told me here, and also in Lucca, that silk first came from a big land far to the east (past India) called China, imported some three hundred years ago by Jewish traders called Radanites.[4] Perhaps it was the *modern* process of silk manufacture that Jews learned in China. For it's also said that, much earlier, at the command of the Emperor Justinian, two monks journeyed to China to smuggle out silkworms in the hollows of their bamboo canes. In any case, in Thebes the entire process of silk making is carried on by Jews; they work as handlers of raw silk, as weavers, and as dyers.

In its first stages the making of thread from silk is quite different from the making of other threads which derive from plants. The cocoon of the silkworm has a core of compact, continuous filament which need only be unraveled and reeled to make thread: it needs no spinning. Many raw-silk handlers are women, for unraveling and reeling are simple jobs, although to do them quickly requires knowledge and dexterity. First the handler separates the cocoons that have holes in them from the perfect cocoons. Next he plunges the perfect cocoons into boiling water to soften the gummy binding material, all the while stirring with rods, so that the silk filaments adhere to the ends of the rods. Then he takes the threads of raw silk, their ends separated, and winds them on reels, passing them over a high frame so that they'll dry faster.

The silkworm cocoon has a second part: the layers of loose filament which cover its core. This is called "waste silk" and has to be spun. Also, the filaments from imperfect cocoons—that is, perforated or tangled cocoons—cannot be reeled off but have to be spun like wool or cotton. Some dishonest weavers, after the threads are dyed, combine this waste silk with raw silk, to make a yarn of poor quality.

As individual filaments of silk are too delicate to be wound, the handler takes a few filaments—generally three to eight—to reel them together. Here the handler must work with special dexterity and care, because the filaments toward the center of a cocoon are thinner than those of the outer layers; yet the thread being wound must be all of the same diameter. The handler twists threads together and rewinds them into yarns, and that is the last process in his hands.

The strands of yarn go to the weaver, who threads the end of each strand through an eye of a heddle of the loom. The weaver attaches the strands very close to one another and absolutely parallel. This process of warping is very slow and requires great skill, but it is crucial for the efficiency of the weaving.

The looms for weaving silk are, to be sure, much the same as for weaving other cloths, but silk weaving requires far greater precision than the weaving of other textiles. Silk thread being strong yet light in weight, silk cloth of good quality possesses extraordinary beauty and durability. It sells for very high prices. Buyers consider it an investment, which they can turn into coin if necessary.[5]

In contrast to other lands, where only royalty and ecclesiastics are permitted to use silk, in the Grecian empire it is only the highest quality of this precious cloth which is so restricted. People here particularly value art and luxury; and any subject of this empire, even a slave, is allowed to make and wear a garment of second-quality silk . . . perhaps as a symbol that any Greek is a cut above subjects of other empires.

Franks who pass through Greece on their way to and from Palestine express amazement at the strong colors and intricate patterns of the local silks, and rare is the soldier or administrator who fails to carry silk cloth back north with him. Franks try to purchase raw silk too, but the Greeks are unwilling to sell that out of their empire. They specifically prohibit local dealers in raw silk from selling it to Jews or to other merchants for resale outside the city.[6]

Spain produces silks, of course, but far inferior to those of Greece. The Moslem *ulema* of Spain have discouraged the wearing of silk as too luxurious, so the producers have little call to manufacture silks of finer quality. The Spanish are happy to sell not only finished cloths but also cocoons and raw silk abroad wherever they can, so the best of Spain's supply is exported and the quality of its manufacture declines.

The quality of the finished silks depends firstly on the raw silk but also, importantly, on the skill of the craftsmen. When the Normans attacked prosperous Greek cities in 1147 they abducted many skilled artisans, including Jews and Jewesses of Thebes's silk industry, carrying these captives off to Sicily to develop silk-manufacture there. Still the great silk center of the Italian peninsula remains Lucca in the north, where, too, Jews dominate the industry.

In the Grecian empire it has long been a matter of utmost importance to control the quality of silk cloth. To that end, silk weavers are organized into guilds. The first guilds, developed many generations ago, had no religious aspect; in times of revolt in Thebes and Salunki, the Jewish members fought alongside their Christian associates at the will of the emperor. But Greek Christians being strongly imbued with their religion, the silk guilds of Thebes and Constantinople took on a Christian character. So Jews created their own guilds.[7] Whenever in any locality Jewish handlers or weavers or dyers were sufficient in number to support a guild of their own, they established one. Thus united, they can react to changes in the practices and policies of the Christian guilds. They also limit the admissions and determine the training of apprentices, and they control competition among members, and they deal with government officials.

At present the Greeks seem content to cooperate with their Jews. For one thing, of course, they are anxious to maintain their superior silk industry. For another, they fear attack by Franks and Normans and who-knows-whom-else, and so strive to secure the loyalty of the Jewish community in case of war. They permit Jews to trade freely and directly with the purple–fishers at the eastern edge of the Great Sea. And in sharp contrast to the Norman rulers of southeast Italy, the Byzantine rulers even exempt all workers in silk- and purple-dyeing from personal taxes. The Jewish community of Thebes is treated better than any other I have seen.

Letter from Salunki

From Thebes **a journey of three days brings you to NEGROPONT, a large city on the coast** of the Gulf of Volos **to which merchants resort from all parts. The main exports are wheat from the fields of Thessaly, and silks. Two hundred Jews reside there.**

$$< \; < \quad < \; < \qquad\qquad > \; > \quad > \; >$$

From thence to JABUSTRISA is one day's journey. The city is likewise **situated on the coast and contains** mostly Wallachians and **about one hundred Jews.**

$$< \; < \quad < \; < \qquad\qquad > \; > \quad > \; >$$

RABENICA is distant one day's journey and also **contains about one hundred Jews.**

$$< \; < \quad < \; < \qquad\qquad > \; > \quad > \; >$$

SINON POTAMO (Sinon-of-the-River) **or Zeitun is one day's journey further. It has fifty Jewish inhabitants.**

There are the confines of Wallachia, a country the inhabitants of which are called Vlachi. They are "as nimble as deer" and descend from their mountains into the plains of Greece committing robberies and taking booty. They torture and slay their captives as if for pleasure. **Nobody ventures to make war upon them, nor can any king bring them to submission. They do not profess the Christian faith, they profess no religious creed.**

The Vlachi used to be nomads; for many generations they wandered over a large area of the Eastern Empire. Meeting Christians, they learned something of Christianity. A great number of Vlachi appear to have settled themselves in this area, but the Greeks don't like them. They insult the Vlachi who wish to live as the Greeks live, so that the Vlachi remain alien and harass and rob and kill the Greeks. They are indeed a great menace, bloody murderers who destroy productive lands and beautiful cities.

Spurned by the Christians, the Vlachi have associated themselves with the Jews, for the Byzantines consider the Jews too as alien and outcast. It may also be that the Vlachi thought the Jewish faith easier to follow, Chris-

123

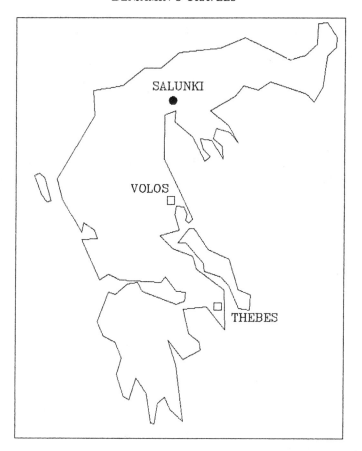

tian dogma being so complicated. **Vlachi names are of Jewish origin; and some even say they have been Jews, which nation they call brethren.** Yet while claiming to adopt Judaism, they never claimed to change their employment—God spare us such converts! Still, **whenever they meet an Israelite, they rob but never kill him as they do the Greeks.** So here, strangely, the Jews have less reason to fear massacre than do the Christians.

< <   < <   > >   > >

From Sinon Potamo it is two days to GARDICKI on the coast of the Gulf of Volos, **a ruined place, containing but few Jewish or Grecian inhabitants.**

< <   < <   > >   > >

Two days further stands the large commercial city of ARMIRO, also **on the coast** of the Gulf of Volos. **It is frequented by the Venetians, the Pisans, the**

Genoese and many other merchants, who there transact business. It is a large city and contains about four hundred Jewish inhabitants.

< <   < <   > >   > >

One day to BISSINA. One hundred Jews reside there.

< <   < <   > >   > >

From Bissina **the town of SALUNKI** (Salonica) **is distant two days journey by sea. It was built by King Seleucus, one of the four Greek nobles who rose after Alexander, and is a very large city,** the site of the most important fair in Macedonia. Multitudes come, of all races and religions, each in its own costume, from Thessaly to the south and from countries as distant as Portugal and Egypt. They transport their merchandise on a wonderful variety of horses, mules, and oxen, and they bring along their dogs and sheep and pigs, whose noises combine in wild cacophony. In the marketplace itself the merchants set up their stalls in two parallel rows of great length, opposite each other, with an aisle between them broad enough to allow the passage of hundreds of buyers intent on examining the commodities of all regions of the earth.[1]

With more Jews than any other Greek city except Thebes, Salunki **contains about five hundred Jewish inhabitants,** the Jews here antedating the Christians. Salunki's position on an inlet of the sea being excellent for commerce, many Jews found the city attractive. The Radanites made it an important port of call, stopping here on their way to Egypt, Arabia, India, and the land named China farther eastward, with brocades, furs, swords, and slave girls, and on their return trip carrying spices back to the land of the Franks.[2]

At the time of the Radanites, the Greek emperor Nicephorus warred with the Slavs to the northeast. He resettled many of his subjects among these Slavs, including Jews from Salunki. The Jews liked living with the Bulgars and persuaded other Jews to come; and they sought to win the Bulgars to Judaism.

The Bulgars had often been vassals of the militaristic Khazars to the east. The Khazars, heathen nomads of Turkish origin, lived northeast of the Black Sea in their own kingdom. Moslem incursions from further east encouraged them to join Islam; but had they done so, they would have had to accept the khalif as their sovereign. Missionaries from the west and southwest tried to make them Christians; but then their spiritual lives would have been subject to the pope. So the Khazars listened attentively to the Jews.

The Jewish religion had the respect of both Moslems and Christians; and the Jewish people, having no kingdom of their own, could not enforce

their will upon the Khazars. Yet if the Khazars were Jewish, they could effectively reject the persuasions of Christians and Moslems. So the Khazar king
became a Jew, and his people were free to continue in their old ways
undisturbed.

Jewish Khazars joined Jews living among the Bulgars in actively proselytizing Bulgars, winning some to Judaism. But then toward the end of the
ninth century, two monks from Salunki called Cyril and Methodius went
among the Bulgars and succeeded in Christianizing them. Salunki became
the Bulgars' holy city.

Trade increased, and with it the wealth of the Khazars. Around the year
960, the Jewish courtier from Cordoba, Hasdai ibn Shaprut, wrote to the
Khazar king Joseph. This king had a magnificent palace in his capital, Astra-
kan. The Khazars' century of prosperity may have weakened them, for they
seem to have died out.

Nowadays Salunki has many Karaites. The Karaites follow a different calendar from the rest of the Jews, so their festival dates are often different
from ours. Their calendar is very important to them. When they celebrate
Succot, they don't content themselves with waving the *lulav* and the *etrog*
as we do; they also use the "four species" in the construction of their
booths.[3] The etrog grows here in the north of Greece, even in Corfu.

About a hundred years ago, the Karaites and the orthodox Rabbanites
were feuding about a festival date. The Karaites complained to the authorities about the Rabbanites, and eventually the Rabbanites had to pay a large
fine. For some thirty years afterward, they had to pay the amount of this
fine every year, as an annual tax on Jews.

The Greeks imposed this additional tax until the turn of the century,
when the first Franks were advancing toward Macedonia on their way to
Jerusalem. Greeks did not join in this "Christian" effort to "rescue" Jerusalem because the pope, fifty years before, had excommunicated all the
Greeks; besides, the Greeks thought themselves too civilized and cultured to
go to war in support of barbarian Franks. The emperor (Alexius Comnenus)
feared, among other things, that the Jerusalem-bound Franks might attract
the interest and then the support of Jews, so to retain the Jews' loyalty, he
abrogated that onerous tax.

In any case the stories which reached the heads of Salunki's Jewish community—about hordes of Franks marching to Jerusalem and all along the
way robbing and massacring Jews—assured that no Jews would join with
the Franks. Men who carried these stories were often refugees from the
north, even from the Rhineland, where the Franks had begun their violence.
Jewish messengers, still suffering shock, spoke of the imminent end of the
world, refering to the *khevlei Moshiakh*, the tribulations which were to herald the coming of the Messiah.

Such wild tidings were not for everyone's ears. The majority of Salunki's Jews heard only of the approach of vast numbers of men from the northwest, on their way to Jerusalem. Some Jews, who knew nothing of the outrages commited by the marchers, rejoiced (as the Emperor Alexius had antici- pated), for they associated the Franks' urgency to reach Jerusalem with the coming of the Messiah.

The inevitable rumors burgeoned. The prophet Elijah (whom the prophet Malachi had named as the precursor of the Messiah) had come down from Heaven, had visited in several towns. Friends of friends had seen the prophet, had touched his garments. Elijah was to come to Salunki! Men donned prayer shawls and spent their days in prayer and repentance; they ceased to occupy themselves with worldly matters like earning a living. They apologized to relatives and friends whom they had wronged. The wealthy distributed their goods among the poor, in anticipation of the end of the world.

At this time the rabbi of Salunki (also chief rabbi of Macedonia) was Tobiah ben Eliezer of Kastoria, famous for his diatribes against the Karaites. R. Tobiah had gained eminence for his legal commentaries (although R. Abraham ibn Ezra has criticized many of his interpretations). This great rabbi Tobiah rejoiced in Elijah's imminent arrival and sent news of it to Constantinople.

The Jews had wished to keep the exciting news inside the Jewish commu- nity, for they feared the reaction of the pietistic Greeks, but the news was too big to be contained. As it turned out, the local Christians (who had been waiting anxiously since the year 1000 for the Second Coming) rejoiced with the Jews and took part in the preparations. The delighted Christians included high-ranking government officials, for the prophet Elijah would naturally be a guest of the city.

The local bishop involved himself. Some say that he shared the Jews' happiness and encouraged them to go off to Jerusalem to meet the Messiah, with the blessings and aid of the king. The other version is that the bishop didn't like Jews encouraging Christians toward heresy, and invited the Jews to leave Salunki "to go to meet your Messiah." Some Jews did leave Salunki. Those remaining in Salunki, or the believers among them impatient to re- ceive Elijah, learned instead that the Franks had captured Jerusalem and murdered the Jews there. Meanwhile, neither Elijah nor the Messiah had appeared. Salunki did not force its Jews to leave, but, ever since, the Chris- tians have treated them with derision.[4]

Now the Jews are much oppressed in this place and live by the exercise of handicrafts. Many are silk weavers, whose families grew prosperous in that industry and who have their own Jewish guilds. Since the Franks have taken over the international commerce formerly carried on by Greeks, the Greeks depend more on the silk export.

The Rabbi Samuel and his children are eminent scholars and the king has appointed him provost of the resident Jews. It is the job of the provost to control the prices of silk products, and weights and measures, in accord with the law. In this way, through his deputy R. Samuel, the king keeps tabs on the Jewish silk weavers.

Perhaps it was some such circumstance which suggested to Moses ibn Ezra the imagery for this verse:

> Thou who art clothed in silk, who drawest on
> Proudly thy raiment of fine linen spun,
> Bethink thee of the day when thou alone
> Shall dwell at last beneath the marble stone.
>
> .   .   .   .
>
> Man is a weaver on the earth, 'tis said,
> Who weaves and weaves—his own days are the thread,
> And when the length allotted he hath spun,
> All life is over, and all hope is dead.[5]

First Letter from Constantinople

MITRIZZI, distant two days' journey from Salunki, **contains about twenty Jews.**

< <   < <   > >   > >

DRAMA, distant from hence two days' journey, contains about one hundred forty Jews. It stands in a valley, near the site of the ancient city of Philippi.

< <   < <   > >   > >

From thence one day's journey to CHRISTOPOLIS, with about twenty Jewish inhabitants. This city is situated on the frontier of Macedonia and Thrace.

< <   < <   > >   > >

Distant three days journey from thence by sea around the peninsula of Gallipolis **stands ABYDOS on the coast.**

< <   < <   > >   > >

Five days journey by the mountains to the large city of CONSTANTINO-PLE. Until Emperor Constantine, who ruled in the fourth century, the city was called by the name of Byzant, which explains why Byzantium is another name for the Eastern or Grecian empire.

The circumference of the city of Constantinople amounts to eighteen miles. One half of the city is bounded by the continent, the other by the sea, two arms of which meet here, the one being a branch or outlet of the Russian Sea (Black Sea), **the other of the Spanish Sea** (Great Sea).

Great stir and bustle prevail at Constantinople in consequence of the conflux of many merchants who resort hither, both by land and by sea, from all parts of the world, for purposes of trade. Merchants from Babylon and from Mesopotamia, from Media and Persia, from Egypt and Palestine, as well as from Russia, Hungary, Patzinakia to the north of the Khazar Kingdom, **Budia** of the Bulgars, and **from Lombardy and Spain, are met with here, and in this respect the city is equalled only by Baghdad, metropolis of the Mohammedans.**

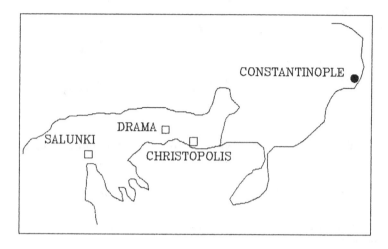

In all this commerce Jews are naturally very active. Jewish traders follow the silk route east to Damascus and Baghdad, some as far as India and China, to buy spices and raw silk, and they go west to Italy and France to sell them. They cross the Russian Sea and go north into the kingdom of Kiev to buy furs and amber from further north and salt from the Azov region; and to sell spices from the east as well as Byzantine manufactures like soap made from olive oil, and jewelry and wine. And, quietly, they sell Greek-produced silk cloth and silk garments.

As in Greece, in Constantinople many Jews work in the silk industry—as weavers, dyers, finishers, and makers of garments. Their work is confined to second-class silks. The producing and wearing of first-class silk is forbidden to commoners, and needless to say, all Jews are commoners. The first-class silk, called "precious," is manufactured by the imperial silk-makers, who work in a wing of the imperial palace under a special guard. These imperial silk makers are naturally the best in the empire, famed for their artistry.

The second-class or "ordinary" silks are made by private guilds, of which in Constantinople there are five: the merchants of raw silk, the spinners, the dyers and clothiers, the traders in domestic silk garments, and the traders in imported silk fabrics. Official regulations determine the commerce between them: for example, a spinner wishing to buy raw silk from an importer must first get permission from the raw-silk merchants. Nor can the spinner sell his processed silk directly to a dyer or clothier, he has to deliver it back to the raw-silk merchant. The job of the private guilds is to prepare and sell their silk goods to Byzantine citizens and to foreigners.

Despite the openness of their custom, even among the private guilds silk making is a regulated business. Due to the Jews' wide international network for their commerce, Jews, explicitly, are restricted by law in the buying and selling of silk. Non-Jewish merchants are forbidden to sell finished goods to Jews, on the grounds that Jewish merchants smuggle them out.[1] Which they do.

Why do the Byzantines attach such great importance to silk? It is both the basis of their prosperity and the symbol of it. The emperor and members of his family, the officers of the court, and the princes of the Church dress in the finest of silks to indicate their authority. Silk is indispensable for court and church not just in Byzantium but also in all other Christian lands; yet little raw silk is produced in the lands north and west of Byzantium, and where in those lands they do make silk cloth (as in Italy and Spain), they do not produce as much or as good silk cloth as that produced here.

The Byzantines limit their export of raw silk and silk cloth so as to maintain their high price and to further their political objectives. When the Byzantines arrange a commercial treaty with another kingdom, they specify the kinds of silk and the amount of silk they will sell. When they grant an export permit to a foreign merchant, it is for a particular quantity and quality. When on occasion they relax the export restrictions on silk, then they derive a large revenue from it by the export duties and by the import of foreign coin. This benefits everyone in Byzantium (not only the court and the silk merchants) for the greater the revenue from foreigners, the lower the taxes each Greek has to pay. If the Byzantines did not restrict the export of their excellent silk, the price of it would fall. Likewise, if silk makers abroad knew the techniques for making the best silk, Byzantium would lose trade.

The law requires an arriving foreign trader to go to register with the prefect, who grants him permission to reside in the city for a limited time (never more than three months). There are strict limits on the amount of silk which a foreign trader might buy: little more than for his own personal use, and none at all of the best quality. It is easy to identify a foreigner on the streets of Constantinople: the merchants resident in the city are all dressed more elegantly than the merchants from abroad. Silk trading is confined to special houses; foreigners, throughout their sojourn, are closely watched—non-Jews, that is. Jewish traders are not limited in the time they may spend in the city or in the empire; and despite the laws against their exporting silk, they are under no surveillance.

In fact it is only Jews who can travel freely between Greek, Roman, and Moslem lands. The Byzantines discourage their own Christian merchants from going abroad, preferring that foreign merchants come to the Greek lands to trade. Many of the foreign traders come not to Constantinople but only as far as a Greek town on the confines of the empire closest to their homeland, and they pay their tribute in those towns. Yet **they say that the city of Constantinople alone receives some twenty thousand florins every day;**

this revenue arises from rent of hostelries and bazaars and from the duties paid by merchants who arrive by sea and land.

The tribute which is collected at Constantinople every year from all parts of Greece, consisting of silks and purple cloths and gold, fills many towers. These riches and buildings are equalled nowhere in the world.

The country is rich also in consequence of producing all sorts of delicacies as well as abundance of bread, meat and wine. The Greeks who inhabit the country are extremely rich and possess great wealth of gold and precious stones. Nothing on earth equals their wealth. They dress in garments of silk (often made in Thebes) ornamented by gold and other valuable materials. In their appearance, they are like princes. Unlike the Christians of the West, among whom only monks are literate, many Byzantines educate their children beyond reading and writing to calculate and to understand classical literature. These peoples are well skilled in the Greek sciences and live comfortably, "every man under his vine and fig tree." And they ride upon horses.

Although Constantinople's Jews include craftsmen in silk, merchants and many rich men, no Jew is allowed to ride on horseback. The one exception is R. Solomon ha-Mitzri (the Egyptian), who is the king's physician and by whose influence the Jews enjoy many advantages even in their state of oppression. He is one among many Jewish physicians, some of them at court, although the Church here too tells Christians not to consult Jewish physicians. But the Christians consult them anyway.

In general Jews here deal freely with Gentiles. Jews are free to enter any occupation; as usual, they work mostly in silk, or in copper and silver, or in leather, or as farmers on their own lands. Some are rich, some poor. Among the poor Jews are a few obliged to work as executioners, ever since a Jew was ordered to put out the eyes of the Emperor Romanus a hundred years ago.[2] Here as elsewhere, people delight in executions but shun the executioners.

Although in other Greek lands a Jew is free to live where he wishes, at Constantinople the Jew dwells apart, having been expelled beyond the one arm of the sea. The quarter inhabited by the Jews is called Pera; the Greeks call it Galata. It's not an unattractive quarter, nor is it poor;[3] Jews may own its houses, which are of wood. The Jewish cemetery is here. Pera is enclosed by the channel of Sophia on one side, and its residents can reach the city by water only, whenever they want to visit it for purposes of trade. The Jews have their own quay in the old city, just like the Venetians.

In days of yore, as far back as the Emperor Constantine at least, the Jews lived in the old city, in the quarter of the central city called the Chalkoprateia, amidst the bronze and copper workers. But over a hundred years ago some Jews began settling in Pera. Starting shortly thereafter, a series of great external events threatened the Byzantine wealth and peace. At the turn of the century, the Emperor Alexius Comnenus allocated special quarters of Constantinople for each community, with Pera as the Jews'.

The Byzantines lost their army at the Battle of Manzikert in 1071 and greatly feared that the victorious Seljuk Turks would come farther west and attack Constantinople. It was in this plight that Alexius Comnenus asked the West for military aid to drive the Turks back. But by so doing he aggravated Western anxiety about the safety of Western pilgrims in Turkish and Moslem lands, with the well-known result that thousands upon thousands of Franks rushed southeast to invade Jerusalem.

The Byzantines refused to join the Franks in what these said was their mission to take Jerusalem, since **at Constantinople is the metropolitan seat of the pope of the Greeks, who are at variance with the pope of Rome.** Besides, the Greeks considering themselves far superior to the Franks, to be carriers of a greater civilization, they preferred to stand aloof from the Franks' impetuous invasions.

Once the Franks had succeeded in their objective, had established themselves in the conquered Holy Land which they called the *Latin* Kingdom of Jerusalem, the unsatisfied among them cast around for other lands to invade, other properties to acquire. The great wealth of Byzantium had always attracted greedy hordes. The Byzantines found that the Christians they had approached to be their allies had instead become another menace. Their fear was realized in 1147, when a Norman Frank army, led by King Louis, attacked and plundered Greek lands on its way to Palestine. That was twenty years ago, but since then small groups of Franks keep passing through.

The Greeks fear the Franks, whom the Roman pope encourages. They also fear the heathen hordes from the north in the region of the Danube, the raiders of Hungary and Patzinakia, and Turkish tribes. Moreover, they live in dread of the Seljuk Turks from the east, Moslems intent upon spreading their religion. If the Seljuk Turks were to conquer Byzantium, the Greeks would lose their religion along with their liberty.

It is the Greeks' old custom to hire foreign soldiers to defend their lands.[4] **They have no martial spirit themselves and, like women, are unfit for warlike enterprise. The Greeks hire soldiers of all nations, whom they call barbarians, for the purpose of carrying on their wars with the Sultan of the Thogarmin who are called Turks.** The soldiers include Vlachi, Bulgars, Khazars, Russians, and Alani; the most able and loyal among them are the Varangians, who speak English and Danish, for they originated in those countries in the West, their ancestors having come here to escape the Vikings.[5]

Doubtless it is the threat of war from all sides that makes the Greeks suspicious of the Jews in their midst, of the Jewish community with its connections to so many other kingdoms. As I said before, the Greeks here feel themselves to be a superior people, and yet their reluctance to defend themselves in war shows them to be cowardly. Although they fear powerful nations, they can molest a small unprotected people with impunity. They try intermittently, the current emperor determining the amount of force, to persuade the Jews to adopt Christianity. From time to time, a prince or a bishop will enforce some restrictions against Jews or abolish some privileges, on religious principle or on whim. In this city of the Greeks' imperial power, the Jews live less securely than do Jews in the smaller Greek cities to the west.[6]

Although the residential area of the Jews is pleasant enough to the eye,[7] **they live here under heavy oppression, and there is much hatred against them which is engendered by the tanners, the workers in leather, who pour out their filthy water in the streets and even before the very doors of the Jews, who, being thus defiled, become objects of hatred to the Greeks.** Tanning is so malodorous that it is everywhere despised; and so it is left to Jews. In the Greek lands especially, but also in the Moslem—think of the long tradition of fine leather work in Cordoba.

In every time and place, some Jews must be tanners in order to supply the paraphernalia for our rituals—leather parchment for Torah scrolls, tefillin straps, contents of mezuzot—all of which must be made from ritually clean animals. Someone has to make our sandals and shoes, our bottles and bags, horse bridles for the rich, and book bindings. As it is written in the Talmud, "The world can exist neither without a perfume-maker nor without a tanner—happy is he whose craft is that of a perfume-maker, and woe to him who is a tanner by trade."[8] The occupation is so vile that the ancient rabbis made special regulations for it: a tanner must not put a mezuzah on his door, he must not do his work in the center of town but on the outskirts, and if his wife finds the smell unbearable and wishes to be free of him, he must divorce her.

The same filth and smell that disturb today's Greeks must have disturbed Jews in biblical times and ever since. Tanning is a dirty job in all its various processes: scraping dung, flesh, and hair off skins; soaking the skins to soften them; working salt into them to retard rotting; soaking them for over a year in a series of oak-bark and oak-gall liquors. For full penetration of the hide the first of the liquors must be old and mellow, the last of them fresh and strong; after a certain time the tanner hauls his hides out of one liquor, drains them, and then drops them into the next liquor. When the old liquor becomes too old, the tanner pours it out.

Perhaps after the Messiah comes, all Jews will be physicians and silk workers. Meanwhile some Jews are executioners and tanners—honest work, admittedly, but work for which they are scorned, and on that pretext all Jews are scorned. **Their yoke is severely felt by the Jews, both good and bad, they are exposed to be beaten in the streets and must submit to all kinds of bad treatment. But the Jews are rich, good, benevolent and religious men, who bear the misfortunes of the exile with humility.**

Second Letter from Constantinople

Constantinople, the metropolis of the whole Grecian Empire, is also the residence of the emperor, King Manuel Comnenus. Twelve princely officers govern the whole empire by his command and every one of them inhabits a palace at Constantinople and possesses fortresses and cities of his own.

King Manuel has built—or rather had rebuilt, at the start of his reign—a large palace for his residence on the seashore, besides the palace built by his predecessors; this edifice is called Blachernes. The pillars and walls of this palace are covered with sterling gold. All the wars of the ancients as well as his own wars are represented in pictures. The throne in this palace is of gold and ornamented with precious stones. A golden crown hangs over the throne suspended on a chain of the same material, the length of which exactly admits the emperor to sit under it. This crown is ornamented with precious stones of inestimable value. Such is the luster of these diamonds that, even without other light, they illustrate the room in which they are kept. Other objects of curiosity are met with here which nobody can adequately describe.

The Hippodrome, meaning horse market, is a public place near the wall of the palace, set aside for the sports of the king. The splendid games and lavish entertainments that take place, the opulence of the furnishings and clothing to be seen, make the Hippodrome the favorite theater of the Greeks. Every year the birthday of Jisho the Nazarene is celebrated there by public rejoicings. On these occasions you may there see representations of all the nations who inhabit the different parts of the world, and surprising feats of jugglery. Lions, bears, leopards and wild asses, as well as birds that have been trained to fight each other, are also exhibited, and all this sport, the equal of which is to be met with nowhere else, is carried on in the presence of the king and the queen.

A statue in the Hippodrome shows a man on a horse, with his hand stretched out. It is Joshua, the Jewish military leader at Jericho, who raised his hands to keep the sun from setting and thereby conquered that city. There are many statues here of men from the Bible. The great emperor Constantine brought them from Jerusalem, including one of Moses, and they are among the greatest treasures in the empire. Doubtless they were placed here for the edification of Christians; in any case, Jews are devoted to these statues of Bible figures.

Constantinople is full of churches and monasteries. The place of worship called St. Sophia contains as many altars as the year numbers days and possesses innumerable riches. These are augmented every year by the contributions of the two islands and of the adjacent towns and villages. All the other places of worship in the whole world do not equal St. Sophia in riches. It is ornamented by pillars of gold and silver and by innumerable lamps of the same precious materials.

The people of the Eastern church seem very affected by the arts and rituals of their religion. They adore their icons, which are distributed everywhere, and they delight in opulent church ceremonies as much as they relish the splendid Hippodrome games. The many icons make a Westerner constantly aware of the division of the Christians into Western church and Eastern church, and remind a Jew of the Jewish division into Rabbanites and Karaites.

They gave the name "Rabbanites" to the traditional Jews who accept the teachings of the rabbis (in other words, the Oral Law) and try to live accordingly. The Jews here who reject the Oral Law call themselves Karaites, from *Karaim, b'nai-mikra*, meaning followers of the Bible. They believe the source of religious law to be only and directly the Bible—"God sent us the Torah, through Moses, which contains the perfect truth"—and that any changes or additions to it are sacrilege. **The number of Jews at Constantinople amounts to two thousand Rabbanites and five hundred Karaites. They live on one spot but a wall divides them,** to reduce their quarrelings.

The Rabbanites are learned in the Law; many of them are manufacturers of silk cloth, many others are merchants, some of them being extremely rich, with a house in Constantinople and another house in the provinces.[1] The Karaites too are scholars and lovers of Torah, but they care nothing for Talmud, and they express their disdain very strongly. They seek to segregate themselves from all persons of other belief, be they Christians, Moslems, or Rabbanite Jews. It was the Karaites who moved away from central Constantinople in the last century to set up a community of their own here in Pera.

The Karaites avoid Rabbanites as violators of God's law. They are far more severe than we are in matters of kashrut. Many abstain from meat and chicken, holding that to partake of these would be inappropriate since the destruction of the Temple. (For Karaites "the destruction of the Temple" always means the First Temple.) Those who do eat meat will not eat the meat of an animal pregnant at the time of death; as Rabbanites do not forbid such meat and their butchers sell it, no Karaite will patronize the Rabbanite butchers.[2] On the other hand, the Karaites dispense with the supervision of slaughter on which the Rabbanites insist, so Rabbanites will not buy from Karaite butchers either.[3] The Karaites don't eat eggs (because of the prohibition against *eber min ha-hai*, eating the limb of a living animal) or honey (which might contain bits of bees). If the tiniest drop of a banned food should fall into a huge quantity of their permitted food, then all of it is prohibited for them to eat; they reject the rabbis' ruling of "a sixtieth part."

The Karaites forbid marriage to Rabbanites; just as they prohibit marriages between kinsmen, which marriages are allowed by the rabbis. And they believe that each person should fulfill God's commands as young as possible, without waiting as Rabbanites do for a child to reach maturity. Consequently they betroth girls as early as four years of age. The families might agree that the girl remain with her parents until puberty; nonetheless, she is a married woman, since the marriage ceremony with the seven benedictions is performed at the betrothal. The Karaites permit women to seek divorce, just as men; and they allow daughters to inherit their parents' property, just as sons.

Karaite worship and ritual are very different from ours. They assemble in minyan but twice daily, mornings and evenings. They recite the *Sh'ma* but not the *Shemonah-Esreh* (*Amidah*), and they chant many more psalms during their service than we do. At prayers the men wear zizit but they don't wear tefillin. (I must admit that we in Spain have also become lax about laying tefillin.) Karaites have no mezuzot on their doorposts, for they believe only figurative the verse about writing God's commandments "upon the doorposts." They say that the rules about tefillin and mezuzot were made by rabbis, long after God gave us the Torah.

They likewise ignore our festival calendar. They celebrate Purim, but not the Fast of Esther. They observe Passover and Succot for seven days, as though in Eretz Yisrael. They make their Passover matzoh of barley flour rather than wheat, as a reminder of the "bread of affliction" mentioned in the Torah. They count fifty days from the first Passover Shabbat to arrive at their Shavuot, which thus always begins on a Sunday. Chanukah they don't celebrate at all, since it is not mentioned in the Torah. On the seventh day of every month they fast. They explain that since the destruction of the Temple, it is incumbent upon Jews to mourn and weep.

Their Sabbath observance is very rigorous. The only activities permitted are those necessary for worship or for essential bodily functions. They allow no fire, forbidding even fires kindled before Shabbat, so that their Sabbath food is cooked on Friday and eaten cold on Saturday, which day they spend in darkness and cold. They are very strict, permitting no heat or light on Shabbat even for a woman in childbirth, for the Torah says "Ye shall kindle no fire throughout your habitations upon the Sabbath day" and makes no exceptions. And in accordance with the Bible verse "Abide ye every man in his place, let no man go out of his place on the seventh day," no Karaite leaves his house on Shabbat except to worship in the synagogue. They deny themselves even the warmth of sexual activity—while for us sex on the Sabbath is a special joy, for them it (like work) is forbidden.

Their stark and dismal Sabbath flouts our joyous Shabbat. Our rabbis insist that, Shabbat being a day of thanksgiving, we make special effort if necessary to keep our homes and synagogues warm and well-lit, that we dine on good foods, that we drink wine and thank the Lord for it in the kiddush ceremony. Perhaps you know that this blessing over the Sabbath wine was originally for the home, but it was considered so important to the celebration of Shabbat that it was recited in the synagogue as well, on Friday night, so that travelers or others without proper homes should not miss it. Contrast the Karaite ascetics, who eschew all intoxicating beverages. Misinterpreting the kiddush ceremony, they once even insulted Saadia Gaon for "lightheadedness": "this inebriate drinks during the very time of prayers!"

Karaites cite the Book of Amos, where the Lord demanded, "Shall not the day of the Lord be darkness, and not light? even very dark, and no brightness in it?" And the Lord continues: "I despise your religious feasts" and "I will turn your feasts into mourning." That's very clear, Karaites insist: Jews' holidays are ordained for fasting, Jews' Sabbath delight is to come not from the preparation of food but from prayer and study.

Some say that this ascetic spirit, and the first Karaites, existed in early Talmudic times, when rabbis began to claim authority for their interpretations of the Bible. Others say that rejection of the rabbis' teachings started in Babylonia a few hundred years ago, under the leadership of the scholar Anan ben David, influenced by Moslems who were unhappy with interpretations of the Koran. Coincidence or not, with the great expansion of the Mohammedan religion to the west, Karaism likewise spread.

Whatever their origins, the Karaites venerate two Babylonians, Anan and Benjamin, who lived in the eighth and ninth centuries. Anan, being a scholar of the House of David, expected to be named exilarch, that is, the political leader and chief judge of the community. He loved Torah, yet he insisted that others not follow his ideas about observance but rather their own consciences: "Search assiduously in the Torah and do not rely on my opinion." "Heresy!" cried the rabbis, and instead of naming Anan exilarch, they gave the post to his younger brother. It's said that some of the orthodox rabbis tried to kill Anan.

But in a time and place of scholars and of questioning faith and practices, Anan attracted disciples. One of his successors, Benjamin al-Nahawendi, took Anan's dictum and made it into a Karaite principle: the free and independent individual study of the Scriptures. Karaism was to allow, indeed was to be based on, multiple interpretations of the Bible. Even today in matters of faith, it seems, no two Karaites agree with each other. This Karaite principle nowhere takes into account men like me who are not scholars and who would not feel able to interpret the law for themselves. In any case, while they flaunt their tolerance of each person's interpretation of Torah, "each person" for them does not extend as far as any Rabbanite.

Judah ben Elijah Hadassi led Constantinople's Karaites, until his recent death. His big book defending Karaism he titled *Eshkol ha-Kofer* (A cluster of henna), the phrase to be found in the Song of Songs, which is Solomon's (therefore suggesting wisdom). This R. Judah had to have known that the word *cluster* was regularly used for erudite and wide-ranging texts[4] . . . used by the Talmudists(!). Hadassi, to whom the Talmudists were anathema, writes about all the laws which have occupied the rabbis since ancient times, criticizing their interpretations.[5] He organized his book according to the Ten Commandments, for each of the ten explaining the related mitzvot (commandments) and halakot (laws) in Karaite belief and practice.[6] Acknowledging that Sabbath joy is permitted, he argues that a people in exile should willingly forego pleasure to celebrate with public mourning.[7] He points out that Shavuot begins on Sunday every year because Leviticus ordains the counting of the seven weeks from the day after the *Sabbath* of the Passover,[8] and not, as the Rabbanites have somehow misinterpreted, from the day after the Passover begins.[9] He attacks the way that the Talmudists and later rabbis interpreted the Bible and raised their opinions into law, and he scorns the Talmud because it contains legends.

A new book, which the Rabbanites say completely refutes Hadassi, only recently arrived here from Spain, with the title *Sefer ha-Kabbala* (The book of tradition)." Its author, Abraham ibn Daud, maintains that we can understand Scripture only with the aid of rabbinic teaching. He narrates the transmission of Jewish law generation by generation from Moses down through the rabbinim and geonim and the new academies in Spain, even through the Almohad persecution in Andalucia (which drove the author from his native Cordoba to Toledo) and the resettlement of Andalucia's Lucena Academy in Toledo. He recounts the story that I heard in Bari, about the four shipwrecked rabbis who came to teach Torah in four different places on the coast of the Great Sea, one place being Andalucia. He contends that religious leadership has passed down through inheritance, that the rabbis in Spain are the legitimate heirs of the geonim.[10]

Note that this defense of the rabbinic tradition comes from Spain. In Byzantium it would seem that—even within the Rabbanite community—the judgments of rabbis are not so highly valued, for parties to a dispute here seldom consult a rabbi; they prefer to settle the matter in private compromise or even to submit it to a Byzantine judge. Not that ibn Daud mentions this; indeed, he barely mentions the many Jews of the Grecian empire. To be sure, his purpose is to write the history which rebuts the Karaites' arguments.

It seems to me that the Karaites are an acerbic bunch, very argumentative. Arguing may be their only pleasure. Just as they deny themselves even a little wine to salve their spirits, so they deny themselves medicines to cure their bodies. (Like Christians, they refuse the physician as God's auxiliary; come to think of it, that's like their refusing to accept the judgments of rabbis.) They deny themselves the solace of visiting the graves of their ancestors, and the spiritual focus that often accompanies worship at the tomb of a scholar.

Yet the Karaites are avid proponents of return to the land of our forefathers. While Eretz Yisrael was under Mohammedan rule, many Karaites settled there. After the Franks' conquest and massacres and their banning of Jews from Jerusalem, naturally only a few Karaites dared to go there, but now that the Holy Land seems calm, albeit in Christian hands, some Karaites here are talking of going up, of joining their few surviving brethren there.[11]

Local Karaites also speak of communities of like-minded Jews all around the Great Sea: in Egypt, in many Greek towns, in Syria and Babylon to the east, and in Moslem and Christian Spain. The two Karaite communities in Toledo and Talavera, of which I was vaguely aware, were established under Moorish rule before the Christian conquest. Toledo being a great city where scholars explored the mysteries of the sciences and the philosophies, it makes sense to me that there new ideas took hold, so there apostates flourished. Here I'm told that in Toledo the Karaite sect comprised the great mass of Jews, who in Moorish times used to be harassed and maltreated by Jewish courtiers; and in our own days the Andalucian refugees from the Almohads, Jews pious and bitter, resumed the persecution.[12] Despite this animosity toward Karaites in Spain, now that the peninsula is half Christian and since Toledo has become a more important center of rabbinic teaching, the Karaites are trying to expand their communities there.

Letter from Cyprus

Two days from Constantinople stands RODOSTO, containing a congregation of about four hundred Jews.

<   <   < <   > >   > >

To GALLIPOLI two days. Of the two hundred Jews of this city the principal are: R. Elijah Kapid ("the short"), **R. Shabbetai the little, and R. Isaac Megas (this term means "tall" in the Greek language).**

<   <   < <   > >   > >

To Kales or KILIA two days. Fifty Jews inhabit this place.

<   <   < <   > >   > >

Two days to MITILENE, one of the islands of the sea. Ten places of this island contain Jewish congregations.

<   <   < <   > >   > >

Three days from thence, journeying south by sea along the coast of Asia, across from the city of Smyrna **lies the island of CHIOS, containing about four hundred Jews.** Numerous Jews came to Chios in the middle of the last century, on which account it was commanded in 1062 that Jews who had recently settled on the island should leave. They dispersed: now in many small towns of Greece and Asia one finds communities of a few Jews.

The trees which yield mastic are found here on Chios. All the villagers live in the mountainous part of the island where their only work is to cultivate mastic trees and gather the mastic. The trees are green all year round; and as tall as a very tall man. In summer workmen cut vertical incisions in the bark (not in the wood) of the tree trunks and of the big branches. The resin that falls from these cuts is almost colorless, tinged light yellow or green.

These aromatic mastic drops, the main business of Chios, are the reason why the Jews came here and why the Arabs and Byzantines made war over the island. Egyptians especially buy much of this mastic for embalming, for

141

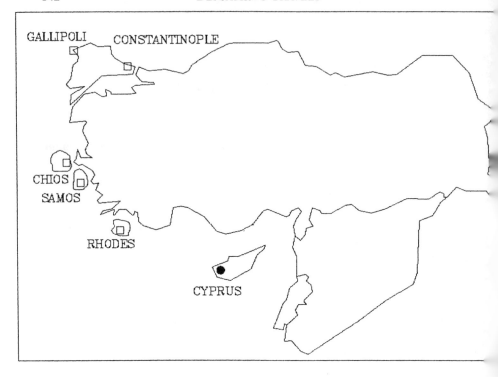

they embalm more of their people than we do. In the Christian West too, I suppose—I recall the king and his whole court in Rome, still lifelike after a thousand years. . . . And did you know that the body of El Cid was embalmed, enabling it to sit on a chair (in a monastery at Valencia) for ten years before it was buried?

The inhabitants of Chios chew the gummy mastic drops for pleasure and relaxation.

< <   < <   > >   > >

Three days to the island of SAMOS with about three hundred Jews. Here too mastic is cultivated. **These islands contain many congregations of Jews.**

< <   < <   > >   > >

From Samos **to RHODES, three days by sea. Four hundred Jews reside here.**

Across from Rhodes on the mainland of Asia, in the country of Phrygia is a town called Chonae. The Jews there produced leather and cloths o' excellent quality. They also had good relations with the Christian community. Then the Franks passed through there, or news about the Franks. Some twenty years ago, the town's Jewish craftsmen offered a gift of their work to decorate the local church. This "impertinence" so incensed the bishop that he expelled the Jews from the town. Never before had such a thing happened in Greek lands.

From Rhodes, four days to CYPRUS, a big island. More Jews live here than on the other islands.

In this island, besides the Rabbanite and Karaite Jews, there is a community of heretic Jews called "Kaphrasin," meaning "Cyprians." Or so R. Abraham ibn Ezra called them. But as they are heretics, we could call them "Apicorossin" (meaning "Epicurians"), which word in the Talmud denotes heretics. These Jews, Kaphrasin, **are** apicorossin **(epicurians).** Blending the two words they might well be **called "Kaphrossin."**

The Jews excommunicate them everywhere. They don't follow our kosher diet, but permit the use of certain fats forbidden to us, in the belief that the only fats banned are those from the kinds of animals once sacrificed at the Temple. Further, **these sectarians profane the evening of the Sabbath, and keep holy the evening of Sunday.** They consider a day as being from one sunrise to the next. Some of these Kaphrossin actually celebrate the Sabbath on Sunday, doubtless due to Christian influence.

The Kaphrossin—locally called Mishawites—originated near Baghdad, some three hundred years ago, as disciples of the Jewish scholar Mishawayh, or Meswi. It was his idea that the day runs from sunrise to sunrise. In fact he established a calendar according to which the festivals were celebrated not on certain dates but instead on certain days of the week, every Yom Kippur falling on Shabbat and every Passover starting on Thursday; but the Mishawites here no longer follow that calendar.

At a time when Byzantium was strong and was making many conquests, and Jews from the Mohammedan lands were migrating into the Greek lands, some Mishawites settled in Cyprus. Here they adopted Christian ways, on which ground the Karaite rabbi Tobiah ben Moses criticized the Mishawites in his legal treatise **Otzar Nehmad.** Thus Rabbanites, Karaites, and Mishawites live antagonistically among the Christians on this island.

The Mishawites' skill in calendar calculation brought them to the attention of the Byzantines. In the reign of King Basil about 150 years ago, the Greek Christians were in conflict over the method to use to set the annual date of Easter. King Basil called in a certain Moses of Cyprus as a calendar expert to advise him on the matter, then praised him highly. So the Mishawites felt even friendlier toward the Greek Christians.

Letter from Antioch

From Cyprus **to CORYCUS two days. This is the frontier of Aram, which is called Armenia. Here are the confines of the empire of Toros, king of the mountains, sovereign of Armenia, whose sway reaches unto the city of Dhuchia and unto the country of the Thogarmin who are called Turks.**

$$< < \quad < < \qquad\qquad > > \quad > >$$

Two days to Malmistras which is TERSOOS (Tarsus), situated on the coast. Thus far reaches the kingdom of the Javanites who are called Greeks.

$$< < \quad < < \qquad\qquad > > \quad > >$$

From the Byzantine port of Tarsus, **the large city of ANTIOCH is distant two days. It stands on the banks of the Makloub, which river flows down from Mount Lebanon.** The Hebrew name of the river, in the Talmud, is the Feer; the Franks call it the Far;[1] and an ancient name for it is the Orontes. **The city was founded by King Antiochus, and it is overlooked by a very high mountain** in the south called Mount Silpius.

A wall surrounds this height as well as the city, the southern fortifications thus appearing as an extension above the natural steep wall arising from the valley. Yellowish sand in color, the wall is immense, its circumference being a full day's journey. **This place is very strongly fortified,** with four hundred towers incorporated into the wall, so that troops stationed on top can observe every corner of the city and a great area outside it. Emperor Justinian built the original wall. **The other side of the city is surrounded by the river,** another obstacle to invaders.

On the summit of Mount Silpius is situated a well called the well of Daphnis, which is distant about one parasang from the center of Antioch. **The inspector of the well distributes the water by subterranean aqueducts and provides the houses of the principal inhabitants of the city therewith.**

Until the Franks came, the city seemed invincible. It was then the northernmost city of the Mohammedans, on the border with Syria, thus a major fortress. Because the wall enclosed Antioch's well, the city could maintain its water supply even in times of siege, and because the walls were so long, a besieged Antioch could smuggle in supplies. But Antioch's location and strength meant that it could not remain a Moslem fortress if the Franks were to succeed in conquering the Holy Land. For the Franks, this city was the last major obstacle on their path to Jerusalem.

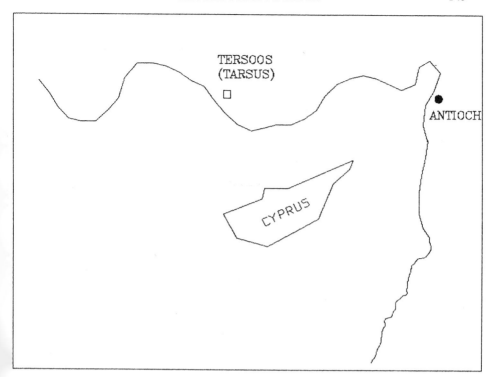

The Christian army reached Antioch in October 1097, led by Bohemond, prince of Otranto and a Norman of the fiercest sort. He could not blockade Antioch entirely, given the wild, mountainous terrain to the south, but the Greek and Armenian residents of the city offered to aid him. Although then under Moslem rule, this coast had once been the domain of the Eastern church and most inhabitants of Antioch were Greeks and Armenians, two kinds of Christians, many of whom welcomed Christian "rescue." Antioch's Syrian Christians, on the other hand, remained loyal to their Mohammedan rulers rather than side with the Franks.

The besiegers faced the urgent problem of finding food. To feed themselves the Franks even sacrificed some of their horses. As winter approached, Bohemond had to send his raiding parties farther and farther into the countryside for whatever was edible, notwithstanding the certain Moslem ambuscades. The Arabian archers were practiced in shooting while riding. The Franks, although their horses were heavier, were not used to long-distance fighting from them: their knights, skilled in fighting mounted, knew mostly close combat with lances, while their bowmen were used to fighting on foot. The Franks lost more lives than did the Moslems, through starvation and in the battles that continued all the winter.[2]

Meanwhile, members of Antioch's various religious communities involved themselves in some complicated spying. In time, Bohemond felt overwhelmed by self-appointed spies on his behalf, and came to the conclusion that some of the men purporting to be Armenians spying on his behalf were actually Turks masquerading as Armenians. He dealt with this duplicity directly: he commanded a meal of captured spies, setting his soldiers to slitting the Turks' throats and his cooks to roasting the carcasses on spits.[3] Thus Bohemond relieved the food shortage, at least for the moment, and the remaining unsolicited spies fled his camp in short order.

With the help of genuine spies among Antioch's Armenians, and with naval aid from Genoa and England, after many months of struggle Bohemond took control of Antioch in the early morning of 3 June 1098. The citadel held out, but by sunset he had killed every Turk in the city.[4]

Since then Antioch has been in the empire of the Franks—it is the main city of their principality of Antioch—but it has been hotly contested by Byzantines and Turks. In 1149 a prince of Antioch, Raymond de Poitiers, joined forces with the Assassins in an effort to crush the aggressive Moslem prince Nureddin, ruler of Aleppo and Edessa. But the Moslem forces annihilated those of Raymond. As symbol of victory and token of homage to the khalif of Baghdad, Nureddin sent him Raymond's skull.[5]

From the Franks' arrival in the East, Antioch has likewise been site and focus of continual hostilities between Eastern and Latin Christians. Now the Frankish city is a suzerainty of Byzantium, since Jerusalem's King Baldwin married Theodora, the niece of the Byzantine emperor Manuel Comnenus, in 1158.

Emperor Manuel made his official entry into Antioch on Easter Sunday of 1159, accompanied by King Baldwin, the two sovereigns on horseback, prancing along the carpeted, flower-strewn, banner-bedecked streets to the sounds of drums and trumpets. King Baldwin, however, wore no crown and carried no arms; and Antioch's Lord Prince Renaud walked alongside the emperor, holding the horse's bridle. The Latin patriarch, Almery of Limoges, in the colorful regalia of his office, led the Byzantine emperor to the Cathedral of Saint Peter, to the sound of hymns, for the purpose of the visit was to show cooperation between Frank and Byzantine, and so between the churches of the Latin and Eastern rites.

Local people talk with relish about that week of ceremonies and parties: about the jousts in which Emperor Manuel performed well enough but the Byzantine knights proved inferior to the Franks, about the gifts distributed to the populace, about the rich meals laid on for them.[6]

If for Renaud, prince of Antioch, the moment was bittersweet, worse had yet to come. Eighteen months later, in November '60, when the herds were being moved from the mountains to the plain, Prince Renaud raided northeastward and was returning to Antioch with his booty of horses and camels and cattle, only to be caught in an ambush laid by one of Nureddin's kinsmen. The Mohammedans took Prince Renaud as captive to Aleppo, where Nureddin still holds him.[7] The principality of Antioch is now **in the possession of** Renaud's son, **Prince Bohemond Poitevin, surnamed "le Bègue"** because of his speech impediment.

Second in importance only to Jerusalem in the Frankish empire, Antioch is a great commercial center despite its distance from the coast—its port lies three parasangs to the west, at Saint Simeon (Le Soudin to the Franks). Beasts carry the merchandise from the port city to Antioch's bazaars, which are thronged with merchants from every port around the Great Sea and from the vast Moslem lands in the East. Antioch's particular manufacture is a plain cloth without any stripes or patterns that sells in great quantities. One finds mills right in the city, likewise gardens and even orchards. Aqueducts and pipes in a remarkable system carry water to the houses.[8] Here too are the most luxurious baths in the world, which Emperor Manuel visited when he came to Antioch.

To this magnificent city the Franks, upon seizing Jerusalem, brought back some of their Jewish captives. Now **the city contains about ten Jews, who are glass manufacturers.**

They say that on this coast glass has been made since the most ancient times, and that Jews have always been among the glassmakers. Jews may have a predilection for glass because for us glass is like fish: it is a product of the sea, and it can be used with both meat dishes and milk dishes.

Spain's glass bowls and pitchers seem common and ordinary compared with the ones I have seen from Venice and around the eastern coasts of the Great Sea. Here they make glassware exceedingly elegant, colorful, decorated with images, even in the shape of animals and plants.

The process of making glass is everywhere the same. At Antioch the workshops are located where the river empties into the sea. First the workmen collect the sand, then they wash it and heat it. Here if the sand isn't clean—or in places where sand is of a lesser quality—then workmen use that sand to make coarse green or dull-colored bottles. It takes well-prepared sand to make fine clean glass.

Other workmen wade into the sea to collect plants, which they then burn. The master glassmaker mixes a small quantity of the resulting ash with a large amount of the sand. He won't tell me how much—he says it's a trade secret. I gather the proportion is not fixed: that it depends on the kind of plants and the cleanliness of the sand, just how to mix the two ingredients so as to produce glass successfully. It's his knowledge of such things that makes him a master glassman.

Central to the whole operation is a huge furnace, twice as tall as a man. Its shape is that of a dome, so that the heat is deflected downwards. At the furnace, stokers work continually. They scoop some mixture of glass and ash into a fire-clay pot, which they then hang in the furnace as one in a circle of pots above the fire; the mixture will heat and begin to fuse. At this stage of early fusing, they remove a pot from the furnace and leave it to cool. They take odd bits of finished glass, of the same composition as the mixture, grind them up and toss the grounds into the cooling, partially fused mixture, then they return the pot to the furnace for a day or two, until its contents are fully fused. It's at this point that the glass is shaped, either as sheets for windows and mirrors or for blown vases and bottles.

The craftsman who does the blowing dips a hollow iron tube into molten glass. By blowing into the tube he expands the formless blob into the shape of a bulb. Blowing into the tube while whirling it about, a skilled workman can produce glass containers of many intricate shapes, and even decorate a vessel with feet or handles.

The finished glass is sent to Tyre and Beirut, whence it is exported to other countries, especially to the lands of the West.

Glass manufacture attracted Jews for particular reasons. Not only are glass vessels used for storing and cooking, they are also important in trades in which Jews specialize. In pharmaceuticals, glass vessels of varied shapes, sizes and colors serve as recipients for the different "simples." In the mints, which employ many Jews, assayers use glass weights as standards for coins.

Everywhere, but especially in this hot climate, glassmaking demands great skill and precision, and it is uncomfortable work. Not many men want to do it. That's probably why Jews are allowed to specialize in it.[9]

Letter from Beirut

Southward **two days from Antioch to Lega which is LATACHIA,** on the coast, **with about two hundred Jews.**

Here reside numerous Italians, whose language one hears often in the markets and streets. Genoa, Pisa, and Amalfi have merchant colonies here, to which the Franks grant official recognition. Not only in this town but also in Antioch live such communities from Pisa and Genoa, and in Antioch's port, Saint Simeon, the Genoese have yet another colony. The Italians hardly associate with the Franks other than for business; they keep to themselves in their offices and shops in their own streets, where they trade according to the ways of their home countries.[1]

<   <   <   <   >   >   >   >

From Latachia **two days to JEBILEE, the Ba'al God of Scripture,** which stands in the rich plain under Mount Lebanon.

In this vicinity resides the nation which are called Assassins, who do not believe in the tenets of Mohammedanism but in those of one whom they consider like unto the prophet Kharmath. They fulfil whatever he commands them to do, whether it be a matter of life or death. He goes by the name Sheikh al-Chashishin, or their old man, by whose commands all the acts of these mountaineers are regulated. His seat is in the city of Kadmus, the Kedemoth of Scripture in the land of Sichon.

The Assassins are faithful to one another by the command of their old man and make themselves the dread of every one, because their devotion goes far enough to gladly risk their lives, and to kill even kings, if commanded to do so. They imbibe the substance hashish, from which their name Assassin comes, with strong effects; they say it gives them a foretaste of paradise and dissolves any concern about their behavior or even life itself.

The extent of their country is eight days' journey. When the Franks first came to these shores, the Assassins cooperated with them against the Moslems; now **they are at war with the Christians, and with the Count of Tripoli,** and with all the Mohammedans.[2]

<   <   <   <   >   >   >   >

Two days farther south along the coast is a city called TORTOSA. Like

149

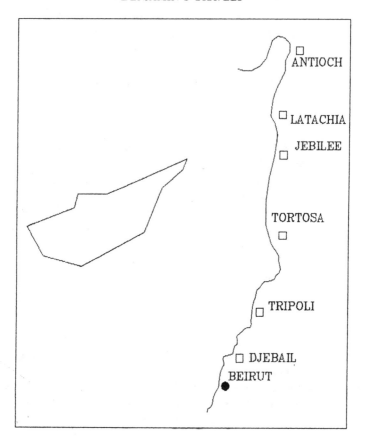

our Tortosa at the mouth of the Ebro, it is a good small harbor. Raymond de Saint Gilles, count of Toulouse—the Count Raymond of the unsuccessful campaign against Tudela in 1087—went on to lead Franks in the first invasions of the Holy Land. He captured Tortosa in 1102 and made it his home while he sought to take Tripoli.[3]

TRIPOLI has the military advantage of location on a rocky peninsula. Count Raymond needed two years and the help of the Genoese navy to conquer the city; in due course he was named ruler of the Franks' county of Tripoli. He died here in 1105.

Because this region was settled by Raymond de Saint Gilles and his followers from around Toulouse, the people here speak a sort of *langue d'oc*, which sounds quite different from the Normans' *langue d'oeil*, which is spoken in Antioch.[4]

The city of Tripoli, its walls battered by the sea, its form a square a thousand cubits on each side, is an old and great city. A busy port, it serves a rich hinterland that includes Damascus. Abounding in trees, Tripoli produces much fruit and timber, and it manufactures paper of good quality. The city continued to prosper under the Franks.

But some time ago Tripoli was visited by an earthquake, which destroyed many Jews and Gentiles. Numbers of the inhabitants were killed by the falling houses and walls, under the ruins of which they were buried. More than twenty thousand persons were killed in Palestine by this earthquake.

Thanks be to God, the local Jewish community survived. Many of its people had come here as captives and as refugees during the years of the Frankish conquests. The fortress that Count Raymond built at the south of the city, on a hill between two wadis, which he used as his base for conquering Tripoli—that still stands.[5] He called the fortress Mont-Pèlerin; now it's known simply as the Castle Saint Gilles.[6]

< <   < <   > >   > >

One day's journey from Tripoli to the other DJEBAIL which was the Gebal of the children of Ammon. It contains about one hundred and fifty Jews and stands on the coast of the Holy Land.

You find there the ancient place of worship of the children of Ammon. The idol of this people sits upon a cathedra or throne, constructed of stone and richly gilt; two female figures occupy the seats on his side, one being on the right, the other being on the left, and before it stands an altar, upon which the children of Ammon offered sacrifices and burned incense in times of yore.

The Greeks call the city Byblos. It's famous among them as the birthplace of Adonis and the site of the Temple of Adonis.

This city is governed by seven Genoese; the supreme command is vested in one of them, Julianus Embriaco by name; he is of the noble Embriaco family of Genoa. This Djebail contains about two hundred Jews.[7]

< <   < <   > >   > >

Farther along the coast two days to BEIRUT, which is Beeroth. In biblical times, this was a city of the tribe of Benjamin. The excellent cedars of Lebanon, of which we read in the Song of Songs, are no longer to be seen. In fact there no longer exists any land of Lebanon, for the Franks made its northern part into their county of Tripoli and incorporated its southern part (including Beirut) into their kingdom of Jerusalem.

This is where young King Baldwin died, early in 1162. A big man, strong, accustomed to good health, only thirty-three at the time, he was passing through Tripoli when he fell ill. Count Raymond of Tripoli had him treated by his own physician, a Syrian. Even though King Baldwin's condition had not improved, he left Tripoli for Beirut—to return to his own kingdom—

and after his death, rumors raged that in Tripoli he had been poisoned. The people grieved, Mohammedans as well as Franks, for this king was especially loved and respected.[8]

Before the Franks came, indeed for many centuries, Beirut's Jews produced the famous glass which they exported in large quantities across the Great Sea to Christian lands. The Franks besieged and conquered Beirut in the spring of 1110. The siege surprised many Jewish merchants who were sojourning here; trapped in the city, they were killed. The then King Baldwin (the first of that name) had commanded that the people of Beirut be left unharmed; but unruly Italian fighters massacred them anyway. They destroyed at least thirty-five houses belonging to Jews.

Those Moslems and Jews who survived the massacres could stay in the now-Frankish city or leave, as they chose. Most of the Jewish survivors fled. It seemed that this Jewish community, in Beirut since the earliest times, had come to an end. The Franks inaugurated a grand commerce with the Italian ports, trading with them almost exclusively; this trade being profitable, they are ever fearful of raids from Druze tribesmen. A few Jews have taken up life here again, and now Beirut has **about fifty Jewish inhabitants.**

Letter from Tyre

From Beirut it is **one day's journey to Saida which is TSIDON of Scripture.**
It lies on the coast of the Great Sea, an attractive city long famous for
activities of the sea, namely trade, glass blowing, and purple dyeing.

In the year 1107 Tsidon was besieged by the Franks with the help of
Danish and English ships blockading the port. The people of Tsidon offered
King Baldwin a huge sum of money if he would leave them in peace; he
needed the money, so he called off his fighters. But after taking Tripoli in
1109 and Beirut in the spring of 1110, King Baldwin (now with a fleet of
ships under young King Sigurd of Norway) returned to Tsidon and finally
captured it in the last weeks of that year. The conquerors looted the city but
did not destroy it; they allowed its Jewish and Moslem residents to choose
to stay or to leave. Those who decided to stay had to pay a punitive twenty
thousand dinars, which reduced them to poverty.

As a Christian city Tsidon thrives. It is **a large city with about twenty
Jewish inhabitants.** The markets are very busy with traders from far and
near, who sell all sorts of merchandise at cheap prices. The city is surrounded by a stone wall with four gates, beyond which are lush gardens and
trees. Sugar cane is a principal crop. Water is plentiful; an aqueduct carries
water from the mountains in the east into the city for people to drink.

In the center of Tsidon is a certain spring of water famed for its fish. The
fish are small, about the length of a finger but fatter; they have tiny fore and
hind legs, which are partly hidden; their male and female organs are evident.
In the spring months men catch these fish and dry them. When a man feels
inclined toward more sexual activity than that for which he has the force,
he scrapes one of these dried fish and eats it: it is an aphrodisiac.

Within twenty miles to the east of Tsidon, in the mountainous area near
the confines of the Latin Kingdom, **resides a nation who are at war with the
inhabitants of Tsidon** and who regularly raid the seacoast at Beirut as well:
**the name of this nation is Druzes. Their abodes are on the summits of the
mountains and in the ridges of the rocks, and they are subject to no king
or prince.**

Mount Hermon, a distance of three days journey, confines their territory.
The Arabs call this mountain Jebel al-Sheikh, which means "the chieftain
mountain," for its impressive peak can be seen and admired from a long

153

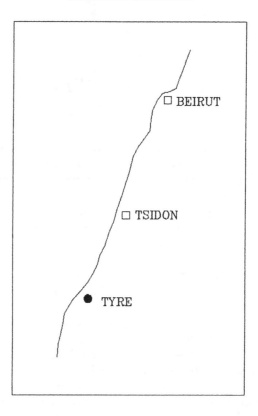

way away. The Bible mentions this mountain: its lions and leopards, its dew, and its cedar trees.[1] Now, though, the mountain stands bereft of trees, for in days long past men cut them down for wood to make masts for ships.

I've heard that **the Druze nation is very incestuous: that a father cohabits with his own daughter, and once every year, all men and women assemble to celebrate a festival upon which occasion, after eating and drinking, they hold promiscuous intercourse.**

They say that the soul of a virtuous man is transferred to the body of a newborn child, whereas that of the vicious transmigrates into a dog or some other animal. "This their way is their folly."

They are called heathens and unbelievers because they confess no religion. But as they keep their community closed to outsiders, those outsiders who speak about them may in fact not know the Druze beliefs. I have also been told that the ancestors of the Druzes were Moslems of the Shi'ite sect, and that just like Moslems the Druze consider Moses, Jesus, and Mohammed to be prophets. Also that they venerate Jethro, the father-in-law of Moses, and make pilgrimage to his grave in the Galilee to the east. And that for these matters they use the Syriac language, although for everyday matters they speak Arabic.

As the Druze isolate themselves, **Jews have no permanent residence among them. Some tradesmen however and a few dyers travel through the country occasionally, to carry on their trades or sell goods, and they return to their homes when their business is done. The Druzes are friendly toward Jews; they are so nimble in climbing hills and mountains, that nobody ventures to carry on war with them.**

<   <   <   <   >   >   >   >

From Tsidon, **one day's journey to New Tsour,** called in Syrian "TYRE" and in Arabic "Sour," **a very beautiful city, the port of which is in the very town** as the city lies on a round headland surrounded by the sea on three sides. Until Alexander the Great, Tyre was an island; to invade it in war, he built the narrow road connecting the city with the mainland.[2]

Long, large rocks in the sea help to form an excellent harbor, which faces west. **This port is guarded by two towers, within which the vessels ride at anchor. The officers of the customs draw an iron chain from tower to tower every night, thereby effectively preventing any thieves or robbers to escape by boat or by other means.**[3] A port equal to this is met nowhere upon earth. Tyre's harbor can take bigger ships than Acre's, although the city of Acre is bigger than the city of Tyre (New Tsour).

If you mount the walls of New Tsour, you may see the remains of "Tsour the crowned" which was inundated by the sea. The first Tsour, on the mainland, was so called because of its position on a rock (the Hebrew "Tsûr" being "rock"). **It is about the distance of a stone's throw from the new town; and whoever embarks may observe the towns, the markets, the streets and the halls at the bottom of the sea.**

New Tsour, now Christian, uses the name Tyre. The city is fortified in a manner to be seen nowhere else. Its walls rest upon land for only a short distance—the part of the walls built into the sea, of hewn stone, are set in bitumen to keep the water from destroying them.[4] The weakness of the city, militarily, is that the peninsula lacks wells; all its drinking water comes from the mainland, by aqueduct.[5] When the forces of the first King Baldwin besieged Tyre during the first four or five months of 1112, the city succeeded in holding out and the Franks were finally forced to retreat.[6] By then Tyre had become a haven for refugees from cities already conquered by the Franks. But at the second siege of Tyre, starting mid-February 1124—the Franks by this time under the second King Baldwin and greatly aided by Venetian sea power—the city bowed to the fate which seemed inevitable and capitulated rather than suffer great damage in battle.

The victorious Christians here too allowed Jewish and Moslem residents to choose whether to stay or to leave, those staying having to pay twenty thousand dinars tax. The leaders of the Moslems left, abandoning their poor and weak. Most Jews remained, and they have been treated decently.

As soon as the city came under Christian rule, merchants from Europe arrived in great numbers—Tyre has communities from Barcelona, Marseille, Genoa, and Pisa, and of course from Venice, whose ships were instrumental in winning the city for the Franks.[7] The republic of Venice makes Jews unwelcome—as I may already have written you from Italy—but here in Tyre the Jews live in the Venetian colony, which not only is inhabited by Venetians but is under the government of the Venetian Republic. The Jewish residents pay their taxes to the Venetians.[8] The Venetians, who in Venice don't want Jews, here are very happy to have them as their subjects. In fact, the French Christian kings of Jerusalem wanted to take control of Tyre's Jews, but the Venetians wouldn't allow it—ironic!

The wealth of Tyre is such that some of the houses rise to five or six stories, and most houses have their own well or cistern. **The city is very commercial, and one to which traders resort from all parts.** Merchants come especially to buy the beautiful tyrian glass, the long-necked vases of glass and pottery. Jews from North Africa come also to trade in spices and flax.

Tyre has a yeshiva, which R. Elijah ben Solomon transferred here from Jerusalem about a hundred years ago when the Holy City fell to the Seljuks; now this yeshiva is the spiritual center for Jews from a wide area. Tyre's Jewish community is strong and contains Jews from several countries, including the *dayyan* Ephraim Misri (of Egypt) and R. Meir of Carcassonne, who respectively lead the parts of the Jewish community following Egyptian and French customs. Many men here are sons and grandsons of refugees and migrants from other cities in Palestine, who came here when their cities were conquered by the Franks. **About four hundred Jews reside in this excellent place.**

Some of them, especially physicians, of course, provide their services to Christian nobles, although the bishops inveigh against Christian knights calling upon Jews.[9] Some of the Jewish craftsmen weave an extremely fine white cloth from yarn sent by the Jews of Jerusalem.[10] Another product of the earth around Tyre **is sugar of a fine grade, for men plant it here and people come from all lands to buy it.** A few of **the Jews of Tyre are shipowners,** apparently the last of the Jewish ship-owners along the coasts of the Great Sea, for now most ships are built in Italian ports by Christians. And Jews here are **manufacturers of the far-renowned Tyrian glass, the purple dye** for which **is also found in this vicinity.**

This coast stinks, due to the dried and drying bodies of the purplefish. That's a kind of shellfish, from which comes the purple dye used for glass and also for cloth. Silk-weavers in Thebes obtain purple dye from shellfish in the waters closer to them, but here on this coast, around Tsidon, Tyre and Haifa, is the great center of purple dyeing. It has always been so: the

Phoenicians were purple dyers, and purple dyeing is mentioned in the Book of Ezekiel.

In ancient Rome and among the early Christians, the rulers reserved to themselves the right of wearing purple; likewise in early Byzantium, whose people called the best purple "imperial purple." To them purple was so important as a symbol that when an heir was born to their reigning monarchs they dubbed him Porphyrogennetos, literally "born in the purple."[11]

Tyrian purple is the color of kings because of its rarity and its fastness, that is, it remains in the cloth forever. The first reason for its expense is that each purplefish gives only a few drops of the liquid from which the dye is made; the second reason, that preparing the dye is a costly process. The dyers keep the details secret. Broadly, however, this is the procedure. In the spring of the year, the purplefishers drop baskets containing bait into the sea, thus luring the shellfish to cling to the baskets.[12] Each year they catch thousands upon thousands of these shellfish. They open each creature and remove from it the organ containing its few drops of creamy liquid. They pile these organs together and salt them for days. Then they rinse them, and boil them for weeks, regularly skimming and sieving the liquid as it turns darker.

When the color is strong enough, it is used to dye cloth. The cloth comes from the vat a yellow color, but in the sunlight it gradually darkens to red or purplish. If the dyers want a stronger color, the true tyrian purple or royal purple, they dye the cloth again. The brilliance and the darkness of the boiled liquor depend upon the kind or kinds of purplefish used, so the dyers control this very carefully. The shade also depends on the salts (i.e., mordant) used to improve the fastness of the dye in the cloth.

Falsifiers of the tyrian purple abound, recipes for false purples being given even in books. Purple colors can be obtained from shellfish other than purplefish, or by dyeing a cloth blue and then red. But these lack the particular beauty and the fastness of tyrian purple.

Letter from Haifa

From New Tsour, **one day to ACRE, which is the Acco of Scripture on the confines of the tribe of Asher. This city is the frontier town of Palestine,** but still it is outside Eretz Yisrael.

For us Jews (although not for Franks) the Holy Land boundaries are specific and very important, because the ancient rabbis made particular laws for inhabitants of the Holy Land, for instance, regarding taxation and farming. Many people feel that the very soil of the Holy Land has a special sanctity. It says in the Talmud that "burial in Israel is like burial under the altar";[1] accordingly, the Jews of Acre placed their two cemeteries within the Holy Land: one to the east of the city; the other (for the more eminent members of the community) to the south of the city at the foot of Mount Kharmel below the cave of Elijah.

Like the other towns along this coast, Acre is built on an elevation to preclude damage by waves. The beach of Acre extends far beyond the city toward the south, its wide sandy stretches the site of frequent horse races. The city itself is compact, so much so that from outside, its massive walls and great towers appear as a fortress.

After the Franks invaded the Holy Land and took Jerusalem, they waited five years before attacking Acre. During those years, with the Christians perpetrating horrors in their conquest of Jerusalem and then of Haifa, Acre's Jews exerted themselves mightily to succor the survivors.

At the same time, the Franks busied themselves arranging naval support from Venice, Genoa, and Pisa, for without sea power, the Franks could not hope to win the Mohammedans' coastal cities. The Franks had to grant the Italian cities substantial trading rights in any city they would help to conquer.[2] In May 1104, while King Baldwin's soldiers held Acre under siege from the land side, Italians attacked by sea; the city collapsed within twenty days. The Franks and Italians devastated the city and massacred its Moslems and Jews, leaving as few survivors in Acre as elsewhere.

Eventually peace returned to Acre, and Jews drifted back. Now the Jewish community, **which contains about two hundred inhabitants**, lies in the new outlying quarter called Mount Musard. The rabbinical court has been reestablished.[3]

After a few years of ruling their Kingdom of Jerusalem, sending myriads of soldiers and officials back and forth between Palestine and Europe, the Franks decided that the dangers of traveling over land through the Greek

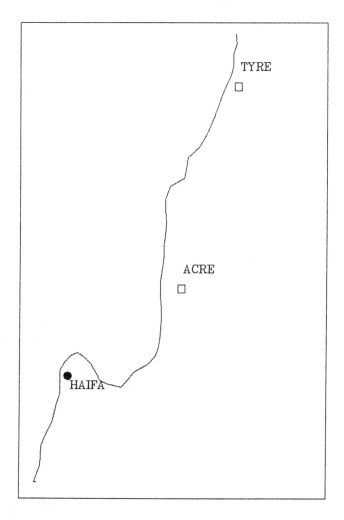

and Turkish kingdoms exceeded the hazards of sea travel and henceforth journeyed mostly by ship.[4] **In consequence of its situation on the shore of** the Great Sea **and of its large port,** Acre **is the principal place of disembarkation of all** administrators and **pilgrims who visit Jerusalem by sea.** Acre's harbor cannot hold the biggest ships (as can the harbor at Tyre), but at Acre the harbor faces south and ships can enter even when great winds prevent their entrance at other ports.

As at Tyre, the harbor here is well protected. It is defined by sea walls and resembles an arcade, the back of which is the town and the front of which extends into the sea; the passage (that is, the harbor) is arched over with chains. To permit the entrance of a ship, the chains are lowered until they sink into the sea, and the ship simply passes over them. Normally the chains are stretched taut, so as to prevent the entrance of unwelcome ships. This system of mole and chain is common along this coast. Acre's harbor is further guarded by an island, called the Tower of Flies, which was once an execution ground.

Several men have told me of a Jewish family here from Spain (from Andalucia) who, as I am planning to do, went on to Egypt. A physician named Moses ben Maimon arrived here after a long voyage from Morocco, full of accounts of the fury of the sea. In Acre he sojourned half a year, the warmest months, in 1165, during which time he made pilgrimage to Jerusalem and Hebron, before going to live in Egypt, where, evidently, he has already established a reputation for his knowledge of the Law.

At the gateway to Palestine, Acre prospers. In its Old City merchants from Italy predominate, but there are also many from Damascus, because that inland city ships its products to the West through Acre.[5] Acre welcomes merchants from Europe, the East, and North Africa, whatever their religion, and lets them travel in peace, once they have paid their tolls. The whole city bursts with travelers, who crowd the roads, making it difficult to move. The local officials are polite enough, but (especially compared to Tyre) Acre is filthy, smelling of dung and garbage. In every street one sees pigs—and crosses.

Acre's visitors of all religions go to see a certain spring of water on the eastern side of the town, called the Spring of the Ox. That is where Adam found the ox with which he was to work the earth.

King Fulk (the father of the current King Baldwin) came to Acre with his Queen Melisende and a great entourage in the autumn of 1143 and visited the Spring of the Ox. As they all rode around there, one of the court spotted a hare and they all chased after it. King Fulk, excited, was riding very quickly with his lance at the ready when his horse stumbled and fell. The king toppled from his horse; his heavy saddle fell onto his head, wounding him grievously. He died three days later, and was laid to his eternal rest at Acre's Church of the Holy Sepulcher.[6]

A river runs near the city, and the sand of its riverbanks serves to make glass. All along this coast they make the famous purple glass; and they also decorate glass with a lovely yellow color by a method which they say is old, but which is to be seen nowhere else: they paint the glass with silver salts and then fire it. The sand here at Acre is said to possess particular qualities, which account for Acre having been, in ancient times, the first place where glass was made. Funny, they didn't tell me that at Tyre.

< <   < <   > >   > >

From Acre, **three parasangs to HAIFA, which is Gath Hachepher.** This is the entrance to the Holy Land. Here was the northern limit of settlement of the Jews who returned from the Babylonian Exile, and for that reason the rabbis consider it the boundary. Here the land is sacred to us. Here, and only within Eretz Yisrael, can a man live Torah in its entirety.

The ancient rabbis made a distinction between two kinds of laws, those pertaining to the community and those pertaining to the person. Communal laws dealt with matters such as the calendar, taxation, and capital punishment; personal laws dealt with matters dependent on the behavior of an individual, such as the honoring of one's parents and the observance of Shabbat and kashrut and marital purity. Laws for the community required the vote of ordained scholars, whose legislation would have force only in their own state, that is, the Jewish state. (It was established in very ancient times that Jews living outside the Jewish state must follow the communal laws of their country of residence.)[7] More than a third of halakha is concerned with the community and the land, the Holy Land, and these laws do not apply to a Jew in Exile; they apply only to Jews in Eretz Yisrael.

Haifa being the first city of the Holy Land that most Jewish pilgrims and settlers see, it is fitting that Haifa is beautiful to the eye. **One side of it is situated on the coast,** on a bay; **on the other it is overlooked by Mount Kharmel. The river Mukattua** (the river Kishon) **runs down the mountain and along its base.**

Under the Mount Kharmel are many Jewish sepulchers. Local Jews have buried their dead in these caves from ancient times, and many Jews journey to the Holy Land carrying the bones of their relatives and friends so that these might lie in sacred ground. **Near the** Kharmel **summit is the cavern of Elijah,** the Tishbite of Gilead, **upon whom be peace,** who, in accordance with God's command, rebutted the priests of Baal and caused the rains to come. **On the summit of the hills you may still trace the site of the altar which was rebuilt by Elijah o.b.m. in the time of King Ahab, and the circumference of which is about four yards. Two Christians have built a place of worship near this site, which they call St. Elias.** Christian monks inhabit some of the Kharmel caves.

Under Moslem rule, Haifa had more Jewish inhabitants than Moslem. This city was a well-fortified trading center, protected by an Egyptian garrison. When the Franks first entered the Holy Land, they bypassed Haifa in their rush for Jerusalem, but the following summer (that is, summer 1100) Franks and Venetians invaded. They set up their huge siege tower and besieged the city; and they attacked it with numerous powerful catapults, concentrating their bombardment on the citadel. The defenders—who naturally included many Jews—fought so well that, after fifteen days, the Franks despaired of conquering the city and were preparing to withdraw. But Christian reinforcements came, enabling the aggressors to storm the citadel and breach the walls in a vicious battle. Some of Haifa's people managed to flee. The Franks and Venetians slew all who remained in the city.[8] Since then, no Jews live in Haifa.

Letter from Nablus

CESAREA, the Gath of the Philistines of Scripture, inhabited by about ten Jews and two hundred Cuthaeans. The latter are Samaritan Jews, commonly called Samaritans. The city is very elegant and beautiful, situated on the seashore, and was built by King Herod who called it Cesarea in honor of the Caesar (meaning Emperor).

< <   < <   > >   > >

Half a day's journey to KAKUN, the K'eilah of Scripture; in this place are no Jews.

< <   < <   > >   > >

Half a day's journey to ST. GEORGE, the ancient Luz. One Jew only, a dyer by profession, lives here.

< <   < <   > >   > >

One day's journey to SEBASTE. This is the ancient Shomron, the ancient city of the ten tribes after their revolt from the House of David, **where you may still trace the site of the palace of Ahab, King of Israel,** but the guides tell the Christians that the ruins are of a church which the Empress Helena built.

In ancient times the city was also called Samaria. Then the Greeks changed its name to Sebaste—"Sebastos" is Greek for "Augustus." King Herod built the Temple of Augustus here, which the Romans rebuilt when they took over the city. The Roman city had a forum and next to it a basilica, of which you can still see the pillars, and a forum which a colonnaded street connected to the western city gate.

It was formerly a very strong city, and is situated on the mount, in a fine country richly watered and surrounded by gardens, orchards, vineyards and olive groves. No Jews live here.

< <   < <   > >   > >

From Sebaste, **two parasangs to NABLUS, the ancient Shechem on Mount Ephraim,** situated in the valley between Mount Gerizim south of Nablus **and**

162

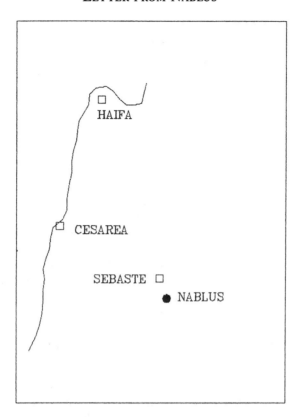

Mount Ebal. Mount Gerizim is rich in wells and orchards, whereas Mount Ebal is dry like stone and rock: the city of Nablus lies in the valley between these two hills.

It is the abode of about one hundred Cuthaeans, who observe the Mosaic law only and are called Samaritans. The schism of the Samaritans from the Jews occurred in ancient times: the prophet Ezra tells the story in the Bible.[1] When Nebuchadnezzar conquered Jerusalem in the year 3163 of the Jewish calendar (597 years before the common era), some Jews managed to escape to Samaria (modern Sebaste), although most of the Jews were sent into exile in Babylon. A century and a half later, the descendants of the exiled Jews returned to Jerusalem and set about rebuilding their city and their Temple, refusing the offer of Samaria's Jews to participate. Insulted, the Jews from Samaria embarked on a long series of petty efforts to sabotage the Jerusalem constructions. We know, of course, that despite the malefactors, the Jews in Jerusalem did complete the Second Temple; but meanwhile the two Jewish groups became estranged, the Jews of Samaria continuing to live in that region.

In the following century, when the great Alexander of Macedon destroyed the city of Samaria (3428 in our calendar; 332 before the common era), the Samaritans fled to Mount Gerizim, where in due course and with the permission of King Alexander they built a great synagogue much like the Temple in Jerusalem. They considered their edifice on Mount Gerizim to be the Temple, a presumption which the Jerusalem Jews thought a sacrilege. During two centuries the two groups anathematized each other; then around 3632 (128 B.C.E.), under the leadership of their high priest John Hyrcanus, some Jerusalem Jews smashed the temple on Mount Gerizim and, for good measure, devastated the nearby Samaritan town of Shechem.

The Samaritans repaired Shechem and continued to inhabit it as the center of their religious community—until the Romans, in their conquest of Palestine (3830 by the Jewish calendar; 70 C.E.) destroyed it again. The Romans had the town rebuilt nearby and named it "new city" like the Naples south of Rome, but, Arabic having no sound for the Latin p, this town became known as Nablus. The old Shechem lay on what is now the periphery of the modern Nablus, near Jacob's well. With its new name, the city remained the Samaritan stronghold; the Samaritans did not mix with other Jews, nor, for that matter, with any other people.

Joseph ben Matthias, also known as Josephus Flavius, who lived during the Roman destruction of Palestine and wrote a grand history of it, called the Samaritans hypocrites. "When they see the Jews in prosperity," he averred,

> [the Samaritans] pretend that they are allied to them and call them kinsmen; as though they were derived from Joseph, and had by that means an original alliance with them. But when they see them falling into a low condition, they say that they are no way related to them; and that the Jews have no right to expect any kindness from them; but they declare that they are sojourners, that come from other countries.[2]

Nonetheless, during the era of Moslem rule, the Samaritans had to share their city with Moslems, Persians, and Jews, who all fought incessantly against one another. The Moslems in particular felt affection toward Nablus, calling it "little Damascus," but that did not keep them from abandoning the city at their first sight of the Franks.[3] Once in control, the Franks modified the city name to Naples and, appreciating how easy it would be to defend the city militarily, constructed a citadel and a palace, and made it a royal city.[4] Like many towns conquered by the Franks, now **this place contains no Jewish inhabitants.**

How do the Samaritans, observers of Mosaic law, differ from Jews? Well, most fundamentally, they have no Mishnah, nor any law after the Torah. They believe that Moses, restored to life, or one of his descendants, will come as the Redeemer. **They have priests, descendants of Aaron the priest, o.b.m., whom they call Aaronim. These do not intermarry with any other** than priestly families; but they are priests only of their own law, who offer sacrifices and burnt offerings in the synagogue of Mount Gerizim. They do this in accordance with the words of Scripture, "Thou shalt put the blessing on Mount Gerizim," and they pretend that this is the Holy Temple. They always orient their synagogues toward Mount Gerizim.

Since the destruction of the Temple in Jerusalem and its replica on Mount Gerizim, a millennium has passed, but Samaritans still wrangle with rabbinic Jews about which was the "sacred" one.

The men of **this sect carefully avoid being defiled by touching corpses, bones, those killed by accident, or graves**, which avoidance they believe God commanded in the Book of Numbers.[5]

They change their daily garments whenever they visit their synagogue, upon which occasion they wash their body and put on other clothes. These are their daily habits. They don't lay tefillin.

Their Sabbath ritual includes four prayer services: that on the Sabbath Eve lasting for about an hour until the setting of the sun, the morning service starting before dawn; the service at the end of the Sabbath lasting for about half an hour until the setting of the sun; and also, between the morning and the evening service they hold a two-hour service starting at noon, but they hold this noon service only on the Sabbaths of the regular months and the Sabbaths that fall during the counting of the Omer, that is, between Passover and the Feast of Weeks (Shavuot).

The Samaritan calendar is like the Jewish calendar in having months of twenty-nine and thirty days, although the Samaritans count their years like the Moslems do. They have their own method of establishing a new month. They follow neither the modern Jewish practice of determining a new month according to calculation, nor the ancient Jewish and the modern Moslem practice of insisting on the visual sighting of the new moon. The Samaritans believe that the new moon being a gradual development from the later phases of the preceding moon, the only really new occurrence each month is the conjunction of the moon with the sun, and they have always calculated that. They give the months no special names, calling them the first month, the second month, and so on, as in the Torah. They start their year in the month of Passover.

The Samaritans observe their festivals on different days than the Jews: the two groups can celebrate a given festival on dates a month apart. The Samaritans base the liturgy for their holidays and festivals on that of their Sabbath. They celebrate neither Chanukah nor Purim, for the Torah doesn't mention them. **On Passover and holidays they offer burnt offerings on the altar which they have erected on Mount Gerizim, from the stones put up by the children of Israel after they had crossed the Jordan.**[6] They pretended to be of the tribe of Ephraim and are in possession of the tomb of Joseph the righteous, the son of our father Jacob, upon whom be peace, as is proved by the following passage from Scripture: "the bones of Joseph, which the children of Israel brought up with them from Egypt, they buried in Shechem."

The Samaritans live here in Palestine as Jews live in the kingdoms of Moslems and of Christians: as a minority people, sometimes tolerated, sometimes despised. The Jewish community considers the Samaritans heretics and ignores them. Long ago the Emperor Justinian decreed Samaritans to be not Jews but Christians, but the Christians don't treat them well either and from time to time even persecute them. When Palestine was under Mohammedan rule, the Samaritans looked to Moslems for protection . . . but around thirty years ago, in 1137, Moslems attacked Nablus and decimated its inhabitants.

What the Samaritans have in common with the Karaites and with the Mishawites in Cyprus is that they reject the Oral Law and have developed their own ways under the influence of the Christians and the Moslems among whom they live. But the Jewish communities which accepted the Oral Law and which obey the teachings of the rabbis were always subject to the same influences.

In Tudela, when I was growing up and where I heard more religious disputations than I could ever remember, there were three religious communities: a Moslem people, and a Christian people, and a small proud Jewish people. Clear lines separated them. When in my youth I became aware of the Karaites, I thought of them as Jews with different traditions, and they *were* Jews. I never realized that their peculiar traditions had grown from the influence of Islam. I had no idea that the Christians are of two distinct branches, two always-wrangling factions. Nor could I have imagined a people like the Druze, who are neither Jewish nor Christian nor Moslem—yet take their prophets from all three.

The people who are more-or-less Jews! Karaites, Vlachi, Khazars, Kaphrossin, Samaritans. The closer I get to Jerusalem, the more of the Jews are heretics.

First Letter from Jerusalem

Four parasangs from Nablus is situated MOUNT GILBOA, which Christians call Monto Jelbon. This is the site where Saul and his sons battled against the Philistines, and lost.[1] **The country is very barren hereabouts.**

< <   < <   > >   > >

Five parasangs further is the valley of AJALON, called by the Christians Val de Luna, because this is where the moon shone when Joshua caused the sun to stand still.[2]

< <   < <   > >   > >

One parasang to GRAN DAVID, formerly the large city of Gib'on. It contains no Jewish inhabitants. From here Jerusalem is just three parasangs distant—a half day's journey!

< <   < <   > >   > >

JERUSALEM is small and strongly fortified by three walls, an ancient and beautiful fortress.[3] "Beautiful in situation," says the psalm, "the joy of the whole earth!"[4] Verily, for **it contains a numerous population composed of Jacobites (Syrian Christians), Armenians, Greeks, Georgians, Franks, and in fact of peoples of all tongues. Two hundred Jews dwell in one corner of the city, under the Tower of David.** This is the city of David, the hill city chosen by King David as his capital.

This is the city to which Ezra the scribe returned from Babylonian exile, with his Levites and priests, to teach Torah and to reestablish Jewish worship, customs, and morality. In so doing, he intensified the idea of Jerusalem as spiritual capital for the Jews, however dispersed they might be. The generations of the historian Josephus and the writers of Mishnah considered Jerusalem the center of the world.[5] For a thousand years and more, Jews have offered this city homage in prayers and poems. Jews build their synagogues to face Jerusalem; yet today Jerusalem has no proper synagogue.[6]

In Oria I copied a poem by R. Amittai ben Shefatia, written three centuries ago but sadly apposite now:

167

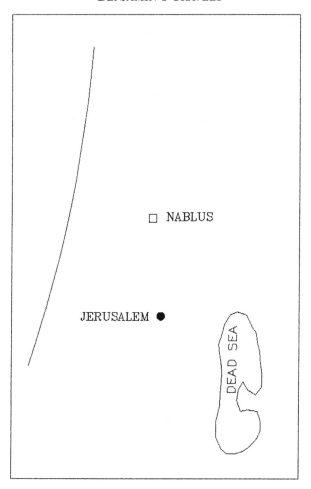

> Lord, I remember and am sore amazed
> To see each city stand in haughty state,
> And God's own city to the low grave razed,
> Yet all the time we look to Thee and wait.[7]

The life of Jerusalem's Jews while the Jews in Exile were "waiting" is a subject on which scholars here are wont to lecture. . . . When the Romans destroyed the Temple and expelled the Jews from Jerusalem, the Jewish capital city was reduced to a provincial town. So it remained for centuries, under Christian rule. Jews didn't return to Jerusalem in any great numbers until the Mohammedans, in the very first years of their religion, conquered the city from the Byzantine Christians; the new rulers let the Christian residents remain and they permitted the Jews to reside. As in Moslem Spain, Christians and Jews lived in Jerusalem as dhimmis.

Mohammedans consider Abraham the father of their religion because he submitted to God in agreeing to sacrifice his son Isaac: "Moslem" means "submitted." They believe it was here in Jerusalem that God tested Abraham's devotion, specifically on the rock of Moriah (the mount where Solomon would build the Temple). They believe that, millennia later, it was from this rock of Moriah that Mohammed ascended into Heaven, he and his horse al-Burak being escorted by the angel Gabriel up a ladder of light; and that by this means Mohammed came into the presence of God, who instructed him as to the way his followers should worship Him. Some years after Mohammed's death, the khalif Abd al-Malik had a huge temple built at Moriah, which temple the Moslems named the Dome of the Rock. **Omar ben al-Khatab erected a large and handsome cupola over it and allowed nobody to introduce any image or painting into this place, set aside for prayers only.** The Moslems venerate Jerusalem, but they do not consider it a sacred city as they do Mecca and Medina in Arabia. Moslems at prayer turn toward Mecca, as Jews turn toward Jerusalem. Moslems living at a distance do not yearn for Jerusalem, as Jews always did and do.

Jerusalem under the Moslems remained a small town, while the Jews in Exile looked toward Babylon for leadership. But Jerusalem was never far from the Jew's mind and heart—do we not pray daily, "If I forget Thee, O Jerusalem, let my right hand forget her cunning . . . "?[8]—and many many Jews like me have wanted to see the Holy City for themselves.

In biblical times it was incumbent on Jews who lived in this land to visit Jerusalem at the three festival seasons each year and to celebrate the festivities at the Temple. Ever since, in remembrance of the Temple and of those days, Jews exhort: "Next year in Jerusalem!" Little distinction being made between the city of Jerusalem and the Temple in Jewish reverence, Jerusalem is often referred to as *beth ha-Miqdash*, Hebrew for "the Temple." (Even the Arabs call the city *al-Muqaddas*, and, from the same root, *al-Quds*.)[9]

Some Jews in every generation have come to Jerusalem to trace the routes of the celebrants of long ago and to worship at the Temple site. They come because of the holiness of the land, encouraged by dicta such as that of R. Johanan: "He who walks four cubits in Israel is assured of a place in the world to come."[10] Can you imagine setting foot in the Holy Land without visiting the Holy City? Still, the Torah's prescription to go up to Jerusalem was a communal law having to do with the land, and as such it does not apply to Jews in the Exile.

Think of the similarity of the Hebrew word *hogeg* (literally, a celebrant) and the Arabic word *hajji* (for one who makes a hajj, or visit to sanctuaries).[11] Every Moslem, wherever he lives, is duty bound to make hajj to Mecca if he is able to do so; but a Jew living in the Exile has no obligation to visit Jerusalem, however able to do so he may be. In this matter we Jews are more like the Christians who visit Santiago or Rome or Jerusalem, not because their religion requires them to do so but because they have a religious urge or a simple wish to see the holy places. Maybe Christians and Moslems took their idea of pilgrimage (as they took so many ideas) from the Jews.

When Jerusalem was under Moslem rule, most of the Jewish visitors came from lands nearby, namely from Egypt, from Syria and the Grecian empire, from Persia. Their favorite month of sojourn was Tishri, including as it does Rosh ha-Shanah, Yom Kippur, and Succot. Now that the Frankish rulers again allow Jews to reside here and to visit, Jews come from as far away as Russia.[12] The great number of Christian Franks coming here to live and to visit has brought about numerous publications of *itineraria*, which tell sojourners about this land and direct them to its important religious sites. But we Jews had a few such books before the Franks: I've seen a *Guide to Jerusalem* written two hundred years ago.

All activities, and especially pleasant ones, have their detractors, I suppose. How many times, en route to Eretz Yisrael, was I told by good and pious men that to come here is no mitzvah, no religious duty?! I would think of Judah ha-Levi, who when planning his trip here must have heard similar cavils. Do you recollect the last chapter of his *Book of Kuzari*, where he has his hero, his Haver, tell the Khazar king of his intention to move to the Holy Land?

And "the king answers that a pure heart and strong desire can reach God from anywhere and warns of the perils of the journey."

Our Haver replies: the Land of Israel is the Holy Land because here were given for all peoples the precepts by which to live. This land was chosen by our father Abraham, and this land was apportioned among the ten tribes. This land is "the inheritance of the Lord" and "the gate of Heaven." God promised that wherever we go, he would bring us back here to the Land of Israel. And we all would have been brought back, except that the people did not wish to return—only a small number wished to do so; the rest preferred to stay with their fields and their chattels, albeit as vassals to strange lords.[13]

R. Judah himself, as you know, decided to spend his last years in accord with the ancient precept to "reside in the land of Israel, even among a majority of idolaters, rather than outside of Israel, even among a majority of Jews."[14]

In truth, many of our rabbis who disparage these journeys aren't so much against the visits to Palestine as they are against the common pilgrim custom of repairing to gravesites. The Karaites and Samaritans, indeed, prohibit worship at tombs. Even if in our tradition it's common to visit the graves of our ancestors and our scholars, some rabbis condemn it. The passage in

Torah about the burial of Moses in the land of Moab,[15] that "nobody knows the place of his burial"—they take it to mean that Jews should not make a shrine of any burial place.

Yet not only in Spain but in several places along the road I traveled, one sees rabbis' graves attended by a number of worshipers, communing (I presume) with the departed rabbi in hopes of being inspired by his knowledge or sanctity. Here, Franks mark many graves of our forefathers distinctively, with a small dome (Hebrew: *kipah*) or with a clump of trees. Naturally all Jews go to pray at these tombs. Even if they are fewer in number than the Christians, one sees Jews at tombs everywhere: at those of Elijah at Haifa, of Joseph at Nablus, of Rachel at Bethlehem, of Abraham, Isaac, and Jacob and their wives at Hebron; and many others. Even **the large place of worship called Sepulcher and containing the sepulcher of that man** (as the Talmudists designated Jisho the Nazarene) **is visited by all pilgrims.**

On seeing Jerusalem for the first time, a Jew recites: "Our holy and our beautiful house, where our fathers praised Thee, is burned with fire and all our pleasant things are laid waste."[16] Then he rends his garments as a sign of mourning. He grieves for a holy site razed not once but three times. How much do Jews today reflect on the Temple which the Romans destroyed, and how much on the synagogue with hundreds of Jews inside which the Franks burned with fire?

Of course the Jewish pilgrim visits the Temple site first. Next, in common practice, he makes a tour of the city's gates, praying for forgiveness and for mercy, for the return of the Temple to the Jews and of the Jews to the Holy Land. **Jerusalem is furnished with four gates, called gate of Abraham, of David, of Zion, and of Jehoshaphat. The latter stands opposite the Holy Temple, which is occupied at present by** the rebuilt Dome of the Rock, **a building called Templo Domino by the Franks. In front of it you see the western wall, one of the walls which formed the Holy of Holies of the ancient Temple, it is called gate of Mercy and all Jews resort thither to say their prayers near the wall of the court yard.** How it aggravates Jews' grief at the long-ago loss of the Temple to see on its site another edifice—so conspicuous, so magnificent—built by Moslems and now used by Christians.

At Jerusalem you also see the stables that were erected by Solomon and which formed part of his house. Immense stones have been employed in this fabric, which we see as a series of caves running from what used to be the Jewish quarter (now it is the Syrian quarter) past the site of the Temple and extending to the southeast.

You see to this day the vestiges of the canal near which the sacrifices were

slaughtered in ancient times, and all Jews inscribe their names upon an adjacent wall.

If you leave the city by the gate of Jehoshaphat, you may see the pillar erected on Absalom's place and the sepulcher of King Usia, and the great spring of the Shiloach which runs into the brook Kidron. Upon this spring you see a large building erected in the times of our forefathers. On the western slope of the valley is the spring called Gihon, where Solomon was anointed king; the Gihon is the main source of water for the city. Very little water is found at Jerusalem. The inhabitants generally drink rain-water, which they collect in their houses, in cisterns.[17] Villages near Jerusalem have springs, but the Holy City itself, being at the top of a hill, has none. Water is neatly drained from the city by sewers that the Romans built.[18]

From the valley of Jehoshaphat the traveler immediately ascends the Mount of Olives, as this valley only intervenes between the city and the mount. After the ruins of the Temple, the Mount of Olives is the most important site at Jerusalem. King Solomon built upon this mount. The prophet Zechariah is buried at its foot, in large and ancient burial grounds. Christians consider the mount holy, believing it to be the site of the arrest and crucifixion of Jisho the Nazarene; the Franks recently renovated an octagon-shaped church which the Byzantines built here long ago. After Byzantine rule of Jerusalem came the Arabs, Moslems who banned Jews from the Temple site, whereupon the Jews built a place of worship here on the mount. The entire Jewish community would ascend the Mount of Olives on the seventh day of Succot, Hoshana Rabba, for on that day the chief rabbi would announce the dates of the festivals for the year to come, and he would harangue against the Karaites and their calendar, and sometimes fights would break out between the two groups.

From the mount there is a clear view of the Dead Sea, called in ancient times Lake Asphaltes, with slimy shores due to the bitumenlike soft stone that washes up from under the water.[19] Two parasangs from the sea stands the salt pillar into which Lot's wife was metamorphosed, and although the sheep continually lick it, the pillar grows again and retains its original state. You also have a panorama of the whole valley of the Dead Sea and of the brook of Shittim, even as far as Mount N'bo.

The Valley of Jehoshaphat and the Mount of Olives are to the east of the city. If you go to the southwest, Mount Zion is also near Jerusalem, and upon it stands no building except a place of worship of the Nazarenes. There also are to be found three Jewish cemeteries, where formerly the dead were buried. Some of the sepulchers had stones with inscriptions upon them, but the Christians destroy these monuments and use the stones in building their houses. In earlier times Mount Zion was located within the city walls, but in the last century a new wall was built which left Mount Zion outside.

Across the wall from Mount Zion, not far from it but inside the wall, in the southwest part of the city, stands the eight-sided Tower of David. Above ten yards of the base of this building are very ancient, having been constructed by our ancestors. The remaining part was added by the Mohammedans and the city contains no building stronger than the Tower of David, the final redoubt of the Moslems at the Franks' conquest.[20] Now the Franks use it as their administrative center, for military garrison, customs offices, and food stores. The king's palace adjoins the tower,[21] and nearby are the dwellings of Jerusalem's few Jews.

Second Letter from Jerusalem

Jerusalem is surrounded by high mountains, and on Mount Zion are the sepulchers of the House of David and of those kings who reigned after him. In consequence of the following circumstances, however, this place is hardly to be recognized at present.

Fifteen years ago, one of the walls of the place of worship on Mount Zion fell down, which the patriarch ordered the priest to repair. He commanded him to take stones from the original wall of Zion and to employ them for that purpose. About twenty journeymen were hired at stated wages, who broke stones from the very foundations of the walls of Zion.

Two of these laborers, who were intimate friends, one day were taking their ease together, and then after a friendly meal returned to their work. The overseer questioned them about their tardiness, but they answered that they would still perform their day's work, and would employ thereupon the time during which their fellow laborers were at meals.

They then continued to break out stones and happened to meet with one which formed the mouth of a cavern. They agreed with one another to enter the cave and to search for treasure, in pursuit of which they proceeded onward until they reached a large hall, supported by pillars of marble, encrusted with gold and silver, and before which stood a table with a golden scepter and crown. This was the sepulcher of David, King of Israel, to the left of which they saw that of Solomon in a similar state and likewise the sepulchers of all kings of Jehuda, who were buried there.

They further saw locked trunks, the contents of which nobody knew, and desired to enter the hall: but a blast of wind like a storm issued forth from the mouth of the cavern, strong enough to throw them down, almost lifeless, on the ground. There they lay until evening, when another wind rushed forth, from which they heard a voice, like that of a human being, calling aloud: "Get up and go forth from this place."

The men came out in great haste and full of fear proceeded to the patriarch and reported what had happened to them. This ecclesiastic summoned into his presence R. Abraham al-Constantini, a pious ascetic, one of the mourners of the downfall of Jerusalem, and caused the two laborers to repeat what they had previously reported. Rabbi Abraham thereupon informed the patriarch that they had discovered the sepulchers of the House of David and of the kings of Jehuda.

The following morning the laborers were sent for again; but they were found stretched on their beds and still full of fear: they declared that they would not attempt to go again to the cave, as it was not God's will to reveal it to any one. The patriarch ordered the place walled up, so as to hide it effectively from every one until the present day.

The above-mentioned R. Abraham told me all this. He is R. Abraham ha-Hasid al-Constantini al-Parush, the Parushim being a small group of men living closely among themselves, hardly talking to anyone outside the group nor even to each other, but devoting almost every hour of their lives to the study of Torah. R. Abraham spends time with me and with other visitors to Jerusalem in hopes of persuading us to remain here and follow his way of life. He himself came here as a young man, but others of the Parushim are sons of men who came here from the south of France, moved by their grief for the destroyed Temple; they came in the wake of Christians from France settling in the kingdom of Jerusalem. These Parushim have a particular method of studying Torah: they look not only at the verses and words of Scripture, but at the individual letters. By considering each letter's numerical value,* they seek a text's deeper meaning. Thus they determine the way they shall pray, and endeavor to speed the coming of the Messiah.

The Parushim are few, while the Holy City's Karaites are numerous, their ancestors having come from Persia long ago. Like the Parushim, these Karaites devote themselves to mourning for the Temple and to praying for the arrival on earth of the Kingdom of Heaven. And now they mourn for our brethren massacred here in the time of our grandfathers—as do we all.

You might suppose that in Jerusalem the Karaites' grief would subdue their asperity, but here too they taunt and criticize the Rabbanites: having rejected the long rabbinic tradition, they continually argue against its worth. Although they denounce the teachings of the rabbis their scholars study them, it seems, in search of some comment or phrase which they can mock. They even ridicule the integral prayer of the Palestinian Rabbanites' Yom Kippur services, the Kol Nidre, calling it dishonest to annul vows.[1]

Jerusalem contains more Karaites than Rabbanites. This has been the situation for many generations, at one time the Karaites outnumbering the Rabbanites even more than they do now. The particular piety of Karaites stirred them to leave their Babylonian home (then the center of rabbinic Judaism) for the Jewishly provincial Palestine, where they would be free to devote themselves entirely to their prayers. Here Jews were living decently. The local Rabbanites did not give all their time to study: they worked, in dyeing and tanning, and a few of them in banking. As Karaites came to lead the Jewish community and speak on its behalf to the Moslem sovereigns,

---

*Letters of the Hebrew alphabet are used for writing numbers. See letter from Lucca, p. 84, above.

the Rabbanites encouraged more followers of the rabbinic tradition to come
here to study and to settle. They moved the Palestine Academy (Yeshiva
Eretz Yisrael) from Tiberias to Jerusalem, and for a long time the rosh
yeshiva at Jerusalem was called the Gaon of Tiberias.

Around the beginning of the last century, Jerusalem again knew warfare,
battles being fought incessantly over a large region by the Fatimids and
Seljuks and Bedouin Tayys and such peoples. Earlier Jews had been humiliated to see the site of the Temple being used for non-Jewish rituals; now
Jews had to suffer additionally while Gentiles were devastating the Holy
Land. As the years passed and the warfare continued, Jerusalem's Jews
became poorer and poorer and had to appeal increasingly to communities
abroad for sustenance; and many Jews left the city.[2]

The Byzantines came here about a hundred years ago to help their coreligionists; they strengthened the fortifications of the city's Christian quarter.
At the same time, a new Jewish quarter was created, in what is now the
Syrian quarter, in the northeast of the city. (Although the Franks razed it
and turned it into the Syrian quarter, this area of the city is still called the
Juiverie.) The Seljuk Turks seized Jerusalem in 1072, and five years later
the Palestine Academy moved to Tyre. By then, Jerusalem's Jewish population had decreased significantly, to hardly more than a few dyers and their
families.

During hundreds of years, from the time that the Byzantines ruled Jerusalem, Christians have come here on pilgrimage. When the Seljuk Turks took
over the city, they continually harried Christian pilgrims and even killed
them. The Christians of the Eastern church feared Turkish invasion of their
own soil and asked aid from the West in preventing it; whereas the Western
church concerned itself only with assuring free passage to Jerusalem for
Western pilgrims. The Church in the West preached its holy war to oust the
Seljuk Turks. While the Franks were grouping their forces on the Palestine
coast in summer 1098, the Seljuk Turks were conquered and driven out of
Jerusalem . . . by the Fatimids, who in their previous long rule of the Holy
Land had never molested Christian (or Jewish) travelers. The Fatimid king
begged the Franks to spare Jerusalem, promising freedom of worship and
free access for pilgrims. But the advantageous change of sovereignty did
not deter the Franks.[3]

Early in 1099, at the end of the short, cold winter, the people of Jerusalem
prepared for a long siege. They brought into the city all the animals from
the surrounding area and they organized continuing supplies of food and
water. They poisoned the water sources outside the city, leaving the pool of
Siloam from which to obtain drinking water.[4] Their governor, Iftikhar ad-
Daula, expelled the city's Christians as potential saboteurs. He also, in his
position of commander of Jerusalem's garrisons, took stock of the munitions

and found them adequate. He had sent to Egypt for military support, to supplement his own soldiers, whom he knew to be loyal to him; the Egyptian soldiers were on their way.

The Franks arrived at the beginning of June and besieged the city for six weeks. They finally won it by bombarding two parts of the wall—in the north and in the southwest—vulnerable because, since the land outside the walls there is high, the terrain does not slope steeply downward as from the rest of the walls.[5] In the southwest, near Mount Zion, the forces from the south of France fought under Raymond of Saint Gilles. Geoffrey de Bouillon led men from the north of France and from Flanders against the wall in the north and northeast, where the Fatimids' forces included many Jews because the Jewish quarter lay just behind this wall. The Franks fought furiously in their compulsion to liberate the Holy City from the Moslem infidels. For the Mohammedans, on the other hand, it was not a holy war—it wasn't as though non-Moslems were attacking Mecca! The Moslem forces faltered. Geoffrey de Bouillon, the first of the Franks to succeed in scaling the wall, later became the first ruler of the Kingdom of Jerusalem.

Inflamed with their conquest, the Franks rampaged through Jerusalem, intent on destroying the venerable city they had vowed to rescue. Without restraint they sliced down Jews and Moslems. They pushed numerous Jews into synagogues, which they then set on fire. They took a small number of Jews as prisoner, of whom the few lucky ones were sold as slaves along the Italian coasts, most of these slaves redeemed soon afterward by the local Jewish communities. (After many months of subjugating the Holy Land, it would not have served the Franks to take many prisoners to sell as slaves, for following any major battle, when the victor sells slaves, the price of these drops in consequence of the rise in the number being sold.) The Franks kept some of their Jewish and Moslem captives busy in Jerusalem for several months, clearing the streets of the maimed and bloodied corpses. From these stinking streets only a few very fortunate Jews managed to flee, carrying their tales of horror to Askalon, Egypt, and elsewhere in the Moslem lands.[6]

As Jerusalem under the Fatimids had contained mostly Moslems and Jews, the Franks soon realized themselves to be rulers of a new kingdom without inhabitants. One of their first decrees banned any Moslem or Jew from entering the city. Directly they brought in tribes of Arab Christians from across the Jordan and settled them in the heretofore-Jewish quarter in the northeast part of the city. Only Christians were to dwell in the Franks' Kingdom of Jerusalem, which they would administer in the French manner. Just a year after his grand conquest, Geoffrey de Bouillon was fatally wounded by an arrow; it was his brother who was crowned King Baldwin of the Latin Kingdom of Jerusalem, on the Christian eleventh day of November of the year 1100.

The Franks, with their armies and navies from many European lands, went on to subdue the other towns of the Holy Land, extending the Kingdom of Jerusalem from the Great Sea east to the river Jordan and from Aqaba in the south to Beirut in the north and establishing other kingdoms further north as well. Everywhere they went they slaughtered Moslems and Jews; the Jewish communities were destroyed, their survivors dispersed. The story of the Jews in Palestine since then has been told by grieving individuals trudging from town to town inquiring about lost relatives.

Throughout, Christian pilgrims flocked from Europe to Jerusalem. Gradually the Franks devoted less of their effort to war and more to administration. Palestine's towns could live peacefully again, with their new populations of Eastern Christians and Syrians, Western Christians who came as pilgrims and stayed, and the few Jews who were drifting back. Although most Jews would have preferred living under Moslem rather than Frankish sovereignty, the Christian towns (that is, those already won by the Franks) offered the greater security. But the Jews were still barred from living in Jerusalem.

The Franks' Jerusalem grew prosperous, thanks to its soldiers and administrators and the thousands upon thousands of pilgrims and the Church officials and the royal court. From the first the Franks encouraged local Eastern Christians and even Arabs to trade in the city.[7] Jerusalem quickly organized itself for selling to the many men who would buy luxuries; but then it found it had few people to produce them. Not even the beautiful cloths so characteristic of the East were being made locally. Jews had traditionally been among the most skilled of dyers, and now they could live only in the kingdom's small towns, where they worked individually or in pairs. So the Franks finally granted the right of residence in Jerusalem to several families of Jewish dyers. **The king sold the exclusive privilege of carrying on this trade in Jerusalem to the Jews, who rent the dyeing-house by the year.**

So the Jews were once again permitted, albeit grudgingly, to come back into the City of David, the City of Peace, to dwell with adherents of the new religions. At least the Jews live here in peace, even if the Christian groups are always fighting among themselves. The native Christians, who naturally outnumber the ruling Franks, belong to Eastern (Byzantine) sects.[8] The Franks keep trying to subject the native Christians to the same taxes they impose on the kingdom's non-Christians.[9] And the Eastern Christians are particularly incensed that the Franks have taken over their big old churches for the Latin rite.[10]

Disregarding the Christians' acrimony, I find it convenient to be once more in a land where the main language is Arabic. Arabic-speakers comprise not only native Christians, but descendants of the Frank conquerors as well; indeed, many of these have native mothers and grandmothers. Most of the soldiers in the royal army are sons of unions of Franks with native women.[11]

Letter from Askalon

Two parasangs from Jerusalem is BETHLEHEM of Jehuda. The country abounds with rivulets, wells, and springs of water. Twelve Jews, dyers by profession, live at Bethlehem.

Approaching from Jerusalem, **within half a mile of Bethlehem, where several roads meet, stands the monument which points out the grave of Rachel,** wife to Jacob, mother of Joseph and Benjamin. It lies "within the border of Benjamin," according to the first Book of Samuel.[1] **This monument has been constructed of eleven stones, equal to the number of children of Jacob, who** laid them on their mother's tomb.[2] **It is covered by a cupola which rests upon four pillars; and every Jew who passes there inscribes his name on the stones of the monument,** for Rachel is the Mother of the Nation, the matriarch of Israel.

Not only Israelites but Christians and Moslems too venerate Rachel and visit her tomb. The Franks say that here lie also the remains of David and Solomon.

From Bethlehem, **six parasangs to HEBRON. The ancient city of that name was situated on the hill and lies in ruins at present, whereas the modern town stands in the valley** with its trees of olives and figs and many other fruits, **in the field of Makhphela.** Our father Abraham bought the cave at the end of this field to use as a burial site.[3] This is the place to which most pilgrims come after visiting Jerusalem; from ancient times Jews have come here to prostrate themselves and thus do honor to their forefathers.

Here is the large place of worship called St. Abraham, which during the time of the Mohammedans was a synagogue. It was built by King Solomon. **The Gentiles have erected six sepulchers in this place, which they pretend to be those of Abraham and Sarah, of Isaac and Rebbekah, and of Jacob and Leah: the pilgrims are told that they are the sepulchers of the fathers, and money is extorted from them.**

But if any Jew come, who gives an additional fee to the keeper of the cave, an iron door is opened, which dates from the times of our forefathers who rest in peace, and with a burning candle in his hand the visitor descends into a first cave, which is empty, traverses a second in the same state, and at last reaches a third, which contains six sepulchers: that of Abraham, Isaac and

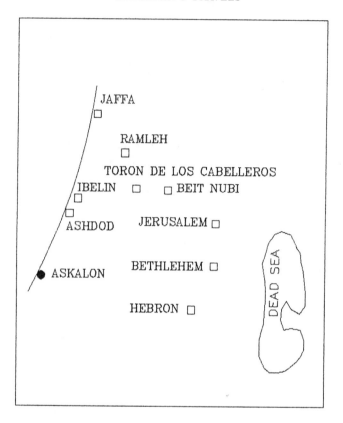

Jacob and of Sarah, Rebbekah and Leah, one opposite the other. All these
sepulchers bear inscriptions, the letters being engraved, thus upon that of
Abraham, "This be the sepulcher of our father Abraham upon whom be
peace," even so upon that of Isaac and upon all the other sepulchers. A lamp
burns in the cave and upon the sepulchers continually, both night and day,
and you there see tubs filled with the bones of Israelites, for it is a custom of
the House of Israel to bring thither the bones of their relicts and of their
forefathers and to leave them there, unto this day.

On the confines of the field of Makhphela, about an hour's ride distant,
stands the house of our father Abraham, who rests in peace, before which
house there is a spring, and in honor of Abraham nobody is allowed to construct any building on that site.

The Franks, within a few days of conquering Jerusalem, took the unprotected Hebron and fortified it.[4] Here, blessed be His Name, the invaders
did not molest the Jews, who had departed at the first sign of danger.[5]

< <   < <   > >   > >

From Hebron, **five parasangs to BEITH JABERIM, the ancient Maresha, in which place there are but three Jewish inhabitants.**

Five parasangs to TORON DE LOS CABELLEROS, which is Shunem, inhabited by three hundred Jews.

From Toron de los Cabelleros, three parasangs to **ST. SAMUEL DE SHILOH, the ancient Shiloh, within two parasangs of Jerusalem. When the Christians took Ramleh, which is Ramah, from the Mohammedans, they discovered the sepulcher of Samuel the Ramathi near the Jewish synagogue and removed his remains to Shiloh, where they erected a large place of worship upon them, called St. Samuel of Shiloh to the present day.**[6]

Three parasangs to **PESIPUA, which is Bib'ath Shaoul, or Giv'ath Benjamin; it contains no Jews.**

Three parasangs to **BEITH NUBI, which is Nob the city of the priests. The two Jews who live here are dyers.**

RAMLEH, where you still find walls erected by our forefathers; this is evident from the inscriptions upon the stones. The city was formerly very considerable, now it contains about three Jews, whose synagogue is in the marketplace.[7] **A Jewish cemetery in the vicinity extends for two miles.**

From Ramleh, **five parasangs to JAFFA, the ancient Japho on the coast.** In the time of the Fatimids, Jaffa had a large Jewish community, with a rabbinical court. The city owed its importance as a commercial center to its port, where Jewish and Christian pilgrims landed on their way to Jerusalem. The Franks, en route to Jerusalem, arrived here in the early summer of 1099; when the Fatimid officials here saw the approaching forces, they fled. With such ease did the Franks obtain this important harbor. The Jews of Jaffa took refuge in Askalon. The Franks naturally use Jaffa's port for their men and supplies; they have made Jaffa the capital of the region, minting its own coins. Genoa and Marseille have colonies here.[8] **Jaffa contains one Jew only, a dyer by profession.**

From Jaffa, **three parasangs to IBELIN, the Jabneh of antiquity,** situated on a small rise where, in days of yore, eminent scholars held their disputations. When the Romans were besieging Jerusalem, some Jews smuggled the rabbi Johanan ben Zakkai out of the city in a coffin, and he managed to obtain the Romans' permission to transfer hither the work of the Sanhedrin. Here the rabbis decided that, despite the destruction of the Temple, the Jews should continue to celebrate the Passover; and here they proclaimed the start of each new month. **The site of the academy may still be traced. No Jews live here.**

From Ibelin, **two parasangs to Palmis, or ASHDOD, formerly a city of the Philistines, at present in ruins, and containing no Jews.**

From Ashdod **two parasangs to ASKALON, which is in fact the new Askalon, built on the coast by Ezra the priest, o.b.m., and originally called Benebra, distant about four parasangs from ancient Askalon, which lies in ruins at present. In the city stands a fountain, called Bir Ibrahim-al-Khalil, which was dug in the time of the Philistines.**

This city is very large and handsome; the Arabs call it Arous as-Scham (Bride of Syria) because it is so beautiful. The region excels in produce: Talmudists spoke of its orchards,[9] and travelers nowadays remark on its red onions.[10] **Merchants from all parts resort hither for purposes of trade, it being conveniently situated on the confines of Egypt.**

When the Franks created the Kingdom of Jerusalem and decimated its Jews, many of the Jewish survivors fled southward toward Egypt, ruled by the Fatimids. They arrived in Fatimid Askalon dizzy with hunger, scarred from blows, virtually naked. In this desperate situation, as at any community crisis, the local Jews closed their businesses and started to fast. The community obliged every man to go to the synagogue and pledge a contribution toward the funds required for relief.[11] Askalon's Jews made extraordinary efforts to absorb the refugees, and then to purchase the sacred scrolls and silver which the Franks had removed from synagogues and then offered for sale.

But the Jewish community was small, and the need was great. The community sent messengers abroad to Egypt and farther to collect funds, for use along with the Askalon Jews' own money to attend the refugees' immediate needs and then move them on to Egypt. They sent them mostly by sea, but the sea voyage was debilitating, even killing, and at least one benefactor, a certain Abu al-Fadl Sahl, paid for caravans of refugees to journey to Egypt across the desert.[12] Some men of Askalon impoverished themselves to pay ransoms for Jewish captives sold or being sold into slavery, going so far as to give their sons in hostage in order to borrow the redemption money. A long time ago some Jews felt obliged to follow that grievous course—in desperate situations of Talmudic times—but never in the Moslem lands had Jews felt so desperate as to barter their sons.

The Franks attempted to take Askalon in 1111, but the Fatimids caused many deaths among them and they had to withdraw.[13] For forty years the Franks plotted to win the city with its harbor. But the Fatimids were equally determined to hold it, even more so after the Franks captured Tyre in 1124 and left the Fatimids with Askalon as their northernmost town. They had built defenses of exceptional strength, including a semicircle of enormously thick, high walls that extended into the sea, and they maintained the fortifications conscientiously, desperately. Invasion of Askalon by sea is virtually impossible, because at this point on the coast the winds generate high waves, terracing the underwater sands so that ships can find no berth; yet small boats can come into the port with supplies. Nonetheless, against the possibility of siege or blockade, the Fatimids kept the city well-provisioned with food and arms. Askalon would be very difficult to conquer.

But the third King Baldwin, young, coveted it. He sent his navy to the waters around Askalon. In January 1153 he himself led his fully equipped army. Their great siege-engines included a huge tower of which the arms could be extended over city walls so that flaming faggots could be dropped right into the city. Accompanying the army were notables of the monastic orders, and the archbishops of Nazareth, Cesarea, and Tyre. Their crosses held high, they camped outside the walls for two months while the inhabitants of Askalon inside the impregnable walls went about their business—for the Franks could blockade and harass Askalon with impunity, yet they could not enter.

With the coming of spring, Christian pilgrims arrived in the Holy Land to celebrate Easter, and that year they happened to come in greater numbers than usual. King Baldwin drafted all the pilgrims into the siege of Askalon, promising them payment; and he commandeered the ships in which they had traveled, ordering them into his fleet patrolling Askalon. The enlarged army and navy sat outside Askalon for another three months.

The Franks had set up their wooden towers adjacent to the wall, and on a certain July day some men of Askalon sought to destroy one of the towers by setting it ablaze. The wind carried flames to the wall, which began to smoulder. The Franks, astonished, wondered what might result if they set a real fire to the walls. They collected a lot of wood and piled it in the space between their ruined tower and the city wall, drenched the wood in oil, and lit their fire. It took several hours. The following morning the Franks and the besieged alike were awakened by the crash of falling wall.

Many people here clearly recall how the men of Askalon patched up their wall and tried valiantly to defend themselves, how they held out during several days of bloody battling but finally had to yield to avoid extermination.[14] The Franks allowed the residents the usual choice between staying and leaving. Most of the Mohammedans left. The Jewish community survived. Now Askalon contains **about two hundred Rabbanite Jews, besides about forty Karaites and about three hundred Cutheans or Samaritans.**

First Letter from Tiberias

From Askalon **back to St. George, which is LYDDA, and in one day and a half to SERAIN, the ancient Jisre'el, a city containing a remarkably large fountain. One Jewish inhabitant, a dyer by profession.**

<   <   <   <   >   >   >   >

Three parasangs to SUFURIEH, the Tsippori of antiquity. Here are the sepulchers of Rabbenu ha-Kodesh the exilarch Judah ha-Nasi, and of his student **R. Chija who came back from Babylon; and of Jonah ben Amittai the prophet. They are buried in the mountain, which also contains numerous other sepulchers.**

Sufurieh was once the principal city of the Galilee and a seat of the Sanhedrin. Josephus the historian, who as governor of the Galilee tried to put down the "insolent" Jews' rebellion against Rome, wrote of how he won Sufurieh and then lost it to the Romans.[1]

Now the small castle here belongs to the Franks.[2] The garrison guards a region inhabited mostly by Moslems. Here the Moslems are peaceful subjects, in part because the taxes imposed on them by the Franks are lower than those they would have to pay to the neighboring Moslem rulers.[3] Or so traders tell me. Some Jewish craftsmen, who live in nearby villages, wander throughout the Galilee to trade.[4]

<   <   <   <   >   >   >   >

From Sufurieh, **five parasangs to TIBERIAS. This city is situated on** the west bank of **the Jordan, which here bears the name of the Sea of Kinnereth or Lake of Tiberias.** The city was built here in ancient times doubtless because from this point on the lake it is easy to ascend the mountains, which begin very close to the lake. Tiberias is thus a long and narrow city that curves for a long stretch along the water, but buildings dot the lower mountain slopes too. The houses are built of the dark rocky soil of Tiberias. It's a beautiful city.

Here are the falls of the Jordan, in consequence of which the place bears also the name of Ashdoth Hapisga, which means "the place where the rapid rivers have their fall." The Jordan afterwards empties itself in Lake Asphaltes, which is the Dead Sea.

187

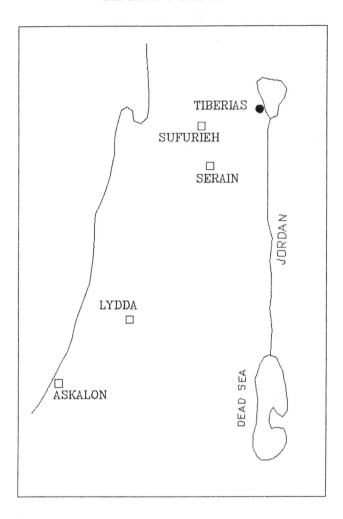

The water of the Sea of Kinnereth is very sweet and abounds with fish. All around its shore grow palms and crops. Some say, nonetheless, that this place is unhealthy, too hot in summer and too damp. Of the men of Tiberias they say "that for two months they dance, and for two more they gorge; that for two months they beat about, and for two more they go naked; that for two months they play the reed, and for two more they wallow." Then they explain that people in Tiberias "dance from the number of fleas, then gorge off the fruit; they beat about with fly-laps to chase away the wasps from the fruits and the meats, then they go naked from the heat; they suck the sugar canes, and then have to wallow through their muddy streets."[5]

The hot waters, which spout forth from under ground, are called the warm baths of Tiberias. The waters remain hot even in winter, needing no fire to heat them. You can cook eggs in these waters, and even scald the skin of chickens.

The waters from the hot baths drain into the lake, as does all household water, such as that used for those eggs and chickens. Now the lake is the source of drinking water for the Tiberians, although travelers often comment that the water has a peculiar flavor. Legend has it that once a governor forbid further draining of wastes into the lake. The citizens complied, shortly afterward the lake water began to stink and was no longer potable. The governor had the drains opened again, and the lake wate became as sweet as before.[6]

The hot baths of Tiberias are eight in number, some sweet, some salty. At the large bath called Hammäm ad Damakir, the water is salty and very hot; people who wish to bathe in it must mix it with cold water. At the small bath Hammäm Lülü, the water is sweet and merely warm, and it is this water which the Tiberians use in their houses.

Since ancient times sufferers from chronic diseases have come from far and wide to bathe in the waters. Each of the different waters is said to relieve a different kind of illness. The early rabbis considered baths and mineral waters helpful for general health and strength and as positive aids for certain skin diseases.[7] Each bathhouse promotes its cures for particular ills: ulcers or scabies, rheumatism or backache. Three days of the bath will cure the sufferer, God willing. Jews here tell tales of ancestors who tried to organize the community to petition the king to dismantle the bathhouses, so that the sufferers would have recourse only to physicians.

The ancient Romans loved hot baths, as you must know, and the Romans knew of these baths located in the most beautiful part of the Galilee. When Herod Antipus ruled Galilee, in the days of the Second Temple, he founded this city and named it after the Emperor Tiberius (the second of that name). During the construction of the city, it was rumored that some workmen digging the excavations had found human bones; consequently people thought that the land where Tiberias was being built had earlier been a burial ground. Since the Torah says that any Jew shall be unclean for seven days after the slightest contact with graves,[8] pious Jews scrupled at living there. Nonetheless, most dwellers in early Tiberias were Jews.

Herod had been anxious to ensure a sufficient population for his city, even bringing in beggars and prisoners to populate it. He need not have worried. In the next generation, about 70 C.E., the Roman forces under General Titus destroyed the Temple and many Jews fled from Jerusalem to Tiberias. Roman Palestine remained a battlefield for a long time. When in the year 135 the Jews were expelled from all Judea, they too took refuge in the Galilee. **In the vicinity is the synagogue of Khaleb ben J'phuneh and, among numer-**

ous other Jewish sepulchers, those of R. Johanan ben Zakkai and of R. Jonathan ben Levi; they are all situated in lower Galilee.

Tiberias contains the tomb of R. Meir, the great rabbi of those earliest days here. He married the scholarly Bururiah, daughter of R. Hanina ben Teradyon, one of the ten martyrs of Rome. R. Meir, by trade a scribe, considered the study of Torah the most important thing in life. He said that even if a man were a heathen, if he studied Torah he would be as worthy a Jew as a high priest.[9] Because R. Meir wrote that men other than Jews could attain eternal happiness,[10] it is said that he was a convert to Judaism. He despised idleness, warning that it led to crime;[11] he thought unimportant which trade a man followed, so long as it was clean and the man did it well.[12] He advised men to work in order to provide themselves with the necessities of life but after that to devote themselves to study of Torah: if you neglect your Torah-study, you will find many reasons for neglecting it, but if you study and live Torah, you will find that God takes care of you.[13]

Scribes like R. Meir endlessly copied the Torah—the Pentateuch and the many succeeding books—under strict standards copying and re-copying so that every Jewish community might have at least one copy of all the sacred writings[14] and the judicial interpretations of them. Jews needed to have easy access to the code if they were to conduct themselves properly as Jews. Newly exiled and now widely scattered, the Jews would find it increasingly difficult to learn and observe Torah, and the scholars who had settled in Tiberias realized that. They re-established the patriarchate here, and set out to compile, in writing, the decrees and opinions of their eminent predecessors.

One of R. Meir's disciples, R. Judah ben Solomon, succeeded his father as patriarch of Tiberias and held that office for almost fifty years; he became known as Judah ha-Nasi (Judah the Prince). A very wealthy man, he used his money to develop elementary schools and to support scholars. Insisting that "it is the unlearned who bring trouble into the world,"[15] he summarized all the previous work by generations of scholars regarding the rules for Jewish life and compiled it in the book of Oral Law which we call the Mishnah. The Mishnah was the first part of the Palestinian Talmud, which would be written wholly in Tiberias.

Tiberias continued under Roman rule for another century after Judah ha-Nasi's death. The interests of the Romans were gradually shifting eastward from Rome. In the fourth century—I must have written you this from Constantinople—the Roman emperor Constantine established a second capital of the empire at the city of Byzant (and changed its name to Constantinople). Newly Christian, King Constantine encouraged Christians to visit the Holy Land to see the original cross of the crosses which symbolize their religion. These Byzantines came to Tiberias continually from then on, and scorned its Jewish residents.

The Byzantines hated the Persians. (not because the Persians were Moslems; this was before Mohammed started his religion). When the Persians invaded Palestine in 614, the Tiberian Jews thought they would prefer Persian rule to Byzantine. Benjamin of Tiberias, a very rich man and a leader of Palestine's Jews, arranged for the Jews to support the Persian armies, which, from the point of view of the Byzantines, was of course treason. Several years later, in 628, when the Byzantines won, Benjamin of Tiberias had to swallow his pride and go to deal cordially with the Byzantine emperor, Heraclius. He did more than that. He played host to the emperor in Tiberias and, being a master negotiator, he obtained from the emperor an amnesty for all Jews who had aided the Persians. And then . . . and then Benjamin of Tiberias converted to Christianity!

Upon which, the Christian prelates in Jerusalem persuaded Emperor Heraclius to revoke the amnesty. The emperor went further, condemning many Jewish supporters of the Persians to death and forbidding Jews to live in and around Jerusalem. Just as this was going on, the Arabs conquered Tiberias, and under the Arabs the Jews had generally lived in peace. So again Tiberias welcomed Jews from Jerusalem.

Through all the warfare and commotion, the scholars of Tiberias persevered in establishing clear liturgy and laws for the dispersed Jewish community. They thereby created ever more documents to be copied by ever more scribes. The scribes of religious material—in Hebrew, *masoretes*—came from particular families, employed generation after generation in reproducing the sacred scrolls.[16] In dealing with the manuscripts, they often came upon differences between copies of a given text: it goes without saying that however meticulous the scribes, texts could hardly have been copied from other copies over a thousand years without unintentional errors creeping in. To say nothing of deliberate deviations from a text.

The Masoretes possessed manuscripts from their predecessors, who had tried to establish one single version of the Bible. Now the new Arab rulers, having adopted the religion of Mohammed, were engaged in a similar endeavor to fix a single version of Mohammed's scriptural Koran, and this added impetus to the Jewish efforts. The Masoretes examined different versions of the Bible, debated about alternative words, and chose the word to be used in the authoritative new scrolls. It was they who decided on the spelling for each word, and who developed the notation for chanting.

Vowel signs were already being used to clarify Hebrew pronunciation; but however helpful these were, said the Masorete editors, they could not be used in the Torah, because when God at Sinai engraved the tablets of the Law, the writing didn't have vowel signs. (These, they knew, their grandfathers had invented.) That is why to this day we have no vowel marks in the Torah scrolls from which we read during our synagogue worship.

When the Karaite scholars arrived on the scene, they disagreed. (This should not surprise you.) They argued that their Bible—and *only* their Bible, not any glosses by rabbis—was the Word of God. Their Bible in its entirety. And since their Bible included marks for vocalization, why then, these too were holy. (When I was in Constantinople, I looked through a book about Karaite practice by one of their recent leaders, Judah Hadassi, o.b.m., and I recall that he wrote on this matter of vocalization, insisting that vowels and accents should appear in the Torah scrolls, since such markings were included on the tablets that God gave us at Sinai. . . .)

Scores of years of efforts, to provide a definitive Torah for the whole community of dispersed Jews, were spent by the wise and pious rabbis of the Palestine Academy here. It is *their* Torah which ever since, to this day, has been *our* Torah. And so it is that Tiberias has the best Torah manuscripts in all the world.

Second Letter from Tiberias

Under Moslem rule, Tiberias was a center for textiles and tapestries—Jews naturally among the principal manufacturers—and still today the lake is always dotted with boats carrying cloths abroad. The great conquest that so ravaged the rest of Palestine left Tiberias unharmed: when the Franks first pushed into the Holy Land, in 1099, Tiberias yielded immediately, without resisting, to Tancred of Otranto. (You recall that I visited Otranto, "from which the Law shall go forth"?) The Franks made Tiberias the capital of their Galilee province and they strengthened the city walls. Throughout, they have kept the city prosperous. The marketplace extends the full length of the city, wall to wall.

Tiberias contains about fifty Jews. The principal among them include R. Abraham the astronomer, who delights in climbing the nearby mountains and in looking out over the wide expanse of the lake and in observing the vast cupola of heaven with its moon and stars. One of a long tradition of astronomers in this region, he is a fund of knowledge.

It is written in the Bible and in the Talmud that Israel should compute the course of the sun and the planets.[1] R. Abraham ibn Ezra went so far as to say that no intelligent person could understand the Talmud's discussion of the new moon unless he had studied astronomy and knew the movements of the sun and the moon.[2]

In ancient times many peoples in the East studied the heavens and the stars, but from their earliest days the Jews distinguished themselves from the others by concentrating on the sun and the moon: the sun, to determine the start of Shabbat, and the moon, to determine the length of months.

The ancient Babylonians having had a calendar based on lunar cycles, the Hebrews had learned from them about "months" and had even brought the Babylonian names of months into the Hebrew language. The Babylonians had determined that a lunar cycle lasts twenty-nine and a half days, an inconvenient month in a world with days and nights and especially awkward for Jews anxious to know for certain when the new month was to begin. Jews thought it imperative to establish the first day of months because the Torah commands the observance of festivals in phrases like "the first day" or "the tenth day" of a month. Yet when one of the religious festivals was being held in the kingdom of Judah, Israel's King Jeroboam was apparently free to select his own date for it for his own people,[3] indicating that his kingdom in the north didn't necessarily follow the same calendar as

Judah in the south. Without knowing when a month began, how could the Jews be sure of celebrating their festivals at the ordained time?

To circumvent the twenty-nine-and-a-half day problem, the Jews decided to add a half day to one month and subtract a half day from the next, thus developing a calendar with twelve alternating twenty-nine-day and thirty-day months. Officially a new month began when a witness saw the new moon and went to have it ordained by the High Court in Jerusalem. Each Rosh Hodesh (first day of the month) was now beyond dispute.

Or was it? The people of the north never accepted the Judean way of establishing a new month. The northern scholars considered the "new moon" (as the Judeans called it) to be simply a continuing development out of the "old moon," and they stressed instead the moment when the moon is directly between the sun and the earth (that is, the conjunction of them) and the moon therefore invisible. The northerners decided that when conjunction of sun and moon occurs during the night or during the early hours of the morning (namely, at least six hours before noon), that day is the first day of the month, which will have thirty days; whereas when the conjunction occurs later in the day, the next day will be the first of the new month, which will have twenty-nine days.

Long before the Romans destroyed the Second Temple and expelled the Jews from Jerusalem, "the northerners" had become "the Samaritans," and in so becoming, they had earned the enmity of the Jewish community centered around Jerusalem. These Jews and the Samaritans remained hostile to each other even after the exiled Jews had re-established their capital in Tiberias. All around the Galilee the new months would be proclaimed by means of fire signals. When Judah ha-Nasi became patriarch, the Samaritans were sending fire signals around the Galilee at whimsical intervals, in order to confuse the Jews about the time of the new moon.

By then astronomers were sure of their ability to determine the time of the new moon by calculation, so Judah ha-Nasi decided to do away with the use of fire signals and henceforward employ messengers to inform the scattered Jewish communities that the new month was imminent.

The method of calculating the new moon stayed secret for several generations. Then King Constantine came to power in the Roman Empire and thus ruled over the Galilee; he made Christianity the official religion, and he persecuted the Jews. Among other things, he banned the High Court from proclaiming the leap year, which was a very grave matter as Jews all over the world looked to Palestine for information about their calendar and festivals. The patriarch of the time, the second Hillel, felt obliged to inform all the Jewish communities about the way to calculate the dates of the new moon and the festivals so that they could themselves determine them. This was fine insofar as their holiday observance was concerned; but as the Jews in the Exile no longer had reason to turn regularly to Palestine, in time the center of world Jewry shifted away.[4]

Calculating the new month was just part of the work of astronomers, for they had realized a basic weakness in the twelve-month calendar: it was shorter than the solar year. God commanded our annual commemoration of the plagues that he sent to release us from slavery in Egypt, plagues which occurred in the month of the barleycorn;[5] in biblical times, that was called "the first month"; to us it is Nissan, so Nissan should always occur when the barleycorn ripens. But the Jewish scholars had seen that if they were to follow their twelve-month calendar into the future, they would soon be celebrating Nissan's spring festival of Passover in mid-winter and eventually the harvest festival of Succot in spring. So they adapted the ancient Babylonian idea of intercalation,[6] and by adding a month to each of seven years in a recurring cycle of nineteen years, they arrived at a calendar of which the years averaged out to the 365 days that the sun takes to encircle the earth.

The Samaritans likewise adopted a calendar with seven leap years in every nineteen years. However, whereas the Judeans had decided once and for all which seven years of the nineteen were to be leap years, the Samaritans decided not to do that but instead to declare their leap years when they saw the need.

By observing the heavens and calculating and debating, the Jewish astronomers were working out their complicated calendars during the same generations when scholars were sharpening their arguments later to be compiled as the Talmud. The scholars weren't satisfied that they had the perfect calendar—that is, the calendar we Jews use now—until around the year 4100 of that calendar, counting from the year of Creation. That was some three hundred years after the destruction of the Second Temple and the start of the Exile.

Around the time that the Jews were becoming satisfied with their calendar, Christian scholars were trying to resolve dating problems of their own. They were unhappy that the dates of major Christian holidays were being fixed on the basis of the Jewish calendar. This was not just a desire to throw off their heritage of Judaism. Early Christians dated the execution and resurrection of Jisho from the Passover holiday in the year of his death; they decided that that man had risen from the dead on a Sunday, the third day of Passover. But of course it's just coincidence that the third day of Passover was a Sunday; it doesn't usually happen that way. The Christian scholars, the ones in the Western branch of the church, decided that their Easter should be celebrated always on Sunday, on the Sunday following the full moon next after the vernal equinox. Even so, they chose this particular day in relation to the Sunday closest to the fourteenth of Nissan, the start of Passover.

Three centuries passed. Around our year 4460 (the year 700 C.E.) a monk in England named Bede interested himself in the old problem of perfecting calendars. The Christians by now had their calendar with a calculated year of 365 days 6 hours. Bede knew this period to be longer than the real solar year of 365 days 5 hours 49 minutes, so he tried to change the calendar. He failed at that; consequently, Christians still have a calendar less accurate than the Jewish one. Bede succeeded, however, in introducing the practice of counting the years of the Christian calendar from the year of their Jisho's birth, the practice long since used for official business by every resident of Christian countries.

Bede was a great astronomer, whose interests went beyond calendars. He made discoveries about the tides in various ports. He wrote about the seven planets circling the earth, and about the earth's being a sphere; but many leaders of his church reject this latter idea, for the prophet Ezekiel clearly mentioned "the four corners" of the earth.[7]

Then the Karaites came out of the East with their own calendar, according to which they might celebrate Rosh ha-Shanah on any day of the week. In the calendar of Jerusalem and the Talmudists (that is, the calendar of the Rabbanites, the one which we use), Rosh ha-Shanah never falls on Sunday, Wednesday, or Friday; so that Yom Kippur cannot fall on Friday or Sunday, nor Hoshana Rabba (the seventh day of Succot) on Saturday. The Yom Kippur of the Karaites, however, can fall on the day before or the day after Shabbat. What's more, although the Rabbanites had long since accepted the start of a month on the basis of calculation, the Karaites still insisted on visual observance. This practice provoked questions about the sighting of the new moon when it was cloudy, or about the possibility of two pious men in different locations sighting the new moon at different times. The Karaites themselves debated such points; but they became angry with the Rabbanites' taunts about them. Controversies over the calendar became so heated and pervasive that it seemed the Jews would divide irrevocably into a Rabbanite community and a Karaite community.

The Karaites rebuked the Samaritans too, because their new months were determined by conjunctions and calculations rather than on the basis of observation. Nevertheless, the core of world Jewry, which followed the rabbinic tradition, accepted the jurisdiction of the Babylonian scholars in matters of the calendar as in all other Jewish matters.

Around the year 920 C.E. the head of the Palestine academy was R. Aaron ben Meir, who lived in Ramleh. He was so much at odds with Palestine's Karaites that he traveled to Baghdad to complain about them and their treatment of Rabbanites. Having seen Baghdad and returned to Palestine, he sought to regain for Palestine some of the authority over world Jewry that the Babylonian academies now held. On Hoshana Rabba, the day for proclaiming the next year's calendar, R. Aaron announced as twenty-nine-day months two months which, according to the Babylonian calendar, were to have thirty days.

As you know, the dates of all other festivals are fixed to accord with the date of Passover. As set by the geonim of Babylonia, Passover 4681 would begin on a Tuesday, and thus Rosh ha-Shanah 4682 would begin on a Thursday. But because of R. Aaron's two shorter months, the beginning of his Passover would fall two days earlier, on the Sunday; thus Rosh ha-Shanah 4682 would begin on Tuesday. The Babylonian geonim tried, by lectures and letters, to win the Palestinians to their dates, stressing the danger to the Jewish community as a whole if all Jews did not celebrate their festivals at the same times. But when Passover arrived, R. Aaron had many followers in Babylonia as well as in Palestine and in Egypt who celebrated it on the earlier date.

Just then Saadia ben Joseph, a young rabbi, was traveling through Palestine on his way from Egypt to Babylonia. Already very knowledgeable about astronomy and the calendar,[8] he took a professional interest in the argument about Passover dating. When he arrived in Babylonia he associated himself with the geonim and wrote his *Sefer ha-Zikkaron* (Book of memory), full of mathematical and astronomical explanations more than sufficient to refute R. Aaron's arguments for the earlier date. Never again did Jerusalem contest Babylonia's jurisdiction over the calendar.

The sages had known the principles of astronomy since Talmudic times, if not before. They knew that the earth is the center of creation and that heaven is the blue canopy above the earth. They knew about the major stars, their locations in heaven, the curved routes along which they traversed heaven, and their distances from the earth. Still, Jews were never at the forefront of astronomical discovery, for God prohibited the making of images of the sun and the moon, the stars, the angels, or the planets;[9] and that, decreed the rabbis, meant that Jews could not even make sketches on a panel of any of God's servants in heaven.

When Mohammed established his religion and his followers went as conquerors to the lands around the Great Sea, Moslem scholars studied the stars so as to determine the direction of Mecca, their holy city, from the different regions of their empire. To learn about planetary motions, they studied Ptolemy's *Almagest*, which they translated from Old Greek into Arabic. The Jews, in turn, translated some works of the Mohammedan astronomers out of Arabic, into Hebrew and Latin and European vernaculars. This wasn't like the field of pharmacology, where Jews learned by trading in the products; astronomy was a science of *ideas*, and Jews learned its new ideas by translating.

The Moslems built magnificent observatories, of which the best contained the most advanced armillary spheres, quadrants, and astrolabes, supplementing a grand variety of sundials and water clocks, alidades, and double-pointed alidades called compasses. The astronomers among the Jews had to have regarded all this with envy. Few Jews could find a place of work in the Moslems' grand observatories, and for financial and religious reasons the Jews had no equivalent observatories, so Jews interested in astronomy had to work along theoretical lines. Yet Jews deemed the Moslem astronomers' calendar seriously deficient, for the Islamic year is significantly shorter than the solar year (just like the calendar of the ancient Hebrews). The Moslem calendar consists of twelve months, into which no month is ever intercalated, so that their year has 354 or 355 days. It takes 103 Moslem years to measure the same duration as 100 of our years.

Based on Arabic models, R. Abraham ibn Ezra wrote many papers delving into various aspects of astronomy: theoretical astronomy, mathematics, and the calendar. He also wrote an original work on the astrolabe, *Kli ha-Nehoshet* (A copper instrument), which instrument astronomers use for measuring the altitudes, positions, and movements of heavenly bodies. He wrote it in Hebrew, remarking on the difficulty of translating some of the technical terms into that language.[10]

R. Abraham ibn Ezra was the second of the great astronomers to write in Hebrew. The first was Abraham bar Hiyya, a scholar from Barcelona who died some thirty years ago. His book *Hibber ha-Meshihah*, which today's astronomers hold in high regard, deals with geometry and algebra. He wrote on trigonometry as well—astronomy relates to all the mathematical sciences, but to trigonometry most closely. Bar Hiyya also refined some mathematical tables of the ancient Greeks, although in this he was not extraordinary: mathematician-astronomers love compiling tables, and they compile new ones every time they obtain a new instrument. He wrote a complete textbook on astronomy, the first in Hebrew, called *Zurat ha-Eretz* (The form of the Earth). The most original of bar Hiyya's work is apparently his *Sefer ha-Ibbur* (The book of intercalation), which treats a specifically Jewish concern, the celebration of the festivals at the proper time; it is said to be the first work in Hebrew devoted just to the calendar.[11] That these two Abrahams of astronomy—bar Hiyya and ibn Ezra—wrote their scientific work in Hebrew illustrates how Jewish scholarship in Spain has been separating itself from the Mohammedan.

R. Abraham ibn Ezra wrote extensively also about astrology, not only in his commentaries on the Bible but also in several treatises on the wisdom of the heavens, as well as writing horoscopes;[12] he had had the rare opportunity to observe the heavens from many different parts of the world. Yet astrology is a science about which the sages have been of two minds. First, they distinguish definitely between, on the one hand, the study of the heavens, especially of the sun and the moon, from which study the scholars and mathematicians developed our calendar; and, on the other hand, the study of the heavens, especially of the stars, from which study the scholars and seers advise about people's lives. The sages don't speak against the first kind of study, but many of them have spoken against the second kind. These say that star-gazing, as they call astrology, is against God's will, or that the fortunes of men, being determined only by God, cannot be influenced by the stars. But Saadia Gaon, astronomer and sage, considered astrology a true science.

It was the predominant view of the learned rabbis who compiled the Talmud that the stars did have influence on men's lives and that skilled observers might be able to forecast such influence, but they doubted that the astrologers were sufficiently skilled to do so. Many of our ancestors just accepted unquestioningly that the same mysterious powers determining day and night and the seasons could also determine their personal fortunes. This conception of heavenly bodies, and of the zodiac, was the central idea of the *Sefer Yezirah* (Book of Creation), which is said to have been written by R. Akiba, or even longer ago, by our forefather Abraham.[13] This ancient book, which presupposes astrology to be a worthy science, has won the high regard of even modern sages, as, for example, Judah ha-Levi.[14]

Shabbetai Donnolo, the tenth-century physician and pharmacologist, was one of the enthusiastic astrologers who wrote on *Sefer Yezirah*, and he said he wrote his lengthy commentary after considerable astrological study and reflection. Physicians make particular use of astrology. From observation of the heavenly bodies, earlier generations of physicians learned on which days of the week it is dangerous to operate on their patients or to have them bled—for example, that it is risky to undergo these treatments on a Wednesday that falls on certain dates of the month, especially the last days of a month. The great knowledge required to select a propitious date for medical treatment may be another reason why Jewish physicians are especially respected among Gentiles. These, knowing that Jews come from the East, believe them to be descendants of the Chaldeans, who excelled in astrology; therefore non-Jews often credit Jewish practitioners of astrology with a particular skill in it.[15]

Doubtless the ordinary Jewish men and women who practice as astrologers and fortune-tellers benefit from this belief in Jews' mastery of the science, and just as likely they are indifferent to the scholarly discussions about whether astrology is even valid as a science. The people who purchase astrological forecasts are legion; this is fortunate for scholarly astronomers who, in the Jewish community at least, generally earn their living as astrologers.

The scholars' argument—whether our fortunes are determined by God or by the stars—shows no sign of abating. Judah ha-Levi sought to resolve it when he had the haver of his *Kuzari* concede that heavenly bodies influence our lives on earth but then go on to explain that the heavenly bodies are controlled by God.[16] R. Abraham ibn Daud (the Andalucian who refuted Judah Hadassi on the Karaites) seems to believe that the stars control all aspects of men's lives because God gave them that control; but that God also gave man the power of controlling his own behavior, so that he might exempt himself from the domination of the stars.[17] And R. Abraham ibn Ezra essays to resolve the matter as it affects Jews: "It is known from experience that every nation has its own star and constellation and similarly there is a constellation for every city; but God bestowed His greater favor on Israel by rendering them starless and Himself their advisor."[18]

This has been a long letter. I'll give the final word to another Spaniard, Solomon ben Judah ibn Gabirol, not only the greatest poet of the last century, but also an astrology enthusiast:

Who shall tell Thy praises?
For Thou madest the Moon the chief source whereby to calculate
Appointed times and seasons,
And cycles and signs for the days and the years . . .

.   .   .   .

Who shall understand Thy secret?
For Thou hast encompassed the sphere of this shining one
With a fourth sphere, wherein is the Sun
That completeth his circuit in a perfect year.
And his body is one hundred and seventy times greater than that of the earth,
According to indications and devisings of intellect.
And he is the apportioner of light to all the stars of the heavens,
And giveth to kings salvation
And majesty, dominion and awe,
And reneweth marvels on the earth,
Whether for war or for peace,
And rooteth up kingdoms,

And establisheth and exalteth others in their stead
And hath power to abase and uplift with a high hand,
But all according to the will of the Creator who created him in wisdom . . .

.   .   .   .

Who can know Thy pathways?
For Thou hast made palaces for the seven planets
In the twelve constellations,
And to the Ram and the Bull Thou hast imparted Thy strength in uniting
    them,
And the third is the Twins, like two brothers in their unity
And their human likeness.
And the fourth is the Crab,
And on him, as on the Lion, hast Thou bestowed of Thy splendor,
And on his sister the Virgin, who is near unto him,
And on the Scales and the Scorpion placed by his side,
And on the ninth that was created in the form of a man of might, whose
    strength runs not dry,

For he is the Archer, mighty of the bow.
And thus too by Thy great power are created the Goat and the Water-Bearer,
While alone is the last constellation,
"For the Lord did appoint a great Fish."
And these are the constellations high and exalted in their degrees,
"Twelve princes according to the nations."[19]

Letter from Damascus

Northwest of Tiberias **to GISH, which is Gish Chales** in the Talmud, **with about twenty Jewish inhabitants.**

Nearby are the Waters of Meron, where the several Canaanite kings gathered with their forces to fight against the Israelites; they were beaten by Joshua and his army.[1]

The hillsides here are covered with fat sheep, whose wool is described in the Talmud as being of extremely fine quality. Can it be that this region gives its name to the merino sheep who produce the wool that is woven by our Jewish weavers in and around Saragossa?[2]

< <   < <   > >   > >

Then the village of **MERON**. Here are buried Simon ben Yochai and his son Eleazar; these two, threatened by the Romans, lived for thirteen years in a cave. And **in a cave near this place are the sepulchers of Hillel and Shammai and twenty of their disciples.** Inside this cave is a large stone bowl; when a pious man enters the cave to pray, the bowl becomes filled with water, while otherwise the bowl stays empty.[3] The rabbis interred here, who lived and taught in the time of the Romans, led the first school of scholars to make rules for the interpretation of Torah. They made this region a center of Jewish scholarship, in consequence of which the Galilee contains a great number of gravesites visited by Jewish pilgrims to Eretz Yisrael.

Also in Meron are to be found the remains of a synagogue of Roman times. Although the synagogues in this region are usually square, this synagogue is twice as long as it is wide. Its main entry, with some wide steps, faces toward Jerusalem; it stands against rock, into which its west side is cut.

< <   < <   > >   > >

From Meron, **six parasangs to ALMA, containing fifty Jewish inhabitants**  **and a large cemetery of the Israelites.**

< <   < <   > >   > >

From thence **half a day to KADES, which is Kadesh Naphthali on the banks on the Jordan. Here are many sepulchers,** but **the place contains no Jews.**

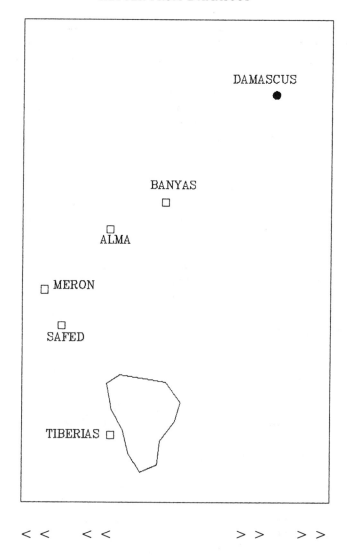

< <   < <   > >   > >

From Kades, one day's **journey to Belinas** or BANYAS, **the ancient Dan,** the town lying just southwest of Mount Hermon. The surrounding plain produces cotton, wheat, and rice. **The traveler here may see a cave from which the Jordan issues. Three miles further this river unites its waters with** those of the Arnon, a rivulet of the ancient land of Moab.

In front of the cave you may still trace vestiges of the altar of Mikha's image, which was adored by the children of Dan in times of yore. There is also the site of the altar erected by Jeroboam ben N'bat in honor of the golden calf.

And here in biblical times as now **were the confines of the land of Israel** toward the hinder sea. This frontier lies on the main road from the Galilee, even from the coast at Acre and Tyre, to Damascus. So Banyas has always been well known to traders. And, at least in recent times, to armies.[4] For a long time the Franks attempted to seize this oasis of Banyas, but were foiled by Assassins or routed by Damascenes. In 1157—at the time of the severe earthquake—the Moslems yielded Banyas to Frankish besiegers, but Nureddin never accepted its loss, kept attacking, and in October 1164 (while the Franks en masse were invading Egypt) Nureddin's forces re-conquered Banyas, which so far remains under Moslem rule.[5]

The Jews of Banyas live in two communities, one following the Palestinian ritual and the other the Babylonian ritual.[6] During the period when no Jews could dwell in Jerusalem or even visit it because of the Franks' ban, an unusual encounter took place here.

A Frank by the name of Obadyah had converted to Judaism and was living as a Jew in Damascus, supporting himself by writing Hebrew poetry for the community.[7] He attracted followers by his accounts of his experiences and his visions. Obadyah moved here to Banyas one year just before Rosh ha-Shanah, he with his followers, and here he met the Karaite, Solomon ha-Kohen. The latter told Obadyah that in two and a half months, that is, at Chanukah, God was going to bring all the Exiles to Jerusalem. Obadyah was skeptical and asked the Karaite how he could so prophesy.

"Because," announced Solomon, "I am the man for whom Israel is waiting."

A Messianic claim?—Obadyah demanded how Solomon, as a Kohen, could be the Messiah, for the Messiah was to come from the tribe of Levi. Doubtless Obadyah also knew that the Messiah would be of the family of David, a descendant of Ruth the Moabite, a proselyte—that is, someone like Obadyah himself.

When Obadyah talked of going to Jerusalem, Solomon begged him not to anticipate the Divine ingathering of all the Exiles. But Obadyah, unwilling to bend to Solomon, insisted that he would betake himself to Egypt, whence he would lead all the Jews to Jerusalem. And off to Egypt he went.[8]

< <   < <   > >   > >

From Banyas **two days to DAMASCUS, a large city** with an excellent climate **and the frontier town of the empire of Nureddin, King of the Thogarmin which are vulgarly called Turks.** The Turks were ruling Damascus at the time the Franks conquered Jerusalem; the Damascus Jews ransomed some of the Palestinian Jews sold into slavery, then, after the second big invasion of To'im, Damascus received more refugees from Palestine.[9] Now there are probably more Jews in Damascus than in the entire Frankish domain.[10]

When the Franks had occupied virtually all of Palestine, they tried again and again to conquer Damascus too. Damascus being the natural point for the grouping of Moslem soldiers to invade the Frankish kingdom, the Franks would not consider their rule of Palestine secure until they controlled Damascus. The city suffered many years of warfare. Then, during the Franks' long siege of Askalon in 1153, they transferred all their forces southward to the coast, and in the aftermath Damascus was taken by the Aleppan general Nureddin.[11] Now king, he has linked Syria with Egypt.

The Talmud refers to Damascus as "the gateway to the Garden of Eden."[12] Indeed, **this place is very large and handsome, enclosed by a wall and surrounded by a beautiful country, which in a circuit of fifteen miles presents the richest gardens and orchards** of plums and pomegranates, figs and apricots, **in such quantity and beauty as to be without equal on earth.** The city streets, although dark and narrow, are fragrant with spices.

The rivers Amana and Parpar, the sources of which are on the Hermon (a mount on which the city leans), run down here. The Amana follows its course through Damascus and the waters are conducted by pipes into the houses of the principal inhabitants as well as into the streets and markets and the numerous bathhouses. **The Parpar runs through the gardens and orchards in the outskirts and richly supplies them with water.** From the mountain the waters rush down so, that the noise can be heard at a great distance. The continuous roar of the waters drowns out the banging of the metalworkers in the bazaars.[13]

They say that because of the abundant waters, in ancient times (even before man used the camel for carrying) this place was a city of traders, who came in their caravans from Babylonia and from the lands of the Turks, from the valley of the Nile and from the coast of the Great Sea. Damascus was a town of the Roman empire, and still today the bazaars are located under the Romans' colonnades.[14] **A considerable trade is carried on here by merchants of all countries,** of all religions and all colors, each group with its own bazaars, caravanserai, place of worship, and even cemetery.[15] Special offerings of the Damascus bazaars include brocades and linen, raw silk, and small furniture with smooth surfaces patterned of tiny bits of wood (a wooden mosaic).[16] And Damascus has been manufacturing paper for hundreds of years, paper of cotton.[17]

People here decorate their houses with wondrous textiles: carpets on floors and walls, long cushions on the benches which are set along the walls. These serve as divans, for the people of the East use no chairs at all.[18] Damascus is renowned for brocade, a textile woven with a woof of unmottled raw silk. The local weavers work in intricate designs, which they repeat endlessly the breadth and length of the cloth,[19] and they are so skillful, they produce cloth of such rare beauty, that traders come for it from far and wide. Damascene brocade is even more precious than the best of the brocades from Greece.[20] The weavers here, Mohammedans, surpass weavers in Greek lands, although Islamic books label weaving a despised profession, just as the Talmud does.[21]

Jews of Damascus engage in a wide range of employments, most common being manufacture of textiles and glass. Some khalifs have drafted Karaite Jews for work in the royal textile factory and in the royal mint.[22] Jews work as financiers and as tax collectors; as tradesmen and artisans of all sorts; and in this city where medical care is of high standard and is accessible to all, naturally one finds Jewish physicians.

Damascus has two hospitals, of which the newer is a large free hospital established a dozen years ago by the prince Nur al-Din Zengi.[23] There are also several academies. The inhabitants of Damascus are well organized into cooperative societies for commerce and finance.[24] The city is busy, spirited, and chaotic. The Mohammedans live in the western part of the city around the citadel as well as around the Great Mosque farther north; the Christians live in the northeastern quarter; the Jews in the southeastern quarter.[25]

Many of the three thousand Jews who inhabit this city are learned men and rich. Here is the residence of the President of the Palestine Academy, by name R. Ezra, the brother of whom, Sar Shalom, is the principal of the Jewish court of law. Also the city contains two hundred Karaites and about four hundred Samaritans. All these sects live on friendly terms, but they do not intermarry.

Among the Jews here are many grandsons of refugees from Palestine. At the end of the last century, when Jerusalem was in a great state of commotion, the Palestine Academy moved first to Tyre, then to Hadrach, which is near Damascus, and finally into Damascus. The academy is governed by a council of ten, just as is the academy at Baghdad; R. Ezra has been selected as principal from among these ten. Baghdad appoints all the principal teachers and judges for Damascus. The local Jewish community also maintains close ties with the Jews of Cairo.

Jews worship at many places within the city. Then there are two synagogues on the outskirts, the smaller synagogue named after the prophet Elisha and a large one named after R. Al'asar ben 'Asarja, a teacher of Mishnah.

Damascus contains a Mohammedan mosque called "the synagogue of Damascus" which building is equalled nowhere upon earth. They say that it was the palace of Ben Hadad[26]—at other times a Roman temple,[27] then a Christian church—and that one wall of it is built of glass by witchcraft, for in no other place can there be found so much window glass, all of gilt and bright colors.[2] This wall contains as many openings as there are days in the solar year and the sun gradually throws its light into the openings. They are divided into

twelve degrees, equal to the number of hours of the day and by this contrivance everybody may know what time it is.

On the other walls are pictures of the greatest towns in the Moslem empires, with their buildings and trees. The pictures are formed as mosaics, with bits of glass of various single colors, or multicolored, or even of gold. To make the gold bits they lay a thin sheet of gold on a surface and then cover it with a thin sheet of colorless glass. To form the designs, and even lettering, they use Arabic gum to make the plaster with which they cover the walls, and into the wet plaster they set the bits of glass. Some entire walls are covered with gold mosaic—they say this mosque used twenty mule-loads of gold. The result is an ornate art like that of the Byzantines.

The palace contains houses richly ornamented with gold and silver, formed like tubs and of a size to allow three persons to bathe in them at once. In this building is also preserved the rib of a giant, which measures nine spans in length and two in breadth, and which belonged to an ancient giant king, of the name of Abkhamas. This name was found engraved upon a stone of his tomb, which also contained the information that he reigned over the whole world.

Letter from Aleppo

One day's journey from Damascus to JELA'AD which is Gil'ad and contains about sixty Jews. The city is large, richly watered, and surrounded by gardens and orchards.

\< \<   \< \<   \> \>   \> \>

Half a day's journey further stands SALKHAT, the city of Salkhah of Scripture.

\< \<   \< \<   \> \>   \> \>

Northward three days' journey from Damascus stands **BA'ALBEK**, a city so ancient that they say Adam lived nearby. **The city is mentioned in Scripture as Ba'alath in the valley of Lebanon, which Solomon built for the daughter of Pharaoh,** the queen of Sheba. **The palace is constructed of stones of enormous size, measuring twenty spans in length and twelve in breadth. No binding material holds these stones together and people claim that the building could have been erected only by the help of Ashmedai.**

Within the palace is a well called the Bir ar Rahmah, which means Well of Mercy; it contains no water. They say that as long as Ba'albek lives in peace, the well shall remain dry, but if the city is ever besieged, the well will fill up with water. The water will last for as long as people need it and then disappear again.

The city lives in peace because it is high on a mountain. In winter the people of Ba'albek use charcoal braziers to heat their houses and they wear fur coats when they go out. Even in summer when the days are very hot, the nights are cool.

A great spring takes its rise at the upper side of the city, through which its waters rush like those of a considerable river. They are employed in the working of several mills, situated within the city, which also encloses numerous gardens and orchards of grapes and figs. In the surrounding valley grow apricot and mulberry trees, and poplars for shade and for wood; also great amounts of wheat and beans. The city, despite the cold, is prosperous and agreeable.

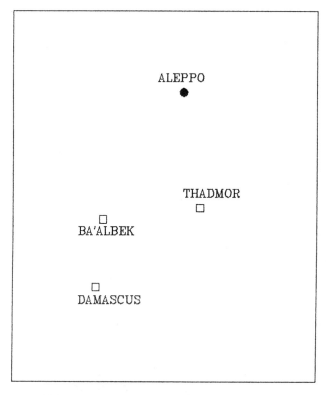

Wheresoever I turn my eyes
Around on earth or toward the skies,
I see Thee in the starry field,
I see Thee in the harvest's yield.
In every breath, in every sound,
An echo of Thy name is found.

The blade of grass, the simple flower,
Bear witness to Thy matchless power.
My every thought, Eternal God of Heaven,
Ascends to Thee, to whom all praise be given.[1]

Abraham ibn Ezra wrote that. Come to think of it, he must have passed through here on his way to Baghdad.

Despite the beauty of this country, my mind keeps returning to Jerusalem. Of course I had known before going there that the Franks had marched and sailed and fought and killed in order to liberate a city holy to Christians from the "infidel" Moslems. Jerusalem was the Holy City of Jews a thousand and more years before the advent of Christians; if one is to call people "infidels," then Christians are just as much infidels as Moslems. The air was heavy for me in Christian-ruled Jerusalem—I feel more comfortable now that I am again in this lush and Moslem land.

I suppose it's in the national character of the three peoples that there's greater affinity between Jews and Moslems than between Jews and Christians. The reason would seem to lie largely in their religious practices and prescriptions, but history has played its part too. Once the Moslems came to dominate the lands around the Great Sea, it was Jews and Moslems, not Christians, who traded in the many Moslem kingdoms. Likewise it was Jews and Moslems who developed interests in the sciences. Moslems, like Jews, gave high priority to scholarship, and it's traditional for Moslem students, like Jewish, to travel from one place to another to study with a particular *sheikh*, or master. In contrast, any scholarship, even any literacy, among Western Christians is to be found in monasteries and scarcely affects the life of the ordinary Christian family man.

It follows that they differ in their regard for bodily health. Although all three faiths have furnished great and good physicians, most Christians behave with less appreciation of medicine than do Moslems and Jews. When a Moslem or a Jew is ill, he is free to seek treatment from a physician of any faith, whereas Christians are banned by their popes from consulting a Jew.[2]

The dispersal of learning among Moslems and Jews reflects the way they organize their religious communities. As the locus of Jewish scholarly life is the synagogue, so the locus of Islamic scholarly life is the mosque . . . which all men are obliged to attend. Both faiths give great importance to law, and study of the law is incumbent upon every Moslem and Jewish man. The *ulema* (learned men) are community leaders and interpreters of law, whose recognition and influence depend on their personal attainments; the *imam* who leads the congregation in prayer is appointed to do so for a short period for a small stipend—in the aggregate of their functions they are similar to rabbis and very unlike Christian priests, whose ordination imbues them with a mystique as intermediary between man and God and who live apart from the other members of their faith.

All three religions require fasting and restrict meat-eating. But Christians eat pork with impunity, whereas the meat of pigs is prohibited to Moslems as to Jews. Islam also adopted other aspects of kashrut, forbidding their faithful to partake of blood or of animals which had died other than by slaughter.

The Moslems' ritual washing before community prayer appears analogous to the Jews' ritual hand-washing before meals, and to these several-times-daily acts of ritual purity the Christians have no equivalent.

The three faiths regulate their religious lives by three different calendars. Jews and Moslems live by lunar calendars and celebrate the start of each new month. Christians live by a solar calendar, excepting only their series of "movable feasts" with dates based on the Jewish lunar-determined Passover.

Just as Jews hold their communal prayers after daybreak, before sunset, and after dark, with no precise moment ordained for the recitation of prayers, so the Moslems set their prayer times according to the sun: at dawn, just after noon, before sunset, just after sunset, and after dark. The Christians, on the other hand, set their prayer times at hours determined by man, the monks scheduling their offices for midnight, for the third, sixth, and ninth hours, and so forth, which they call "canonical hours."

When we see the three faiths at worship, the most obvious dichotomy concerns art. Christians adorn their churches with paintings and sculptures of their holy personages, which practice to Jews and to Moslems seems idolatrous: Moslems, like Jews, build and decorate their houses of worship without representing the human form. Also, while Jews and Mohammedans often make merry with music, both groups prohibit instrumental music in their houses of worship.

Even in naming themselves, the Christians are "odd men out," for they frequently identify a man by a personal characteristic, such as Long John or Baltazar the Bold, whereas Moslem and Jewish nomenclature usually identify a man by patronymic, e.g., the physician-philosophers Abu Ali ibn-Sina (Latin: Avicenna) and Moses ben Maimon (Greek: Maimonides).

These are ideas that have come to me in thinking about why it is that the Jews generally live better in Moslem kingdoms than in Christian.

< <   < <   > >   > >

THADMOR is surrounded by a wall, and stands in the desert far from any inhabited place, and is four days' journey from the above-mentioned Ba'alath. The Romans and Greeks called the city Palmyra, a rendering of the name "Thadmor," which is related to the Hebrew "tamar," meaning palm tree, for the city is a grand oasis. It is the midpoint of the route between the Great Sea and the valley of the Euphrates in Babylonia, and is situated also on the paved road from Damascus to Babylonia.

Like Ba'alath, **this city was also built by Solomon, of equally large stones.** Because even in ancient times this was a meeting point of many trade routes, Solomon needed to hold this city in order to control the commerce between Palestine and Babylonia. Nowadays commerce on this important route is often interrupted due to the Frank raids.[3]

This city has two congregations, Palestinian and Babylonian,[4] **and contains two thousand warlike Jews. These are at war with the Christians and with the Arabian subjects of Nureddin, and they aid their neighbors the Mohammedans.**

< <   < <   > >   > >

From Thadmor, **half a day to CARIATEEN, which is Kirjathaim. One Jew only, a dyer by profession, lives here.**

< <   < <   > >   > >

From Cariateen, **one day to HAMAH, the ancient Chamath, on the Orontes, under Mount Lebanon.**

Some time ago this city was visited by an earthquake, in consequence of which fifteen thousand men died in one day, leaving only seventy survivors.

< <   < <   > >   > >

Half a day from Hamah **to REIHA which is Chazor.**

< <   < <   > >   > >

From Reiha, **three parasangs to LAMDIN, from whence it is a journey of two days to Aleppo.**

< <   < <   > >   > >

ALEPPO, the Aram Tsoba of Scripture, the Halab of the Moslems. Near the town wall is a castle which contains the altar where, it is said, sacrifices were offered by our father Abraham. He used to keep his flocks in the cave under the castle, and when he milked his sheep and people came for their milk, they would ask, first of each other while they stood around, and then of Abraham: "Halaba ya lâ?" ("Milked yet, or not?"), for which reason the place around Abraham's cave was called Halab (meaning "milked").

There being neither spring nor river, the inhabitants drink rainwater, which is collected by a cistern (Arabic: algub) at every house.

This is **the royal city of Nureddin,** although he rules under his prince in Baghdad, the khalif of the Abbasids. Nureddin is a just and pious ruler, and the Jews live here in peace. Before the time of Nureddin, the Moslem rulers lacked strength, wherefore the Franks succeeded in capturing Palestine, but Nureddin is an able general who has waged war against the Franks and recaptured Edessa, to the north. He is determined to drive the Franks from Syria and Palestine. May he be blessed in his endeavors!

In the midst of the city is his palace surrounded by an uncommonly high wall of white stone: constructed not of rubble stone, but rather of blocks cut, shaped, and planed by skilled quarriers, so that buildings here have a symmetry like nowhere else in the world.[5] This is a very large place and a fine city with trade from all the Moslem lands. In the market streets the shops have double wooden shutters, closed at night. For trading, the shopkeeper raises the upper part of the shutter, thereby making it into a roof providing shade and arranges the lower part of the shutter as a counter to display his wares. All the shops and the houses in Aleppo stand very close together, in long rows, each row being reserved for a particular craft. A whole row gives the appearance of a single shop. All the crafts of the world are to be seen in Aleppo.[6]

The city's gates are called the gate of Antioch, the gate of Paradise, the gate of Allah, and the Jews' gate. **The city has** five thousand **Jewish inhabitants,**[7] **the principal of them being R. Moses el-Constantini and R. Seth.** Aleppo's Jewish community has close contacts with the Palestine academy at Damascus and with the great yeshiva at Baghdad.

Letter from Baghdad

From Aleppo **to BALES which is P'thora on the Euphrates, two days.** This city was conquered by the army of Tancred and then recaptured by the Turks of Zengi. **Even at present you still find remains there of the tower of Bil'am ben Be'or (may the name of the wicked rot) which he built in accordance with the hours of the day,** like the palace of Ben Hadad in Damascus. **This place contains about ten Jews.**

From Bales **half a day to KALA' JIABER, which is Sela' Midbarah. This city remained in the power of the Arabs even at the time when the Thogarmin or Turks took their country and dispersed them in the desert; it contains about two thousand Jews.**

From Kala' Jiaber **one day to RACCA, which is Khalneh on the confines of Mesopotamia, being the frontier town between that country and the Thogarmin or Turks; it contains about seven hundred Jewish inhabitants, the principal of whom are R. Sakhai, and R. Nadib who is blind. One of the synagogues was built by Ezra the Scribe, when he returned to Jerusalem from Babylon.**

From Racca, **one day to the ancient place of CHORAN. Its twenty Jewish inhabitants also possess a synagogue erected by Ezra. Nobody is allowed to construct any building on the site, where the house of our father Abraham was situated; even the Mohammedans pay respect to the place and resort thither to pray.**

Two days journey from thence is a town on the **sources of the El-Khabour, the Chabor of Scripture. This river takes its course through Media and loses itself in the Kizil Ozein. About two hundred Jews dwell near this place.**

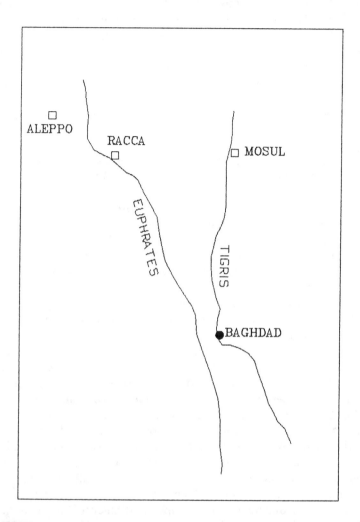

To **NISIBIS two days; it is a large city, richly watered, and contains about one thousand Jews.**

From Nisibis, **two days to JEZIREH BEN OMAR, an island in the Tigris.** This river having been specified in the week of Creation, on seeing it one thanks God, "Who hath made the work of creation." The waters are beneficial for the body and mind.[1]

This town is **on the foot of Mount Ararat and four miles distant from the place on which the ark of Noah rested; Omar ben al-Khatab removed the ark**

from the summit of the two mountains and made a mosque of it. The Moslems say that Noah was the favorite Bible figure of Mohammed.

There still exists in the vicinity of the ark a synagogue of Ezra the Scribe, which is visited by the Jews of the city on the Ninth of Ab. The city of **Jezireh Omar ben al-Khatab contains about four thousand Jews**, and it is a market-place for trade especially with Mosul to the south and Armenia to the north.

< <   < <   > >   > >

From Jezireh distant **two days stands MOSUL, mentioned in Scripture as Ashur the Great,** the metropolis of Assyria, now called Persia. **Mosul, situated on the confines of Persia, is of great extent and very ancient.**

The buildings here are all of stone, yet the city lacks any grand market-place or house of worship. There are, to be sure, some synagogues: **Mosul contains the synagogues of Obadiah, of Jonah ben Amittai**, whose tomb is here and whose memory is honored by the Turks as well as Jews, **and of Nachum ha-Elkoshi**, who likewise is buried here. The city **contains about seven thousand Jews, the principal of whom are R. Zakkai, the Prince, a descendant of King David; and R. Joseph, who is astronomer of Seifed-din, the brother of Nureddin, King of Damascus.**

Mosul stands on the banks of the Tigris and is connected by a bridge with Nineveh. In ancient times Nineveh was a very large city, a city of wicked people. As God commanded, Jonah warned them that their city would be destroyed. The residents of Nineveh heeded Jonah and God relented,[2] but years later the earth opened up and swallowed the city.[3] **Although Nineveh lies in ruins,** now **there are numerous inhabited villages and small townships on its site,** among them Ninive, Nunia, and Nimrod.

Farther along the Tigris, not far from Mosul, is a place of tar, a large black hole in the earth, from which spurts a black material, something between soft stone and thick liquid. This tar is collected in vessels which have been set about on the ground for this purpose. The tar, set aflame, loses its liquid and becomes bitumen, which is then cut into pieces for shipment. It is widely used for medicaments, as at Capua and Salerno. In the delta region of the Tigris and Euphrates, where little wood or stone is to be found, people manufacture a construction material by mixing bitumen with sand and vege-table fibers. Bitumen is commonly used in building watercourses, as for the immense coastal walls of Tyre.[4]

< <   < <   > >   > >

From Mosul, **three days** across the desert **to RAHABAH,**   ich is Recho-both by the River Euphrates and contains about two thousand .   s. **The city is surrounded by a wall, is very handsome, large, and well-fortified; the environs abound with gardens and orchards.**

< <   < <   > >   > >

From Rahabah, **one day to KARKISIA, the ancient Kharkh'mish, on the banks of the Euphrates,** into which, nearby, runs the river Khabur (Araxes). Where the rivers come together there are fine views and marshlands, also cultivated fields and gardens, and clumps of tamarisks. The town **contains about five hundred Jewish inhabitants.**

From here it is two days to El-Anbar, which is Pumbeditha in Nehardea, whence I shall travel after visiting Baghdad and Sura.

< <   < <   > >   > >

From Karkisia, one week **to CHARDAH or Chadrah with fifteen thousand Jews.**

< <   < <   > >   > >

From Chardah, **two days to OKBERA, the** city on the Tigris **which was built by Jekhoniah King of Judah. It contains about ten thousand Jews and stands two days from Baghdad.**

< <   < <   > >   > >

BAGHDAD on the Tigris is the most populous city in the world. Yet Jews often refer to the city as "Babylon," which is really the name of the old town, famous for the Tower of Babel, located on the river Euphrates fifteen parasangs south of Baghdad. And sometimes we call Baghdad "Babylonia," the name by which this whole country of Mesopotamia was known in ancient times. The confusion of names arose because the Jews exiled from Palestine in the days of our fathers came to the country of Babylonia. Just as Palestine was the home of most Jews during the biblical era, Babylonia has been the home of most Jews during the Exile. It is written in a Midrash that "the land of Israel extends to the Euphrates River."[5] Baghdad, however, is a fairly new city—the Abbasids built it in the eighth century as their capital.

Now Baghdad is a great metropolis and the center of Babylonian Jewry. **This city contains twenty-eight Jewish synagogues, situated partly in Baghdad and partly in Al-Khorkh on the other side of the River Tigris, which** runs **through and divides the city.**

The people can walk across the river on a wide bridge which is supported by several small barges; iron chains attach the barges to one another at both ends, and attach the end barges to posts sunk deep at each riverbank. There are ferry boats too, especially for carrying animals and merchandise and produce. The region around Baghdad **is rich in palm-trees, gardens and orchards, so that nothing equals it in Mesopotamia, and it contains many wise**

philosophers well-skilled in the sciences, and magicians proficient in all sorts of witchcraft, as well as multitudes of weavers excelling in brocades.[6] Our forefathers used Babylonian weavings of bright reds and blues to decorate the Temple.[7]

Yet, as I said, Baghdad the metropolis is new. One of the early khalifs of the Abbasid dynasty, the khalif Harun al-Rashid, made Baghdad the wondrous city immortalized in the stories of the Thousand and One Nights. As khalif, Harun fought against the Byzantines and made friendly overtures to the Western Christians: it was he who sent to Charlemagne the elephant which was driven by the Jew Isaac. Harun al-Rashid was pious and himself traveled frequently on pilgrimage. He was wise and a great patron of learning: he established the great university of Baghdad with a medical school and hospital. By then Baghdad had a factory for manufacturing paper, so that books were common.[8] Harun's successor established an academy for astronomy and philosophy, and since that time other colleges have been founded here, Jewish colleges among them. As Moslems desirous of knowledge travel from one master teacher to another in the way that Jewish scholars do, Baghdad resounds with young men's diversions and disputations.

Baghdad is the large metropolis of the Abbasid **khalif Emir al-Mumenin** (commander of the faithful), al-Mustanjid **of the family of their prophet, who is the chief of the Mohammedan religion. All Mohammedan kings acknowledge him and he holds the same dignity over them as the Pope enjoys over the Christians.**

The palace of the khalif at Baghdad extends for three miles; it contains a large park of all sorts of trees, both useful and ornamental, and all sorts of beasts, as well as a pond of water led thither from the River Tigris. And whenever the khalif desires to enjoy himself and to sport and to carouse, birds, beasts and fishes are prepared for him and for his councillors, whom he invites to his palace.

This great Abbasid is extremely kind toward the Jews, many of his officers being of that nation. He understands all languages, is well-versed in the Mosaic law, and reads and writes the Hebrew language. He enjoys nothing but what he earns by the labor of his own hands and therefore manufactures coverlets which he stamps with his seal and which his officers sell in the public market; these articles are purchased by the nobles of the land and from their produce his necessaries are provided.

The khalif is an excellent man, trustworthy and kindhearted towards every one, but generally invisible to the Mohammedans. The pilgrims, who come hither from distant countries on their way to Mecca in Yemen, desire to be presented to him and thus address him from the palace: "Our Lord, light of the Mohammedans and splendor of our religion, show us the brightness of thy countenance," but he heeds not their words. His servants and officers then

approach and pray: "Oh Lord, manifest thy peace to those men who come from distant lands and desire shelter in the shadow of thy glory," and after such petition he rises and puts out of the window one corner of his garment, which is eagerly kissed by the pilgrims. One of the lords then addresses them thus: "Go in peace, for our Lord, the light of the Mohammedans, is well pleased and gives you his blessing." This prince being esteemed by them equal to their prophet, they proceed on their way, full of joy at the words addressed to them by the lord, who communicated the message of peace.

All the brothers and other members of the khalif's family are accustomed to kiss his garments, and every one of them possesses a palace within that of the khalif, but they are all fettered by chains of iron, and a special officer is appointed over every household to prevent their rising in rebellion against the great king. These measures are enacted in consequence of an occurrence which took place some time ago and upon which occasion the brothers rebelled and elected a king among themselves. To prevent this in future it was decreed that all the members of the khalif's family should be chained, in order to prevent their rebellious intentions. Every one of them, however, resides in his palace, is there much honored, and they possess villages and towns, the rents of which are collected for them by their stewards; they eat and drink and lead a merry life.

The khalif leaves his palace but once every year, namely, at the time of the feast called Ramadan. Upon this occasion many visitors assemble from distant parts, in order to have an opportunity of beholding his countenance. He then bestrides the royal mule, dressed in kingly robes, which are composed of gold and silver cloth. On his head he wears a turban, ornamented with precious stones of inestimable value, but over this turban is thrown a black veil. (Black is the color used to represent the Abbasids and to distinguish them from their enemies the Fatimids of Egypt, who use green.) On this Moslem festival he covers the brilliant gems with black as if to say: See all this worldly honor will be converted into darkness on the day of death.

When he goes out on this occasion the khalif is accompanied by a numerous retinue of Mohammedan nobles, arrayed in rich dresses and riding upon horses, princes of Arabia, of Media, of Persia, and even of Tibet, a country distant three months' journey from Arabia.

The procession goes from the palace to the mosque on the Botsra gate, which is the metropolitan mosque. All those who walk in procession are dressed in silk and purple, both men and women. The streets and squares are enlivened by singing, rejoicing, and by parties who dance before the great king, called khalif. He is loudly saluted by the assembled crowd who cry: "Blessed art Thou, our Lord and King." He thereupon kisses his garment and, by holding it in his hand, acknowledges and returns the compliment. The procession moves on, into the court of the mosque, where the khalif mounts a wooden pulpit and expounds their law unto them. The learned Mohammedans rise, pray for him and praise his great kindness and piety, upon which the whole assembly answers "Amen!" He then pronounces his blessing and kills a camel, which is led thither for that purpose, and this is their offering, which is distributed to the nobles. These send portions of it to their friends, who are eager to taste of the meat killed by the hands of their holy king and are much rejoiced therewith.

He then leaves the mosque, and returns alone, to his palace, along the banks of the Tigris, the noble Mohammedans accompanying him in boats until he enters this building; he never returns by the way he came, and the path on the bank of the river is carefully guarded all the year round, so as to prevent any one treading in his footsteps. The khalif never leaves the palace again, for a whole year.

He is a pious and benevolent man and has erected buildings on the other side of the river, on the banks of an arm of the Euphrates which runs on one side of the city. These buildings include many large houses, streets and hostelries for the sick poor, who resort thither in order to be cured. According to Moslem tradition in Babylonia, each khalif provides for a hospital. At the times of great gatherings and festivals, the khalif sends physicians into the crowds around the mosques, to care for anyone who may have need. There are about sixty medical warehouses here, all well provided from the king's stores with spices and other necessaries; and every patient who claims assistance is fed at the king's expense, until his cure is completed.

There is further the large building called Dar-al-karaphtan (meaning "the abode of persons who require being chained") in which are locked up all those insane persons who are met with, particularly during the hot season; every one of whom is secured by iron chains until his reason returns, when he is allowed to return to his home. For this purpose they are regularly examined once a month by the king's officers, appointed for that purpose, and when they are found to be possessed of reason, they are immediately liberated.

All this is done by the king in pure charity, towards all who come to Baghdad, either ill or insane, for the king is a pious man and his intention is excellent in this respect. He requires that physicians work in hospitals and pass examinations and have the police attest their morality before they are granted a license (from a senior physician authorized by the khalif to grant licenses, or sometimes from the khalif himself), which license allows a physician to treat the sick without supervision.[9] In medicine the East surpasses the West, and nowhere else even in the East does one find practitioners of the medical sciences as skilled as in Baghdad.

Most Moslem scholars are practicing physicians,[10] just as among the Jews Physicians must be scholars. Naturally our Jewish physicians are learned in Judaism. Wherever he lives in the Jewish world, an aspiring physician must prove himself as a yeshiva scholar before beginning the study of medicine, for how else can his capacities be judged?

Only after having prepared in Hebrew, Arabic, and Talmud, and after mastering the intricacies of Jewish law, can the aspiring physician immerse himself in the ideas of the Greeks and the Arabs. The course of study for advanced students at the Babylonian academies has traditionally included Greek philosophies and medical ideas. And theology: a knowledge of theology is essential for those men who are learning foreign ideas and who will sometimes be working in the non-Jewish communities, where they will be surrounded by foreign influences. The yeshivot teach Jewish ethics and the idea that to help maintain the human body, to help prolong life, is a sacred vocation.[11] Moreover, Jewish physicians must be familiar with every aspect of medicine known to their Moslem and Christian colleagues, lest a patient's non-recovery be attributed to his Jewish physician's treating him in a manner different from the usual.[12]

Babylonia's Jewish doctors have had to prepare themselves entirely within the Jewish academies, being virtually barred from other medical studies in Baghdad.[13] The Mohammedans made this city a great medical center, which attracted many aspiring physicians of their own faith; even for a Moslem it is difficult now to obtain a post at a hospital, so they have no need of Jews. There is an old law which limits Jews to the use of Hebrew and Syriac in studying and teaching medicine. The royal physicians in Baghdad are Syriac Christians.

If the other religious communities consider it important to have their own physicians, how much more so for the Jews! Not only to assure excellent care to our Jewish people—all the physicians care equally for the ill regardless of religion—but to have eminent representatives who can deal on a basis of common interest and equality with men of the ruling faith. Indeed, physicians account for a very great number of spokesmen for Jewry.

The Jewish aspiring physician in Babylonia, in addition to studying at an academy, works alongside an older physician (his father, if he's lucky), helping wherever possible, in the early stages of his studies especially, by bleeding patients under the physician's eyes. (Although once licensed as a physician, he'll send his patients to others for bloodletting; most physicians, Jews and Gentiles, hate letting blood.) At a later stage he might pay an eminent physician to instruct him and supervise him. From first to last, he reads through these physicians' libraries: tomes of Hippocrates and Galen and the hundreds upon hundreds of commentaries on them which describe new diseases and explain how to prepare drugs.

Like his Moslem counterpart, the Jewish student will learn about a great number of diseases, and about how their causes may relate to climate, to what people eat, to how they take care of their bodies. The variety in all these things, including the diseases themselves, becomes known to Moslem and Jewish physicians partly through their intercourse with co-religionists living in so many different parts of the world.

If he proves himself able, the Jewish aspiring-physician receives the license from senior physicians of the Jewish community, which is autonomous in such matters. With his license, the young physician can practice independently; he can set up by himself or with a partner in one of the shops in the marketplace, furnishing it with a great variety of bottles and boxes and with the scales and mortar for mixing medicaments and with his shield over the door.[14]

Sickness can have an unpleasant odor, but because of the medicaments the shop of physician or druggist always smells so good! The pomegranate-flavored syrup of honey and vinegar, and the licorice jam—both often used here—are but two of the potions among the dozens whose smells commingle in the shop. Shabbetai Donnolo wrote his handbook with some 120 drugs, and since then the pharmacists have found many more drugs and have compiled many more handbooks. A series of regulations here requires druggists to know the contents of the handbooks and to consult them before prescribing for an unusual case. Of course a physician may work in a shop with a druggist, but a physician may be his own druggist. Much illness which a physician treats is uncomplicated: he must provide the sufferer with artificial teeth, or he prescribes cassia for a case of constipation. Yet as the human physician can do only so much, he generally completes his prescriptions with a notation like "with God's help, this will cure." The physician Judah ha-Levi, our beloved poet, expressed the idea this way, in a prayer:

> My God, heal me and I shall be healed;
> Be not angry with me, lest I be consumed.
> My medicines are of Thee, whether they be good or evil, whether strong or
>   weak.
> It is Thou who choose, not I.
> Thou alone know what is wrong and what is fair.
> Not upon my power of healing do I rely,
> Only for Thine healing do I watch.[15]

In Salerno it seemed to me that physicians confined themselves to cities; but here in the East that seems not to be true. As Jews live dispersed in Babylonia, so Jewish physicians are to be found everywhere in the land: in the villages as well as in the towns and cities. Not at court, perhaps— although there are stories about some khalifs using the services of Jewish physicians.

If the Jewish aspiring-physician failed to obtain a hospital post, it is likely that as a practicing physician sooner or later he will work in a hospital— even if the hospital is in his own home. Although the khalifs' hospitals are open to all who are seriously ill, and although it is said that the officers of these hospitals are sensitive to the dietary requirements of Jews, many Jewish people avoid going into hospital for fear of breaking kashrut. So most Jewish physicians assume the care, in their own house, of their seriously ill patients who are also their friends or who are wealthy enough to afford it.

Baghdad is inhabited by about forty thousand Jews, who enjoy peace, comfort, and much honor under the government of the great king. Among them are very wise men and presidents of the colleges, whose occupation is the study of the Mosaic law. The city contains ten Jewish colleges, those from Sura and Pumbeditha transferred here in the last century, and eight smaller ones. These academies receive contributions from Jewish communities throughout the Exile; the money from Spain comes regularly. Indeed, the Jewish communities of Spain seem more devoted to the academies in Babylonia than some of the communities at lesser distance.

The heads of these Talmudic academies or colleges, from the old days in Sura and Pumbeditha, are officially titled rosh yeshivot, but often they are called geonim or, here, "batlanim" (the idle), because their sole occupation consists in the discharge of public business. During every day of the week they dispense justice to all the Jewish inhabitants of the country, except on Monday, which is set aside for assemblies under the presidency of the Rabbi Samuel ben Eli, master of the College Gaon Jacob. Rabbi Samuel on that day dispenses justice to every applicant and is assisted therein by the ten batlanim, presidents of the colleges.

Rabbi Samuel, a descendant of the Prophet Samuel, has no sons. He has a daughter who is very learned; she gives lessons in Bible and Talmud. She teaches from behind a window of her house, for the sake of modesty. The men in the garden below listen to her but cannot see her.[16]

The principal of the presidents of the colleges is R. Daniel ben Hisdai, who bears the titles of Prince of the Captivity and Lord and Exilarch of all Israel, and who possesses a pedigree which proves his descent from King David. Every exilarch claims descent from the royal House of David, which stayed in Babylon when Ezra led the Jews from their captivity back to Jerusalem. R. Daniel is addressed by Jews as "Lord, Prince of the Captivity," and by the Mohammedans as "Saidna ben Daud," noble descendant of David; as the Moslems honor the prophet David, so they do honor to the exilarch as his descendant. He holds great command over all Jewish congregations under the authority of the Emir Al-Mumenin (commander of the faithful) the lord of the Mohammedans, who has commanded all people to respect him, and the emir has confirmed R. Daniel's power by granting him a seal of office. Every one of his subjects, whether he be Jew or Mohammedan or of any other faith, is commanded to rise in the presence of the Prince of the Captivity and to salute him respectfully under penalty of one hundred stripes.

Whenever he pays a visit to the king, he is escorted by numerous horsemen, both Jews and Gentiles, and a crier commands aloud: "Make way before our lord the son of David, as becomes his dignity!" On these occasions he rides upon a horse and his dress is composed of embroidered silk; on his head he wears a large turban, covered by a white cloth and surmounted by a chain or diadem.

For thus Mohammed commanded concerning him and his descendants. And the exilarch is seated on his throne opposite that of the khalif in compliance with the command of Mohammed to give effect to what is written in the Law: "The scepter shall not depart from Judah, nor the rulers' staff from between his feet, as long as men come to Shiloh, and unto him shall the obedience of the people be." The Mohammedans accept that until the coming of the Kingdom of Heaven to earth, the Jews will always have a Jewish ruler, in whichever country he may live; as the khalif of Baghdad is a Moslem ruler, so the exilarch in Baghdad is the Jewish ruler, to be obeyed by all.

The authority of the Prince of the Captivity extends over the following countries: namely, over Mesopotamia; Persia; Khorassan; S'ba which is Yemen; Diarbekh; all Armenia and the land of Kota near Mount Ararat; over the country of the Alanians, which is shut in by mountains and has no outlet except by the iron gates which were made by Alexander; over Sikbia and all the provinces of the Turkomans unto the Aspisian mountains; over the country of the Georgians unto the river Oxus (these are the Girgashim of Scripture); and as far as the frontiers of the provinces and cities of Tibet and India. Permission is granted by the Prince of the Captivity to all the Jewish congregations of these different countries to elect rabbis and ministers, all of whom appear before him in order to receive consecration and the permission to officiate, upon which occasions presents and valuable gifts are offered to him even from the remotest countries.

At the time of the installation of the Prince of the Captivity he spends considerable sums in presents to the king, or khalif, his princes and nobles. The ceremony is performed by the act of the laying on of the hands of the king or of khalif, after which the prince rides home from the king's abode to his own house, seated in a royal state carriage and accompanied by the sound of various musical instruments; he afterwards lays his hands on the gentlemen of the academy, consecrating them.

The metropolitan synagogue of the Prince of the Captivity is ornamented with pillars of richly colored marble, plated with gold and silver; on the pillars are inscribed verses of the Psalms in letters of gold. The ascent to the Holy Ark is composed of ten marble steps, on the uppermost of which are the stalls set apart for the Prince of the Captivity and the other princes of the House of David.

The Prince of the Captivity possesses hostelries, gardens and orchards in Babylonia and extensive landed property inherited from his forefathers, of which nobody dares deprive him. He enjoys a certain yearly income from the Jewish hostelries, the markets, and the merchandise of the country, which is levied in the form of a tax, over and above what is presented to him from foreign countries; the man is very rich, an excellent scholar and so hospitable that numerous Israelites dine at his table every day.

Jews come from many lands to Baghdad, to see the opulence of the Prince of the Captivity and to query him or the masters of the colleges about religious practice and law in their home communities. They say these visitors are but a trickle compared with the flood of Jews who in earlier times sought judgments in Babylonia. They say too that the wealth and status of Baghdad's leading Jews make them arrogant and quarrelsome; the geonim argue with the exilarch and with each other.

The Jewish community lives here autonomously, untroubled by outside forces. In this part of the world the khalifs have generally ignored the Moslem ban against the construction of churches and synagogues; at least they have allowed Jews to circumvent the ban by enlarging old synagogues or reconstructing places of worship formerly used by non-Jewish dhimmis.[17] Occasionally a khalif decrees that Jews must wear a particular article of clothing, but fortunately these harassments have been short-lived. Forty or fifty years ago Jewish men were required to wear yellow badges, but no one of our generation has ever worn one.[18] Now, here, only the fringes on the Jews' outer garments distinguish them from the voluminous wraps of Gentile men. Jews entering synagogues to pray remove their footwear, like Moslems.[19] It is the custom of the East to show respect by going with bare feet and a covered head.[20]

Many of the Jews of Baghdad are good scholars and very rich. Merchants of all countries resort hither for purposes of trade, as the precious merchandise from the East destined for Europe comes through here. Especially dyes from India: brazilwood, kermes, indigo. These dyes are used locally too, in making the splendid brocades. Everyone wears robes of bright colors, and golden-colored caps under their turbans.[21] As elsewhere, Jews predominate among the traders in dyestuffs.[22] If the Jews are prosperous, they are just partaking of the good things that Baghdad offers.

Particularly at their meals. You know the old saying, "Sleep in a Christian bed and enjoy Jewish food." Around here they expand it to: "Of the good things of this world the Moslems enjoy most sex, the Christians money, the Persians status, and the Jews food."

Letter from Sura

Three days' journey south of Baghdad, **BABYLON** is situated on the banks of the river Euphrates. **The ancient Babel now lies in ruins but the streets still extend thirty miles.** Today's Babylon is a small village, yet from it the whole region takes its name.

Within about twenty miles from thence live twenty thousand Jews, who perform their worship in the synagogue of Daniel, who rests in peace. This synagogue is of remote antiquity, having been built by Daniel himself; it is constructed of solid stones and bricks.

In ancient times Nebuchadnezzar was the king of Babylon who destroyed the First Temple and all of Jerusalem by fire, before taking Jerusalem's leading Jews to exile in Babylonia.[1] **Of the palace of Nebuchadnezzar the ruins are still to be seen,** in a valley well known to every one. People are afraid to enter it on account of the serpents and scorpions by which it is infested, nonetheless **the traveler may behold Nebuchadnezzar's palace with the burning fiery furnace into which were thrown Chananiah, Mishael and Asariah.**[2]

HILLAH lies on the river Euphrates **at a distance of five miles** southward from Babylon. Hillah is a new town, the Abbasids having made it a regional capital and enclosed it in a wall about seventy years ago. Therewith, it flourished into a commercial center. Although Jews dwelt in this place long before the Abbasids came, in the last decades many more Jews have settled here. Now Hillah **contains about ten thousand Jews and four synagogues, in which public worship is performed daily.**

The tower of Babel **built by the dispersed generation is four miles from thence. It is constructed of bricks; the base measures two miles, the breadth two hundred and forty yards and the height about one hundred canna. A spiral passage, built into the tower, leads up to the summit, from which there is a prospect of twenty miles, the country being one wide plain and quite level. The heavenly fire, which struck the tower, split it to its very foundation.**

From Hillah **half a day to NAPACHA, which** contains **two hundred Jews, and the synagogue of R. Isaac Napacha, in front of which is his sepulcher.**

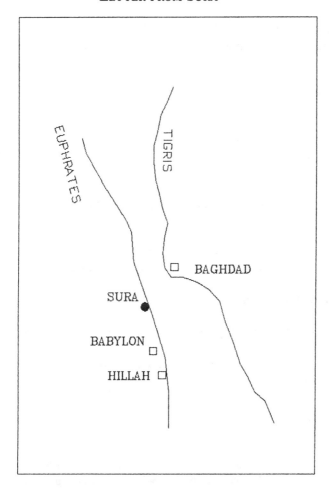

Three parasangs from Napacha on the banks of the Euphrates stands the synagogue of the prophet Ezekiel, who rests in peace. The place of the synagogue is fronted by sixty towers, the room between every two of which is also occupied by a synagogue. In the court of the largest stands the Ark and behind it, in a man-made cave, is the sepulcher of Ezekiel ben Busi ha-Kohen. The monument is covered by a large cupola and the building is very handsome. It was erected by J'khoniah, King of Jehuda, and the thirty-five thousand Jews who went along with him, when evil M'rodakh released him from prison, which was situated between the River Chaboras and another river. The name of J'khoniah and of all those who came with him are inscribed on the wall, the king's name first, that of Ezekiel last.

The place is considered holy even to the present day, and is one of those to which people resort from remote countries in order to pray, particularly in late spring at the time of Shavuot and at the season of the New Year and

Atonement Day. Great rejoicings take place there about the time of the New Year, which are attended even by the Prince of the Captivity and the presidents of the colleges of Baghdad. The assembly is so large that their temporary abodes cover twenty-two miles of open ground, and it attracts many Arabian merchants, who keep a market or fair.

On the Day of Atonement the proper lesson of the day is read from a very large manuscript Pentateuch in Ezekiel's own handwriting.

A lamp burns night and day on the sepulcher of the Prophet and has always been kept burning, since the day he lighted it himself; the oil and wicks are renewed as often as necessary.

A large house belonging to the sanctuary contains a very numerous collection of books, some of them as ancient as the Second Temple, some even coeval with the First Temple, it being the custom that whoever dies childless bequeaths his books to this sanctuary.

The inhabitants of the country lead to the sepulcher all foreign Jews who come from Media and Persia to visit it in consequence of vows they have performed.

The noble Mohammedans also resort thither to pray, because they hold the prophet Ezekiel, upon whom be peace, in great veneration. They call him by the name Khazkil and they call this place "Dar m'licha" (agreeable abode); the sepulcher is also visited by all devout Arabs. Within half a mile of the synagogue are the sepulchers of Chananiah, Mishael and Asariah, each of them covered by a large cupola. Even in times of war neither Jew nor Mohammedan ventures to despoil or profane the sepulcher of Ezekiel.

Three miles from the sepulcher of Ezekiel stands the city of AL-KOTSONAATH with three hundred Jewish inhabitants and three sepulchers, in front of each of which is a synagogue in which Jews pray daily.

To AIN JAPHATA three parasangs, this place contains the sepulcher of the prophet Nachum the Elkoshite who rests in peace. In Persian villages nearby are other sepulchers.

To KUFA one day, this city contains about seventy thousand Jews and the sepulcher of King J'khoniah of Jehuda which consists of a large building with a synagogue in front of it.

< <   < <   > >   > >

From Kufa **one day and a half to SURA**, the remains of this important city lying a few miles upriver from Babylon, on the Euphrates where that river divides into two. **This is the place called in the Talmud Matha M'chasia and was formerly the residence of the princes of the captivity and of the principals of the colleges. The following sepulchers are at Sura: that of R. Sherira and of his son R. Hai, that of Rabbenu Saadia al-Fayyumi, and of many other princes of the captivity, descendants of the House of David, who formerly resided here, before the city was ruined.**

Long before the city of Baghdad existed, before there existed a religion of Mohammed or even of Jisho, Jews were dwelling in Sura; their history here extended over a thousand years, during which time Jews throughout the world looked to Sura for their religious leadership. The earliest Jews exiled in Babylon lived dispersed in villages, sundered from Palestine and isolated from any strong Jewish community—they were unsure how to live as Jews.

In order to teach them about Jewish law and custom, R. Abba Arika established an academy here, about the year 4000 (240 C.E.). "Rav," they called him, or "Master," because he was a great scholar and pious, and he wrote many prayers, among them the Alenu, which we recite every day. He gained such fame as a lecturer that in the week preceding each of the three festivals people came to hear him from throughout the land. Even the exilarch came from Baghdad to hear the Rav. So many people arrived that they had to sleep in the open on the banks of the canal. Among his regular students were hundreds who had come to live in Sura. From these educational beginnings would develop the Talmud.

The rabbis who compiled the Talmud worked at various academies in Babylonia but especially in Sura and in Pumbeditha (which lies three days upriver from Sura). They studied, debated, and recorded points of diet and health, marriage and divorce, prayer and ritual. Palestine too had its *amoraim*—compilers of Talmud—but there due to poverty and Christian persecution, they could not work as well. In time, as the amoraim in Babylonia lost touch with those in Palestine, and as their work on the Talmud covering all aspects of life became known to Jews in distant lands, Babylonia came to assume the sovereign position in world Jewry. So much was Babylonia the center of Jewish scholarship and of Jewish life that Babylonian rabbis forbid their disciples to emigrate, even to Palestine.[3]

As the Talmud developed, the amoraim had their work copied and sent abroad. This encouraged distant Jews to pour over the texts they had at hand and, when in doubt, to write for authoritative interpretations of Scripture, advice on festival observance, and so forth. When, for example, the Jews from Lucena requested help in arranging the prayers for their daily worship, Sura responded with a sequence for the services that other communities too have adopted. Babylonian scholars were queried about financial concerns: Can a debt be paid in installments? Who is responsible to pay the tax of a poor widow?

By 500 C.E. the Talmud was complete. Now the academics addressed themselves to matters raised by those who had trouble understanding points of Talmud. Sura and Pumbeditha were no longer just the major academies, but the only ones of significance. Sura ruled the south and Pumbeditha the north of Babylon. Each academy had evolved into a yeshiva, like a *collegium* or the Greek *sanhedrion*, of which the head was the rosh yeshiva or gaon; on the occasions when Pumbeditha and Sura spoke with a single voice, they sometimes, in memory of ancient days, referred to themselves as "the Great Sanhedrin." The two geonim, of Sura and Pumbeditha, were in no way dependent upon the exilarch in Baghdad; nevertheless they went every year before Passover to do him honor at the assembly of nobles and scholars called the Great Kallah. In the days when the Sura Academy was still in Sura, the geonim installed each new exilarch here with ceremony like crowning a king and festivities lasting a week or more.[4]

The yeshivot, no longer taking in students, functioned as high court. Developing their opinions from words of the Bible, the geonim judged matters of ritual and civil law. They professed not to *make* the law, for "the Law is God's,"[5] but they voted on matters of importance to the entire Jewish community, and each decision had the force of a decree, so that they were in fact legislators. This was the situation in Babylonia—while Pumbeditha and Sura dealt primarily with legal matters, Palestine concerned itself with the spiritual as in philosophy and poetry. Regarding halakha, even the scholars of Palestine were greatly influenced by the Babylonians.

The rulers of Babylonia adhered to the new religion of Mohammed. The Moslems adopted many of the fundamental ideas of Judaism, including belief in the one God, the circumcision of infant boys, obedience to a Scripture, and ritual slaughter of animals for food. But they didn't accept other of our Jewish practices. As you know, they don't observe the Sabbath as a day of rest: they named Friday a day of assembly for prayer but did not forbid work on that day. Moslems don't eat pork or blood, but otherwise they ignore our dietary laws. (Here in the East they commonly enjoy the meat of camels.)

Babylonian Jews saw Moslems, pious Moslems, leading a life which seemed not only easier than Jewish life but perhaps even more sensible as, under the geonim, Judaism grew increasingly rigorous and legalistic. Starting with the biblical prohibition against seething a kid in its mother's milk, the rabbis produced tomes of complex injunctions relating to chickens (which have no milk) and to cooking utensils. The commandment to honor the Sabbath and observe it as a day of rest from work led rabbis to spend lifetimes debating about how far from home a man might walk on the Sabbath and how much "work" was involved in wearing a false tooth or carrying a baby. The scriptural ban against lending money at interest within the Jewish community caused the rabbis to forbid partnerships, profit-sharing, and many other arrangements between a lender and a borrower.[6] Jews saw pious Moslems studying their Koran, which they considered to be the Word of God, and drawing from it their code for religious life; so why could not Jews practice from Torah directly?

Because, responded the geonim, every man could not possibly give a valid interpretation to each Torah text. The rabbis explained that if each man were to interpret the Torah for himself, not only would some individuals err in ritual observance and commercial behavior but—at least as dangerous— the differences of opinion would shatter the Jewish world. The Law that God gave Moses had descended through generation after generation of interpreters (that is, the rabbis) right through to the geonim, who currently held the authority to rule, to tax, and to judge the Jews. What the geonim determined, that was the Jewish Law, no getting away from it.

Jews were obliged to follow the dictates of the geonim under penalty of flogging or even excommunication. Locally, as a last resort to have their decisions enforced, the geonim might call on Moslem officials. Outside the Moslem world, naturally, the geonim had no such sanctions, but in Europe, too, a Jewish community, for lack of any other authority, would consider a gaonic decision as binding. Geonim insisted on their supremacy, collective and individual. Commonly a gaon, in writing his answering letters or responsa to questioning communities, demanded that their future queries (and financial contributions) be directed to himself or to the yeshiva led by him.[7]

Although the geonim were insisting on the unique authority of their interpretations to avoid dividing the Jewish world, the very competition among geonim resulted in splits in Jewish communities. Whenever individuals in a community differed on a point which had been questioned (and it was this difference which occasioned the request for a judgment), or whenever they disagreed with the judgment of the gaon, these individuals stayed away from the synagogue, and this on religious grounds, for it was regarded as unlawful to say a prayer when led by an unworthy person.[8]

All this pettifogging and feuding served to push some Jews from the rabbis' fold—after all, how "right" could the Jewish Law be, if rabbis could interpret it in so many different ways?[9] To free themselves from rabbinical authority, some Jews simply converted to Islam. Other Jews in Babylonia wanted to practice a Judaism without rabbinic authority; a large group of these were the original Karaites, who made it their earliest principle that every man should study the Bible and interpret it for himself.

I have already written you quite a bit about the Karaites, who are still a major force in all the world eastward from the Greek lands. Just as Islam spread quickly during the seventh century, Jewish Karaism spread quickly during the ninth, and it spread through the lands of the Moslems. By the start of the tenth century, it posed a real threat to traditional rabbinic Judaism.

Saadia ben Joseph, then a young rabbi in Egypt, addressed that problem by writing a book against Karaism's founder, Anan. Egypt's Karaites forced Saadia to flee the country, and after several years of travel he settled in Babylonia. He soon established himself here, by providing the geonim with the astrological information they needed to win the calendar battle against ben Meir. Saadia continued to give evidence of his brilliance. Although he was a foreigner and of humble family, when the gaonate of Sura fell vacant in 928, six years after the Ben Meir retreat, Saadia was named gaon.

He was very clear about what, how, and why he wanted to teach. At the start of his *Book of Beliefs* he wrote:

> I saw . . . men sunk, as it were, in seas of doubt and overwhelmed by waves of confusion, and there was no diver to bring them up from the depths nor a swimmer who might take hold of their hands and carry them ashore. But inasmuch as my Lord had granted me some knowledge by which I might come to their assistance and had endowed me with some ability that I could put at their disposal for their benefit, I thought that it was my duty to help them therewith and my obligation to direct them to the truth.[10]
>
> . . . . I implore any learned man who may read this book and find in it some mistake, to correct it. . . .
>
> . . . . I further implore . . . all those of my readers who strive after wisdom to read this book with an open mind, to try honestly to see my point of view, and to clear their minds of obstinacy, hasty judgment, and confused thinking so that they may derive from it the maximum of profit and advantage. . . .[11]

Moving from his general introduction into his argument for reason in faith:

> Some think that a Jew is forbidden to speculate or philosophize about the truths of religion. This is not so. Genuine and sincere reflection and speculation is not prohibited. What is forbidden is to leave the sacred writings aside and rely on any opinions that occur to one concerning the beginnings of time and space. For one may find the truth or one may miss it. . . .
>
> Our investigation of the facts of our religion will give us a reasoned and scientific knowledge of those things which the Prophets taught us dogmatically, and will enable us to answer the arguments and criticisms of our opponents directed against our faith. Hence it is not merely our privilege but our duty to confirm the truths of religion by reason.[12]

In his dedication to building rabbinic Judaism a bulwark against the Karaite tides, Saadia also set about translating the Bible into Arabic. There had been no Bible in Arabic, the vernacular of the Karaites; Karaite scholars had developed their whole religious system around each man's studying the Bible, yet only with Saadia's translation could every Karaite read it. Perhaps even scholars could better comprehend Scripture in their mother tongue.

To his translation Saadia added a commentary, persuasive in its arguments for the validity of Oral Law. He published an edition of the Hebrew prayer-book, with Arabic annotations on laws and customs. He wrote all his work in Arabic, even a Hebrew grammar explaining Hebrew's difficult words and phrases. They say it is thanks to Saadia's work that the tide of Karaism receded.

Given the appreciation that the leading rabbis had shown for Saadia's intellectual gifts before they named him gaon, you'd think that they would have allowed him some time of calm to proceed with his important writing in their behalf. But Saadia was to gain his quiet years in a rather different manner. . . .

Both gaon and exilarch were judges. The first duties of the exilarch were those of a chief justice: judging civil and criminal cases, and appointing judges and other administrative officers. A gaon, as scholar, was responsible for the judgments over religious matters, while the more secular exilarch was responsible for the judgments over all other matters. But since our Jewish civil law is included within the religious code—that is, besides religion there are no "other matters"—inevitably exilarch and gaon fought over who held responsibility over what.

Saadia had become gaon of Sura with the favor of the exilarch in Baghdad, R. David ben Zakkai. In his first two years in office Saadia Gaon had shown himself to be incorruptible. Then, in the year 930, the exilarch decided a case in a way that would have brought him (the exilarch) a tenth part of the great sum at issue. The implementation of this decree, as of every legal decision, required endorsement by the two geonim of Sura and Pumbeditha. Saadia Gaon would not sign; he knew the decision to be illegal, for every judge is forbidden to decide any case in which he has an interest.[13] The exilarch was angered by Saadia's inflexibility; more than that, he was furious that one of his own appointees would dare to contradict him. He threatened Saadia with deposition, but Saadia still refused to sign. Babylonia's Jewish community split into a faction supporting the exilarch (led by the exilarch's courtiers and the gaon of Pumbeditha) and a faction supporting Saadia Gaon (composed of scholars and community leaders). Eventually the exilarch did depose Saadia, who was to spend the next five years living in a kind of exile in Baghdad . . . and writing.

The exilarch appointed another man as gaon of Sura. Saadia, as the rightful gaon, excommunicated R. David ben Zakkai and named another man as exilarch in his stead. This leadership-contest between two Sura geonim and two exilarchs exasperated the community. Leading Jews, driven mostly by their respect for Saadia, strove to end the hostilities, finally bringing about a reconciliation between Saadia and David ben Zakkai on Purim 937. They reinstated Saadia, who returned to Sura. He spent five more years here as gaon, until he died at age fifty.

Saadia was one of the greatest sages of all time, yet as it behooved every rabbi to advance the knowledge of the Law, even the lesser geonim and their disciples wrote learned treatises on particular laws and compiled legal codes. Many of these writings developed from discourses of scholars to students. To use the proper terminology, they called a lecturer *haver*, which meant a member of the yeshiva at Sura or Pumbeditha, while *rabbi* or *rav* meant a prominent scholar qualified to give legal opinions; students were known as "sons of a master," for they needed the guidance of a teacher.

Its position at the pinnacle of legal scholarship made Sura a Jewish capital city, which like any capital city lived on tribute from its subjects. Nonetheless most of the men of Sura spent part of each working day in remunerative employment. They worked as merchants or as artisans or especially as farmers, since this region is very fertile. Irrigated with water from the Euphrates, it produces rich yields of barley, wheat, and fruit, including grapes for a flourishing wine industry. The Jews around Sura made the wine and traded in it, and raised cattle.[14]

As anywhere, few of the men here were scholars. Most knew just the Pentateuch and the basic rules of kashrut, Shabbat, and the festivals. Those men who were pious or haverim knew all of the Bible and the religious and civil law as put forth in the codes. The furthest advanced in learning were the "members of the academy," or doctors of the law, who knew the Mishnah and the Talmud and the commentaries on them; only these doctors of the law had the authority to issue legal opinions or could be sent as judges to other cities.

Twice every year, in the month of Elul at the end of summer and the month of Adar at the end of winter, students, haverim, geonim, everyone would come together at the academies for a period of study, the kallah. The students would query their teachers about the texts (from Bible or codified law) which they had been studying at home during the preceding five months. They posed many hypothetical questions, the "what-ifs" that occurred to them when reading an assigned text. Students and teachers would discuss the texts and questions at length, and would attend lectures. At the end of the kallah the teachers would assign other texts to study during the coming months. The texts and lectures dealt not only with matters of observance but with any matter covered by the Law, that is, any part of life.

The instruction of the kallah enabled ordinary men, working at ordinary occupations, to qualify as judges. As Jewish communities throughout the world addressed the geonim with myriad uncertainties about religious observance and about relationships between people, each academy needed many judges for its *beth din*, or court. Every case, no matter how small, was considered by three judges, who didn't need to be scholarly but rather able to apply the law to the infinite variety of life's situations. The senior judges long debated whether an ordinary judge should refer to the text of Torah in explaining his decisions, but they eventually agreed that a judge's decision would be less open to dispute if he justified it by the opinions of earlier judges. Especially at the kallah in the month of Adar at the end of winter, the geonim would present queries sent from abroad. To some of the more complicated questions, the geonim themselves sat in judgment, and their answers to these often became the basis of further ordinances or codes.

Customarily the answers and decrees would be dispatched every year at the end of Passover, with merchants leaving Baghdad. Equivalent to rulers' proclamations, circulated through the Jewish world, the responsa served to strengthen the dispersed Jews' feeling of nationhood. In this way the Law went forth from Sura, during several centuries, until about 130 years ago when the academies moved to Baghdad and the authority moved to southern Spain.[15]

Letter from Pumbeditha

From Sura **two days to SHAFJATHIB, site of a synagogue which the Israelites erected with earth and stones** they had **brought** with them **from Jerusalem and which they called "the transplanted of Nehardea."** Nehardea's inhabitants were mostly Jews, and during the centuries of Roman rule the city of Nehardea was the prosperous center of Jewish life in Babylonia and the seat of a great academy. Situated near the place of the present Shafjathib on the Euphrates between Sura and Pumbeditha, Nehardea was razed by the Persians about 260 C.E. in one of their wars against the Romans.[1]

$$< < \quad < < \qquad\qquad > > \quad > >$$

From thence, a day and a half to El Jubar, or PUMBEDITHA ON THE EUPHRATES, where Jews have lived since the days of the Second Temple and **which** today **contains about three thousand Jews.**

Here are **the synagogues, sepulchers and colleges of Rab and Samuel.** These two, natives of this region and close friends, lived in the generation after Judah ha-Nasi just a thousand years ago, in the time when rabbis were *Rabbis.* Samuel became the head of the academy already established at Nehardea. He was a scholar not only of Torah but also of medicine and astronomy: he once boasted that he knew the paths of heaven as well as the streets of Nehardea.[2] Like some other learned scholars he devised a perpetual calendar, although he never released it because back in those days calendars were the domain of the academy in Palestine.

Rab, from boyhood more of a religious scholar, journeyed to Palestine and studied there with Judah ha-Nasi; he returned to Babylonia and worked as a merchant, prospered, and with his earnings he set up his own academy at Sura. It was then that he became known as "Rab," meaning "Master," and many were the students who appreciated his greatness and spoke of going to study at "the Master's house"—which is why that term was used as a name for the academy at Sura and why it is used to designate any house of study even today.[3]

Nehardea perished just a few years after the death of R. Samuel, but then rose the academy here at Pumbeditha. Sura served the south of Babylonia, Pumbeditha the north. Although Pumbeditha's academy was to last for eight hundred years, and although it had its great scholars and its great moments, Pumbeditha was always considered secondary to Sura: it was thought that

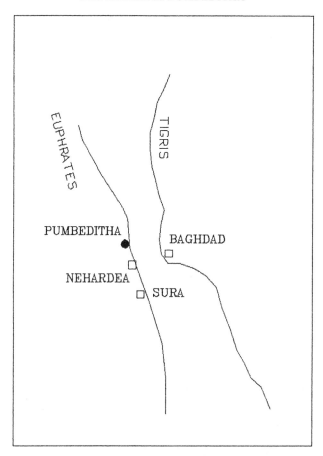

Pumbeditha, being a commercial center, offered scholars too many distractions from learning Torah and too many temptations from living Torah. Talmudists elsewhere looked down on Pumbeditha as materialist and dishonest, opinions which they wrote into Talmudic texts.

The Jews of Pumbeditha, going about their business (commercial and scholarly) would respond by quoting Rabbi Akiba: "Live not in a city whose heads are scholars!"[4]

For several centuries Sura and Pumbeditha shared the scarcely disputed leadership of world Jewry. When the new Mohammedan religion came to Babylonia, it built up the city of Baghdad and it stimulated Jewish heretics and sects who questioned the rabbis' authority. All the while the geonim continued to study and to teach Torah, to issue responsa, and to collect funds from the communities of the Exile. The Jews lived undisturbed in their dhimmi autonomy under the khalifs who ruled over an immense empire; doubtless it seemed appropriate to the khalifs that the Jews of the world also looked to Babylonia as their capital. Baghdad flourished, and Jews shared in its prosperity; the khalifs grew pompous and autocratic, and the Jewish leaders emulated them.[5]

The local Jewish leaders striving to be potentates, as reflected in the continual conflicts between the exilarch and the geonim—that was the poison leading to the death of the Babylonian hegemony. Meanwhile, those Jews who sought independence from gaonic rule were suppressed, most effectively by Saadia Gaon, who from Sura impugned both benMeir and the Karaites and wrote strong defenses of rabbinic authority. But R. Saadia turned out to be the last of the great geonim of Sura. After him, such greatness as remained in the gaonate issued from here in Pumbeditha, the academy-city with commercial interests.

In the generation after R. Saadia, Pumbeditha's gaon was R. Sherira, a descendant of the House of David and a great authority on Jewish history. When he was ninety-eight years old he appointed his son, R. Hai, to share the office of gaon with him. R. Sherira and R. Hai attracted many scholars from throughout the Jewish world, and vast sums in donations as well. This resurgent activity at Pumbeditha came to the ears of the khalif, frightening him; he had both rabbis arrested and briefly imprisoned. The experience further weakened the frail R. Sherira, who died at the age of one hundred.

R. Sherira and R. Hai were so highly respected and so beloved that at the Sabbath service just after R. Sherira's death the congregation paid them a singular honor. The worshipers read aloud from the First Book of Kings about the last days of King David, and when they reached the verse "And Solomon sat upon the throne of David his father . . ." they lovingly substituted "And Hai sat upon the throne of Sherira his father, and his kingdom was firmly established."[6]

Hai Gaon was to prove worthy of their honor. During his forty years in the office, he wrote over a thousand responsa, collecting his information from his Christian and Moslem friends as well as from Jewish sources.[7] He compiled a lexicon; he wrote a commentary on the Talmud which is used in the Italian yeshivot as well as in the Spanish.[8] He made one ruling bemoaned by our schoolboys: that the Spanish communities must continue to teach the Aramaic translation of the Torah, as its use goes back a thousand years.[9] Hai Gaon himself was fluent in Hebrew, Aramaic, Greek, Persian, and Arabic; he did all his writing in the last of these.[10] He was also a poet, and in Spain we recite one of his poems, the "Sh'ma koli asher yishma bekoloth," on the eve of Yom Kippur.[11] Probably the most significant of his decisions—did he realize that he himself would be the last of the Babylonian geonim?—was that in case of conflict between the Babylonian Talmud and the Palestinian Talmud, the Babylonian was to rule.

Hai Gaon died, aged ninety-nine, in 1038. The news would have reached

Saragossa, where young Solomon ibn Gabirol was composing his poems, at about the same time that his patron Yekutiel was jailed and executed. Solomon wrote:

> Weep, my people, put on cord and sackcloth,
> Break all the instruments of music and song,
> For Rab Hai, our master, the last remnant
> Left to us in the world, has gone.
> What shall we bemoan and lament first of all,
> And for what shall we first grieve and mourn?
> For the ark which now lies hidden in Zion,
> Or for Rab Hai, buried in Babylon?[12]

Deprived of their academies and their glory, the Babylonian cities needed other pursuits. In Pumbeditha the shift was easy, for Pumbeditha had always provided alternative occupations to scholarship, employing Jews as artisans, vintners, and farmers.[13] Jewish families have long been the owners of most of the region's olive presses.[14] Traditionally too Jews here have been active in trade. Since ancient times the principal trade route between Persia and the Great Sea has passed near Pumbeditha, causing local commerce to flourish, in the same way that Pamplona has thrived because of the route to Santiago. Pumbeditha's canal is the northernmost of several canals between the Euphrates and the Tigris. Apart from its advantageous commercial situation, Pumbeditha enjoys a pleasant climate and plentiful water, which facilitate cultivation of the land. Crops of all sorts abound, the principal fruit being dates and the principal textile crop being flax.

Silk is the cloth of kings; wool is the main cloth of the Holy Land; ordinary people in hot countries wear linen made from flax. Jews have prospered in Babylonia since biblical times by applying their skills to flax and linen.

If the producer wants his flax for good-quality linen, he can't just sow it haphazardly. Flax seeds sparsely planted will yield flax plants with good seeds but inferior fiber; to get a fine fiber for making thread, he must sow the flax seeds very densely. The flax sown for fiber must be harvested before the seeds are ripe, otherwise the plant will become too woody. Flax must be harvested in a particular way, pulling it from the ground by its roots, as has been done since ancient times: the workman seizes several stalks with one hand, removes them from the soil by pulling upward, and transfers the stalks to the other hand very carefully so that the stalks are parallel and the root ends even. He piles the stalks, in shocks, in the fields until they are dry.

The worker in the fields delivers his bundles of dried flax stalks to a farmworker at a bench on which a comb is mounted. This worker draws the stalks through the comb to remove the seeds. The task of the next farmworker is to immerse the stalks in water so that the flax fiber will separate from the woody core of the plant. Along the banks of the Euphrates large bales of flax stalks are dipped into the water, the farmworker using poles to restrict the movement of the bales in the current. Nor can the bales of stalks simply be left to soak in the water; they must be turned. The crucial decision at this stage is when to remove the bales of stalks with their fiber loosened from their core before the fiber disintegrates. The loosening process can take a week or two or three—it depends on the conditions of the soil in which the plants were grown and on the water's temperature and current: the loosening goes faster in warm, clear water than in cold water or water with greenery or discarded matter in it. Drying the stalks, again by setting them in open shocks, is the final task of the farmer.

The next steps of flax preparation are performed by the flax workers. First they beat the stalks with mallets to break up their wooden parts. Then, having laid the stalks over the edge of a bench, they rasp them with a knife to dislodge the brittle woody particles and separate them from the loosened fibers. The workers go through this rasping process a second time, to remove the last woody bits. The fibers are still attached to one another and cannot be spun, but the wastes of raw flax at this stage can be spun and are sometimes made into sackcloth.

The next and last stage of fiber preparation is particularly delicate, for on it especially depends the quality of the yarn. A skilled flax worker uses combs to disentangle the fibers, taking extreme care that they not break while they separate from one another. The combing creates a lot of dust. Flax combs are actually circles of wooden teeth set into boards. The first step of this combing process uses large teeth, the second step slightly smaller teeth, and so through a few combings until the final one with very fine teeth. And then the flax fiber is ready to be spun.

Fibers combed just two or three times before being spun will produce a cloth for bedclothes or underclothes; fibers combed several times and finally with the finest combs will be used for luxury cloths.[15]

In consequence of these numerous procedures and the variations possible at each stage, each piece of finished linen cloth may be quite different from others, less smooth or fine, more durable or lustrous. When a Babylonian Jew takes his chosen yarn (that is, the spun fibers) to the weaver to have a garment made, he always takes slightly more than he thinks will be required because he knows that afterward it would be next to impossible to match any yarn.[16] Most of us, at one time or another, have had trouble matching a yarn or a cloth—and now I appreciate why.

Letter from the frontier of Khuzestan

Travelers tell me that from Mesopotamia southward **twenty-one days journey through the desert of Sheba or al-Yemen one finds the abodes of the Jews who are called B'nai Rekhab, men of Thema.**

The seat of the government is at Thema or Tehama. This city is large and the extent of their country is sixteen days journey toward the northern mountain range. They possess large and strong cities and are not subject to any of the Gentiles, but undertake warlike expeditions into distant provinces with the Arabians, their neighbors and allies, "to take the spoil and to take the prey." These Arabians are Bedouin, who live in tents in the deserts and have no fixed abode, and who are in the habit of undertaking marauding expeditions in the province of Yemen. The Jews are a terror to their neighbors.

Their country being very extensive, some of them cultivate the land and rear cattle. A number of studious and learned men, who spend their lives in the study of the Law, are maintained by the tithes of all produce, part of which is also employed towards sustaining the poor and the ascetics, who are called "mourners of Jerusalem." These eat no meat and abstain from wine, they dress always in black, live in caves or in low houses, and keep fasts all their lives except on Sabbaths and Holy-days, as the Talmud prohibits fasts on those days. **They continually implore the mercy of God for the Jews in Exile and devoutly pray that He may have compassion on them for the sake of His own great Name, and they also include in their prayers all the Jews of Tehama and of Telmas.**

The latter contains about one hundred thousand Jews, who are governed by Prince Sal'mon who is descendant of the royal House of David, who rests in peace, which is proved by his pedigree. In doubtful cases they solicit the decisions of the Prince of the Captivity, and set aside forty days of every year during which they go in rent clothes and keep fasts and pray for all the Jews who live in Exile.

The province of which Thanaejm is the metropolis contains forty cities and two hundred villages and one hundred small towns and is inhabited by about three hundred thousand Jews. Thanaejm is a very strong city, being fifteen square miles in extent and large enough to allow agriculture to be carried on within its boundaries; within which are also situated the palace of the prince Sal'mon and many gardens and orchards.

Telmas is also a city of considerable magnitude; it contains about one hun-

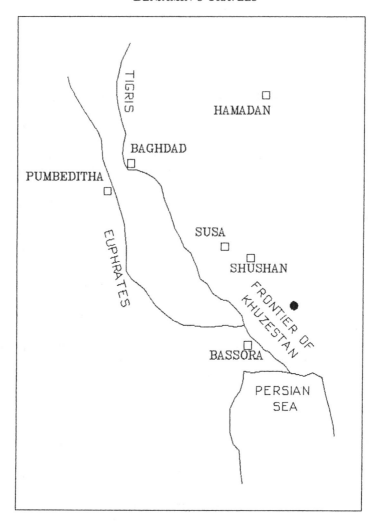

dred thousand Jews, is strongly fortified and situated between two very high mountains. Many of its inhabitants are well-informed, wise and rich.

It is reported that these Jews are of the tribes of Reuben, Gad, and half the tribe of Manasseh, who were led away captives by Shalmanesser, King of Ashur; and who repaired into these mountainous regions, where they erected the above-mentioned large and strong cities. They carry on war with many kingdoms and are not easily to be reached because of their situation, which requires a march of eighteen days through uninhabited deserts and thus renders them difficult of access.

The distance from Telmas to Chaibar is three days journey. Chaibar is also a very large city and contains among its fifty thousand Jewish inhabitants many learned scholars. The people of this city are valiant and engaged in wars with the inhabitants of Mesopotamia, with those of the northern districts and with those of Yemen, who live near them; the latter province borders on India.

Basra or **BASSORA ON THE TIGRIS**, where the Tigris and the Euphrates empty into the Indian Sea (Persian Gulf). This city, a creation of the Moham-medans and surrounded by large groves of date palms, is a major port with merchants coming from the Great Sea in the west and from China in the east, and **with two thousand Israelites, many of whom are learned and wealthy.**

Two days to a place on the River Samarra or Shat-el-Arab **which is the frontier of Persia and contains fifteen hundred Jews.**

The sepulcher of Ezra the priest and scribe is in this place, where he died on his journey from Jerusalem to King Artaxerxes. In front of the sepulcher a large synagogue and a Mohammedan mosque have been erected, the latter as a mark of the veneration in which Ezra is held by the Mohammedans, who are very friendly towards the Jews and resort thither to pray.

Four miles from thence begins KHUZESTAN, Elam of Scripture, a large province, which however is but partially inhabited, a portion of it lying in ruins. Among its ruins are the remains of SHUSHAN, the metropolis and palace of King Achashverosh, which still contains very large and handsome buildings of ancient date. Its seven thousand Jewish inhabitants possess four-teen synagogues, in front of one of which is the sepulcher of Daniel who rests in peace. Daniel built his synagogue near Babylon but retired here.

The River Ulai divides the parts of the city, which are connected by a bridge. That portion of the city which is inhabited by the Jews contains the markets; to that quarter all trade is confined and there dwell all the rich. On the other side of the river the people are poor, because they are deprived of the above-mentioned advantages and even lack gardens and orchards.

The poor were jealous, and believed **that all honor and riches** pertaining to those on the other side of the bridge **originated from the** prosperous quarter's **possession of the remains of the prophet Daniel. A request was made by the poor to move the sepulchers to the other side,** to the poor quarter, **but it was rejected; upon which a war arose and was carried on between the two parties for some time. The strife lasted until "their souls became loath" and they came to a mutual agreement that the coffin which contained Daniel's bones should rest one year on one side of the river and alternate years on the other side.**

Both parties faithfully adhered to this arrangement, until it was interrupted by the interference of Sanjar Shah ben Shah, who governs all Persia and holds

supreme power over forty-five of its kings. This prince is called in Arabic "sultan al-fars al-khabir" ("supreme commander of Persia") and his empire extends from the banks of the Shat-el-Arab unto the city of Samarkand and the Kizil Ozein, encloses the city of Nishapur, the cities of Media, and the Chaphton mountains, and reaches as far as Tibet, in the forests of which country that quadruped is met with, which yields the musk; the extent of his empire is four months and four days journey.

When this great emperor, Sanjar King of Persia, came to Shushan and saw that the coffin of Daniel was removed from side to side, he crossed the bridge with a very numerous retinue and inquired into the reason for those proceedings. Upon being told what we have related above, he declared that it was derogatory to the honor of Daniel and commanded that the distance between the two banks should be exactly measured, that Daniel's coffin should be deposited in another coffin, made of glass, and that it should be suspended from the very middle of the bridge, fastened by chains of iron.

A place of public worship was erected on the very spot, open to every one who desired to say his prayers, whether he be Jew or Gentile; and the coffin of Daniel is suspended from the bridge unto this very day. The king commanded that in honor of Daniel nobody should be allowed to fish in the river, one mile on each side of the coffin.

< <   < <   > >   > >

Now I shall tell you about events which were first recounted to me in Baghdad and since then many times. But I had much to write from Babylonia, in any case it is fitting that I write this to you from here at the entrance to Persia.

Many days journey northward through Persia, toward the kingdom of the Khazars, lived Jews suffering under their khalif. This followed upon the Franks' conquest of the Holy Land, which made all the khalifs of the world fearful of the Christians. As remote from Palestine as they were, these Jews—like many others—hoped that the massacres augured the coming of the Messiah.

At Mosul about fifteen years ago there arose a good-looking man named Menachem ben Solomon—though he called himself by the name of David el-Roy because it suited his purposes to indicate descent from the House of David: David el-Roy of the city of Amaria, who had studied under the Prince ' of the Captivity Hisdai and under Eli the President of the College of Gaon Jacob in the city of Baghdad. David el-Roy became an excellent scholar, being well versed in Mosaic law, in the decisions of the rabbis, and in the Talmud; he understood also the profane sciences, the language and the writings of the Mohammedans, and the scriptures of the magicians and enchanters. He made up his mind to rise in rebellion against the King of Persia, to unite the Jews who live in the mountains of Chaphton and with them to engage in war against all Gentiles, making the conquest of Jerusalem his final object.

To the Jews of Baghdad he gave signs by false miracles and assured them: "The Lord has sent me to conquer Jerusalem and to deliver you from the yoke of the Gentiles." In a letter he promised to transport Baghdad's Jews to Jerusalem, by night on the wings of angels. Some of the Jews did believe in him and called him "Messiah," but those who stayed up all night awaiting the angels were very embarrassed. When the King of Persia became acquainted with these circumstances, he sent and summoned David into his presence. The latter went without fear and when they met he was asked: "Art thou the King of the Jews?" to which he answered "I am!" Thereupon the king immediately commanded that David should be secured and put into prison in that place, situated in the city of Dabaristan, on the banks of the Kizil Ozein, which is a broad river.

After a lapse of three days, when the king sat in council to take the advice of his nobles and officers respecting the Jews, who had rebelled against his authority, David appeared among them, having liberated himself from prison without the aid of anyone. On beholding David the king inquired: "Who brought thee hither or who has set thee at liberty?" To which David answered: "My own wisdom and subtlety, for in truth I neither fear thee nor all thy servants."

The king immediately commanded that David should be made captive, but his courtiers answered: "We see him not, we are aware of his presence only by hearing the sound of his voice." The king was very much astonished at the exceeding wisdom of David, who thus addressed him: "I now go my way!" and he went out followed by the king and all his nobles and servants to the banks of the river, where he took his shawl, spread it upon the water and crossed it thereupon. At that moment he became visible and all the servants of the king saw him cross the river on his shawl; they took boats and pursued him but without success, and they all confessed that no magician on earth could equal him. He must have known the mystery (known to very few) of the Tetragrammaton, so that by the help of God's Name he performed these feats. That very day David traveled to his home town of Amaria and related to the astonished Jews all that had happened to him.

This King of Persia afterwards sent to the Emir of Mumenin, the Khalif of Baghdad, principal of the Mohammedans, to solicit the influence of the Prince of the Captivity and of the presidents of the colleges in order to check the activities of David el-Roy. The Exilarch Hisdai in Baghdad and the Prince Zakkai in Mosul were already furious that David el-Roy, by using that name, had mocked the princes of the House of David. And now, because of David el-Roy, the khalif of Persia threatened to put to death all Jews who inhabited his empire, and in fact dealt very severely with the Jewish congregations of Persia, whose leaders sent letters to the Prince of the Captivity and the presidents of the colleges at Baghdad demanding: "Why will you allow us and all the Jews of this empire to die? Restrain the deeds of this man and prevent thereby the shedding of innocent blood."

The Prince of the Captivity and the presidents of the colleges thereupon addressed David in letters which run thus: "Be it known unto thee that the time of our redemption has not yet arrived and that we have not seen the signs by which it is to manifest itself, and that by strength no man shall prevail. We therefore command thee to discontinue the course that thou hast adopted, on pain of being excommunicated from all Israel."

Copies of these letters were sent to Zakkai, Prince of the Jews in Mosul, and to R. Joseph the astronomer who also resides there, with the request to forward them to David el-Roy. The last-mentioned prince and the astronomer added letters of their own, in which they exhorted David: but he nevertheless continued in his criminal career.

This he carried on until a certain prince of the name of Sin-el-din, a vassal of the king of Persia and a Turk by birth, cut it short by sending for the father-in-law of David el-Roy, to whom he offered ten thousand florins if he would secretly kill David el-Roy. This agreement being concluded, he went to David's house while he slept and killed him on his bed, thus destroying his plans and evil designs. Notwithstanding this, the wrath of the king of Persia still continued against the Jews, who lived in the mountains and in his country, who in their turn craved the influence of the Prince of the Captivity with the king of Persia. Their petitions and humble prayers were supported by a present of one hundred talents of gold, in consideration of which the anger of the king of Persia was subdued and the land was tranquillized.

< <   < <   > >   > >

From Shushan, **HAMADAN is a journey of ten days** northward across Persia. A thriving commercial center, Hamadan has buildings of clay and a wall with four gates of iron. All around are orchards and gardens. It is situated beautifully, and in summer the Persian king dwells there.

In the time of our forefathers, Hamadan **was the metropolis of Media.** It had a Jewish community then, and now the city **contains about fifty thousand Jews** and a yeshiva directed from Baghdad. **In front of one of the synagogues** in the center of the city **is the sepulcher of Mordechai and Esther.**

< <   < <   > >   > >

I returned to the country of Khuzestan, which lies on the Tigris. This river runs downward and falls into the Indian Sea (Persian Gulf) in the vicinity of an island called KISH. The extent of this island is six miles and the inhabitants do not carry on any agriculture principally because they have no rivers, nor more than one spring in the whole island, and are consequently obliged to drink rain water.

It is however a considerable market, being the point to which the Indian merchants and those of the islands bring their commodities; while the traders of Mesopotamia, Yemen and Persia import all sorts of silk and purple cloths, flax, cotton, hemp, mash (which is a sort of pea), wheat, barley, millet, rye, and all other sorts of comestibles and pulse, which articles they exchange. Those from India import great quantities of spices, and the inhabitants of the island live by what they gain in their capacity of brokers to both parties.

The island contains about five hundred Jews.

Letter from El-Cathif

From the Tigris almost to the Nile without any halt, a long sea voyage. Now I appreciate why Judah ha-Levi wrote as he did, on his approach to Egypt, something like this:

> Call greetings to my daughters and kinsmen, to my brothers and sisters,
> From this prisoner of hope who is possessed by the sea. . . .
> . . . .
> Between him and death lies nothing but a step;
> Aye, between them nothing but the thickness of a plank.
> He is buried alive in a coffin of wood.
> No floor under him—just earth, and not even enough space there for a
>   proper grave.
> On that earth he sits . . . for there's no room for him to stand;
> He lies down . . . but he cannot extend his legs.
> He is sick. He is afraid of the Gentile passengers,
> And of pirates, and of the winds.
> The helmsman and the sailors, come from the rabble—
> They rule as captains and governors here!
> Here benefit accrues neither to the wise man nor to the craftsman,
> But only to those who know how to swim!
> I am troubled by this for a moment
> (How can my heart exult?)
> But only for a moment,
> Until I pour out my soul into the bosom of God,
> Before the place of the Ark and the altars,
> And bestow upon God, who bestows good things upon the unworthy,
> The best of my songs and praise.[1]

< <   < <   > >   > >

On board ship we have little to do except regale each other with stories, mostly of distant places.

To the east is a country called **Chulam, on the confines of the country of the sun-worshipers,** of which the inhabitants **are descendants of Khush, are addicted to astrology and are all black.**

This nation is very trustworthy in matters of trade and whenever foreign merchants enter their port, three secretaries of the king immediately repair on board their vessels, write down their names, and report them to him. The king thereupon grants them security for their property, which they may even leave in the open fields without any guard.

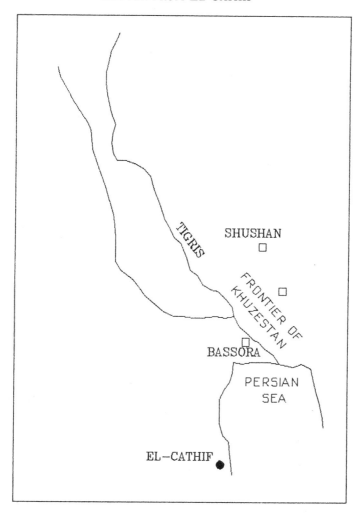

One of the king's officers sits in the market and receives goods that may have been found anywhere, which he returns to those applicants who can minutely describe them. This custom is observed in the whole empire of the king.

From Easter to Rosh ha-Shanah, during the whole of the summer the heat is extreme. From the third hour of the day (nine o'clock in the morning) people shut themselves up in their houses until the evening, at which time everybody goes out. The streets and markets are lighted up and the inhabitants spend all the night in their business, which they are prevented from doing in the day time, in consequence of the excessive heat.

The pepper grows in this country. The trees which bear this fruit are planted in the fields which surround the towns, and every one knows his plantation.

The trees are small and the pepper is originally white, but when they collect it they put it into basins and pour hot water upon it; it is then exposed to the heat of the sun and dried in order to make it hard and more substantial, in the course of which process it becomes of a black color.

Cinnamon, ginger, and many other kinds of spices also grow in this country.

The inhabitants do not bury their dead but embalm them with certain spices, put them upon stools and cover them with cloths, every family keeping apart. The flesh dries upon the bones and, as these corpses resemble living beings, every one of them recognizes his parents and all the members of his family for many years to come.

These people worship the sun. About half a mile from every town they have large places of worship and every morning they run towards the rising sun. Every place of worship contains a representation of that luminary, so constructed by witchcraft that upon the rising of the sun it turns round with a great noise, at which moments both men and women take up their censers and burn incense in honor of this their deity. "This their way is their folly."

All the cities and countries inhabited by these people contain only about one hundred Jews, who are of black color as well as the other inhabitants. The Jews are good men, observers of the Law, and they possess the Pentateuch, the Prophets, and some little knowledge of the Talmud and its decisions.

Farther to the east is the island of **Khandy** (Ceylon), of which **the inhabitants are fire-worshipers called Druzes; twenty-three thousand Jews live among them.** These people are spoken of in Baghdad too, whence they go to trade.[2] These Druzes have priests everywhere in the houses consecrated to their idols, and those priests are expert necromancers, the like of whom are to be met with nowhere else.

In front of the altar of their house of prayer, you see a deep ditch, in which a large fire is continually kept burning: this they call Elahuta, deity. They pass their children through it and into this ditch they also throw their dead.

Some of the great of this country take a vow to burn themselves alive; and if any such devotee declares to his children and kindred his intention to do so, they all applaud him and say: "Happy shalt thou be, and it shall be well with thee." Whenever the appointed day arrives, they prepare a sumptuous feast, mount the devotee upon his horse if he be rich or lead him afoot if he be poor, to the brink of the ditch. He throws himself into the fire and all his kindred manifest their joy by the playing of instruments until he is entirely consumed.

Within three days of this ceremony two of the principal priests repair to his house and thus address his children: "Prepare the house, for today you will be visited by your father, who will manifest his wishes unto you." Witnesses are selected among the inhabitants of the town and lo! the devil appears in the image of the dead. The wife and children inquire after his state in the other world and he answers: "I have met my companions, but they have not admitted me into their company, before I have discharged my debts to my friends and neighbors." He then makes a will, divides his goods among his children, and commands them to discharge all debts he owes and to receive what people owe him. This will is written down by the witnesses, who then allow the departed to go his way, and he is not seen any more.

In consequence of these lies and deceit, which the priests pass off as magic, they retain a strong hold upon the people and make them believe that their equal is not to be met with upon earth.

From thence the passage to China[3] is effected in forty days. This country lies eastward and some say that the star Orion predominates in the sea which bounds it, and which is called Sea of Nikpha. Sometimes so violent a storm rages in this sea that no mariner can reach his vessel, and whenever the storm throws a ship into this sea, it is impossible to govern it, the crew and the passengers consume their provisions and then die miserably.

Many vessels have been lost in this way, but people have learned how to save themselves from this fate by the following contrivance: they take bullocks' hides along with them and whenever this storm arises and throws them into the Sea of Nikpha, they sew themselves up in the hides, taking care to have a knife in their hand, and being secured against the sea water, they throw themselves into the ocean. Here they are soon perceived by a large eagle called griffin, which takes them for cattle, darts down, takes them in his grip and carries them upon dry land, where he deposits his burden on a hill or in a dale, there to consume his prey. The man, however, now avails himself of his knife therewith to kill the bird, creeps forth from the hide and tries to reach an inhabited country. Many people have been saved by this stratagem.

Being myself still inexperienced in the use of such antidotes against the hazards of traveling, and likewise unskilled in the telling of travelers' tales, when it is my turn to speak I like to quote poetry, especially poems of Jews with which my Gentile co-passengers are unfamiliar.

I told them of Solomon ibn Gabirol, and that he spent his youth in the town next to mine, observing his patron's life of luxury which he sometimes celebrated in wine songs; that he never traveled beyond Spain, thus could only imagine the monotony of *our* daily vistas; still . . .

> Of wine, alas, there's not a drop,
> Our host has filled our goblets to the top
> > With water.
> When monarch wine lies prone,

By water overthrown,
How can a merry song be sung?
For naught we have to wet our tongue
     But water.

Of wine, alas, there's not a drop,
Our host has filled our goblets to the top
     With water.

No sweetmeats can delight
My dainty appetite
For I, alas! must learn to drink
(However I may writhe and shrink)
     Pure water.

Of wine, alas, there's not a drop,
Our host has filled our goblets to the top
     With water.

To toads I feel allied,
To frogs by kinship tied;
For water-drinking is no joke,
Ere long you all will hear me croak
     Of water.[4]

We laugh at what we fear, and here naturally we share our anxiety of the waters around us. I recited these lines by Judah ha-Levi in an effort to reassure my audience (and myself):

In the heart of the seas I say to my quaking heart
(Pounding in fear with the roaring of the waves):
If you believe in God who made the sea,
And whose Name will stand for all eternity,
The sea shall not frighten you with its surging waves,
For with you is One who controls the sea.[5]

I think it valid to say that all of us here aboard, in our moments of solitude, ruminate on our past lives and vow, should we survive, to live better. Feeling our lives in danger, how we appreciate life! Moses ibn Ezra provided us with some relevant food for thought:

The world is like a flowing brook,
Men drink of it and are not sated;
They would not be satisfied
Were the sea empty therein.

It is as though the water were strong brine,
And the craving in their hearts impelled them to drink thereof—
Like a torrent it would rush into their throats,
But their thirst would remain unquenched forever.[6]

< <   < <   > >   > >

One country of the East is **Middle India, which is called Aden and, in Scripture, "Aden in Thelasar."** This country is very **mountainous** and is said to be the habitat of lions. **It contains many independent Jews, who are not subject to the power of the Gentiles but possess cities and fortresses on the summits of the mountains, from which they descend into the country of Ma'atum, with which they are at war. Ma'atum (a Christian kingdom) is also called Nubia, its inhabitants are called Nubians.**

The Aden **Jews generally take spoil and plunder from them, which they carry into their mountain fastnesses, the possession of which makes them almost unconquerable. Many of the Jews of Aden visit Egypt and Persia.**

< <   < <   > >   > >

It has taken ten days voyage from the Tigris to arrive at **EL-CATHIF** on the Arabian shore of the Persian Sea, a large city of which the inhabitants are outspoken and courageous Arabians.[7]

They live by diving into the sea, for **in this vicinity pearls are found. About the twenty-fourth of the month of Nissan large drops of rain are observed upon the surface of the water, which are swallowed up by reptiles. After this they close their shells and fall upon the bottom of the sea. About the middle of the month of Tishri some people dive with the assistance of ropes, collect these reptiles from the bottom and bring them up with them, after which they are opened and the pearls taken out.** But it all depends upon the spring rains, for the people here say that if it doesn't rain then, then during the following year they can obtain no pearls.

And they say that the pearls of this sea are the best of all the world. Most of the pearls here are the color of cream, but the most precious pearls are the ones of reddish tint, like roses or lilacs. From the reptiles all pearls come with a delicate color and a rough surface. To make jewelry, a hole is bored into each pearl, the hole going all the way through the pearl if the pearls are to be strung into a necklace or the hole going halfway through if the pearl is to be attached as for a brooch. Making holes in pearls is very skilled work, which is often performed by Jews.

The city has about five thousand Israelites.

Letter from Cairo

During this longer leg of the voyage (it seems interminable) the travelers tell too of the lands south of Egypt, like the country of Assuan. The road thence leads through the desert of Sh'ba, on the banks of the Nile, which comes down here from the country of the blacks. This country is governed by a king whom they call Sultan al-Chabash and some of the inhabitants resemble beasts in every respect. They eat the herbs which grow on the banks of the Nile, go naked in the fields, and lack the intelligence of other men, for instance they cohabit with their own sisters and with whomever they find. The country is excessively hot and when the people of Assuan invade the country of al-Chabash they carry wheat, raisins and figs, which they throw out like bait, thereby alluring the natives. These they capture in great numbers, bring them back to Assuan and sell them in Egypt and in the adjoining countries, where they are known as black slaves, being the descendants of Cham.

They say that from Assuan to Chaluah is twelve days. Chaluah contains about three hundred Jews and is the starting point of the caravans, which traverse the desert al-Tsahara in fifty days on their way to Savila, the Chavila of Scripture, which is in the country of Ganah. This desert contains mountains of sand and whenever a storm arises the caravans are exposed to the imminent danger of being buried alive by the sand. Those which escape, however, carry iron, copper, different sorts of fruits, pulse, and salt; gold and precious stones are brought from thence in exchange. This country lies westward of Khush or Abyssinia, and it is said that Chaluah stands thirteen days journey from Kuts.

On the frontiers of Egypt, KUTS, an ancient city, is now very large, with thirty thousand Jewish inhabitants. It is a meeting-place of merchants from Aden and India, Abyssinia and Yemen,[1] and many other places of the world.

From thence five days to FAYYUM, which is Pithom, a very fertile area. Here can be seen the traces of a canal constructed by Joseph.[2] The Mohammedans tell how the officials of Pharaoh, wanting to disparage Joseph when

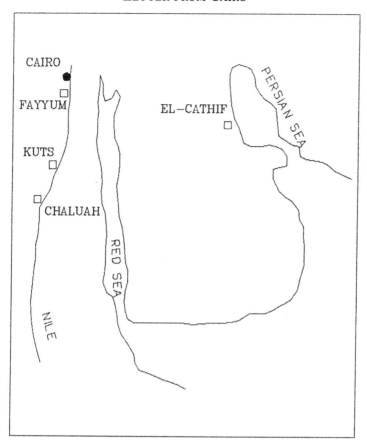

he was getting on in years, persuaded Pharaoh to set Joseph a task that he'd be unable to accomplish. Whereupon Pharaoh commanded Joseph to double the district revenues in a few years. In response, Joseph diverted a narrow arm of the Nile so as to form a canal which at flood-time would inundate the district. The crops were thereby increased to such an extent that the district revenues doubled.[3]

Now canals cross the land at close intervals, bringing Nile water to crops throughout the valley. At the time of the annual flooding, which occurs around Rosh ha-Shanah, the canals drain the raging waters from the river. In the spring of the year, when the waters are low, everywhere along the canals peasants can be seen dipping their buckets attached to either end of long poles.[4]

Also to be seen here, **even to this day**, are **some remains of the buildings erected by our forefathers.** This is the native district of R. Saadia ben Joseph, gaon of Sura; it **contains about twenty Jews.**

< <   < <   > >   > >

CAIRO **stands on the banks of the Nile. The city is large, containing many markets and bazaars,** and some dwellings that stand five, six or even seven stories.[5] As you would expect in a prosperous commercial city, it has some **very wealthy Jewish inhabitants.**

Commonly the rich people of Cairo receive water delivered to their houses by camels or donkeys or by men water carriers. Each house has a pit or pool built specially to hold its used water and wastes; from some of these pits a large pipe carries the water away, but most of them are emptied by workmen who sell the wastes to gardeners outside the city and earn a good living thereby. The city streets are very hot and dusty. Through the crush of merchants and buyers, numerous camels lumber with a leather barrel of water on each flank, Nile water, which the camel drivers sell to the thirsty.

The metropolis of Cairo has two parts: the newer, for the khalif and his officials and called **Tso'an, is enclosed by** an immense **wall; whereas** the older part of Cairo, which some people call Fustat and others Misr, **is open and the Nile washes one portion of it.**

Fustat, previous to the Mohammedans a Byzantine city, centers around a walled edifice called the Fortress of the Greeks or the Fortress of the Candles, situated on the east bank of the Nile. Most of the city's Christians and Jews live in Fustat; it **contains about two thousand Jews.** There is no special Jewish quarter,[6] and Jews mingle freely with Gentiles.

The Romans built a grand canal here from the Nile to the Red Sea, and for that reason Fustat has always been a major river port and the commercial center of all Egypt.[7] The sellers to the public have their stalls right on the riverbank, so as to offer their wares just as soon as they are unloaded. To facilitate the delivery of the merchandise, the plank bridges which cross nearby canals are pulled up for certain periods every day. Fustat's money exchange, called the *dar al-sarf*, operates under some sort of official control; it's always very busy, selling coin from all foreign countries that trade in Alexandria. The Moslem ban on alcohol notwithstanding, Fustat has a Street of the Wine-Sellers, where they sell wine quite openly.[8] Jewish vendors sell kosher wine, not only to Jews but also to the non-Jewish, non-Moslem foreigners, who particularly appreciate it. Nonetheless it does seem that Egypt's Moslems are more likely to imbibe than are the Moors in Spain.[9]

The Jews congregate around the Square of the Perfumers, the place of much of their business. On this square are the shops not only of perfumers but also of druggists, herbalists, spice merchants, dye-sellers, and so forth, of all those who deal in the plants or parts of plants that come especially from the East and are used for coloring cloth, preserving food, curing illness, stimulating virility, or decorating one's body. Some shops sell only large quantities of these items to smaller shops, which in turn sell in small quantities to the public. However, Fustat's perfumers, because they sell such small quantities anyway of very expensive products, will each deal with smaller shops and also with a lady buying just for herself.[10] Pharmacists here have their own shops, never going into partnership with a physician as they do elsewhere;[11] each pharmacist will make up medicaments for several physicians. Jews are active here in all these occupations.

A word on dyestuffs, of which there are a number beyond counting. All countries import a wide variety of them, to use in addition to the dyes they obtain locally. It is remarkable how different nations use different colors. The Palestinian Jews wear mostly black and red.[12] In Baghdad yellow clearly predominates for women's garments (as prescribed, to be sure) but also for household textiles; here in Egypt it's very rare to see women's clothing of yellow.[13] Here the women wear garments of white and blue. This is true despite a local belief (common in Palestine as well as in Egypt) that blue is unlucky. Indeed many people will not utter the word; when they want to describe something blue they say green instead.[14] Jews here don't wear green, that color being reserved for Moslems.[15]

Local Jews talk constantly about moving into New Cairo, that part, built just two hundred years ago, being the cleaner and more elegant. Some rich Jewish families have one house in New Cairo and another house in Fustat; some wealthy families have abandoned Fustat completely. The Jews remaining in Fustat are not so rich but they are not poor either, generally, and despite having to bear a greater burden for community services than before, they are friendlier than the Jews of New Cairo. The two parts of the city are close together—indeed, at certain places one is unsure whether it is Fustat or New Cairo—but the main Jewish streets of the two are distant by rather more than a permissible Sabbath's journey, so the two groups lead separate lives.

Here in Fustat **are** the **two** principal **synagogues, one of the congregation of Palestine (called the Syrian), the other of the Babylonian Jews (or those of Iraq).** The two vie ardently for congregants.[16] The smaller synagogue is the Babylonian;[17] immigrants from Babylonia about three hundred years ago converted it from a church.[18] The "Ezra" synagogue of the Palestinians has a large courtyard, with its well for hand washing before prayers and it has its own fine orchard (whose gardeners are Jewish).[19] And this synagogue is where, on Mondays and Thursdays,[20] the judges meet: the Jerusalem Academy came here about forty years ago, from Damascus. The synagogue is much older than that, indeed in the last century it was rebuilt. Its storage rooms for old papers contain not only questions to the rabbis and the usual miscellany of business letters, medical prescriptions, and marriage contracts, but also documents from Jerusalem which the Franks seized and then offered for sale to Egypt's Jewish community.[21]

The particular pride of this community is a Talmud copied five hundred years ago, since it's doubtless more authentic than most of the copies available today.[22]

The Babylonians and the Palestinians **follow different customs regarding the division of the Pentateuch into parashiyyot and sedarim. The Babylonians read one parasha every week, as is the custom throughout Spain, and finish the whole of the Pentateuch every year; whereas the Syrians** or Palestinians **have the custom of dividing every parasha into three sedarim and concluding the reading of the whole Pentateuch once in three years**, which is the custom also in the lands to the north of the Great Sea. Notwithstanding their differences of ritual, Fustat's Babylonians and Palestinians **uphold however the long-established custom of assembling both congregations and performing public service together on the day of Rejoicing in the Law** (the last day of the Feast of Tabernacles) **and on that of the Giving of the Law** (the Feast of Weeks, Shavuot). In the prayer services, the Palestinians chant many piyyutim,[23] (their own piyyutim, not the Spanish-Babylonian ones).

Perhaps it is due to the continuing civil commotion in this land, but it seems that the Jews are not very observant; they don't even have a *mikva*, although Fustat's academy is the principal in Egypt. In times past Fustat has had some very wise and learned men, but the few scholars who dwell here now have come from other countries. Lectures and discussions are always taking place at the synagogues, and meetings about communal business, collecting money or deciding where it is most needed. In mosques, all worshipers face Mecca, like a turning toward God; but in synagogues the world over, we Jews sit along the walls facing each other, so that we are always aware of other people.

The Fustat community raises its funds in this way: after the High Holydays every man must vow how much he will give every week. Each synagogue does this separately, but they put the money together so that it is the Jewish community as a whole that buys the necessities and provides for the poor.

Those in need can obtain two loaves of bread a week, on Friday for Shabbat and on Tuesday. Clothes—always new clothes, never used—are distributed at least twice a year not only to the poor but also to persons who serve the community in the lower ranks. (Naturally Fustat has shops selling already-worn garments . . . a whole bazaar of them, in fact, of great appeal to the ladies who buy and sell their clothing there.[24)] At both the Palestinian and the Babylonian synagogues, by the way, the beadles are women, and they are paid partly in coin and partly in bread and clothing; it may be that they are employed out of charity. For those travelers (away from home and family) who fall ill, the synagogue is a haven. For unfortunate Jews who are away from home, ill, and without money, the pious foundations will provide the needed bed and medicines.

For travelers just needing a place to sleep, the synagogues no longer serve; the community has a few hospices, called *funduqs*. In fact, Fustat's community owns quite a bit of property, some of it donated by Jews who moved to New Cairo; with so many leaving at around the same time, they couldn't sell their houses for any decent price and so left them for the synagogue to use.[25] The community also owns some towers in the Fortress of the Greeks and rents them out as workrooms or dwellings. The Jewish community obtains a large part of its money from the rents of its properties, which are located all around the city.

But sojourners here no more than elsewhere can remain "travelers" indefinitely. After a month of residence the solvent Jew must begin to assume his responsibilities as a contributing member of the community, his responsibilities increasing as his stay lengthens, in accord with the rules of Talmud,[26] and his name accordingly being added to the list of contributors on a Fustat synagogue's wall.[27]

Rabbi Nathaniel, the Lord of Lords, is the president of the Jewish Academy. In his capacity of primate of all the Jewish congregations of Egypt he exercises the right of appointing rabbis and ministers. He is one of the officers of the great king, who resides in his fortress of Tso'an . . . at the pleasure, it is said, of his viziers.[28] The palace, in which the king lives with his household, is surrounded by barracks for thousands of soldiers, which barracks are surrounded by the wall. **The prince appears in public twice every year: once at the time of their great holiday,** Ramadan, **and the second time at the moment of the inundation of the Nile.**

Tso'an is the metropolis of all those Arabians who obey the Emir al-Mumenin (Commander of the Faithful) **of the Shi'a sect of Ali ben Abi-Taleb. All the inhabitants of his country are called rebels, because they rebelled against the** Sunni **Emir al-Mumenin al-Abassi who resides at Baghdad. Between these two there is continual hatred.** The leaders of Moslem prayers here pronounce anathema against the khalifs of Baghdad, just as in Baghdad at public prayers they excommunicate the Egyptians. The principal religious buildings of the Mohammedans are all in New Cairo, including al-Azhar, which is like a big Moslem yeshiva.

The Fatimid kings don't disturb the Jews, provided the Jews pay their taxes and live peaceably. The poll taxes here are very high, accounting for much of the local poverty (and doubtless for many of the occasional conversions to Islam).[29] All dhimmis, of course, must pay the poll tax. The taxes on silk manufacture and on dyeing and so forth are separate, and these are usually collected by Jewish merchants operating as tax-farmers.[30]

Envy of the Jews is not unknown among the local Mohammedans; indeed, they have an old poem which runs:

> The Jews of these times do a rank attain,
> The goal of their desires; for now they reign.
> Theirs is the power, wealth to them doth cling,
> To them belong both councilor and king.
> Egyptians! Hear the words I counsel you:
> Turn Jews, for heaven itself has turned a Jew.[31]

Egyptian Jews have known only one period of persecution, and that was some 150 years ago, under the Khalif Hakim, who had been raised by his Christian mother and other Christians. This wanton and brutal khalif issued mad decrees against Christians and Jews, tried to force dhimmis to turn Moslem, and had synagogues and churches burned and confiscated.[32] He also attacked the Moslem religion, and in Moslem prayer services had his own name substituted for that of Allah. The Moslems rioted—against Khalif Hakim, not against the Jews,[33] blessed be the Name of God. Nowadays synagogue worship includes prayers for the continued well-being and tolerance of the khalifs.[34] Jews are ever anxious that the next khalif or jurist might behave like Khalif Hakim, banning or burning synagogues.[35] No one here voices the fear that Moslem leaders might behave like Franks, banning and burning Jewish people.

Jews here are as free as anyone else to choose their occupation. The Moslem rulers often employ Jews in court, as agents, financiers, and physicians. And although the Fatimids do not require the sedentary peoples to send men for army or navy service, some Jewish physicians choose to work with the Egyptian military forces.[36] More often than not, it's a physician whom the Jewish community names as nagid, which Egyptian title corresponds to the Arabic ra'is al-Yahud (head of the Jews). They always choose him from among those Jews working at court, for the nagid represents all Egypt's Jews to the khalif.[37]

About thirty-five years ago the nagid was Samuel ben Hananiah, who served as physician to the Khalif al-Hafiz. One day this khalif asked R. Samuel to prepare a poison to kill his son, the prince Hassan, but R. Samuel refused. The khalif obtained a drug from a Christian physician and murdered his son; but he later repented and had the Christian physician killed. Then he appointed R. Samuel chief physician of the court. That was the position of R. Samuel when he invited Judah ha-Levi to Cairo; and the two became friends.

The current nagid, R. Žuta, is the chief collector of taxes and a stormy petrel. One leader of the Fustat Jews who works to resolve the community's controversies is R. Moses ben Maimon, from Andalucia, who came here to live only a few years ago. Before coming here he spent some months in Eretz Yisrael, where he made such an impression that they told me about him there. A great scholar, this R. Moses has written extensively about the calendar (he hates astrology!) and he has recently completed a grand commentary on the Mishnah, *Kitab al-Siraj* (Book of the lamp).[38] Although in his youth he studied medicine, he only recently took up its practice here. He was content to spend his days studying and writing, but a year or two ago his brother (who had been supporting the family) died young and tragically, at sea. Beyond seeing patients, R. Moses tries to persuade people in the community to live in ways conducive to physical and mental health so as to mitigate their ailments and even prevent them.[39] Often he cites Talmud to the effect that bodily health leads to spiritual health.[40]

This learned R. Moses endeavors to reduce all frictions among Jews; he strives for a single united Jewish community. It follows that he resents the Karaites and their influence. He keeps reminding them that the Sabbaths and festivals are to be celebrated joyfully, not with weeping and fasting.[41]

Not that many of the Jews here are Karaites, although the local Karaites tell me that this Karaite community is second in size only to that of Constantinople. Generally speaking, they are prosperous and pious—more scholarly than the Rabbanite Jews. There have been some Karaite-Rabbanite marriages. The Karaites have their own leader, like a *nasi*, and grandly they call him the "prince of the whole diaspora of Israel." They are more discreet about their synagogues, calling them *majlis* (meaning "the place where one sits") or just halls, probably because dhimmis are supposed to keep their worship inconspicuous. Of course, the Karaites built their synagogues after the Moslems had forbidden new places for non-Moslem worship—at the time of that ban, no Karaites even existed![42]

In any case, the Fatimid rulers don't enforce the Moslem ban; there are small synagogues here of recent construction. It is something of a joke: on one Fustat synagogue is inscribed as its founding date the year 336 of the Seleucid era—that is, before the destruction of the Second Temple![43]

To return to the local Karaites. Generally they work as merchants of one sort or another. Some of them no longer deal in merchandise but act as bankers to the court. Thus they live well. It's not unusual for a Karaite merchant, when he begins to feel the weight of his years, to turn to the ascetic life which Karaism extols and to relinquish his worldly goods.

The Karaites rarely own farms or fields, although Rabbanites commonly own farmland. Non-Jewish Egyptians perform all the work on the soil, but the Jewish farmers supervise their work, at least the making of the cheese and the pressing of the grapes. Most of the grapes grown here, as it happens, are used for wine; nor do the Egyptians cultivate much else in the way of fruits for eating. Strange, as they like to eat fruits, consider them delicacies in fact; they buy imported and expensive fruits—fresh fruits and dried fruits, and nuts too—and serve them (usually glazed with sugar) in great quantities,[44] often in fine silver bowls of Fustat manufacture.[45]

Jews here too work predominantly in textiles. The Egyptians' main textile plant is flax, of which they claim to cultivate at least twenty varieties. Jews don't employ themselves in the actual growing of it or in preparing the fiber, but once it has been spun and combed out, Jews sell the thread, in Egypt and abroad. If the flax is to be woven into linen in Egypt, the Christian Copts do the weaving and Jews trade the linen. The weavers of Fustat make a cloth of linen warp and cotton wefts; it is thick, generally dyed dark, and sold mostly locally.

Egypt grows no cotton, but imports the raw cotton from Tunisia and India.[46] Silk is produced, in Egypt's south, but it's not very good; the weavers of it are Egyptians, the traders are Jews, and whenever they can, they mix the locally produced silk with silk imported from Syria and then sell the woven cloth as Syrian.[47] Wool is hardly woven here, as in this climate no one wears woolen garments—Egyptians keep their numerous sheep for cheese.

Much merchandise passes through Egypt on its way from India and China to the West. The Fatimid rulers have encouraged trade by protecting the merchants' sea routes and land routes, and by allowing the merchants to trade what and where they wish. The Jewish merchants thrive.

But during the last dozen years King Amaury invaded Egypt several times. The rule of Egypt is also contested among Mohammedans, between, on the one hand, some Egyptian viziers, and, on the other hand, Saladin the young nephew and recent heir of the great general Shirkūh who fought in the name of Baghdad's Emperor Nureddin. The local merchants, especially, fear that the good times may not long endure.

Letter from Gizeh

Rain, frost or snow is almost unknown here, the climate being very warm. The river overflows once every year, in the month of Elul in late summer, inundating the whole country and moistening it to the extent of fifteen days journey. The water remains standing on the land during that and the following month, whereby it is moistened and made fit for agriculture.

The proprietors of land cause ditches to be dug along their fields, into which the fishes are swept with the rising waters. When the river retires into its bed the fish remain in the trenches, the proprietors collect them and eat them; fresh, the fish can be roasted or fried. Other proprietors sell their fish to merchants, who cure them and sell them thus all over the country; fish for curing must measure at least a finger length. These fish have abundant fat, which the rich of this country use instead of oil to light lamps. Those who eat of the fish and drink Nile water after it need not fear any bad consequences, Nile water being an excellent preventive against illness.

A marble pillar, constructed with great skill, has been erected in front of an island. Twelve yards of this pillar protrude above the level of the river and whenever the water rises to a height sufficient to cover the pillar, they know that it has inundated the whole land of Egypt to the extent of fifteen days journey. Whereas if only one-half of the pillar be covered, it shows that one-half of the country is yet dry. A certain officer measures the rise of the river every day and makes proclamation in these words: "Praise God, for the river has risen so and so much." The measuring and proclamation is repeated every day. Whenever the water submerges the whole pillar, it produces great plenty in the whole land of Egypt.

To persons who ask why the river rises, the Egyptians respond that it is caused by heavy rains which fall in the country of Abyssinia, the Chavila of Scripture, which country is higher than the level of Egypt; this forces the river out of its bed and inundates the whole country. Whenever the overflowing of the Nile is suspended, they can neither sow nor reap, "and the famine is sore in the land."

The time for sowing in Egypt is the month of Marcheshvan in the fall after the river has retired into its usual bed. In Adar in early spring they cut barley and in the next month, Nissan, the wheat. In that same month the following fruits are ripe: a kind of acid plum, called cherry; nuts; cucumbers; gourds; St. John's bread; beans; spelt-corn; chick-peas. Also all sorts of herbs, such as: purslane; asparagus or fennel; grapes; lettuce; coriander; succory; cab-

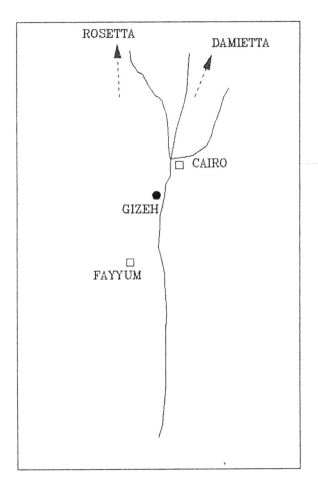

bage; and wine. On the whole the country abounds with good things, the gardens and orchards are watered partly from wells and partly from the Nile.

From Cairo to ancient Memphis is a distance of two parasangs. The latter lies in ruins, but the sites of the walls and the houses may still be traced at this day. Memphis, the biblical Mitsraim, was in the time of our forefathers an important city with numerous temples and palaces, but the prophets foretold its destruction.[1]

OLD MITSRAIM is three miles in extent. Here are the remains of the granaries of Joseph, of which there are a large number.

The pyramids, which are seen here, are constructed by witchcraft, and in no other country or other place is any thing equal to them. They are composed

of stones and cement and are very substantial. The sandy ground which they cover is as great in extent as all of Tudela!

In the outskirts of the city is the very ancient synagogue of our great master Moses, upon whom be peace. On the west bank of the Nile, in the area of Gizeh, at a place called Dimmah, it is the principal site of pilgrimage for Jews in Egypt. Whole families come in the month of Sivan, at Shavuot, for this is the place where Moses dwelt when he was imploring Pharaoh to free the Jews. It is said that this synagogue was built more than a thousand years ago, namely forty years after the destruction of the Temple; and that the huge tree inside the synagogue has been there ever since the days of Moses.[2] **An old, very learned man is the overseer and clerk of this place of public worship. He is called Shaikh Abou-Nassar.**

< <   < <   > >   > >

Above Cairo **the Nile divides into four arms. One of them goes to Damietta, which is Khaphtor. and there falls into the sea; a second flows toward Rashid or Rosetta, which is near Alexandria, and there falls into the sea; the third takes the direction of Ashmun, the large city on the frontier of Egypt.**[3]

The banks of these four arms are lined on both sides by cities, towns and villages, so close to one another that they touch, and each of them is crowded and flourishing, with its own markets and artisans. All the valley of the Nile is **enlivened by numerous travelers, who journey both by river and land.** All along the roads water carriers sell drinks, in cups of brass or silver; they carry the water in goatskin bags, fastened across their shoulders by linen straps. **In fact, upon the whole earth there is no country as populous and as well cultivated as Egypt, which is of ample territory and full of all sorts of good things.**

Judah ha-Levi, who visited Cairo and Alexandria on his way to Jerusalem when he was already advanced in years, wrote of his enjoyment in being here. Once, asked his opinion of Egypt, he replied:

> Wondrous is this land to see,
> With perfume its meadows laden,
> But none of it more fair to me
> Than yon gentle maiden.
>
> Ah, time's swift flight I fain would stay,
> Forgetting that my locks are grey.[4]

First Letter from Alexandria

From Old Mitsraim **eight parasangs to the land of Goshen**, where Jacob lived after this land had been given to Joseph.[1] **BELBEIS is a large city, and contains about three hundred Jewish inhabitants.**

< <   < <   > >   > >

Half a day to ISKIIL AIN AL SHEMS ("fountain of the sun"), which is in ruins. Here are remains of the buildings erected by our forefathers, tower-like buildings constructed of bricks.

< <   < <   > >   > >

One day's journey to AL-BUBIZIG, on the eastern bank of the Nile, in which region abound the poppies from which opium is made.[2] **About two hundred Jews live here.**

< <   < <   > >   > >

Half a day to SEFITA, at the upper end of the island where the Nile separates into two arms, in which town a great number of boats assemble which go on the sea for big fish,[3] and which contains **about two hundred Jews.**

< <   < <   > >   > >

Four parasangs to DAMIRA. Even along this busy waterway with much commerce between towns, most towns have dye works, brickyards, and factories to supply most of their own needs, to avoid paying expensive transport charges. **This place,** a small market town which manufactures beautiful cloths,[4] **contains about seven hundred Jews.**

< <   < <   > >   > >

Five days to MAHALEH, with about five hundred Israelites.

< <   < <   > >   > >

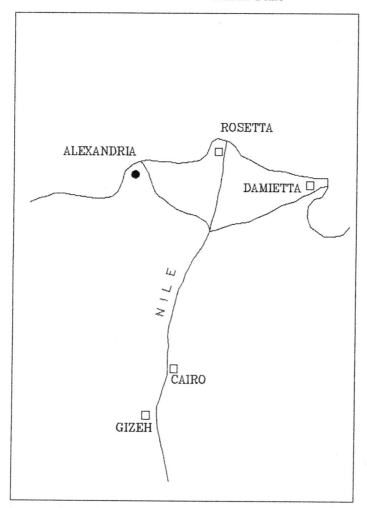

From thence two days to ALEXANDRIA, the largest city in Egypt. **Alexander of Macedon, who built this extremely strong and handsome city, called it after his own name.** He conquered Palestine, following upon which Jews were brought to this city as prisoners, thus started the Jewish community in Alexandria.

As a flourishing coastal city, Alexandria incites the aggression of conquerors. The only large Arab port on the Great Sea, the city is now being contested by groups of Moslems even while it is a prime target of the Franks, who in recent years have besieged the city during long periods by blockading the ports. Many people here were wounded in the catapult bombings; and many more suffer from the grave illnesses which started with the famine. The Jewish physicians keep telling people to avoid crowding in the narrow streets, so as not to become sick through contact with others.

The city is built upon arches which are hollow below and which carry water from the Nile to the western part of the city.[5] **The streets are straight and some of them are of such extent that the eye cannot see all of them at once; the street which runs from the Rosetta to the Sea Gate is a full mile in length.**

On the seashore is a marble sepulcher, upon which are depicted all sorts of birds and beasts, all in very ancient characters, which nobody can decipher, but it is supposed that it is the tomb of a king of very ancient date, who reigned even before the flood. The length of the tomb is fifteen spans, by six in breadth.

In the outskirts of this city was the school of Aristotle, the teacher of Alexander. The building is still very handsome and large and is divided into many apartments by marble pillars. This is where Alexander built his grand library, which lasted seven hundred years until it was burned by warring Christians in the first years of the Eastern church. **There were about twenty schools, to which people flocked from all parts of the world, in order to study the Aristotelian philosophy.** These schools taught about how all of life may be considered as pertaining to two areas: the lower being the material and the higher being the spiritual, or that which man comprehends with his mind.

The schools continued throughout the time of the Romans. One of their Jewish students, from a wealthy leading family of Alexandria, was Philo, who at the time of the first year of the common era was twenty or twenty-five years old. (He lived under the same Roman rule as the governor-historian Josephus, Philo living just a generation earlier, albeit the two Jewish writers were about as different as two men could be.)

In later years Philo would write about himself:

> There was once a time when by devoting myself to philosophy and to contemplation of the world and its parts I achieved the enjoyment of that Mind which is truly beautiful, desirable and blessed; for I lived in constant communion with sacred utterances and teachings, in which I greedily and insatiably rejoiced. No base or worldly thoughts occurred to me, nor did I grovel for glory, wealth or bodily comfort, but I seemed ever to be borne aloft in the heights in a rapture of soul.[6]

As even under the Romans the language of the schools (and indeed of Alexandria) was Greek, Philo knew the Pentateuch in its Greek translation, and he wrote his own books in Greek. He valued the Bible and endeavored to relate it to that essential of Greek philosophy, rationalism.

From his Greek teachers he learned about the classification of knowledge. Neither the Greek scholars nor the Roman officials comprehended the existence of the One God, so, addressing himself to them and to Jews imbued with Greek views, Philo presented his Judaism by describing the Pentateuch as a legal code. He introduced his book by recounting the story of Creation.

doing so partly for those of his readers who might be ignorant of it, and partly to show that biblical laws proceeded directly from natural laws.

He wrote out the stories of Abraham, Isaac and Jacob, and of Moses of Egypt, explaining how they had become heroes by living in accord with God's law . . . and this before the giving of the Torah. He taught the importance to all men of a life pleasing to God, insisting that good and worthy leaders could come from any people. "No one can be considered a man, who does not hope in God,"[7] but, through God's laws, a man might mature into "a loyal citizen of the world."[8]

Philo's observation of the world around him assured him of God's existence:

> Who can look upon statues or paintings without thinking at once of a sculptor or painter?. . . . And when one enters a well-ordered city . . . what else will he suppose but that this city is directed by good rulers? So he who comes to the truly Great City, this world, and beholds hills and plains teeming with animals and plants, . . . the yearly seasons passing into each other, . . . and the whole firmament revolv- ing in rhythmic order, must he not . . . gain the conception of the Maker and Father and Ruler also?[9]

I'm told that Philo was the first philosopher to have considered reason in relation to faith, reason being that which can be proven or be arrived at by thinking, faith being that which cannot be so proven and must be accepted on the basis of authority. He contrasted the Greek gods, who are subject to the immutable laws of nature just as men are, to the One God, who can suspend the laws of nature as he did when he showed Moses the burning bush that didn't burn up.[10] In this way Philo indicated the inadequacy of the pagans' gods and the superiority of the one Jewish God. He distinguished God's essence from God's nature, explaining the difference between man's ability to know that God exists and man's inability to know what God is like. He argued that a man's belief in the One God must be based on faith. Through his many treatises of this kind, Philo gained fame and respect.

Under the Romans, Alexandria was the largest city of the Greek province of Aegyptus. The city's inhabitants were mostly Greeks, but many were Jews. In their immense empire, the Romans granted citizenship to very few of those from their eastern provinces, and naturally almost all the Alexandrians who were citizens were Greek; nonetheless Philo's family held citizenship. Citizens did not pay the poll tax, nor did Greeks; but virtually all Jews, being neither Greek nor citizen, had to pay an onerous tax. It was a time of conflict between Greeks and Jews, and between Greeks and their Roman sovereigns: that is to say, the Greeks were anti-Roman and anti-Jew, so that in the Greek-Roman conflicts, the Jewish community favored the Romans. The Jews wanted to become citizens, for exemption from the poll tax and also for the honor. Their ambition aggravated the Greeks' animosity, to the point where Greeks supported anti-Jewish hooligans.

When Philo was a mature man, quarrels broke out between the Roman governor in Egypt and the new Roman emperor in Rome, Caligula, one result of which was rioting against the Jews in Alexandria. The local Greeks destroyed synagogues and murdered Jews, and they forced the remaining Jews to dwell in a quarter of their own in the delta area, apart from other people. The Greeks had always resented the Jewish dedication to the One God to the exclusion of local gods, and now, wanting to curry favor with Emperor Caligula in Rome, they placed statues of him in what was left of the synagogues in the Jewish quarter. The Roman governor of Egypt took the side of the Greek rioters against the Jews.

The Alexandrian Jews selected a delegation to go to Rome and entreat the emperor to improve their situation. They were aware that their representatives would have to deal very cleverly against great odds and would run particular personal risks due to Caligula's madness. They chose Philo to lead the mission because his family had had dealings at high levels in Rome, because as a wealthy citizen he desired good relations with Rome, while as a scholar he felt indebted to the Greeks, and because of the very high regard in which they held him as philosopher.

At the beginning of the year 40 C.E. the delegates sailed to Rome. They spent many months there awaiting royal audiences and occasionally speaking with the emperor, in constant fear that some whim on his part would mean the loss of many, many Jewish lives as well as their own. While trying to win benefits from him, they had to remain composed in the face of his continual insults, inquisitions, taunts, tirades, and tantrums.

Caligula, in apparent sincerity, labeled crazy those who would not worship him, for he felt entitled to be worshiped throughout the empire, which was, after all, his. Philo writes amusingly—it's amusing *now*—of how the Jewish delegates explained to Caligula that the Jews would not worship statues and that, although they would not make sacrifices *to* him, they would make sacrifices *for* him and indeed had already been making offerings in his name. Caligula, however, saw no point in that; he demanded to be sacrificed *to*.

Eventually Philo's delegation was able to leave Rome with the satisfaction of having won Caligula's acquiescence that Jews need not bow down before his statue . . . on the condition, easy enough to meet, that Jews would not interfere when others celebrated his divinity. Who knows if Caligula might have changed his mind again? Fortunately, within a year he died.[11]

Although Philo was one of Alexandria's leading citizens, he did not live here gladly, he would have preferred a life of contemplation.[12] Once, in the Holy Land, he came to know a Jewish community called Essenes, people who lived peaceably and piously among themselves near the Dead Sea, far from urban wrangling and royalty, deliberately ignorant of Greek culture and convinced that contemporary kings were corrupt; Philo praised them highly.[13] Probably he envied them, for he considered big cities like Alexandria to be too crowded, too sinful, and too noisy.[14]

Second Letter from Alexandria

As in Roman times, the Alexandria of today **is very mercantile and affords an excellent market to all nations.** Despite the hostile activities of the Franks throughout this region, despite even the frequent bloody battles between Moslems and Christians in Palestine, in Babylonia, and here in Egypt, the Moslem rulers keep Alexandria open for trade, so as to earn the revenue thereof. **People from all Christian kingdoms resort to Alexandria, from Valencia, Tuscany, Lombardy, Apulia, Amalfi, Sicily, Rakuvia, Catalonia, Spain, Roussillon, Germany, Saxony, Denmark, England, Flanders, Hainault, Normandy, France, Poitou, Anjou, Burgundy, Mediana, Provence, Genoa, Pisa, Gascogne, Aragon and Navarre.** The Italians especially fight for trade here, even though the pope in Rome condemns Christian commerce with Mohammedans.[1] **From the west you meet Mohammedans from Andalucia, Algarve, Africa and Arabia; as well as from the countries towards India, Chavila, Abyssinia, Nubia, Yemen, Mesopotamia, and Syria, besides Greeks and Turks.**

The city is full of bustle and every nation has its own *fondaco* here. Cairo's Jews call a hospice for travelers a *funduq*; *fondaco* is the original word, for the Italians developed this institution. A full-fledged fondaco is like a small fortress, in which merchants from a foreign city live—they are not allowed to reside elsewhere in this city—and there they have storerooms for their merchandise, their own church, also baths and gardens. Each fondaco has a leader, a consul, who maintains the fondaco, assures the good behavior of its members, and represents it to the Egyptian officials. Egyptian guards lock the gates of the fondachi at the hours of Moslem prayers and at night.

In return for the privilege of establishing a fondaco, the foreign city regularly delivers war matériel to Alexandria: iron and weapons, wood to build ships and pitch to maintain them. These arrangements apparently work well in peacetime, but in times of war (as when the Franks were blockading Alexandria or threatening Cairo) Alexandria imprisons foreign merchants and confiscates their merchandise.[2]

Withal, the traders come. "For the sake of gain," Philo wrote over a thousand years ago, "merchants cross the seas and compass the wide world, letting nothing stand in their way, summer heat or winter cold, violent gales or contrary winds . . . , the society of friends . . . , all the greatest amenities of civic life.[3]

The foreign merchants come here not only to buy, but even more, to sell the products of their home countries. All kinds of merchandise pass through

272

here: grammar books, and saffron for seasoning and coloring; bananas[4] and dried fruits, and cowrie shells for ornaments. Finished jewelry and gemstones, pearls and onyxes, corals from the coastal waters of Tunisia and of the lands north of the Great Sea to be sent east to India and beyond. Vast amounts of silk from Spain and Sicily to be sent farther east and north through the Moslem empire. From Sicily and from Tunisia, olive oil, soap, and wax, and animal skins in the form of furs, hides, leather, and shoes.

Alexandria trades too in some products originating in Egypt. Egypt exports its flax to Tunisia and Sicily; its cloths and mats, to India; and its sugar; and pens, made of the reeds from the lake at Maryut.[5] And books, including Hebrew ones, produced at the great paper manufactory in Fustat.[6] Egypt's own products, however, account for a very small part of its trade. For several generations, Alexandria has been famous and prosperous because it ships products of the West to the lands of the East, and even more, products of the East to the kingdoms of the West.

From Arabia and Persia, India and China, the Egyptians buy flax and wool to send on to Spain and dyestuffs to send to all lands around the Great Sea. **From India they import** pepper, nutmeg, clove, ginger, sesame, Chinese wood, or cinnamon—**all kinds of spices, which are bought by Christian merchants.** Not only in spices, but in all such things as herbs, drugs, and cosmetics, there is so much commerce that the shops on Alexandria's Square of the Perfumers trade only with other traders, selling only to keepers of smaller shops, not selling directly to the public, as do shops in Cairo.

Nowhere on earth is such a great port to be found as at Alexandria. Except maybe for Constantinople. I've never seen anything approaching such vast quantities of merchandise. You can't imagine it all! Merchants tell me this port has come upon bad times, that Egypt was much more prosperous before the Italians moved into the trade,[7] but I see the streets and quays so full, I hear so much hustle-bustle, that I can't believe there used to be more. Yet the individuals in Alexandria who are not employed in this commerce are always complaining that the local markets offer them nothing, that all the good products are for sale in Fustat.

All the grand commerce does pass through Fustat, and has always done so, since the government is seated there and controls all the business, the better to tax it. Foreign merchants choose their goods for exportation in Fustat, and they pay the duties on them in Fustat, for they must show Fustat receipts in the Alexandria port before they can depart with their merchandise. They even buy in Fustat the foreign coin they need for traveling.[8]

Alexandria differs from Cairo in several respects, among which is that Cairo is quieter and more stable with settled inhabitants, whereas many people in Alexandria are just passing through, like the merchandise, or if they are resident, they are often unsure whether they wish to stay. Both cities have many foreigners, but in Cairo the foreigners are not so conspicuous, whereas in Alexandria the unsettled foreigners are often in conflict with men who were born here. Animosity against Jews is an Alexandrian tradition going back a thousand years.[9]

The Jews of Alexandria maintain close relations with the Jews of Cairo. In times of trouble—as when Jews have to be ransomed, in this century from Frank invaders and in the last century from Moslem pirates—the Jewish communities all over Egypt cooperate. Jews dwell in most of Egypt's towns, big and small; the largest Jewish community is here, for **Alexandria contains about three thousand Jews.**

Jews here work in the international trade not only as merchants, agents, and so forth, but also as officials connected with seafaring and commerce: Jews are among those who superintend the port and who board ships as assessors for the duties.[10] Some local Jews are oyster fishers. The traders specialize in textiles and leather goods; in dyes, spices, and pharmaceuticals; in metals, raw or wrought; and in certain foods including honey and dried fruits. Indeed, in this grand market–metropolis, Jews deal in most things; although not in grains or in animals or in weapons.

Speaking of animals. I think I wrote you how Fustat supports its community by members' donations. Here in Alexandria the Jews rely on a meat tax, so that the rich bear most of the burden. Some of the Jewish communities in the Holy Land—so tiny they are!—likewise raise their funds through taxing meat.

In Alexandria as in Fustat, the main synagogue is Palestinian and the smaller is Babylonian. The ideas of the Jewish scholars of Babylonia, so important to us in Spain, are not paid much attention in Egypt, which has been greatly influenced by the Greeks: first by the Greek scholars of Philo's time, then (since the Moslems began) by Greek ideas as translated and transmitted by Mohammedans. To be sure, there were and are Jews among the translators.

If modern Egypt is weak in Jewish scholarship, earlier Egypt produced at least two outstanding Jewish scholars. Isaac ben Solomon Israeli, a physician-philosopher, about the year 900 received an appointment to the court of the khalif in Kairouan, the first khalif of the Fatimid dynasty, and in Kairouan R. Isaac taught medicine. Although esteemed as an eye doctor, he wrote his books about diet, about urine, and about fever. He lived one hundred years and he never married; he asserted that his books would keep his memory alive longer than any children he might have.[11]. . . One of R. Isaac's younger friends, R. Saadia ben Joseph, the later gaon at Sura, came from a village in the district Fayyum in Upper Egypt, through which I passed. . . . Come to think of it, both these scholars gained renown for what they did after they sailed from Egypt.

The port of Alexandria is formed partly by a pier which extends a mile into the sea. Here is also erected a high tower, called a lighthouse, from Alexander's day, remarkable because it is so high and so solid. They say that this very lighthouse was the model for the Moslems' minarets; in any case the Arabic word *mānarāt* means "lighthouse."[12]

This lighthouse contained Alexandria's ancient observatory. **On top of the tower stands a glass mirror. All vessels, which approached with hostile intentions from Greece and from the western side, could be observed at fifty days distance by means of this glass mirror, and precautions taken against them. Many years after the death of Alexander, there arrived a Greek vessel commanded by a man of the name of Theodoros, who was of extreme cunning. The Greeks were subject to the Egyptians at this time and the above-named skipper brought a valuable present to the king of Egypt, consisting of silver, gold, and silk garments. He rode at anchor in view of the mirror, the customary station of all merchantmen who arrived, and he invited the keeper of the lighthouse with his servants to visit him every day until they became very intimate and paid one another frequent visits. Upon a certain day he invited the keeper and all his servants to a sumptuous meal and plied them with so much wine that both he and his servants became drunk and fell into a sound sleep. The skipper and his crew seized this opportunity to break the mirror, after which feat they left the port that very night. From that time the Christians began to visit Alexandria with small and large vessels; they took the large island of Crete as well as Cyprus, which are in possession of the Greeks unto this day; and the Egyptians have not been able to withstand the Greeks ever since.**

This story reminds me of how Samuel ha-Nagid put the wine problem into verse:

> Red to the eye, sweet on the tongue,
> Savored in India though Spanish libations—
> Fermented juices are weak in the cup,
> But can rule heads of men who rule nations.[13]

The lighthouse is still a mark to all seafaring men. By day the smoke from it can be observed at the distance of one hundred miles, and **at night it shows a light** which appears like a star and **which serves as a guide to all mariners.**

Letter from Messina

From Alexandria **two days to DAMIETTA. The place contains about two hundred Jews.**

< <   < <   > >   > >

From thence half a day to SUNBAT, the inhabitants of which sow flax and weave fine linen, which forms a very considerable article of exportation and makes them prosperous.

< <   < <   > >   > >

Four days to AILAH, which is Elim; it belongs to the Bedouin Arabs.

< <   < <   > >   > >

Two days to R'PHIDIM, which is inhabited by Arabians and contains no Jews.

< <   < <   > >   > >

From R'phidim **one day to MOUNT SINAI. The Syrian monks possess a place of worship on the summit of the mount, at the base of which is a large village. The inhabitants, who speak the Chaldean language, called it Tour Sinai; the mountain is small, is in possession of the Egyptians and is five days distant from Misr.**

Is this the mount that Moses ascended to receive the moral laws by which we are to live? We don't know, that is, Jews do not claim to know, although the Christians believe that holy place to be here. In the generations after Moses heard God's voice and received His Law, long long before the start of the religion of Jisho the Nazarene, then Jews likely made pilgrimage to the mount chosen by the Lord for His great revelation. But knowledge of the place has been lost to us, and according to the sages,the place is unimportant; God's commandments are important.

From Mount Sinai the Red Sea is one day's journey; this sea is an arm of the Indian Sea.

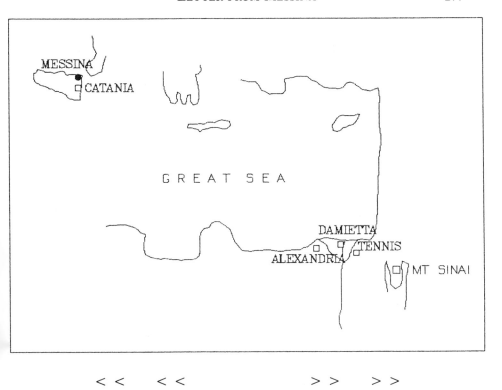

From Mount Sinai **back to Damietta, whence by sea to TENNIS, the ancient Chanes, an island of the sea, containing forty Israelites. Here are the confines of the empire of Egypt.**

From thence twenty days by sea to MESSINA on the shores of the island of Sicily, located in the middle of the Great Sea. **The island begins at Messina, where many pilgrims meet.** For travelers from France and Spain, Messina is halfway to the Holy Land. And for those like me, returning to Navarre from the Holy Land, Sicily is the last major stopping place of the long voyage.

It extends to Catania, Syracuse, Masara, Pantaleone, and Trapani, being six days in circumference. Near Trapani is found the stone called coral, in Arabic al-murgan. Two days' journey south of Messina lies the city of Catania, where a few years ago the Jews were freed of special taxes and were granted the right to hold their own courts. In '69, early in February, that city was devastated by an earthquake so severe that it even damaged the walls of Messina.[1]

Messina is situated on the strait called Lunir, an arm of the sea which divides the mainland of Calabria from the island of Sicily. The kingdom of Sicily includes Calabria and extends north to Salerno and Naples.

Most of the pilgrims who embark for Jerusalem assemble here at Messina **because this city affords the best opportunity for a good passage.** Here ships take on horses and supplies of food. The harbor is deep and, being on the narrow strait, easy to defend in case of war. But the currents of the strait are very swift due to the sea monsters Scylla and Charybdis. King Roger sent a diver into these waters to learn about the currents.

The great forests nearby provide Messina with materials for building and repairing ships, a thriving industry. From here numerous ships sail to every port in Christendom and to Moslem lands as well; all, even the very biggest, are laden with merchants from every place and merchandise of every sort. Several towns in the north of Italy have in recent years established fondachi here, with wharves and with offices for their own merchants.

Sicily's main export is wheat, of which most goes to North Africa. In times of commotion in North Africa, when Moslems fight among themselves or when Moslem lands are set upon by Berbers or by pagan tribes, the consequent food shortages there swell Sicily's coffers with the tax on grain exports. Sailors on ships all over the Great Sea are nourished by hard bread made of Sicilian wheat. Messina also ships out salt, and coral from west Sicilian waters. From the land come sulphur and iron. From Sicily's industries, fine silks. **Messina is beautifully situated in a country abounding with gardens and orchards and full of good things** like lemons and oranges, almonds and melons.

Right now Sicilians are marking a hundred years of Christian rule. Prior to that Sicily was under Moslem rule, and Messina still sounds and behaves as though it were a Mohammedan city. On the streets most people (including Jews) speak Arabic,[2] and bands play Mohammedan music. Torchlight processions accompany weddings, and professional mourners accompany funerals in accord with Moslem custom. The Moslem women cover themselves completely and some of the older Christian women follow their example. On this island of many natural riches and many peoples, Christians, Moslems and Jews may freely celebrate their religion. About forty years ago the Jews received a charter with that assurance.

Messina contains about two hundred Jews, many of whom have Arabic names and dress in the same way as Moslems. Rather than the ordained three prayer services on workdays, Jews here hold only one. They call their synagogues *moschea* and their community *assembly* or *aljama,* as in Moslem Spain.[3]

Letter from Palermo

Westward two days from Messina stands PALERMO, a large city, bigger than Rome, as big as Baghdad. The surrounding **country is rich in wells and springs, grows wheat and barley, and is well-supplied with gardens and orchards; it is in fact the best in the whole island of Sicily.**

Palermo was the Arab capital of Sicily during the many generations that Sicily was controlled by Mohammedans from Tunisia and from Egypt. Jews, who have had a community in Palermo since the days of the Romans, lived in Palermo under Moslem rule as they lived elsewhere under Moslem rule: as dhimmis, paying the jizya tax, but in general securely and comfortably. Then, during several generations, the Arab rule of Sicily was contested by Normans as a by-adventure of their travels to the Holy Land, and these managed to stay in control.

When the Norman, Robert Guiscard, established his rule over Sicily, he did nothing to abrogate Jews' rights as citizens—Jews could still worship as they wished, could own buildings and lands, and could engage freely in the trades and professions. But the dhimmi tax that Jews had to pay to their Moslem rulers was henceforth to be paid to Robert Guiscard . . . and the Jews would pay that tax in addition to the other taxes they paid as citizens. Then Robert Guiscard made a present of the annual revenue from that tax to his wife, Sichelgaita; and when he died in 1085 Sichelgaita transferred that tax-revenue to the archbishop. (She arranged, however, that each year one-sixth of the tax revenue would go to the archbishop, while as long as she lived the remaining five-sixths she would keep for herself.) That was the situation of the Jews, living like the archbishop's vassals, for some twenty years during which various groups of Normans and other Christians fought over the island.

Robert Guiscard's nephew, Count Roger, had his capital in Calabria on the continent. In his early years, both the Roman church and the Eastern church claimed rights in Sicily, where most of the inhabitants were Arab Moslems. Count Roger came to Sicily and endeavored to secure religious peace, giving rights of person and property to all groups, which improved the Jews' tax situation. On Count Roger's death in 1101, his widow Adelaide became regent, and it was she who made Palermo the Norman capital.

The son of Adelaide and Count Roger, also called Roger, would come of age in 1113; then Adelaide would be free of her royal duties. She, being extremely wealthy, attracted the attention of King Baldwin of Jerusalem,

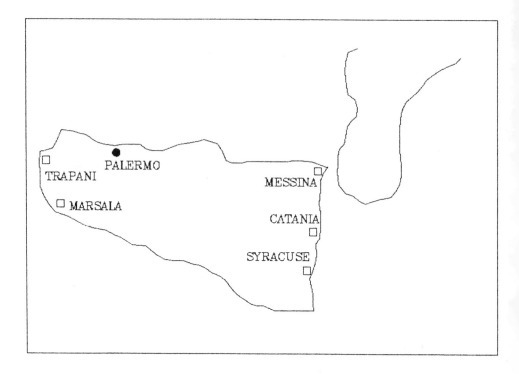

who was then about fifty-five and still married to an Armenian lady whom he had put aside. King Baldwin longed for control of the Great Sea, an end which could be brought into reach by a Sicilian alliance. He sent an emissary to the dowager countess, proposing the marriage. Adelaide accepted, with a condition. She knew that King Baldwin's children had died—during the early battles for the Holy Land—and she realized that at her age she would probably have no more children. Her condition to King Baldwin: in the absence of a child of their own, her son Roger would inherit the Kingdom of Jerusalem.

In the summer of 1113 Adelaide sailed for Acre and her wedding. Just as soon as they were married, King Baldwin set about using her dowry for the military needs of his kingdom. The Franks were pleased by their country's new wealth, less pleased by King Baldwin's bigamous marriage. Adelaide, who had thought she would prefer a second titled marriage to her position as dowager, found herself living far less comfortably in Jerusalem than she had at Palermo. Baldwin was bored by her, and (perhaps in consequence) anxious about living in a state of sin; he also knew his advisers to be furious that he had virtually bequeathed the kingdom without even consulting them. In short, the marriage disintegrated, and by spring 1117 Adelaide was back in Sicily.[1]

Her son Roger, ruling Sicily, powerful and very ambitious, would all his life hate the Franks for having humiliated his mother and for having denied him Jerusalem's crown. He was always at odds with the other kings and princes of Christendom.[2]

In 1130, when the Cardinal Pietro Pierleoni was elected pope in Rome with the name Anacletus and all the other European rulers favored the rival pope because of Pierleoni's Jewish ancestry, Roger gave strong support to Pierleoni as pope. Doubtless this stemmed from Roger's wish to follow an independent course, and it may also have reflected his unquestioned liberality in matters of religion. In addition, I have just learned that Roger and Pierleoni were brothers-in-law,[3] Roger's wife being the pope's sister.

The two men worked to each other's advantage: Roger supporting the insecure Anacletus, Anacletus investing Roger (whose father had ruled as Count Roger) as king.[4]

Of his new kingdom of Sicily (including the southern half of the Italian peninsula) Roger proved a magnificent king. When the other Christian kings persecuted their Jewish subjects and went to fight in the Holy Land, King Roger refused; he continued his father's policy of respect for each religious community. His equal treatment of all people led to Sicily's holding courts in various languages, with professional judges under the surveillance of itinerant justices. He likewise concerned himself about the qualification of physicians throughout his kingdom, and supported Salerno's medical academy, which was independent of the Church.[5] Himself a practitioner of astronomy and astrology, he was an avid patron of the sciences and the arts. He gave Sicily peace, and made of it a great nation.

In the conflict over the papacy, King Roger was driven from southern Italy and Pope Anacletus to his death. Under the new pope, the Church excommunicated King Roger several times, but he did not change his ways.

When he died in 1154, not only Christians grieved but also, very deeply, Jews and Moslems. Within a year of his death, a serious conflict broke out between the chief minister of the new king (the first King William) and some nobles, which conflict resulted in the departure from Palermo of many Moslems.

I myself have benefited from King Roger's patronage of Moslem scholars. King Roger took into his court a great Arab geographer called al-Edrisi, who died about five years ago, from whose elaborate *Book of King Roger* I have learned much about the countries in which I sojourned, because he traveled to many of the same places twenty or thirty years ago and wrote wisely about them. He visited Spain, even praised the Jativa paper[6] (which has served me well). After having seen many big cities, al-Edrisi wrote of Palermo that it is "the greatest and finest metropolis of the world. . . . Its beauties are infinite, its defenses are impregnable, its buildings dazzle the eye."

First among Palermo's important buildings is **a large palace, the walls of which are richly ornamented with paintings and with gold and silver. The pavement is of marble and rich mosaic representing all sorts of figures; in the whole country there is no building equal to this.**

The city is the seat of the viceroy, who is also the archbishop of Palermo. The viceroy rules Sicily in the name of young King William, whose father the first King William died in '66 when the prince was only twelve years old; he is soon to begin his rule as the second King William. **The king's vessels are ornamented with silver and gold and are ever ready for the amusement of himself and his women. The palace is called al-Hacina and contains all sorts of fruit trees as also a great spring surrounded by a wall and a reservoir called al-Behira, in which abundant fish are preserved.**

Fishing is one of Palermo's great industries. Ships regularly buy the salted tuna fish which comes from the waters here. Many Jews work in the fishing industry and have a good reputation.

The Jews in Sicily (as in the Greek lands) do almost all the work in textile dyeing and silk. Palermo, as a royal city, needs a great deal of silk. Silk dyeing is expensive and requires very able workers not because the dyeing process is different from that used for other cloths, but because silk demands very bright shades.[7] And the great value of raw silk means that the dyer dare not make a mistake.

People say that the silk industry here was begun when King Roger abducted skilled Jewish silk workers from the Greek lands, but in truth silk making is an old craft in Sicily and a traditional craft of Sicilian Jews. Silk was produced here under the Arabs. What King Roger did, when he invaded Greece twenty-five years ago was to bring back very skilled silk workers, most of them Jews, who used the particular methods of Thebes and worked with dedication in the Sicilian silk manufacture and thereby invigorated it. Now Sicily produces silk cloths of a very high quality, along with others of lesser grades. Sericulture here has become important. Sicily exports raw silk as well as silk fabrics, from Palermo and Masara in the west of Sicily and from Syracuse in the east.[8]

The Jewish silk workers have benefited Palermo, and have naturally also enlarged the local Jewish community, which is much bigger than any in Italy. **Palermo is inhabited by about fifteen hundred Jews, and many Christians and Mohammedans.** Jews here are full citizens like any others. They can own any property except Christian slaves. They can work at any occupation. They can be appointed to official posts. They can worship freely, and can settle disputes within the Jewish community in their own courts in accord with Jewish law. Jews can live a very good life in Palermo.

Although for my part, I shall be glad enough to take up life in Tudela, to which, God willing, I shall shortly return.

Letter from Tudela

Dear Friends in Tiberias

"Blessed be He who resurrects the dead!" In the few days since my return to Tudela, people have greeted me thus not once but a hundred times. To be sure I've been away several years, and that's the usual blessing upon seeing someone after a long period of separation, but to me it hardly seems that I have returned from a land of the dead. . . .

With what joy and profound gratitude I think of the places I saw and the stories I heard and especially the people I met: the physicians in Salerno, the Karaite merchants in Constantinople, the remaining Jewish ship owners in Tyre, the intrepid returnees to Jerusalem. Everywhere textile-workers and scholars—how many men are both! I also remember, and shall remember forever, the nights in the hills of Tiberias looking up at the stars. . . .

As they say, "it is good to travel, and it is good to come home." Tudela did not suffer by my absence. Naturally there have been some changes. A couple of years ago, the local Jews moved into the citadel, with King Sancho's promise to maintain its walls in good condition. Of course, should the citadel be attacked by the king's enemies, we are obligated to take part in its defense. Living in the citadel will give us some security in case of riots, and if during any assault we injure or kill an attacker, we shall not be held liable.[1] At least not by the king. . . .

Today is the Monday after my first Shabbat at home. We have held a service of thanksgiving for my safe return. I was thinking of you all, and especially of the survivors of the Franks' massacres and their sons and grandsons, when reciting this prayer of homecoming:

May the Lord in his mercy be full of compassion towards them and us and may He fulfil towards both the words of his Holy Scripture: "Then the Lord thy God will turn thy captivity, and have compassion upon thee, and will return and gather thee from all the nations, whither the Lord thy God hath scattered thee."
Amen. Amen. Amen.

Benjamin

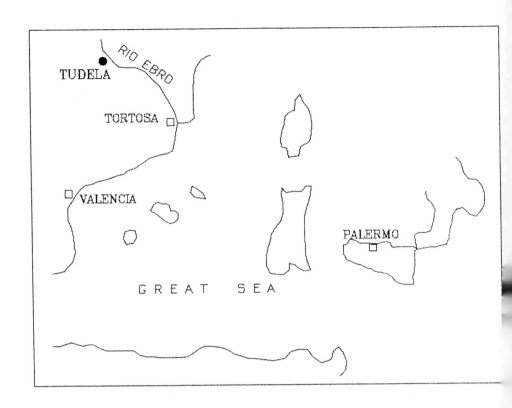

TUDELA

RIO EBRO

TORTOSA

VALENCIA

PALERMO

GREAT   SEA

Glossary

Aljama—(Arabic: "congregation") Self-governing Jewish (or other religious) community in medieval Spain.

Amidah—(Hebrew: "standing") The prayer at the heart of each of the prescribed daily services. Ashkenazim commonly call it the Shemoneh-Esreh (eighteen) because it originally consisted of eighteen benedictions.

Amora (pl. **Amoraim**)—(Aramaic: "speaker" or "interpreter") The school of scholars who taught and expanded the Mishnah, from the time of the completion of that work, ca. 200, until the completion of the Babylonian Talmud, ca. 500.

Ashmedai—(Greek) Name of the prince of demons, i.e., the Devil.

Bar-mitzvah—(Hebrew: "son of the commandment") Term denoting the attainment of religious and legal maturity, upon which a Jew becomes obligated to fulfill all the commandments. This had been fixed at age thirteen for boys, at age twelve for girls, before the Talmudic era; but not until a couple of centuries after Benjamin's time did this transition to adulthood begin to be marked by special ceremony.

B.C.E.—Before the Common Era (= B.C.)

C.E.—Year of the Common Era (= A.D.)

Chanukah (also, **Hanukka**)—(Hebrew: "dedication") Annual eight-day festival starting on the twenth-fifth of Kislev (in December). Tradition holds that it began with Judah Maccabee and his followers.

Dayyan (pl. **Dayyanim**)—(Aramaic: "judge") Term taken from Aramaic into Hebrew to replace the biblical *shofet*. The *Rosh bet din* was the chief justice, and the dayyanim were the associate justices.

Dhimmi—(Arabic) In Moslem law, term denoting "the protected peoples," i.e., Jews and Christians and others whose faith is based on a scripture and who live in an Islamic state. A dhimmi as such has certain legal responsibilities (e.g., payment of a poll tax, refraining from proselytizing Moslems or aiding their enemies) and certain rights (e.g., exemption from military service, judicial autonomy).

Eretz Yisrael—Hebrew: "the Land of Israel."

Etrog—*see* **Four species.**

Exilarch—Term equivalent to the Aramaic *rosh galuta*, "leader of the Exile"—in Babylon, the ruler of the Jewish community.

Four species—The four different plants (etrog, lulav or palm, myrtle, and willow) used in the celebration of the holiday of **Sukkot**, as ordained in Leviticus.

Gaon (pl. **Geonim**)—Title, equivalent to **Rosh Yeshiva**, of the head of the Academy at Sura and of the Academy at Pumbeditha. The two geonim, each vaunting the superiority of his own academy, shared the authority over world Jewry for almost five hundred years, roughly from 600 to 1050.

Haggada—(Hebrew: "telling") The homilies, stories, and anecdotes together comprising the nonlegal part of the old rabbinical literature. Haggada contrasts with **Halakha.**

Halakha—(Hebrew: from the root "to go") The legal side of Judaism, its compass being the relations between persons and between peoples, and all the rites, rights, duties of Judaism.

Haver (pl. **Haverim**, also, **Haber**)—(Hebrew: "member," "colleague") Originally, member of a group pledged to strict observance of the laws of heave-offering (*terumah*), tithing, and purity. Established by the beginning of the common era, groups of haverim lived apart from nonmembers of the group. As haverim were generally scholars and their disciples, *haver* became a synonym for *scholar*. Jews in the Moslem countries used haver in this sense and the term passed into Arabic.

　　Judah Halevi, writing *al-Kuzari* in Arabic, called his scholar-protagonist by the Arabic form of haver.

Imam—(Arabic: from the root "to precede," "to lead") Originally leader, esp. caravan leader, in the Koran the term denotes "model," "example," "prototype." From the beginning of Islam, the term has been applied to the man who indicates the ritual movements of the worship service.

Jizya—(Arabic: roughly, "compensation") Poll tax or head tax, a personal tax as distinguished from property tax, paid exclusively by non-Moslems in Moslem lands.

Kabbala, Kabbalism (also, **Cabala**)—(Hebrew: from the root "to receive") Originally denoting the oral tradition as distinct from written law, around Benjamin's time Jewish mystics adopted the term for their own traditions and since then Kabbala has referred to Jewish mysticism.

Karaite—(Arabic/Hebrew) The name of the sect Kara'im, Ba'alei ha-Mikra (people of the Scriptures), reflects its essential characteristic, the belief in Scripture (that is, the Torah) as the only source of religious law. Correspondingly, the Karaites reject the Oral Law, the rabbinic tradition.

Kashrut—(Hebrew: "fit," "proper") A code of laws defining food and other items as ritually correct. Items in accord with the regulations are said to be **kosher.**

Khalif—(Arabic: "successor," "vice-regent") The political head of the Moslem community.

Kiddush (also **Kiddish**)—(Hebrew: "sanctification") The prayer recited over a cup of wine in the home and the synagogue to consecrate a holy day. Kiddush also denotes the ceremony, which takes place on the eve of the Sabbath or festival and which is celebrated at table in the home as well as in the synagogue.

Kol Nidre—(Aramaic: "all vows") The primary prayer of the evening of the Day of Atonement (Yom Kippur). The recitation annuls all vows made during the preceding year, that is, vows between man and God, vows affecting the self but not other individuals.

The first reference to Kol Nidre as a collective declaration is found in the responsa of the Babylonian geonim beginning in the eighth century, indicating that Kol Nidre was familiar to them from "other lands."

Congregational recitation of Kol Nidre may well have originated in Palestine, as a reaction to Karaite attacks on the Rabbanite practice of annually seeking dispensation from forgotten or too-rigorous vows to God. In Babylonia the geonim (especially of Sura) sharply condemned the recital of Kol Nidre for many generations, but the prayer was popular among the people. Around the year 1000, the era of Hai Gaon, acceptance had been achieved for a Kol Nidre wording that asked God's pardon for the sin of having made a vow or taken an oath and not fulfilled it.

Kosher—*see* **Kashrut.**

Lulav—*see* **Four species.**

Mezuzah (pl. **Mezuzot**)—(Hebrew: "doorpost") The parchment scroll, with certain biblical verses, which is affixed to the doorpost of rooms in the Jewish home. Attributed to Biblical ordinance (Deut. 6:9), the mezuzah has been in common use since before the Talmudic era.

Midrash (pl. **Midrashim**) —(Hebrew: from the root "to seek," "to investigate") A detailed commentary on a specific biblical book or text. A book called a Midrash is generally an anthology, including biblical exegesis, public sermons, and haggadic material. Many Midrashim written before the compilation of the Talmud were "incorporated into it; other and later Midrashim have been published as independent books.

Mikva—(Hebrew: "collection," especially of water) A ritual bath, for use (at separate times) by postmenstruant women, by pious men in certain circumstances, and by converts and by vessels on their introduction into the community. A mikva is constructed according to detailed specifications around a pool of water from a natural spring or river.

Minyan—(Hebrew: "number") The quorum of ten adult males required for most Jewish religious ceremonies, among which public worship.

Mishnah—(Hebrew: from the root "to repeat") Codification of basic Jewish law, compiled by Judah ha-Nasi around 200 c.e.

Mitzvah (pl. **Mitzvot**)—(Hebrew: from the root "to command," "to ordain")

An act of merit performed voluntarily rather than in response to a positive religious commandment; thus, a good deed.

Nagid (pl. **Negidim**)—(Hebrew) The head of the Jewish community in Islamic countries (except under Abbasid rule, where Jewry was led by the exilarchs) and in some Christian countries. In the Middle Ages, beginning in the tenth century, there were negidim in Spain, Kairouan, Egypt, and Yemen.

Nasi (pl. **Nasi'im**)—(Hebrew: "prince") In the days of the Sanhedrin, the head of it. Later the term took on different meanings in different times and places. Nasi could denote the leader of the community, with considerable power, as in Fustat (Egypt) and in Moorish Spain.

Ninth of Ab—Fast day commemorating the Destruction of the Temple. Ab is the name of a summer month.

o.b.m.—"of blessed memory," formula used when uttering the name of the deceased.

Parasha (pl. **Parashiyyot**)—(Hebrew: "divide") A section of the Pentateuch, so designated with regard to the portion to be read each week. In their synagogue service, Babylonian Jews read through the complete Pentateuch each year, and fixed the number of Parashiyyot at fifty-four.

Passover—A major Jewish festival that commemorates the Exodus from Egypt. Celebrated in the spring (starting on the fifteenth day of Nissan), the holiday lasts seven days in Israel and eight in the Diaspora.

Paytan—writer of **Piyyutim**.

Piyyut (pl. **Piyyutim**)—(Greek) Hebrew liturgical poems.

Purim—(Hebrew: "lots") A Jewish festival to commemorate the feast hosted by Mordecai to celebrate the deliverance of the Jews from Haman's plot to kill them. The story is told in the Book of Esther. Purim is so called after the lots cast by Haman in order to determine the month in which the slaughter was to take place. Purim is celebrated for one day (Palestine) or two (Diaspora) in the middle of the month of Adar, which comes in late winter.

Radanites—(perhaps Persian, from the root "knowing the way") Jewish merchants of the ninth century whose activities took them from Spain and France in the west to Russia, India, and China.

Responsa —(Hebrew: "queries and replies") The exchange of letters between a Jewish congregation and a distant authority about some point of ritual or behavior. A tradition of consultation older than the Talmud, the bulk of responsa date from the ninth through eleventh centuries, when they were the threads tying the Jews of the Diaspora to the Babylonian academies; the law as broadcast unremittingly by the **geonim** united the disparate Jewish communities into world Jewry.

Rosh ha-Shanah—(Hebrew: "new year") The autumn festival celebrated on the first day of Tishri (in Palestine; or the first and second days of Tishri in the Diaspora) with prayer and feasting to mark the beginning of the new year.

Rosh Yeshiva—Hebrew: "head of the academy."

Sanhedrin—(Hebraization of the Greek *synedrion*: "assembly") During the Roman period in Jewish Palestine, the Jewish judiciary. Each smaller Sanhedrin had twenty-three judges; the Great Sanhedrin had seventy-one and was the supreme court of Jewish law.

Seder (pl. **Sedarim**)—(Hebrew: "order," "outline"—an order of prayers, or of worship service). (1) The term originally meant the sequence of readings. In the Palestinian tradition, a Seder referred to the portion of the Pentateuch to be read each week at the synagogue service. Generally in that tradition the reading of the Pentateuch extended over three years, and the Sedarim numbered 153. (2) Commonly the word is used for the Passover Seder, the home ceremony of dinner and worship.

Sh'ma—(Hebrew: "hear") The Jew's confession of faith, the declaration of God's unity, the prayer since ancient times recited twice daily in public worship. The command—"Hear, O Israel, the Lord our God, the Lord is one"—comes from Deut. 6:4.

Shabbat—(Hebrew: from the verb for "cease," "rest") The Hebrew Sabbath, a day to abstain from work, to pray, and to rest.

Shavuot—(Hebrew: "weeks") The festival celebrating God's giving the Torah to the Jews. A late-spring holiday observed on the sixth (and seventh) of Sivan, it marked the end of the barley and the beginning of the wheat harvest and is ordained in the Bible as one of the three pilgrim festivals.

Shemonah esreh—*see* **Amidah**.

Shofar—(Hebrew) A ram's horn developed for use as a musical instrument and blown in the synagogue to herald the New Year, as well as on Yom Kippur.

Succot—(Hebrew: "booth," "tabernacle") A harvest and vintage festival of autumn, beginning on the fifteenth day of Tishri and lasting for seven days (in Palestine) or eight days (in the Diaspora). The ancient Israelites held a major festival at harvest time and called it "the feast of the L rd." When the Children of Israel lived in the wilderness after the Exodus they dwelt in huts called succot; in commemoration of which each Jewish household, each year, constructs its own produce-laden succot and takes its meals there throughout the festival.

Taharoth—(Hebrew: "purities") The name of a book of the **Mishnah**, devoted to laws in abeyance since the destruction of the Temple, and thus rarely studied.

Talmud—(Hebrew: "study," "learning") Each of two great compilations of legal material, records of academic discussion about every aspect of Jewish life. The Talmud begins with the **Mishnah**. Two groups of scholars, in Babylonia and in Palestine, recorded their discussions on the laws and teachings of the Mishnah, producing respectively the Babylonian Talmud (completed about 500 c.e.) and the shorter Jerusalem Talmud (completed about 400 c.e.)

Tefillin—(Hebrew, usually translated *phylacteries*) Two black leather boxes containing scriptural texts, which the Jewish man fastens to his left hand and forehead and wears while reciting his daily morning prayers.

During the twelfth century argument raged among scholars over whether the biblical injunction to wear the texts (Deut. 6:8) was literal or figurative, whether the law to do so came from Scripture or from the rabbis.

To'im—(Hebrew: "wanderers") The designation by the Jews of the twelfth century for those who are now called Crusaders.

Torah—(Hebrew: "teaching") Denotes either Scripture or Scripture plus Oral Law. Scholars throughout the ages, including Saadia Gaon, Judah ben Barzilai, Abraham ibn Ezra, Judah Hadassi, and Judah Halevi, have argued about the meaning of "Torah."

Ulema (pl. of **alim**)—(Arabic: "possessors of knowledge, in a broad sense and to a high degree") The body of scholars who make the ultimate decisions about Islamic theology and law. Although the scholars are not organized into any formal association, collectively they are the authority on Islamic law.

Yeshiva (pl. **Yeshivot**)—(Hebrew: "academies") Institutes of Talmudic learning.

Yom Kippur—(Hebrew: "day of atonement") The most important day in the Jewish liturgical year, a day of fasting and atonement. Observed the tenth of Tishri, it is the climax of the Ten Days of Penitence, which begin with **Rosh ha-Shanah**.

Zizit—(Hebrew: "fringes") The fringes or tassels attached to the four corners of special garments worn by men in fulfillment of the biblical commandment (Num. 15:37–41; Deut. 22:12).

Notes

Chapter 1. Tudela's Marketplace

1. On cut and color of garments: *CIBA Review* no. 1, "Medieval Dyeing," 28–29; Goitein, *Mediterranean Society* 1:106–8, 4:160–61, 172; on lack of distinguishing dress: Goitein, *Mediterranean Society* 3:286, 4:195; Abrahams, *Jewish Life*, 302, 308–9; Dimont, *Jews, God, and History*, 225; on right of Jews to carry a sword: Biale, *Power and Powerlessness*, 72.
2. Poem translation from Goldstein, *Hebrew Poems from Spain*, 123.

Chapter 2. Tudela's Jews under Moslem Rule

1. *Apocrypha, Ben Sira* 38:31–34; see also B. Talmud, Nedarim 49b; Bava Kamma 79b.
2. *Mishnah, Derek Eretz Zuta* 4:2.
3. B. Talmud; Kuddushin, 82a-b. J. Talmud. Sanhedrin, 11, Sec.7,f.30b, line 68.
4. Goitein, *Mediterranean Society* 1:161.
5. Abrahams, *Jewish Life*, 247.
6. Leroy, *Jews of Navarre*, 25.
7. Goitein, *Jews and Arabs*, 1955 ed., 74; Goitein, "Jewish Society and Institutions," 175; Stillman, *Jews of Arab Lands*, 62; Ashtor, *Jews of Moslem Spain* 1:23–24 and, regarding where Jews dwelt in particular cities, 294, 300, 315, 320, 331.
8. B.Talmud. Kiddushin, 29a.
9. Ibid., 82a.
10. Runciman, *Crusades* 1:21–23 summarizes the aljama institution, which he calls by the name "milet system." See also Hourani, *Arab Peoples*, 117–19, 135. Leroy, *Jews of Navarre*, 20–25, discusses the aljama of Tudela specifically, from the year 1121.
11. Goitein, *Mediterranean Society* 2:380–81, 391.
12. Poem translation from Waxman, *History of Jewish Literature* 1:223.
13. Poem translation from Goldstein, *Hebrew Poems from Spain*, 85.
14. Schirmann, "Hebrew Poet in Medieval Spain," 236.
15. Poem translation from Waxman, *History of Jewish Literature* l:234; the Hebrew poem is in M. Friedländer, *Commentary of ibn Ezra on Isaiah* 1:xviii.
16. Poem translation from Baron, *Social and Religious History* 7:203–4.
17. Goitein, *Jews and Arabs*, 92; Goitein, *Mediterranean Society* 1:112.
18. Goitein, *Mediterranean Society* 1:112.
19. Baer, *Jews in Christian Spain* 1:32–33; Graetz, *History of the Jews*, 3:255–60.
20. Lines of poem translation from Weinberger, *Jewish Prince in Moslem Spain*, 34–37.

21. Poem translation from Goldstein, *Hebrew Poems from Spain*, 57.

22. Translation from Baron, *Social and Religious History* 7:148.

23. Poem translation from Graetz, *History of the Jews* 3:235. He says that Arabs took pride in the Jewish poets in their midst. See also Stillman, *Jews of Arab Lands*, 58.

24. Baer, *Jews in Christian Spain* 1:35–36.

25. Dubnov, *History of the Jews* 2:614–15.

26. The translation is of lines in Yitzhak Baer, *Toledot haYehudim bi-Sefarad haNotzrit* (Jews in Christian Spain), (Tel Aviv: Am Ovid, 1965), 36.

Chapter 3. Santiago, Reconquista, Crusades

1. Lomax, *Reconquest of Spain*, 34; Leroy, *Jews of Navarre*, 2.

2. Baer, *Jews in Christian Spain* 1:47; Erbstösser, *The Crusades*, 71.

3. Erbstösser, *The Crusades*, 72.

4. Baron, *Social and Religious History* 3:124.

5. The Hebrew poem is in Moses ibn Ezra, *Selected Poems*, 63.

6. Baer, *Jews in Christian Spain*, 1:65.

7. Poem translation by Nina Davis Salaman, in Judah Halevi, *Selected Poems*, 157–58.

8. Adapted from the poem translation by Nina Davis Salaman, ibid., 10–11.

9. The Hebrew poem is ibid., 2.

Chapter 4. Leaving Tudela

1. Poem translation by Nina Davis Salaman, in Judah Halevi, *Selected Poems*, 39–40.

2. *Midrash on Psalms,* 23:3.

3. B. Talmud. Gittin, 70a.

4. Quoted in Goitein, *Mediterranean Society* 1:348.

5. Midrash Rabbah, Ecclesiastes 4:9, sec. 1.

6. Judah Halevi's death at Jerusalem's gates is the traditional story. See Goitein, "Judah Ha-Levi," 56, for discussion of recently discovered documents that suggest he did not so die.

7. Goitein, *Mediterranean Society* 1:205.

8. *Encyclopedia Judaica*, s.v. "Economic History," 16:1275.

9. Goitein, *Mediterranean Society* 1:58–59.

10. Astor, *Jews of Moslem Spain* 1:308.

11. Abrahams, *Jewish Life*, 105–6; Abrahams, *Book of Delight*, 123–24, deals specifically with documents for Jews leaving Spain.

12. Baron, *Social and Religious History* 4:169.

13. McMurtrie, *The Book*, 65, 67; *CIBA Review* no. 72, "Paper," 2634–35f, 2642.

14. A fragment of the chronicle written by Benjamin, on paper, is in the British Library in London.

15. The Hebrew poem is in Weinberger, *Jewish Prince in Moslem Spain*, 118.

16. B. Talmud. Berakhot, 29b.

Letter from Barcelona

1. Poem translation from Waxman, *History of Jewish Literature* 1:220.

2. Poem translation from Goldstein, *Hebrew Poems from Spain*, 63.

3. The translation is of the poem in Zinberg, *Toledot Sifrut Yisrael* 1:39.

4. Solomon ibn Gabirol, *Selected Religious Poems*, xxiv, xxviii–xxix.

5. Lines of poem translation from Graetz, *History of the Jews* 3:268.

6. Stanza of poem translation from Friedlander, *Standard Book of Jewish Verse*, 241.

7. Poem translation by Israel Zangwill in Waxman, *History of Jewish Literature* 1:222.

8. Solomon ibn Gabirol, *Selected Religious Poems*, xlix.

9. Lines of poem translation from ibid., xxii.

10. Adapted lines from the poem translation by Emma Lazarus, in Ausubel and Ausubel, *Treasury of Jewish Poetry*, 179.

11. *Encyclopedia Judaica*, s.v. "Gabirol," says he died about 1057 at age 37, but scholars argue about this. There is general agreement that he died violently and relatively young.

12. Joseph ben Meir Zabara, *Sepher Shaashuim*, xli, xlii.

13. *Encyclopedia Judaica*, s.v. "Charlemagne."

14. Lopez and Raymond, *Medieval Trade*, 162.

15. Singer et al., *History of Technology* 2: 449–84, esp. 472, 475, 481 for technical details on silversmithing, and 490 on coins.

16. Those whom we call crusaders, the Jews of Benjamin's time called To'im.

Letter from Narbonne

1. Saige, *Les Juifs du Languedoc*, 42–43; "Schwarzfuchs, "France and Germany under the Carolingians," 131; *Encyclopedia Judaica*, svv. "Charlemagne," "Narbonne."

2. Saige, *Les Juifs du Languedoc*, 69–70; *Encyclopedia Judaica*, s.v. "Narbonne."

3. Baron, *Social and Religious History* 7:139; Rashdall, *Universities* 2:121.

4. Parkes, *Jews in the Medieval Community*, 58; *Encyclopedia Judaica*, s.v. "Narbonne."

5. *Encyclopedia Judaica*, s.v. "Abraham ben Isaac of Narbonne."

6. Erbstösser, *The Crusades*, 87.

7. Parkes, *Jews in the Medieval Community*, 312–14, 326–27. Sarton, *History of Science*, vol. 2, pt. 1, p.163; *Encyclopedia Judaica*, s.v. "Money-lending," 48.

8. Roth, "Economic Life and Population Movements," 38–39.

9. *Jewish Encyclopedia*, s.v. "Synods"; Graetz, *History of the Jews* 3:377.

Letter from Lunel

1. Saige, *Les Juifs du Languedoc,* 11–12; *Encyclopedia Judaica*, s.v. "Beziers."

2. Sarton, *History of Science*, vol. 2, pt. l, p. 163.

3. Ibid., 352.

4. Ibid., 246.

5. Johnson, *History of the Jews*, 199–200.

6. Graetz, *History of the Jews* 3:390.

7. Twersky, "Provençal Jewry," 190–94.

8. *Encyclopedia Judaica*, s.v. "Economic History," 16:1275.

9. Apocrypha, Ben Sira 14:14; B. Talmud, Ta'anit, 11a,b (Bar Kappara), Bava Batra, 60b.

10. Judah Halevi, *Kuzari*, part 2, sec. 50.

11. Abrahams, *Jewish Life*, 387.

12. *Encyclopedia Judaica*, s.v. "Tibbon."

13. Zinberg, *Jewish Literature* 2:165–66.
14. *Encyclopedia Judaica*, s.v. "Tibbon"; Dan, *Jewish Mysticism and Jewish Ethics*, 22; Sarton, *History of Science*, vol. 2, pt. 1, p. 345; and Twersky, *Provençal Jewry*, 199, give dates for Judah ibn Tibbon's translations: *Hovot ha-Levavot*, 1161, *Kuzari*, 1166–67.
15. *Encyclopedia Judaica*, s.v. "Tibbon."
16. *Jewish Encyclopedia*, s.v. "ibn Tibbon."
17. Baron, *Social and Religious History* 7:138.
18. Abrahams, *Hebrew Ethical Wills*, 53.
19. The Hebrew poem is from ibid., 58. Judah ibn Tibbon included his translation of the verse in his ethical will.
20. Graetz, *History of the Jews* 3:260.
21. See Judah ibn Tibbon's ethical will, in Abrahams, *Hebrew Ethical Wills*, 53, 81–82.
22. Friedenwald, *The Jews and Medicine* 1:11.
23. Abrahams, *Jewish Life*, 254.

Letter from Marseille

1. For Posquières, Asher mistakenly says Beaucaire.
2. Baron, *Social and Religious History* 7:70–71.
3. *Mishnah, Berakhot* 4:4 (R. Eliezer) is one of several examples.
4. Poem translation from Baron, *Social and Religious History*, 7:75.
5. Goitein, *Mediterranean Society* 1:211.
6. Rabinowitz, *Jewish Merchant Adventurers*, 43.
7. Goitein, *Mediterranean Society* 1: 284.
8. Goitein, *Mediterranean Society* 1: 197, 240–47.
9. Goitein, *Jews and Arabs*, 111–12.
10. Ibid., 118–19.
11. Goitein, *Mediterranean Society* 1:155.
12. Lopez and Raymond, *Medieval Trade*, 239.
13. Payne, *The Dream and the Tomb*, 124.
14. Erbstösser, *The Crusades*, 136.

Letter from Pisa

1. Roth, *History of the Jews of Italy*, 75; *Jewish Encyclopedia*, s.v. "Genoa."
2. Milano, *Storia degli Ebrei in Italia*, 69.
3. Byrne, *Genoese Shipping,* 3–8 passim.
4. *CIBA Review*, no. 10, "Trade Routes and Dye Markets," 325; *Encyclopedia Britannica*, 1950 ed., s.v. "Pisa."
5. Milano, *Storia degli Ebrei in Italia*, 72; *CIBA Review,* no. 10, "Trade Routes and Dye Markets," 325.
6. *CIBA Review*, no. 10, "Trade Routes and Dye Markets," 325.
7. Milano, *Storia degli Ebrei in Italia*, 72.
8. *CIBA Review*, no. 10, "Trade Routes and Dye Markets," 325.
9. Roth, *History of the Jews of Italy*, 75.

Letter from Lucca

1. *CIBA Review*, no. 80, "Lucchese Silks," 2903; Milano, *Storia degli Ebrei in Italia*, 73.

2. *CIBA Review*, no. 80, "Lucchese Silks," 2902, 2907.
3. Singer, *History of Technology* 2:198.
4. *CIBA Review*, no. 80, "Lucchese Silks," 2908–09.
5. Ibid., 2909.
6. Ibid., 2911; Goitein, *Mediterranean Society* 1: 242–43.
7. *CIBA Review*, no. 80, "Lucchese Silks," 2909.
8. Ibid., 2908.
9. Ibid., 2908, 2915.
10. Ibid., 2907.
11. *CIBA Review*, no. 10, "Trade Routes and Dye Markets," 325.
12. *CIBA Review*, no. 80, "Lucchese Silks," 2903, 2907, 2908.
13. *CIBA Review*, no. 10, "Trade Routes and Dye Markets," 325.
14. *CIBA Review*, no. 80, "Lucchese Silks," 2908, 2912.
15. Ben Sasson, "The Northern European Jewish Community," 214; *Encyclopedia Judaica*, s.v. "Textiles," 1038.
16. Runciman, *Crusades* 2:254–55.
17. Dan, *Jewish Mysticism and Jewish Ethics*, 27.
18. Poem translation from Goldstein, *Hebrew Poems from Spain*, 129–30.
19. Sarton, *History of Science*, vol. 2, pt. 1, p. 187; *Encyclopedia Judaica*, s.v. (Abraham) "ibn Ezra," 1167.

Letter from Rome

1. Asher, *Travels of Benjamin of Tudela*, 2:17.
2. This is written as though Benjamin were in Rome in 1165.
3. Kelly, *Popes*, s.v. "Anacletus II."
4. Vogelstein, *Jews in Rome*, 144.
5. Kelly, *Popes*, s.v. "Anacletus II."
6. Baron, *Social and Religious History* 4:11; Vogelstein, *Jews in Rome*, 144–45; *Jewish Encyclopedia*, s.v. "Anacletus II"; *Encyclopedia Judaica*, s.v. "Popes."
7. *Encyclopedia Judaica*, svv. "Bulls," "Caixtus."
8. Roth, *History of the Jews of Italy*, 90.
9. Milano, *Storia degli Ebrei in Italia*, 80–82.
10. Vogelstein, *Jews in Rome*, 127; Zinberg, *Jewish Literature* 2:170.
11. The Hebrew poem is in Moses ibn Ezra, *Selected Poems*, 58.
12. Schechter, *Studies in Jewish Liturgy*, 28.
13. Roth, *History of the Jews of Italy*, 92.
14. Zinberg, *Jewish Literature* 2:166–67; Abrahams, *By-paths in Hebraic Bookland*, includes five pages in light style on "Nathan of Rome's Dictionary" and its importance, 60–66.
15. Graetz, *History of the Jews* 3:290, 369. See also Schechter, *Studies in Jewish Liturgy*, 28; and Vogelstein, *Jews in Rome*, 150–51.
16. M. Friedländer, *Commentary of ibn Ezra on Isaiah* 1:xxii–xxiii, provides explanation of Abraham ibn Ezra's long poem, several stanzas of it in Hebrew, and a translation of them into English, from which this excerpt and the following have been adapted. The entire poem in Hebrew is in Kahana, *Rabbi Abraham ibn Ezra*, 22–30.
17. Baron, *Social and Religious History* 8:171; M. Friedländer, *Commentary of ibn Ezra on Isaiah* 1:xxii–xxiii.
18. Vogelstein, *Jews in Rome*, 151.
19. Lines of poem as in n. 16, above.

Letter from Salerno

1. Milano, *Storia degli Ebrei in Italia*, 83.
2. *Encyclopedia Judaica*, s.v. "Capua."
3. *Encyclopedia Britannica*, 1974 ed., Macropædia, s.v. "Petroleum" 14:165.
4. Asher, *Travels of Benjamin of Tudela* 2:27, quoting Edrisi.
5. Ibid., p. 28.
6. Lopez and Raymond, *Medieval Trade*, 54.
7. Asher, *Travels of Benjamin of Tudela* 2:27, quoting Edrisi.
8. Milano, *Storia degli Ebrei in Italia*, 84.
9. Roth, *History of the Jews of Italy*, 79.
10. M. Friedländer, *Commentary of ibn Ezra on Isaiah* 1:xxiv; Waxman, *History of Jewish Literature* 1:176–77; Zinberg, *Jewish Literature* 2:168.
11. Roth, *History of the Jews of Italy*, 62.
12. Details about Christian medicine in Salerno are given in Friedenwald, *The Jews and Medicine* 1:15; Coleman, *Story of Medicine*, 26–29; Rashdall, *Universities* 1:80; and Erbstösser, *The Crusades*, 70.
13. Coleman, *Story of Medicine*, 34–35.
14. B. Talmud. Berakhot, 60a.
15. Friedenwald, *The Jews and Medicine* 1:16.
16. B. Talmud. Berakhot, 60a.
17. Apocrypha. Ben Sira. 38:4.
18. Friedenwald, *The Jews and Medicine* 1:16.
19. Harington, *The School of Salernum*, 75–76.
20. Baron, *Social and Religious History* 8:245, 258.
21. Friedenwald, *The Jews and Medicine* 1:12.
22. B. Talmud. Bava Kamma, 85a.
23. Sarton, *History of Science*, vol. 2, pt. 1, p. 76.
24. Harington, *The School of Salernum*, p. 80. "Meats" is an old word for foods generally.

Letter from Taranto

1. Ps. 116:17.
2. Ahimaaz, *Chronicle*, 63–66.
3. Cohen, *Ibn Daud*, 64.
4. Milano, *Storia degli Ebrei in Italia*, 89.
5. Schechter, *Studies in Jewish Liturgy*, 29. The line paraphrased by R. Tam is Isa. 2:3.
6. Runciman, *Crusades* 1:6, 21, 88–89.

Letter from Oria

1. Friedenwald, *The Jews and Medicine* 2:557.
2. On the obligation to rescue: *Encyclopedia Judaica*, s.v. "Economic History," 16:1275; on Donnolo; Morais, *Italian Hebrew Literature*, 3.
3. Donnolo's lines are translated from the Hebrew in Zinberg, *Toledot Sifrut Yisrael* 1:332; see also Baron, *Social and Religious History* 8:253.
4. Zinberg, *Jewish Literature* 2:137. Donnolo took the phrase from B. Talmud. Sanhedrin, 37a.
5. Baron, *Social and Religious History* 8:245 and Friedenwald, *The Jews and Medicine* 1:151, 2:556 tell the story of Donnolo and Nilus.

6. Friedenwald, *The Jews and Medicine*, 1:15; Singer and Underwood, *Short History of Medicine*, 69–71.

7. Adapted lines of poem translation in Schirmann, "Beginning of Hebrew Poetry," 257.

8. Ibid.

9. Zimmels, "Scholars and Scholarship," 176.

10. Roth, "Italy," 11:104–5.

11. Poem translation by Nina Davis Salaman, in Schirmann, "Beginning of Hebrew Poetry," 252.

12. Ahimaaz, *Chronicle*, 85.

13. Ibid., 87. See also Schirmann, "Beginning of Hebrew Poetry," 252–53.

Letter from Otranto

1. Roth, *History of the Jews of Italy*, 86–87.

2. Goitein, "Jewish Society and Institutions," 177.

3. Song of Songs 4:14.

4. Dubnov, *History of the Jews* 2:596.

5. Colafemmina, "Una nuova epigrafe," 421.

6. Poem translation by Nina Davis Salaman, in Schirmann, "Beginning of Hebrew Poetry," 251.

7. Ahimaaz, *Chronicle*, 67–69; Zinberg, *Jewish Literature* 2:163–64.

8. Mann, *Texts and Studies* 2:117.

9. Ibid., 51.

10. Idelsohn, *Jewish Music*, 106.

11. Mann, *Texts and Studies* 2:116.

12. Poem translation from Baron, *Social and Religious History* 5:152.

13. *Encyclopedia Judaica*, s.v. "Piyyut."

14. Zinberg, *Jewish Literature* 2:167.

15. Ibid.

16. Roth, "Italy" 11:112–13; Milano, *Storia degli Ebrei in Italia*, 64.

Letter from Thebes

1. Sharf, "Jews in Byzantium," 64.

2. Verse of Abraham ibn Ezra, translated in Waxman, *History of Jewish Literature* 1:235.

3. *CIBA Review*, no. 75, "Byzantine Silks," 2745, 2748, 2753.

4. Rabinowitz, *Jewish Merchant Adventurers*, is a history of the Radanites. See also Baron, *Social and Religious History* 4:180–81; Lopez and Raymond, *Medieval Trade*, 31–32.

5. Goitein, *Mediterranean Society* 1:264.

6. Lopez and Raymond, *Medieval Trade*, 22.

7. On antiquity of these guilds: *CIBA Review*, no. 11, "Early History of Silk," 385; Lopez, "Silk Industry," 5–8; on the Jews' guilds; Lopez, "Silk Industry" 24.

Letter from Salunki

1. Geanakoplos, *Byzantium*, 280–81.

2. Lopez and Raymond, *Medieval Trade*, 31–32.

3. Ankori, *Karaites in Byzantium*, 284.

4. Prawer, *Jews in the Latin Kingdom*, 13.

5. Poem translation by Emma Lazarus, in Kravitz, *3,000 Years of Hebrew Literature,* 257–58. The lines quoted are the first and last of ten stanzas, originally in Moses ibn Ezra's *Tarshish*.

First Letter from Constantinople

1. Goitein, *Mediterranean Society* 1:103.

2. Sharf, "Jews in Byzantium," 66.

3. Starr, *Jews in the Byzantine Empire*, 43.

4. Runciman, *Crusades* 1:61–62, 83, mentions the unwillingness of the Greeks to make war.

5. Ibid., 1:47. Finucane, *Soldiers of Faith*, 11.

6. Sharf, *Byzantine Jewry*, 17.

7. Starr, *Jews in the Byzantine Empire*, 43.

8. B. Talmud; Pesahim, 65a (Judah ha-Nasi); Bava Batra 16b (Bar Kappara).

Second Letter from Constantinople

1. Sharf, "Jews in Byzantium," 64.

2. Ankori, *Karaites in Byzantium*, 286.

3. Ibid.

4. Waxman, *History of Jewish Literature* 1:412.

5. Ibid., 413–15.

6. Ibid., 1:413.

7. Ankori, *Karaites in Byzantium*, 268.

8. Lev. 23:15.

9. Ankori, *Karaites in Byzantium*, 275–76.

10. Cohen, *Ibn Daud.*

11. Baron, *Social and Religious History* 4:111–12, argues that the Jews remaining in Jerusalem were mostly Karaites.

12. Baer, *Jews in Christian Spain* 1:77.

Letter from Cyprus

On the Mishawites/Kaphrossin, see Ankori, *Karaites in Byzantium*, 376–89, 408.

Letter from Antioch

1. Runciman, *Crusades* 1:217, in a footnote reports that William of Tyre called it the "Far."

2. Newby, *Saladin in his Time*, 49; Prawer, *World of the Crusaders*, 125–26; Finucane, *Soldiers of Faith*, 63–65, on hunger and the eating of horses and human flesh, 68–69, 87, 94, on fighting from horseback; Runciman, *Crusades* 1:219, 221, on lives lost.

3. Maalouf, *Crusades through Arab Eyes*, 38–39, and 270 for sources and comments; Erbstösser, *The Crusades*, 96; Finucane, *Soldiers of Faith*, 97.

4. Runciman, *Crusades* 1:235.

5. Ibid. 2:325–326.
6. Grousset, *L'épopée des croisades*, 186–89; Runciman, *Crusades* 2:353–54.
7. Grousset, *L'épopée des croisades*, 189–90; Runciman, *Crusades* 2:357.
8. Runciman, *Crusades* 2:316.
9. Goitein, *Mediterranean Society* 1:109–10, on Jews in glass-making.

Letter from Beirut

1. Runciman, *Crusades* 2:294; "Erbstösser, *The Crusades*, 129, 131–32.
2. Maalouf, *Crusades through Arab Eyes*, 102, on Assassin activity in the Crusades.
3. *Grand Larousse,* s.v. "Raymond de St.Gilles"; Runciman, *Crusades* 1:270.
4. Runciman, *Crusades* 2:294.
5. Grousset, *L'épopée des croisades*, 75, on Count Raymond's capture of Tortosa and Tripoli; Runciman, *Crusades* 1:270–75; 60–64.
6. Runciman, *Crusades* 2:60.
7. Benjamin gives both figures.
8. Runciman, *Crusades* 2:361.

Letter from Tyre

1. Lions and leopards: Song of Songs 4:8; dew: Ps. 133:3. cedar trees: Ps. 104:16; Isa. 14:8.
2. Maalouf, *Crusades through Arab Eyes*, 89; *Encyclopedia Britannica*, 1950 ed., s.v. "Tyre," and 1974 ed., Micropædia 10:223.
3. Le Strange, *Palestine under the Moslems*, 343, has a similar description of the port, written in 985.
4. Ibid., 343, reporting an observation of 1047.
5. Runciman, *Crusades* 2:169.
6. Maalouf, *Crusades through Arab Eyes*, 90.
7. Runciman, *Crusades* 2:167–69, 294.
8. Prawer, *Jews in the Latin Kingdom,* 103.
9. Friedenwald, *The Jews and Medicine* 2:556; Erbstösser, *The Crusades*, 150.
10. Probably cotton, of which much was then produced in Palestine; see, for example, Benvenisti, *The Crusaders in the Holy Land,* 386. Le Strange, *Palestine under the Moslems*, 18, reports cotton exported from Jerusalem to Syria in tenth century.
11. *CIBA Review*, no. 4, "Purple," 121; "Erbstösser, *The Crusades*, 40.
12. Spanier and Karmon, "Muricid Snails," 188.

Letter from Haifa

1. B. Talmud. Ketubbot, 11a.
2. Runciman, *Crusades* 2:16.
3. Prawer, *Jews in the Latin Kingdom*, 97, 103.
4. Finucane, *Soldiers of Faith*, 51.
5. Runciman, *Crusades* 2:88.
6. Ibid., 233; Payne, *The Dream and the Tomb*, 149.

7. The idea that "the law of the state is the law" is repeated several times, e.g., in the B. Talmud, Nedarim, 28a and Bava Kamma, 113a.

8. Runciman, *Crusades* 1:316.

Letter from Nablus

On the Samaritans, see Baron, *Social and Religious History* 5:170–77.

1. Ezra 4:1–6.

2. Josephus, *Antiquities*, bk. 9, chap. 14, sec. 3, from an edition based on Havercamp's translation (New York: Bigelow, Brown and Co., 1924). Josephus repeated this idea, in slightly different words, in Bk. 11, chap. 8, sec. 6.

3. Runciman, *Crusades* 2:4.

4. Ibid., 297–98.

5. Num. 19:11–18.

6. Deut. 27:4.

First Letter from Jerusalem

1. 1 Sam. 28:4, 31:1–8; 2 Sam. 1:6, 21.

2. Josh. 10:12–13.

3. Runciman, *Crusades* 1:279.

4. Ps. 48:3.

5. Josephus, *Jewish War*, bk. 3, chap. 3, sec. 5; B. Talmud, Sanhedrin, 37a, n. a(9).

6. *Encyclopedia Judaica*, s.v. "Jerusalem," 1415–18, in a long description of the city under the Crusaders, makes no mention of a synagogue. The *Jewish Encyclopedia*, 1912 ed., s.v. "Jerusalem," 131, refers to one briefly. Prawer, *Jews in the Latin Kingdom*, 106, mentions probably-inconspicuous prayer-places.

7. Amittai ben Shefatia, "Adonoy, Adonoy," *Jewish Quarterly Review*, o.s., 9 (1897): 722, trans. by Nina Davis Salaman. The poem is used in the current Yom Kippur Neilah service.

8. Ps. 137:5.

9. Prawer, *Jews in the Latin Kingdom,* 132.

10. B. Talmud, Ketubbot, 111a (R. Johanan).

11. Prawer, *Jews in the Latin Kingdom*, 132.

12. Ibid.

13. Judah Halevi, *Kuzari*, pt. 2, sec. 22.

14. B. Talmud, Ketubbot, 110b.

15. Deut. 34:6.

16. B. Talmud. Mo'ed Katan, 26a.

17. Runciman, *Crusades* 1:279, 2:316.

18. Ibid. 2:316.

19. *Encyclopedia Britannica*, 1974 ed., Macropædia, s.v. "Petroleum," 14:165.

20. Maalouf, *Crusades through Arab Eyes*, 50; Runciman, *Crusades* 1:286.

21. *Encyclopedia Judaica*, s.v. "Jerusalem," 1416.

Second Letter from Jerusalem

1. Mann, *Texts and Studies* 2:49–51.

2. Goitein, *Mediterranean Society* 1:257.

3. Runciman, *Crusades* 1:229; Maalouf, *Crusades through Arab Eyes*, 46–47.

4. Finucane, *Soldiers of Faith*, 62.

5. Runciman, *Crusades* 1:279; the attack described, 279–87.

6. Baron, *Social and Religious History* 4:109–10; Prawer, *Jews in the Latin Kingdom*, 28–31; Finucane, *Soldiers of Faith*, 104–5.

7. Runciman, *Crusades* 2:156.

8. Ibid., 464.

9. Ibid., 299; Erbstösser, *The Crusades,* 130.

10. Runciman, *Crusades* 2:321.

11. Ibid., 100.

12. Ibid., 294.

13. Prawer, *Jews in the Latin Kingdom*, 103.

14. Runciman, *Crusades* 2:316–17; Erbstösser, *The Crusades*, 130–36 passim.

15. Benvenisti, *Crusaders in the Holy Land*, 378–79.

16. Ausubel, *Treasury of Jewish Poetry*, 427–28, has the poem as translated into English by Nina Davis Salaman.

17. Baron, *Social and Religious History* 4:114–15; "Prawer, *Jews in the Latin Kingdom*, 104, 107; Benvenisti, *Crusaders in the Holy Land*, 21.

18. Goitein, *Mediterranean Society* 2:282.

19. Runciman, *Crusades* 2:101, 302; Prawer, *Jews in the Latin Kingdom*, 98–99.

Letter from Askalon

1. 1 Sam. 10:2.

2. Gen. 35:20.

3. Gen. 23: 9–17.

4. Runciman, *Crusades* 1:304, 2:4.

5. Prawer, *Jews in the Latin Kingdom*, 40–41.

6. This place was probably not the ancient Shiloh. See Asher, *The Travels of Benjamin of Tudela*, 2:95.

7. Goitein, *Mediterranean Society* 2:165–66.

8. Runciman, *Crusades* 2:294.

9. J. Talmud, Shevi'it 6:1.

10. Maalouf, *Crusades through Arab Eyes*, 88.

11. Goitein, *Mediterranean Society* 2:165.

12. Prawer, *Jews in the Latin Kingdom*, 29.

13. Maalouf, *Crusades through Arab Eyes*, 88; Runciman, *Crusades* 2:94–95.

14. Runciman, *Crusades* 2:338–39; Benvenisti, *Crusaders in the Holy Land*, 116–17.

First Letter from Tiberias

1. Josephus, *Vita*, secs. 67, 71.

2. *Encyclopedia Judaica*, s.v. "Sepphoris."

3. Runciman, *Crusades* 2:295, 299.

4. Prawer, *Jews in the Latin Kingdom*, 122.

5. Le Strange, *Palestine under the Moslems*, 335f.

6. Ibid.

7. B. Talmud, Shabbat, 40a, 109a; Ketubbot, 77b.

8. Num. 19:16.

9. B. Talmud, Bava Kamma, 38a (Rabbi Meir); Avodah Zarah, 3a.
10. *Jewish Encyclopedia*, s.v. "Meir."
11. Nathan, *The Fathers*, xxi.
12. B. Talmud, Kiddushin, 82a–b.
13. Taylor, *Sayings of the Jewish Fathers* 4:14.
14. Johnson, *History of the Jews*, 89–90.
15. B. Talmud, Bava Batra, 8a (Judah ha-Nasi).
16. Johnson, *History of the Jews*, 90.

Second Letter from Tiberias

On Jewish calendar development see *Encyclopedia Judaica*, s.v. "Calendar," and *Jewish Encyclopedia*, s.vv. "Astronomy," "Samaritans."
1. B. Talmud; Hullin, 60b.
2. Abraham ibn Ezra, *Yesod Mora*, 18 in the German translation.
3. 1 Kings 12:32–33.
4. Halpern, *People in Post-Biblical Times*, 127.
5. Exod. 9:31, 12:1–3, 14–16; Deut. 16:1.
6. Baron, *Social and Religious History* 8:188.
7. Ezek. 7:2.
8. *Encyclopedia Judaica*, s.vv. "Ben Meir," "Saadia."
9. B. Talmud; Avodah Zarah, 43a,b; Rosh Ha-Shanah, 24a,b.
10. M. Friedländer, *Writings of Ibn Ezra*, 179.
11. Sarton, *History of Science*, vol. 2, pt. 1, pp. 206–7. Zinberg, *Jewish Literature* 2:80–82; *Jewish Encyclopedia*, s.v. "Abraham bar Hiyya," "Astrology."
12. Baron, *Social and Religious History* 8:178–80.
13. *Jewish Encyclopedia*, s.v. "Astrology," "Yezirah."
14. Judah Halevi, *Kuzari*, pt. 4, sec. 25.
15. *Jewish Encyclopedia*, s.vv. "Astrology," "Donnolo."
16. Judah Halevi, *Kuzari*, pt. 1, sec. 77; pt. 4, secs. 8, 9.
17. Baron, *Social and Religious History* 8:181. Ibn Daud's *Sefer ha-Kabbalah* (the anti-Karaite book) and *Emunah Ramah* were both published in 1161. An astronomy book of 1180 has been lost.
18. Abraham ibn Ezra's commentary on Deut. 4:19, quoted in *Encyclopedia Judaica*, s.v. "Astrology," 792. But this idea wasn't original with him; see *Jewish Encyclopedia*, s.v. "Astrology," 243.
19. Lines of poem translation by Israel Zangwill, in Solomon ibn Gabirol, *Selected Religious Poems*, "The Royal Crown" (Keter Malkut), secs. XII, XV, XXII.

Letter from Damascus

1. Josh. 11:5–7.
2. Asher, *The Travels of Benjamin of Tudela* 2:108.
3. Ibid., 107–8.
4. The phrase "from Dan to Beersheba" occurs several times in the Bible. Dan for receiving news of invaders: Jer. 4:15, 8:16.
5. Runciman, *Crusades* 2:343, 370–71; Benvenisti, *Crusaders in the Holy Land*, 147–51.
6. Goitein, *Mediterranean Society* 2:6.
7. Ibid., 159.

8. Prawer, "Obadyah the Norman."

9. *Jewish Encyclopedia*, s.v. "Damascus"; Prawer, *Jews in the Latin Kingdom*, 52.

10. Erbstösser, *The Crusades*, 127.

11. Runciman, *Crusades* 2:340–41. Grousset, *L'épopée des croisades*, 171–72. Benvenisti, *Crusaders in the Holy Land*, 5.

12. B. Talmud; Eruvin, 19a.

13. Le Strange, *Palestine under the Moslems*, 237.

14. *CIBA Review*, no. 10, "Trade Routes and Dye Markets," 333.

15. Ibid.

16. Maalouf, *Crusades through Arab Eyes*, 59.

17. McMurtrie, *The Book*, 64; Le Strange, *Palestine under the Moslems*, 19.

18. Wiet, *Medieval Civilizations*, 319.

19. *CIBA Review*, no. 11, "Early History of Silk," 373.

20. Le Strange, *Palestine under the Moslems*, 240.

21. Goitein, *Mediterranean Society* 1:92.

22. Ibid., 82.

23. Maalouf, *Crusades through Arab Eyes*, 112. Zengi established the hospital in 1154.

24. Goitein, *Mediterranean Society* 1:83.

25. *Encyclopedia Judaica*, s.v. "Damascus," 1240; *Encyclopedia Britannica*, 1986 ed., Macropædia, s.v. "Damascus," 16:985.

26. Amos 1:4. The kings of Damascus were commonly named Ben Hadad.

27. *CIBA Review*, no. 10, "Trade Routes and Dye Markets," 333.

28. Le Strange, *Palestine under the Moslems*, 244.

Letter from Aleppo

1. Poem translation from J. Friedlander, *Standard Book of Jewish Verse*, 420–21.

2. Friedenwald, *The Jews and Medicine* 2:556.

3. *CIBA Review*, no. 10, "Trade Routes and Dye Markets," 318.

4. Goitein, *Mediterranean Society* 2:6.

5. Wiet, *Medieval Civilizations*, 317.

6. Lopez and Raymond, *Medieval Trade*, 77.

7. Asher prefers a nineteenth-century estimate of 5,000 Jewish inhabitants to the 1,500 in the Hebrew version he uses of *The Travels of Benjamin of Tudela* 2:124. Adler, *Itinerary of Benjamin*, 32, says 5,000. *Encyclopedia Judaica*, s.v. "Aleppo," says that the 5,000-figure appears in the "best-preserved manuscript versions" of Benjamin's chronicle.

Letter from Baghdad

1. *Encyclopedia Judaica*, s.v. "Tigris."

2. Book of Jonah.

3. Eliezer, *Pirkei de R. Eliezer*, chap. 43, 343.

4. *Encyclopedia Britannica*, 1974 ed., Macropædia, s.v. "Petroleum," 14:165; Maalouf, *Crusades through Arab Eyes*, 27.

5. *Midrash Rabbah*, vol. 1, *Genesis* 16:3.

6. *CIBA Review*, no. 10, "Trade Routes and Dye Markets," 332.

7. Josephus, *Jewish War*, bk. 5, chap. 5, sec. 4.

8. Goitein, *Jews and Arabs*, 92.
9. Wiet, *Medieval Civilizations* 3:650–51, 654.
10. *Cambridge Medieval History* 4:298; Bernal, *Science in History*, 201.
11. Friedenwald, *The Jews and Medicine* 1:16.
12. Baron, *Social and Religious History* 8:265.
13. *Jewish Encyclopedia*, s.v. "Medicine," 414.
14. On the making of the Jewish physician, see Bernal, *Science in History*, 201; Friedenwald, *The Jews and Medicine* 1:10; Goitein, *Mediterranean Society* 2:247.
15. Adapted from the poem translation by Nina Davis Salaman, in Judah Halevi, *Selected Poems*, 113. Halevi took his first line from Jer. 17:14.
16. Abrahams, *Jewish Life*, 367.
17. Baron, *Social and Religious History* 3:135.
18. Goitein, *Mediterranean Society* 2:285–88, 4:193–95.
19. Abrahams, *Jewish Life*, 309, citing Petachia.
20. Abrahams, *Jewish Life*, 300.
21. *CIBA Review*, no. 10, "Trade Routes and Dye Markets," 318, 332, 334.
22. *Ibid.*, 334.

Letter from Sura

1. 2 Kings 25.
2. Dan. 3 tells the story with the names Shadrach, Meshach, and Abed-nego, names given (respectively) to Chananiah, Mishael, and Asariah by Nebuchadnezzar (Dan. 1:7).
3. B. Talmud, Ketubbot, 110b, 111a.
4. Halpern, *People in Post-Biblical Times*, 164.
5. Deut. 1:17.
6. Johnson, *History of the Jews*, 173, 202, 203.
7. Goitein, *Mediterranean Society* 2:13.
8. B. Talmud, Eruvin, 65a.
9. Baron, *Social and Religious History* 5:22.
10. Saadia, *Book of Beliefs and Opinions*, 7.
11. Altmann, *Saadya Gaon*, 30.
12. Husik, *Mediaeval Jewish Philosophy*, 28.
13. Exod. 23:8. See also B. Talmud, Ketubbot, 105b, Shabbat, 119a.
14. Abrahams, *Jewish Life*, 243. Rejwan, *The Jews of Iraq*, 24; Stillman, *Jews of Arab Lands*, 28, 34–35.
15. Graetz, *History of the Jews* 3:236.

Letter from Pumbeditha

1. Rejwan, *The Jews of Iraq*, 35, 48.
2. B. Talmud, Berakhot, 58b.
3. Halpern, *People in Post-Biblical Times*, 135–40.
4. B. Talmud, Pesahim, 112a (Akiba).
5. Graetz, *History of the Jews* 3:93–94, 231–34.
6. Halpern, *People in Post-Biblical Times*, 177; Graetz, *History of the Jews* 3:234.
7. Rejwan, *The Jews of Iraq*, 134.
8. Ibid.
9. Halpern, *People in Post-Biblical Times*, 178.

10. Rejwan, *The Jews of Iraq*, 134–35.

11. Ibid., 135.

12. Poem translation from Goldstein, *Hebrew Poems from Spain*, 66.

13. Raphael, *Road from Babylon*, 38.

14. Abrahams, *Jewish Life*, 243.

15. *CIBA Review*, no. 49, "Flax and Hemp," 1773–77; Goitein, *Mediterranean Society* 1:105; *Encyclopedia Britannica*, 1950 ed., s.v. "Flax," and in 1974 ed., Micropædia, 4:177.

16. Goitein, *Mediterranean Society* 4:167, 177.

Letter from El-Cathif

1. Adapted from the poem translation by Nina Davis Salaman in Judah Halevi, *Selected Poems*, 30–31.

2. Asher, *The Travels of Benjamin of Tudela* 2:187.

3. It appears that Benjamin was the first European to write (even fleetingly) about China. He wrote his chronicle a hundred years before Marco Polo traveled to China.

4. Poem translation from Waxman, *History of Jewish Literature* 1:221.

5. Adapted from the poem translation by Nina Davis Salaman in Judah Halevi, *Selected Poems*, 28.

6. Lines of poem translation by Solomon Solis-Cohen in Moses ibn Ezra, *Selected Poems*, 46.

7. Asher, *The Travels of Benjamin of Tudela* 2:178.

Letter from Cairo

1. Asher, *The Travels of Benjamin of Tudela* 2:196.

2. Asher, Ibid., 196–97.

3. Adler, *Itinerary of Benjamin*, 69 n. 3.

4. Durant, *The Story of Civilization* 1:138.

5. Wiet, *Medieval Civilizations*, 317.

6. Goitein, *Mediterranean Society* 1:71, 2:290.

7. James Aldridge, *Cairo: Biography of a City* (Boston and Toronto: Little, Brown, 1969), 39–97. Aldridge, not concerned with Jews specifically, nonetheless provides much detail about Fustat at the time of Benjamin's sojourn.

8. Goitein, *Mediterranean Society* 4:253–54.

9. Ibid. 1:122–23.

10. Ibid., 150, 2:263.

11. Ibid., 2:266, 271.

12. Ibid. 1:106.

13. Ibid. 4:174–75; Prawer, *Jews in the Latin Kingdom,* 105.

14. Goitein, *Mediterranean Society* 4:174–75; Abrahams, *Jewish Life,* 323–24.

15. Abrahams, *Jewish Life,* 324; Hourani, *Arab Peoples,* 117.

16. Goitein, *Mediterranean Society* 2:52.

17. Ibid., 26.

18. Ibid., 284.

19. Ibid., 145–46.

20. Goitein, *Jews and Arabs,* 94.

21. Prawer, *Jews in Latin Kingdom,* 30. These papers came to light, or at least to

the attention of Europeans, in the last decade of the nineteenth century, with the unearthing of the "Cairo Geniza." Scholars, especially of Judaica and especially in the West, have been glorying in its abundance of poetry and of social and commercial detail from the High Middle Ages. The primary editor of this material from the 1960s through 1980s was S. D. Goitein. For an explanation of the Geniza's hoard and its importance, see his *Jews and Arabs,* 90–95, and *Mediterranean Society* 1:1–28.

22. Baron, *Social and Religious History* 7:137.

23. Johnson, *History of the Jews,* 202.

24. Goitein, *Mediterranean Society,* 2:109 on the common wearing of old clothing and the distribution to the poor of new clothing, and 1:150 on the shops.

25. Goitein, *Mediterranean Society* 2:113, 4:29.

26. B. Talmud, Bava Batra, 8a.

27. Johnson, *History of the Jews,* 204.

28. Asher, *The Travels of Benjamin of Tudela* 2:201.

29. Goitein, *Mediterranean Society* 2:381, 393.

30. Ibid. 2:359–60.

31. Poem translation from Fischel, *Economic and Political Life,* 89.

32. Goitein, *Jews and Arabs,* 83.

33. Goitein, *Mediterranean Society* 2:28–29; Runciman, *Crusades* 1:35–36.

34. Goitein, *Mediterranean Society* 2:164; see also Johnson, *History of the Jews,* 199.

35. Baron, *Social and Religious History* 3:135.

36. Goitein, *Mediterranean Society* 1:73, 2:380.

37. Mann, *Texts and Studies* 1:394; see also Hourani, *Arab Peoples,* 117–19.

38. Sarton, *History of Science,* vol. 2, pt. 1, p. 373; *Encyclopedia Judaica,* s.v. "Maimonides," 756, 780, s.v. "Astrology," 792–793.

39. *Jewish Encyclopedia,* s.v. "Moses ben Maimon," 74; Sarton, *History of Science,* vol. 2, pt. 1, pp. 371–73. Goitein, *Mediterranean Society* 2:252, gives an exemple of Dr. Maimonides's instructions.

40. For example, in B. Talmud, Eruvin, 83a, and Yoma, 29a.

41. Minkin, *Moses Maimonides,* 277.

42. Goitein, *Mediterranean Society* 2:166.

43. Baron, *Social and Religious History* 3:134–35.

44. Goitein, *Mediterranean Society* 4:246.

45. Ibid. 1:121, 4:146.

46. On Egypt's flax and cotton: Goitein, *Mediterranean Society* 1:104–5; *Cambridge Economic History* (1987 ed.) 2:432; *Encyclopedia Britannica,* 1974 ed., Micropædia, s.v. "Fustian."

47. Goitein, *Mediterranean Society* 1:103.

Letter from Gizah

1. Isa. 19:13; Jer. 2:16, 46:14, 19; Ezek. 30:13.

2. Asher, *The Travels of Benjamin of Tudela* 2:208–9.

3. Benjamin's geographical note is incomplete.

4. Adapted from the poem translation in Waxman, *History of Jewish Literature* 1:228.

First Letter from Alexandria

1. Gen. 45:10, 47:27.

2. Asher, *The Travels of Benjamin of Tudela* 2:210.

3. Ibid., 210–211.

4. Ibid., 211.

5. Ibid., 212, referring to Edrisi.

6. Philo, *Special Laws*, bk. 3, sec. 1, in Goodenough, *Introduction to Philo Judaeus*, 5.

7. Philo, *Rewards and Punishments*, vol. 8 of the Collected Works, sec. 14.

8. Philo, *On the Creation of the World*, vol. 1 of the Collected Works, bk. 1, sec. 3.

9. Philo, *Special Laws*, vol. 7 of the Collected Works, bk. 1, chap. 6, secs. 33–34. See also *Allegorical Interpretations,* vol. 1 of the Collected Works, bk. 3, chap. 32.

10. Wolfson, *Philo* 1:152–56, 429–30. Philo describes the burning bush in *Life of Moses*, vol. 6 of the Collected Works, bk. 1, chap. 12, sec. 65.

11. Philo tells the whole story in his *Embassy to Gaius*, vol. 10 of the Collected Works, where he reports the discussion about sacrifices in chaps. 44–45, secs. 353–67. The emperor, formally named Gaius Caesar Augustus Germanicus, was known by his childhood nickname Caligula ("little boots").

12. Philo, *Migration of Abraham*, vol. 4 of the Collected Works, chap. 9, sec. 47; and *Special Laws*, vol. 7 of the Collected Works, bk. 3, chap. 1, sec. 1.

13. Philo, *Every Good Man is Free*, vol. 9 of the Collected Works, chap. 12, secs. 75–87.

14. Philo, *Contemplative Life*, vol. 9 of the Collected Works, chap. 2, sec. 19.

Second Letter from Alexandria

1. Finucane, *Soldiers of Faith*, 51.

2. Erbstösser, *The Crusades*, 131; Goitein, *Mediterranean Society* 4:29. See Lopez and Raymond, *Medieval Trade*, 84–86, for *fondachi* around the Mediterranean region.

3. Philo, *Migration of Abraham*, vol. 4 of the Collected Works, chap. 39, sec. 217.

4. Goitein, *Mediterranean Society* 4:253, reports bananas.

5. Ibid., 2:234, reports the pens.

6. Goitein, *Jews and Arabs*, 92; Goitein, *Mediterranean Society* 1:154; *Cambridge Economic History*, 1952 ed., 2:432.

7. *Cambridge Economic History*, 1952 ed., 2:433; *Encyclopedia Britannica*, 1974 ed., Macropædia, s.v. "Egypt, History of" 6:490.

8. Goitein, *Mediterranean Society* 1:159, 238, 267.

9. Johnson, *History of the Jews*, 205.

10. Goitein, *Mediterranean Society* 2:379.

11. Kagan, *Jewish Medicine*, 75; *Encyclopedia Judaica*, s.v. "Israeli."

12. Mario Pei, *The Story of Language*, rev. ed. (New York: J. B. Lippincott Co., 1965), 368.

13. The Hebrew poem is in Weinberger, *Jewish Prince in Moslem Spain*, 107, and in Carmi, *Penguin Book of Hebrew Verse*, 297.

Letter from Messina

1. Carrera, *Città di Catania*, 154, reports that the earthquake occurred "in the first hour" of 4 February 1169.

2. Mann, *Jews of Egypt and in Palestine*, 204 n. 1.

3. *Encyclopedia Judaica*, s.v. "Aljama."

Letter from Palermo

1. Runciman, *Crusades* 2:102–5; *Cambridge Medieval History* 5:184.

2. Runciman, *Crusades* 2:199, 207, 251–52.

3. *Jewish Encyclopedia*, s.v. "Anacletus."

4. Baron, *Social and Religious History* 4:11; *Cambridge Medieval History* 5:186.

5. Coleman, *Story of Medicine*, 34; Friedenwald, *The Jews and Medicine* 1:263; Painter, *History of the Middle Ages*, 198.

6. *CIBA Review*, no. 72, "Paper," 2634.

7. Ponting, *Dyes and Dyeing*, 134.

8. *CIBA Review*, no. 10, "Trade Routes and Dye Markets," 324; Goitein, *Mediterranean Society* 1:102; Runciman, *Crusades* 2:275.

Letter from Tudela

1. Baron, *Social and Religious History* 4:35–36. The translated text of King Sancho's franchise is in Chazan, *Church, State and Jew*, 72–73.

List of Works Consulted

N.B.: Books of the Bible are not listed.

Encyclopedic Works

Encyclopedia Britannica (1950, 1974, and 1986 eds.)
Encyclopedia Judaica (1971 ed.)
Jewish Encyclopedia (1912 ed.)
Grand Larousse (1963 ed.)
Cambridge Economic History (1952 and 1987 eds.)
Cambridge Medieval History (1923 ed.)
Talmud, Babylonian (Soncino ed.) (hereafter B. Talmud)
Talmud, Jerusalem (University of Chicago Press ed., *The Talmud of the Land of Israel*) (hereafter J. Talmud)

Collections of Literature and Poetry

Ausubel, Nathan and Maryann, eds. *A Treasury of Jewish Poetry.* New York: Crown Publishing Co., 1957.
Carmi, T. [Carmi Charny], ed. *Penguin Book of Hebrew Verse.* New York: Viking Press, 1981.
Friedlander, Joseph, comp. *The Standard Book of Jewish Verse.* Edited by George Alexander Kohut. New York: Dodd, Mead, 1917.
Goldstein, David, trans. and comp. *Hebrew Poems from Spain.* New York: Schocken Books, 1966.
Kravitz, Nathaniel. *3,000 Years of Hebrew Literature.* Chicago: Swallow Press, 1972.
Millgram, Abraham E. *An Anthology of Medieval Hebrew Literature.* 1935. Reprint. London and New York: Abelard-Schuman, 1961.
Schwarz, Leo W., ed. *A Golden Treasury of Jewish Literature.* New York: Rinehart and Co., 1937.
Waxman, Meyer. *History of Jewish Literature.* Vol. 1. 1930. Reprint. New York and London: Thomas Yoseloff, 1960.
Zinberg, Israel. *Toledot Sifrut Yisrael* (History of Jewish Literature). Tel Aviv: Joseph Sharbarak, 1955.
———. *A History of Jewish Literature.* Vols. 1 and 2. Cleveland: Case Western Reserve University Press, 1972.

Books and Periodicals

Abetti, Georgio. *The History of Astronomy.* New York: H. Schumann, 1952.
Aboth de Rabbi Nathan. See Nathan.

309

Abraham ibn Ezra. *Yesod Mora*. In Hebrew and German. Frankfurt-am-Main: J. Baer, 1840.

Abrahams, Israel. *The Book of Delight and Other Papers*. 1912. Reprint. New York: Arno Press, 1980.

——. *By-paths in Hebraic Bookland*. 1920. Reprint. New York: B. Blom, 1972.

——. *Hebrew Ethical Wills*. 1926. facs. ed. Philadelphia: Jewish Publication Society, 1976.

——. *Jewish Life in the Middle Ages*. 1896. Reprint. London: Edward Goldston, 1932.

——. *A Short History of Jewish Literature*. London: Fisher, Unwin, 1906.

Adler, Marcus Nathan. *The Itinerary of Benjamin of Tudela*. London: Oxford University Press, 1907.

Ahimaaz ben Paltiel. *Chronicle* (Sefer Yuhasin). Translated and edited by Marcus Salzman. New York: Columbia University Press, 1924.

Altmann, Alexander, trans. *Saadya Gaon: Book of Doctrines and Beliefs*. In *Three Jewish Philosophers*. 1945. Reprint. New York: Harper and Row Publishers, Harper Torchbook, in association with the Jewish Publication Society, 1965.

Ankori, Zvi. *Karaites in Byzantium: The Formative Years, 970–1100*. New York: Columbia University Press, 1959.

Arkin, Marcus. *Aspects of Jewish Economic History*. Philadelphia: Jewish Publication Society, 1975.

Asher, A[dolf], trans. and ed. *The Travels of Benjamin of Tudela*. Vol. 1, *Text, Bibliography, and Translation;* vol. 2, *Notes and Essays*. New York: "Hakesheth" Publishing Co., 1840.

Ashtor, Eliyahu. *The Jews of Moslem Spain*. 3 vols. Philadelphia: Jewish Publication Society, 1973.

——. *The Jews and the Mediterranean Economy, 10th–15th Centuries*. London: Variorum Reprints, 1983.

Avenari, H. "Geniza Fragments of the Hebrew Hymns and Prayers Set to Music." *Journal of Jewish Studies* 14 (1965): 87–105.

Avi-Yonah, Michael. *The Holy Land*. New York: Holt, Rinehart and Winston, 1973.

Bachrach, Bernard. *Early Jewish Policy in Western Europe*. Minneapolis: University of Minnesota Press, 1977.

Baer, Yitzhak. *A History of the Jews in Christian Spain*. Translated from the Hebrew. Vol. 1. Philadelphia: Jewish Publication Society, 1961.

Baron, Salo Wittmayer. *A Social and Religious History of the Jews*. Vols. 3–8 of *High Middle Ages*. New York: Columbia University Press, 1957.

Ben Sasson, Haim Hillel. "The Northern European Jewish Community and its Ideals." In *Jewish Society through the Ages*, edited by H. H. Ben-Sasson, 208–19. London: Vallentine Mitchell, 1971; New York: Schocken Books, 1972.

——, ed. *A History of the Jewish People*. Translated from the Hebrew. London: 1976.

——, ed. *Jewish Society through the Ages*. London: Vallentine Mitchell; 1971. New York: Schocken Books, 1972.

Benvenisti, Meron. *The Crusaders in the Holy Land*. Jerusalem: Keter Publishing House, Israel Universities Press, 1970.

Bernal, John Desmond. *Science in History*. Cambridge, Mass.: MIT Press, 1971.

Biale, David. *Power and Powerlessness in Jewish History*. New York: Schocken Books, 1986.

Birnbaum, Philip, ed. *Holy Day Prayer Book, Yom Kippur: Sephardic*. New York: Hebrew Publishing Co., 1958.

Borchsenius, Poul. *The Three Rings: The History of the Spanish Jews*. Translated from the Danish. London: George Allen and Unwin, 1963.

Bréhier, Louis. *La civilisation byzantine*. 1950. Reprint. Paris: Editions Albin Michel, 1970.

Byrne, Eugene H. *Genoese Shipping in the 12th and 13th Centuries*. Medieval Academy of America Publications, no. 5. Cambridge, Mass.: Academy, 1930.

Carrera, D. Pietro. *Delle Memorie historiche della Città di Catania*, per Giovanni Rossi, nel Palazzo dell'illustrissimo Senato. 1639.

Chazan, Robert. *Church, State and Jew in the Middle Ages*. West Orange, N.J.: Behrman House, Library of Jewish Studies. 1980.

Cheetham, Nicholas. *Mediaeval Greece*. New Haven: Yale University Press, 1981.

CIBA Review. Basle, Switzerland: Gesellschaft für Chemische Industrie.

No. 1. "Medieval Dyeing" (September 1937)

No. 4. "Purple" (December 1937)

No. 10. "Trade Routes and Dye Markets in the Middle Ages" (June 1938)

No. 11. "The Early History of Silk" (July 1938)

No. 12. "Weaving and Dying in Ancient Egypt and Babylon" (August 1938)

No. 29. "Venetian Silks" (January 1940)

No. 39. "Madder and Turkey Red" (May 1941)

No. 49. "Flax and Hemp" (April 1945)

No. 57. "Medieval Dress" (June 1947)

No. 72. "Paper" (February 1949)

No. 75. "Byzantine Silks" (August 1949)

No. 80. "Lucchese Silks" (June 1950)

No. 81. "The Early History of Tanning" (August 1950)

No. 85. "Indigo" (April 1951)

Cohen, Gerson D. "The Talmudic Age." In *Great Ages and Ideas of the Jewish People*, edited by Leo W. Schwarz, 143–212. New York: Random House, Modern Library, 1956.

———. ed. *Ibn-Daud, Sefer ha-Kabbalah* (The book of tradition). Philadelphia: Jewish Publication Society, 1967.

Colafemmina, Cesare. "Una nuova epigrafe ebraica altomedievale a Lavello." *Vetera Christianorum* 29 (1992): 411–21.

Coleman, Vernon. *The Story of Medicine*. London: Robert Hale, 1985.

Colson, F. H., and G. H. Whitaker, *Philo*. London: William Heineman, 1929; Cambridge, Mass.: Harvard University Press, 1929, 1962.

Dan, Joseph. *Jewish Mysticism and Jewish Ethics*. Seattle and London: University of Washington Press, 1986.

Danby, Herbert, trans. *See* Mishnah.

Dimont, Max. *Jews, God, and History*. New York: Simon and Schuster, 1962.

Douglas, R. W., and Susan Frank. *A History of Glassmaking*. Henley-on-Thames: Foulis, 1972.

Dreyer, J. L. E. "Medieval Astronomy." In *History and Method of Science*, edited by Charles Singer, 2:102–20. Oxford: Clarendon Press, 1921; New York: Arno Press, 1975.

Dubnov, Semen. *History of the Jews, from the Roman Empire to the Early Medieval Period*. Translated from the Russian. Vol. 2. New York and London: Thomas Yoseloff, 1968.

DuFourcq, Charles-Emmanuel. *La vie quotidienne dans l'Europe médiévale sous domination arabe*. [Paris]: Hachette, 1978 (esp. chap. 9, "Le comportement et l'existence des Juifs").

Durant, Will. *The Story of Civilization*. Vol. 1, *Our Oriental Heritage*. New York: Simon and Schuster, 1954.

(Al-) Edrisi. *Libro del re Ruggero*. 1592. Reprint. Rome, 1883.

Eliezer. *Pirkei de Rabbi Eliezer*. Translated by Gerald Friedlander. New York: Hermon Press, 1965.

Emmanuel, I[saac] S[amuel]. *Histoire de l'industrie de tissus des Israélites de Salonique*. Paris: Lipshutz, 1935.

Erbstösser, Martin. *The Crusades*. Translated from the German. New York: Universe Books, 1979.

Ferorelli, Nicola. *Gli Ebrei nell'Italia meridionale*. Turin, 1915.

Finucane, Ronald C. *Soldiers of Faith: Crusaders and Moslems at War*. New York: St. Martin's Press, 1983.

Fischel, Walter J. *Jews in the Economic and Political Life of Medieval Islam*.1937. Reprint. New York: Ktav Publishing House, 1969.

Friedenwald, Harry. *The Jews and Medicine: Essays*. 2 vols. Baltimore: Johns Hopkins University Press, 1944.

Friedlander, Gerald. *See* Eliezer.

Friedländer, Michael. *The Commentary of* [Abraham] *ibn Ezra on Isaiah*. London: N. Trübner and Co., for the Society of Jewish Literature, 1873.

———. *Essays on the Writings of* [Abraham] *ibn Ezra*. Vol. 4. London: Jews College, 1877.

Gabirol. *See* Solomon ibn Gabirol.

Galanté, Avram. *Les Juifs de Constantinople sous Byzance*. Part 1 of Galanté's *Histoire des Juifs de Turquie*. Istanbul: Isis Yayimçilik Ltd., 1940.

Geanakoplos, Deno John. *Byzantium: Church, Society and Civilization as Seen Through Contemporary Eyes*. Chicago: University of Chicago Press, 1984.

Goitein, S[hlomo] D[ov]. "The Biography of Rabbi Judah Ha-Levi in the Light of the Cairo Geniza Documents." *Proceedings of the American Academy for Jewish Research* 28 (1959): 41–56.

———. "Jewish Society and Institutions under Islam." In *Jewish Society through the Ages*, edited by H. H. Ben-Sasson, 170–84. London: Vallentine Mitchell, 1971; New York: Schocken Books, 1971/1972.

———. *Jews and Arabs: Their Contacts Through the Ages*. 3d rev. ed. New York: Schocken Books, 1955 1974.

———. *Letters of Medieval Jewish Traders*. Princeton: Princeton University Press, 1973.

———. *A Mediterranean Society: The Jewish Communities of the Arab World as Portrayed in the Documents of the Cairo Geniza*. Vol. 1, *Economic Foundations*, 1967; vol. 2, *The Community*, 1971; vol. 3, *The Family*, 1978; vol. 4, *Daily Life*,

1983; vol. 5, *The Individual,* 1988. Berkeley: University of California Press, 1967–88.

Goldin, Judah, translator. *See* Nathan.

Goodenough, Edwin R. *Introduction to Philo Judaeus.* 1940. Reprint. Oxford: Basil Blackwell, 1962.

———. "Philo of Alexandria." In *Great Jewish Personalities in Ancient and Medieval Times,* edited by Simon Noveck, 102–19. New York: Farrar, Strauss and Cudahy, for B'nai Brith, 1959.

Graetz, Heinrich. *History of the Jews.* Translated from the German. Vol. 3. Philadelphia: Jewish Publication Society, 1894, 1898.

Grousset, René. *L'épopée des croisades.* Paris: Librarie Plon, 1939.

Halevi, Judah. *See* Judah Halevi.

Halkin, Abraham S. "The Judeo-Islamic Age." In *Great Ages and Ideas of the Jewish People,* edited by Leo W. Schwarz, 213–63, section, "The Karaites," 241–49. New York: Random House, Modern Library, 1956.

Halpern, Joseph. *History of Our People in Post-Biblical Times.* London: Shapiro, Vallentine, 1965. (Incorporates an enl. and rev. ed. of *History of our People in Rabbinic Times.* London: Shapiro, Vallentine, 1939.)

Harington, Sir John. *The School of Salernum* (rhymed English version of *Regimen Sanitatis Salernitanum*), London, 1608. Reprint. New York: Paul B. Hoeber, 1920.

Harvey, John [Hooper]. *Medieval Craftsmen.* London: Batsford Press, 1975.

Heyd, W[ilhelm von]. *Histoire du commerce du Levant au moyen age.* Translated from the German. 2 vols. Leipzig: O. Harrassowitz, 1885–86. Reprint. Amsterdam, 1959.

Hitti, Philip K. *Lebanon in History.* London: Macmillan, 1957; 3d ed., New York: St. Martin's Press, 1967.

Hourani, Albert. *A History of the Arab Peoples.* Cambridge, Mass.: Harvard University Press, 1991.

Hunter, Dard. *Papermaking: The History and Technique of an Ancient Craft.* 1943. Reprint. New York: Dover Publications, 1978.

Husik, Isaac. *A History of Mediaeval Jewish Philosophy.* 1916. Reprint. New York: Harper and Row Publishers, Harper Torchbook, in association with the Jewish Publication Society, 1966.

Idelsohn, A[braham] Z. *Jewish Liturgy and Its Development.* 1932. Reprint. New York: Schocken Books, 1967.

Idelsohn, Abraham Z. *Jewish Music in its Historical Development.* 1929. Reprint. New York: Schocken Books, 1967

Johnson, Paul. *A History of the Jews.* London: Weidenfeld and Nicholson, 1987.

Joseph ben Meir Zabara. *Sepher Shaashuim.* Edited by Israel Davidson. New York: Jewish Theological Seminary, 1914.

Josephus, Flavius. *Antiquities; The Jewish War; Vita.* In *The Complete Works of Flavius Josephus.* Translated by William Whiston. New York: Holt, Rinehart and Winston, 1970.

Judah Halevi. *Book of Kuzari.* Translated by H[artwig] Hirschfeld from the Arabic. 1905. Reprint. New York: Pardes Publishing House, 1946.

———. *Selected Poems of Jehudah Halevi.* Edited by Heinrich Brody, translated by Nina [Davis] Salaman. Schiff Library of Jewish Classics. Philadelphia: Jewish Publication Society, 1924.

Kagan, Solomon. *Jewish Medicine.* Boston: Medico-Historical Press, 1952.

Kahana, David, ed. *Rabbi Abraham ibn Ezra: Collected Poems with Notes and Introduction.* In Hebrew. Warsaw, 1894.

Karmon, Nira, and Ehud Spanier. "Archeological Evidence of the Purple Dye Industry from Israel," in *The Royal Purple and the Biblical Blue,* edited by Ehud Spanier, 147–58. Jerusalem: Keter Publishing House, 1987.

Kelly, J. N. D. *The Oxford Dictionary of Popes.* Oxford: Oxford University Press, 1986.

Klein, Isaac. *A Guide to Jewish Religious Practice.* New York: Jewish Theological Seminary, 1979.

Koestler, Arthur. *The Thirteenth Tribe.* London: Hutchinson, 1976.

Lapidus, Ira. *A History of Islamic Societies.* Cambridge and New York: Cambridge University Press, 1988.

Leroy, Béatrice. *The Jews of Navarre in the Late Middle Ages.* Translated from the French. Magnes Press, Hebrew University, 1985.

Le Strange, Guy. *Palestine under the Moslems: A Description of Syria and the Holy Land, 650–1500.* 1890. Reprint. Beirut: Khayats, 1965.

Lewis, Bernard. *The Jews of Islam.* London: Routledge and Kegan Paul; Princeton: Princeton University Press, 1984.

Lewy, Hans, ed. *Philo: Selections.* In *Three Jewish Philosophers.* 1945. Reprint. New York: Harper and Row Publishers, Harper Torchbook, in association with the Jewish Publication Society, 1965.

Lomax, Derek W. *The Reconquest of Spain.* New York and London: Longman, 1978.

Lopez, Robert S. "The Silk Industry in the Byzantine Empire." *Speculum* 20 (January 1945): 1–42.

Lopez, Robert S., and Irving W. Raymond. *Medieval Trade in the Mediterranean World.* London: Oxford University Press, 1955.

Maalouf, Amin. *The Crusades through Arab Eyes.* Translated from the French. London: Al Saqi Books; New York: Schocken Books, 1984.

Mack Smith, Denis. *Medieval Sicily, 800–1713.* London: Chatto and Windus, 1968.

Mann, Jacob. *The Jews of Egypt and in Palestine under the Fatimids.* Vol. 1. London: Oxford University Press, 1920.

———, ed. *Texts and Studies in Jewish History and Literature.* Vol. 1 (untitled); and vol. 2, *Karaitica.* Cincinnati: Hebrew Union College Press, 1931, 1935.

Marcus, Jacob R. *The Jew in the Medieval World: A Source Book, 315–1791.* Cincinnati, Ohio: Sinai Press, 1938.

Marcus, Joseph. "Studies in Ahimaaz." *Proceedings of the American Academy for Jewish Research* 5 (1933–34): 85–93.

Marcus, Ralph. "The Achievement of Hellenistic Judaism." In *Great Ages and Ideas of the Jewish People,* edited by Leo W. Schwarz, 122–39. New York: Random House, Modern Library, 1956.

McMurtrie, D[ouglas] C[rawford]. *The Book.* 1937. Reprint. New York and London: Oxford University Press, 1943.

Menendez Pidal, Ramón. *The Cid and his Spain.* Translated from the Spanish. London: Frank Cass and Co., 1934.

Midrash on Psalms (Midrash Tehillim). Translated by William A. Braude. New Haven: Yale University Press, 1959.

Midrash Rabbah. Translated and edited by Rabbi Dr. H. Freedman and Maurice Simon. 10 vols. Vol. 1, *Genesis*; vol. 8, Ecclesiastes. London: Soncino Press, 1939.

Milano, Attilio. *Storia degli Ebrei in Italia.* Turin: Einaudi, 1963.

————. *Storia degli Ebrei italiani nel Levante.* Firenze: Casa editrice Israel, 1949.

Minkin, Jacob S. *The World of Moses Maimonides, with Selections from his Writings.* New York and London: Thomas Yoseloff, 1957.

Mishnah. Translated by Herbert Danby. London: Oxford University Press, 1938.

Montgomery, James Alan. *The Samaritans, the Earliest Jewish Sect: Their History, Theology and Literature.* 1907. Reprint. New York: Ktav, 1968.

Morais, Sabato. *Italian Hebrew Literature.* 1926. Reprint. New York: Hermon Press, 1970.

Moses ibn Ezra. *Selected Poems.* Edited by Heinrich Brody, translated by Solomon Solis-Cohen. Schiff Library of Jewish Classics. Philadelphia: Jewish Publication Society, 1934.

Mullins, Edwin. *The Pilgrimage to Santiago.* London: Secker and Warburg, 1974.

Nathan, the Babylonian. *The Fathers according to Rabbi Nathan* (Aboth de Rabbi Nathan). Translated by Judah Goldin. Yale Judaica series, vol. 10. New Haven: Yale University Press, 1955.

Negev, Avraham. *Archeological Encyclopedia of the Holy Land.* London: Weidenfeld and Nicholson, 1972.

Nehama, Joseph. *Histoire des Israélites de Salonique.* Vol. 1. *Salonica.* 1935. London: World Sephardi Federation, 1959.

Neuman, Abraham. *The Jews in Spain: Their Social, Political and Cultural Life in the Middle Ages.* 2 vols. Philadelphia: Jewish Publication Society, 1942.

Newby, Percy Howard. *Saladin in His Time.* London and Boston: Faber and Faber, 1983.

Noveck, Simon, ed. *Great Jewish Personalities in Ancient and Medieval Times.* New York: Farrar, Strauss and Cudahy, for B'nai Brith, 1959.

O'Callaghan, Joseph F. *A History of Medieval Spain.* Ithaca, N.Y.: Cornell University Press, 1975.

Painter, Sidney. *A History of the Middle Ages.* New York: Knopf, 1953.

Parkes, James. *A History of Palestine from 135 A.D. to Modern Times.* London: Victor Gollancz, 1949.

————. *The Jew in the Medieval Community.* 1938. Reprint. New York: Hermon Press, 1976.

————. *Prelude to Dialog: Christian-Jewish Relationships.* London: Vallentine Mitchell, 1969.

Payne, Robert. *The Dream and the Tomb: A History of the Crusades.* London: Robert Hale, 1984.

Philo. [Collected Works]. 10 vols. Edited by T. E. Page, E. Capps, and W. H. D. Rouse, translated by F. H. Colson and G. H. Whitaker. Loeb Classical Library, Cambridge, Mass.: Harvard University Press, 1929–42.

Pirke Avot. See Taylor, Charles.

Pirkei de Rabbi Eliezer. See Eliezer.

Ponting, Kenneth G. *A Dictionary of Dyes and Dyeing.* London: Mills and Boon, 1980.

Prawar, Joshua. "The Autobiography of Obadyah the Norman, a Convert to Judaism at the Time of the First Crusade." In *Studies in Medieval Jewish History and Literature*, edited by Isadore Twersky, 1:110–134. Cambridge, Mass.: Harvard University Press, 1979.

———. *History of the Jews in the Latin Kingdom of Jerusalem*. New York: Oxford University Press, 1988.

———. *The World of the Crusaders*. London: Weidenfeld and Nicholson, 1972.

Rabinowitz, Louis. *Jewish Merchant Adventurers: A Study of the Radanites*. London: Edward Goldston, 1948.

Raphael, Chaim. *The Road from Babylon: The story of Sephardi and Oriental Jews*. London: Weidenfeld and Nicholson, 1985.

Rashdall, Hastings. *The Universities of Europe in the Middle Ages*. Edited by F. M. Powicke and A. B. Emden. 3 vols. London: Oxford University Press, 1895, 1936.

Rejwan, Nissim. *The Jews of Iraq: 3000 Years of History and Culture*. London: Weidenfeld and Nicholoson, 1985.

Robinson, Stuart. *A History of Dyed Textiles*. London: Macmillan, Studio Vista, 1969.

Roth, Cecil. "Economic Life and Population Movements," in *The Dark Ages: Jews in Christian Europe, 711–1096*, edited by Cecil Roth, 13–48. New Brunswick, N.J.: Rutgers University Press, 1966.

———. *The History of the Jews of Italy*. Philadelphia: Jewish Publication Society, 1946.

———. "Italy." *In The Dark Ages: Jews in Christian Europe, 711–1096*, edited by Cecil Roth. New Brunswick, N.J.: Rutgers University Press, 1966.

———, ed. *The Dark Ages: Jews in Christian Europe, 711–1096*. Vol. 11 of *World History of the Jewish People*, and also vol. 2 of its the Medieval Period Series, edited by Cecil Roth. New Brunswick, N.J.: Rutgers University Press, 1966.

Rowling, Marjorie. *Everyday Life of Medieval Travellers*. New York: Putnam's Sons, 1971.

Rubens, Alfred. *A History of Jewish Costume*. London: Vallentine Mitchell, 1967, New York: Crown, 1973.

Runciman, Steven. *A History of the Crusades*. Vols. 1 and 2. Cambridge (England): Cambridge University Press, 1951, 1952.

Saadia Gaon. *Book of Beliefs and Opinions*. Translated by Samuel Rosenblatt. Yale Judaica series, vol. 1. New Haven: Yale University Press, 1948.

Saige, Gustave. *Les Juifs du Languedoc: Antérieurement au XIV siècle*. Facs. ed. 1881. Reprint. Farnborough: Gregg, 1971.

Salzman, Marcus. *See* Ahimaaz.

Sarton, George. *Introduction to the History of Science*. Vol. 2, pt. 1. Baltimore, Md.: Carnegie Institute of Washington, 1931.

Schechter, Abraham I. *Studies in Jewish Liturgy*. Philadelphia: Dropsie College, 1930.

Schirmann, Jefim. "The Beginning of Hebrew Poetry in Italy and Northern Europe." In *The Dark Ages: Jews in Christian Europe*, edited by Cecil Roth, 249–66. New Brunswick, N.J.: Rutgers University Press, 1966.

———. "The Function of the Hebrew Poet in Medieval Spain." *Jewish Social Studies* 16 (1954): 235–52.

———. "Zur Geschichte der hebräischen Poesie in Apulien und Sizilien." *Mitteilungen des Forschungsinstituts für hebräische Dichtung* 1 (1932): 96–147.

Schwarz, Leo W., ed. *Great Ages and Ideas of the Jewish People.* New York: Random House, Modern Library, 1956.

Schwarzfuchs, S. "France and Germany under the Carolingians." In *The Dark Ages: Jews in Christian Europe,* edited by Cecil Roth, 122–42. New Brunswick, N.J.: Rutgers University Press, 1966.

———. "France under the Early Capets." *In the Dark Ages: Jews in Christian Europe,* edited by Cecil Roth, 143–61. New Brunswick, N.J.: Rutgers University Press, 1966.

Sharf, Andrew. *Byzantine Jewry: From Justinian to the Fourth Crusade.* London: Routledge and Kegan Paul, 1971.

———. "Jews in Byzantium." In *The Dark Ages: Jews in Christian Europe,* edited by Cecil Roth, 49–68. New Brunswick, N.J.: Rutgers University Press.

Signer, Michael A. *The Itinerary of Benjamin of Tudela.* Malibu, California: Joseph Simon Publisher, 1983.

Singer, Charles, et al. *A History of Technology.* Vol. 2, *The Mediterranean Civilizations and the Middle Ages.* Oxford: Clarendon Press, 1956.

Singer, Charles, and E. Ashworth Underwood. *A Short History of Medicine.* 2d ed. New York: Oxford University Press, 1962.

Singer, Charles Joseph, ed. *Studies in the History and Method of Science.* Vol. 2. 1921. Reprint. New York: Arno Press, 1975.

Smith, Denis Mack. *See* Mack Smith, Denis.

Solomon ibn Gabirol. *Selected Religious Poems of Solomon ibn Gabirol.* Edited by Israel Davidson, translated by Israel Zangwill. Schiff Library of Jewish Classics. Philadelphia: Jewish Publication Society, 1923.

Spanier, Ehud, ed. *The Royal Purple and the Biblical Blue.* Jerusalem: Keter Publishing House, 1987.

Spanier, Ehud, and Nira Karmon. "Muricid Snails and Ancient Dye Industries." In *The Royal Purple and the Biblical Blue,* edited by Ehud Spanier, 179–92. Jerusalem: Keter Publishing House, 1987.

Starr, Joshua. "The Epitaph of a Dyer in Corinth." *Byzantinisch-Neugrieschischen Jahrbücher* 12 (1936): 42–49.

———. *The Jews in the Byzantine Empire, 641–1204.* 1939. Reprint. Farnborough: Gregg, 1969.

Stillman, Norman A. *The Jews of Arab Lands: A History and Source Book.* Philadelphia: Jewish Publication Society, 1979.

Straus, Raphael. *Die Juden im Königreich Sizilien unter Normannen und Staufern.* Heidelberg: C. Winter, 1910.

Taylor, Charles, ed. *Sayings of the Jewish Fathers* (Pirke Avot). Cambridge (England): Cambridge University Press, 1897.

Twersky, I[sadore]. "Aspects of the Social and Cultural History of Provençal Jewry." In *Jewish Society through the Ages,* edited by H. H. Ben-Sasson, 185–207. London: Vallentine Mitchell, 1971; New York: Schocken Books, 1971/1972.

Twersky, Isadore, ed. *Studies in Medieval Jewish History and Literature,* Vol. 1. Cambridge, Mass.: Harvard University Press, 1979.

Vicens Vives, Jaime. *An Economic History of Spain.* London: Oxford University Press, 1969.

Vogelstein, Hermann. *History of the Jews in Rome.* Translated from the German. Philadelphia: Jewish Publication Society, 1940.

Waterer, John William. *Leather in Life, Art and Industry.* 2d ed. London: Faber and Faber, 1950.

Weinberger, Leon J. *Jewish Prince in Moslem Spain: Selected Poems of Samuel ibn Nagrela.* Tuscaloosa: University of Alabama Press, 1973.

Weiss-Rosmarin, Trude. "Saadia." In *Great Jewish Personalities in Ancient and Medieval Times*, edited by Simon Noveck, 161–78. New York: Farrar, Straus and Cudahy, for B'nai Brith, 1959.

Whalley, Joyce Irene. *Writing Implements and Accessories.* Newton Abbot: David and Charles, 1975.

Wiet, Gaston. *The Great Medieval Civilizations.* Translated from the French. London: George Allen and Unwin, for UNESCO, 1975.

Wischnitzer, Mark. *A History of Jewish Crafts and Guilds.* New York: J. David, 1965.

Wolfson, Harry A. *Philo: Foundations of Religious Philosophy in Judaism, Christianity, and Islam.* 2 vols. Cambridge, Mass.: Harvard University Press, 1947.

Woolfson, Marion. *Prophets in Babylon.* Boston and London: Faber and Faber, 1980.

Zimmels, Hirsch Jacob. "Scholars and Scholarship in Byzantium and Italy." In *The Dark Ages: Jews in Christian Europe,* edited by Cecil Roth, 175–88. New Brunswick, N.J.: Rutgers University Press, 1966.

Zunz, Leopold. *Literaturgeschichte der synagogalen Poesie.* Berlin, 1865.

Index

Reiha, 212
religious services: conduct, 72
Rhodes, 142
Rodosto, 141
Rome, 85; described, 87–88; Jews in, 87
R'Phidim, 276

St. Sophia (church); described, 135
Salerno: inhabitants, 92–93; medical academy, 93; physicians, 97–98; scholars, 93
Salunki (Salonica), 126, 127; commercial importance, 125; inhabitants, 125
Samaritans, 186; and Islam, 166; and Karaites, 166; beliefs, 163, 164–65, 170; calendar, 194, 196; schism, 163; temple, 164
Samos, 142
Sancho VI, 39
Santiago, 34, 36, 39, 41; shrine, 35
Saragossa, 17, 34, 53
schism, 85
scholars: education, 23–24; support, 23
sea travel: hazards, 281–82
Sebaste: described, 162
Sefer ha-Ibbur, 198
Sefer ha-Kabbala, 139; author, 139
Sefer ha-Shetarot, 57
Sefer ha-Yakar, 96–97
Sefer Yezirah, 199; commentary, 105
Sefita, 266
Seljuks: in Jerusalem, 176
sevilla, 42
ships: building, 278; cargo, 74, 75; construction, 75, 77; types, 75, 77
Sicily: and travellers, 278; kingdom, 278; rulers, 278, 279–80, 282; territory, 277
Silano; author of piyyutim, 113–16
silk industry; buyers, 82; cloth, 81; demand, 82; dyers, 80–81, 130–31; history, 282; manufacturing, 119–21; merchants, 80; patterns, 81; prices, 81, 128; purchase, 80; sales, 82; transport, 80; uses, 82, 131; weavers, 80–81, 130–31, 282
silversmiths, 60
Sinai, Mount: described, 276
Sinon Potamo (Zeitun), 123
slavery, 177
Sorrento, 91
Spain: infrastructure, 35; Jews, 60; Moorish rule, 36
Sunbat, 276

Sura: inhabitants, 220; Jewish capital, 234, 237
synagogues: Alexandrian, 274; hospitality centers, 46, 258; prayerbooks, 22; purpose, 29; seating, 22

Talmud, 10, 257; development, 229; on travel, 45
Talmudists: compositions, 10
Taranto: Jewish community, 103–4
Tarragon, 56–57; inhabitants, 57
taxation, 26
Talmas: described, 241–42; inhabitants, 241–42
Tennis, 277
Tersoos (Tarsus), 144
Thadmor: described, 211
Thanaejam: described, 241
Thebes, 119–22; industries, 120; inhabitants, 120
Thema: described, 241; inhabitants, 241
Thessaly, 119
Tiberias: baths, 188–89; commercial center, 193; conquered, 193; described, 187; inhabitants, 188, 193; religious practices, 189–90, 191; rulers, 189–90
Toledo, 9, 17; history, 36; Jewish community, 36
Torah: prohibitions, 21; readings, 22; study, 190
Toron de los Cabelleros, 183
Tortosa, 17, 56, 149–50
Tower of David; described, 172
trade routes, 41
traders, 74
trading partnerships, 75
Trani: described, 101–2
translators, 68–69
travellers: advice, 45; favored, 64; Jews, 17, 45–46, 74, 258; letters of introduction, 48; Moslem, 74; taxed, 48
travelling: hazards, 45, 281–82
Tripoli: earthquake, 151; inhabitants, 151; language, 150; location, 150
Tsidon (Saida): described, 153; history, 153
Tudela, 17, 31; craftsmen, 20, 21; crops, 38; fall, 37–38; Jews, 40; location, 20; markets, 17, 20; merchants, 35; Moorish rule, 34; part of Navarre, 34; pilgrim route, 34–35
Turks: in Palestine, 204